Villainy in Western Culture

ALSO BY M. GREGORY KENDRICK

The Heroic Ideal: Western Archetypes from the Greeks to the Present (McFarland, 2010)

Villainy in Western Culture

Historical Archetypes of Danger, Disorder and Death

M. Gregory Kendrick

McFarland & Company, Inc., Publishers
Jefferson, North Carolina

LIBRARY OF CONGRESS CATALOGUING-IN-PUBLICATION DATA

Names: Kendrick, M. Gregory, 1953– author.
Title: Villainy in western culture : historical archetypes of danger, disorder and death / M. Gregory Kendrick.
Description: Jefferson, N.C. : McFarland & Company, Inc., Publishers, 2016. | Includes bibliographical references and index.
Identifiers: LCCN 2016004073 | ISBN 9780786498680 (softcover : acid free paper) ∞
Subjects: LCSH: Villains in popular culture. | Villains in mass media. | West (U.S.)—In popular culture.
Classification: LCC P96.V48 K46 2016 | DDC 305.9/0692—dc23
LC record available at https://lccn.loc.gov/2016004073

BRITISH LIBRARY CATALOGUING DATA ARE AVAILABLE

ISBN (print) 978-0-7864-9868-0
ISBN (ebook) 978-1-4766-2533-1

© 2016 M. Gregory Kendrick. All rights reserved

No part of this book may be reproduced or transmitted in any form or by any means, electronic or mechanical, including photocopying or recording, or by any information storage and retrieval system, without permission in writing from the publisher.

Front cover (clockwise from top left) Germanic barbarian, Adolf Hitler, Benedict Arnold, Darth Vader, Carlos Gambino and Mata Hari

Printed in the United States of America

*McFarland & Company, Inc., Publishers
Box 611, Jefferson, North Carolina 28640
www.mcfarlandpub.com*

To my dear friends
in mischief and mayhem,
Gary Borgstedt, David Mattingly
and Yoko Yanari

Acknowledgments

As with my book on the heroic ideal in the West, this book on Western notions of villainy would never have seen the light of day without the good humor, encouragement, and assistance of students, colleagues, and friends. Of these, I am particularly grateful to the many freshmen at UCLA who have taken my first-year seminar on this topic over the last five years, and afforded me the opportunity to develop and explore the ideas and themes presented here. Kudos are also in order for the following individuals who read and edited various drafts of this book's chapters, and provided me with thoughtful advice and criticism—Jonathan Friedman, Richard Hoffman, Anthony (Tony) Friscia, David Mattingly, Joe Menosky, and Yoko Yanari. I wish to extend special thanks as well to my undergraduate research assistants, Sahara Al-Mahdi and Benjamin (Ben) Genta. It was a pleasure to work with them. Mention also needs to be made of my two colleagues in UCLA's first-year cluster course, *Neverending Stories: Multidisciplinary Perspectives on Myth*—Professors Stephanie Jameson and Joseph Nagy—whose insights and work in linguistics and folklore have inspired me, and made me look at my own work in new ways. It has been a joy to teach with them over the years I have spent researching and writing this history.

Table of Contents

Acknowledgments — vi
Introduction — 1

Part One. Drawing Lines in the Sand: The Villain as "Other" — 7
1. "Red in tooth and claw": The Villain as Nature — 11
2. Sybarites and Savages: The Villain as Barbarian — 33

Part Two. Tyrants, Traitors and Tramps: The Villain as Agent of Discord and Disorder — 59
3. "One who rules without law": The Villain as Tyrant — 64
4. "Et tu, Brute?": The Villain as Traitor — 101
5. "Her arms are wicked and her legs are long": The Villain as Femme Fatale — 139

Part Three. The Bad Seed: The Villain as Pathology — 179
6. Gangsters and Grifters: The Villain as Sociopath — 183
7. Rippers and Rapists: The Villain as Psychopathic Murderer — 211

Epilogue. Marplots and Madmen: The Villain as Metaphor — 234
Chapter Notes — 241
Bibliography — 252
Index — 259

Introduction

> LUKE SKYWALKER: *[angrily] I'll never join you!*
> VADER: *If only you knew the power of the Dark Side. Obi-Wan never told you what happened to your father.*
> LUKE: *He told me enough! He told me you killed him!*
> VADER: *No, I am your father.*
> LUKE: *[shocked] No. No! Thats not true! That's impossible!*
> VADER: *Search your feelings; you know it to be true!*
> LUKE: *NOOOOOOO! NOOOOOOOO!!!*
> VADER: *Luke, you can destroy the Emperor. He has foreseen this. It is your destiny! Join me, and together, we can rule the galaxy as father and son! Come with me. It is the only way.*
> —The Empire Strikes Back

As my friends, colleagues, and students all know, I am an unabashed fan of *Star Wars* episodes IV *A New Hope*, V *The Empire Strikes Back*, and VI *Return of the Jedi*. Of these three movies, I concur with the overwhelming majority of *Star Wars* aficionados in adjudging episode V the best of the series. It sports a well crafted story with splendid special effects, stirring action scenes, romance, interesting new characters—Yoda being the most memorable—and the shocking revelation—revealed above—that *the* villain of the galaxy, Darth Vader, is the father of Luke Skywalker, the heroic youth destined to be its savior.

Another element that makes this film so memorable to its many fans is how the figure of Vader, in his black armor, boots, cape, and brilliantly polished *Wehrmacht* helmet, dominates every scene in which he plays a part. Even though the audience is rooting for the other side, it cannot help but be mesmerized, even attracted to, the menace, unstoppable power, and utter ruthlessness of Lucas' Sith Lord. He is without question the most interesting character in *The Empire Strikes Back*, and may very well be the only figure of any real substance or interest in the whole *Star Wars* universe.

What makes Lucas' villain such an odious and yet compelling antagonist?

There is of course that striking wardrobe, the bright red light saber, and the command he exercises over the "dark side" of this supernatural entity called the "force." All of Vader's accouterments play on deeply held Western fears associated with darkness, fire, sorcery, and, more recently, Nazism. Beyond the uniform, however, Vader behaves in a manner that projects confidence and power. While others dither and prevaricate, he acts decisively. In a time where everyone is paralyzed and powerless, he appears to stand out from history and seems quite capable of changing it.

While Lucas' prequel to the original *Star Wars* trilogy leaves much to be desired, it does provide us with backstory on his villain that further contributes to his allure. We find out in these three movies that Vader's alter ego, Anakin Skywalker, was born a slave, worked as a grease monkey building and repairing robotics and cars, and, upon becoming an aspiring Jedi knight, showed himself to be both a rebel and a romantic. Indeed, his path to perdition is lined with only the best of intentions, and, as we find out in episode VI, this ultimately leads to his redemption. In short, we have in Darth Vader the heads and tails of villainy, or to paraphrase the Rolling Stones' *Sympathy for the Devil*, he is the cop who became a criminal, the sinner who becomes a saint.

Why have I gone on at such great length about a fictional character that most of my colleagues in academe find puerile? In part, my interest in Vader stems from the fact that I have a model of him on the desk in my study; his imperial march is the ringtone on my iPhone; and I routinely cheer for him whenever he appears on screen (a habit that has gotten me pelted with popcorn by irate young children on more than one occasion). There's something odd about all of this and, as an academic, I am genuinely interested in figuring out why I find such an obviously villainous character so attractive and exciting.

This Vader fetish aside, I am also beginning this book with a discussion of Lucas' antagonist because he is in many respects the perfect metaphor for the many villainous types addressed in this work. Indeed, Vader's backstory embodies the original meaning of the word "villain," which was derived from the Latin *villanus*, a term used to describe a rural laborer, or a slave, who worked on one of the large country farms known as *villas* in ancient Italy. During the Middle Ages, *villanus* was assimilated into Old and Anglo-Norman French as *vilein* or *villain* and was used, as it had been in Latin, to designate "a low-born rustic." Because of the association of villain with individuals who were "ignoble" and unbounded by accepted codes of gentlemanly conduct, it also became a moniker during the medieval period for any "unprincipled or depraved scoundrel" who was "naturally disposed to base or criminal actions, or deeply involved in the commission of disgraceful crimes." It is striking that some two millennia later, Lucas casts as his villain a young man born on the wrong side of the tracks who works with his hands as a slave on a largely rural planet.

I also argue in this book that the term villain has long been used in Western culture as a "line drawing word," i.e., as a signifier for "others" who are deemed dangerous; individuals who sow discord and disorder; and people who are chronic criminals. Vader is all of these things. His origins and nature set him apart from the paladins of the republic and his fellow Jedi. His impatience with republican corruption, and love for a woman of power and wealth—a "femme fatale," if you will—lead him to a heinous act of betrayal that ushers in a terrible tyranny, which he serves loyally and efficiently. His many cold-blooded crimes—massacres, murders, and xenocide—identify him as a sociopath of the first order. Indeed, Darth Vader is the villain *par excellence*.

Finally, Vader's redemption at the end of Lucas' space opera also points to another key concern of this study, the way in which much of what was once considered villainous has now been called into question, and in some cases redeemed. For example, like the force, the West now recognizes that nature also has a "good side" that is necessary for our survival as a species. Otherness, whether based in foreignness, ethnicity, or class, is no longer in and of itself a reason to villainize a person or people. Tyrants have been deemed "great," traitors sometimes are hailed as patriots (if their side wins), powerful women are today's CEOs, and some psychologists believe that sociopathy can be harnessed for positive ends. As Jagger's Lucifer reminds us, we are living in a time where cops can be criminals, and all the sinners saints. How and why these shifts in thinking have occurred is a question addressed here.

Before turning to these matters, however, I would like to say something about how this book came about, why it is organized as it is, and what kinds of materials have been consulted in addressing its subject matter. This study follows on the heels of an earlier work, *The Heroic Ideal: Western Archetypes from the Greeks to the Present*, also published by McFarland in 2010. Though I originally did not intend to address the subject of villains and villainy at that time, my work on heroes and heroism did raise a number of questions concerning those whose actions highlight what we regard as immoral and unlawful conduct. For example, what has the word villain meant over the last three millennia of Western history, how has it been used during this time, and who or what has been deemed worthy of the rubric? Concurrently, have our notions with regard to villains and villainy changed over time, and, if so, how have these changes in thinking reflected and influenced shifts in the ethical, social, and political thinking of Western society and culture? No less than with my work on the hero, I felt that addressing these queries might shed considerable light on what sociologist Norbert Elias refers to as the Western "civilizing process"—the complex of technology, manners, knowledge, self-perception, and worldview that distinguishes Occidental society from all others.

To this end, I have followed the Weberian method that I used in *The Heroic Ideal*. That is, I examine a number of villainous "types" representative of entities, individuals, and actions that have been associated with villainy of one form or another over the last three millennia. These include nature (*the great enemy of humanity through most of our history*), barbarians, tyrants, traitors, femme fatales, sociopaths, and psychopathic murderers.

Unlike my history of the hero, however, which followed the dramatic expansion of the heroic pantheon from demi-gods to schlumps like the Big Lebowski, this book focuses on types that have been consistently regarded as villainous in the West. For example, while the face and features of the barbarian change over time, the "other" who invades, disrupts, and devastates our communities is almost always regarded as an odious "scourge of God" or "swarm of locusts." Consequently, each of the book's chapters examines in some detail the history of the type with which it is concerned. By way of illustration, the chapter dealing with the tyrant introduces the reader to the various permutations of this word from a rubric for the ruler of a Greek city-state who was not a *basileus*, or king, to a term associated with usurpers, despots, dictators, and faceless bureaucracies. Each of these faces of tyranny is further illustrated by case studies, e.g., Pisistratus of Athens, Peter the Great of Russia, Germany's Adolf Hitler, and the dystopias of oppressive domination found in works such as *1984* and *Brave New World*.

The book is also divided into three parts dealing with how different types of villains have been used by Western societies to identify and delineate insiders from outsiders; political, social, and sexual behaviors that foster discord and disorder; and mal- as opposed to well-adjusted mental health. Part One addresses the villain as an "other," i.e., as *something* or *someone* that poses a real and present danger to the well-being of the human communities that settled in and around the Mediterranean as well as Europe and the Americas. In the first chapter, the reader is introduced to the origins and development of the longstanding animus between Westerners and the natural world. It moves from the many real dangers confronting early humans during the Paleolithic period to an examination of how nature's villainous reputation is further enshrined within the storytelling traditions of pagan and later Christian civilizations and then reinforced and strengthened by such developments as the new science and the industrial revolutions of the modern period. The second chapter examines in some detail how and why Western civilizations from the Greeks to the present have villainized particular societies and social groups by labeling them "barbaric." It moves from the use of this term as a moniker to describe non–Greek speaking peoples to a largely negative catchword that is used over time to describe nomadic tribesmen, non–Christians, non–Westerners, impoverished, uneducated, and unwashed folk in general, and the modern social welfare state.

While the first part of the book examines how notions of villainy are used to distinguish insiders from outsiders, Part Two considers how certain villainous types are used to identify political, social, economic, and cultural behaviors believed to constitute a threat to the order, harmony, and well-being of society itself. Specifically, this part's chapters look at how the actions of the tyrant, traitor, and so-called femme fatale have both challenged and reinforced Western thinking with regard to legitimate governance, loyalty to one's people, and proper male/female roles and relationships. Each chapter also makes use of appropriate historical case studies to further explicate the different facets of its subject matter.

Part Three addresses those villainous types identified as the sociopathic gangster and grifter and the psychopathic murderer. Throughout the history of villainy, these individuals have served as models of evil and/or unprincipled behavior, and, in so doing, have highlighted what we regard as moral and rightful conduct. Each chapter in this part addresses how Western society explains and deals with the problem of what is now called "anti-social behavior." During this discussion, considerable attention is paid to the role of what Barbara Oakley refers to as "evil genes" in determining why these individuals behave as they do, and whether or not their actions can be better understood and even curtailed through neuroscience and psychiatric treatment.

This study ends with a consideration of two distinct, albeit related, phenomena, i.e., the dramatic shrinking of what is considered villainous in the West in tandem with the proliferation of all manner of odd and over-the-top villains in Western pop culture and mass media. Regarding the former of these two developments, it is striking how many of the types treated in this work would no longer be regarded as proper candidates for inclusion in the annals of villainy. For example, everyone is now a tree hugger; barbarians are lovable hirsute folks in Capital One commercials; tyrants are the bureaucratic personnel and practices that make modern mass societies possible; femme-fatales are now regarded as "career girls"; and grifters and serial killers are not only mentally ill individuals in need of treatment but actual heroic figures in not a few films and television series (*Dexter* being the most obvious case in point).

As with my study of the heroic ideal, this treatment of villains makes use of a wide variety of primary and secondary texts. These include poems, plays, novels, histories, and films that are focused in one way or another on the lives and actions of figures that have been and continue to be regarded as villainous. This book is also a deeply syncretistic study that attempts to deepen our understanding of the connections between changing conceptions of villainy and the process by which the West has defined its moral, social, and political values.

Part One

Drawing Lines in the Sand
The Villain as "Other"

> We are all born into systems of lines that mark off nearly all of our experiences. Such lines define the self, others, nature, time, space, and God/gods.... Line-drawing enables us to define our various experiences so as to situate ourselves, others, and everything and everyone that we might come into contact with. Our ancestors passed down to us the set of lines they inherited, and with this we find ourselves in a cultural continuum that reaches back to the sources of our cultural heritage.
>
> —Bruce J. Malina, *The New Testament World*

> They cannot represent themselves; they must be represented.
>
> —Karl Marx, *The Eighteenth Brumaire of Louis Bonaparte*

Imagine if you will the Périgord region in the south of France some 30,000 years ago. It is a densely forested area of valleys, high cliffs, steep banks, and deep gorges carved out of the surrounding countryside by the waters of what we now call the Dordogne River, a wide stream with strong and swift currents that originates in the French Massif Central and flows into the Atlantic Ocean in the west. This lush and verdant landscape is extremely fertile and filled with assorted flora, many of which provide a variety of edible fruits, vegetables, and nuts. It is also home to an array of large and fierce megafauna—mammoths, mastodons, giant elk, aurochs, cave bears, saber-toothed cats—as well as smaller creatures like deer, wood mice, birds, snakes, and lizards.

In addition to this local flora and fauna, there is a hominid species, *Homo neanderthalensis*, or "Neanderthal man," that inhabits this territory. Short and stout—they are roughly five feet, five inches in height and weigh about 185 pounds—these primitive humans have massive muscles, expansive rib cages, capacious lungs, sloped chins and foreheads, big noses, and low domed skulls housing brains that are somewhat larger than our own. Using a range of simple stone tools and sharp, fire-hardened spears, they spend most of their time hunting, killing, and carving up their animal neighbors, and, occasionally, when food is scarce, one another. They clothe themselves with the hides and furs of their prey, and find shelter in the many caves that line the cliffs above the Dordogne River.

At some point during this time period, small nomadic bands of Cro-Magnon men and women, each numbering some 20 to 30 people, arrive in this same region. In appearance, these folks are anatomically modern humans, that is, they are anywhere from five feet, five inches to five feet, seven inches in height. Their arms, legs and chests are well-muscled (though not nearly so large as their Neanderthal neighbors), and their faces feature tall straight foreheads, slight brow ridges, and prominent chins.

One thing that is instantly apparent about these Cro-Magnon visitors is that they are much more sociable and talkative than their Neanderthal kin. They use their capacity for language to transmit to one another information about their bands—where they come from, what they have achieved, who among them are counted as ancestors, how they relate to one another—as well as what they have learned about the natural environment, tool making, hunting and gathering, music, dance, and art. All of this chatter also appears to have been translated into the stuff of a rather sophisticated material culture, i.e., stronger and more durable weapons and tools made out of finely worked stone blades, animal bones, and antlers; woven baskets, nets, and warm clothing; bracelets, armbands, and necklaces; figurines of animals and humans carved out of stone and wood; and manganese and iron oxides that can be used to paint pictures of the local fauna on cave walls.

The other thing that stands out about these Cro-Magnons is how quickly and efficiently they take control of their new home. They scout out the terrain, establish campsites in secure locations, and then begin to systematically exploit the non-human environment for foodstuffs, fibers, fuel, and anything else that can be transformed into useful technologies. Their sociability and communication skills also allow them to organize and coordinate effective defenses against the area's larger predators, as well as to launch hunting parties that trap and bring down mammoths, mastodons, elk, and aurochs. While the men harvest the region's megafauna, Cro-Magnon women and children gather together the edible plants of the Périgord, as well as its smaller animals.

Though it will take several thousand years, these sociable tech savvy Cro-Magnon bands will exterminate both the large predators and the big game animals of the Périgord. They will also considerably reduce the number of smaller animals in the area—snakes, deer, birds, fish—while increasing the numbers of those they choose to domesticate—goats, sheep, pigs, dogs. The region's flora will also be radically altered, as Cro-Magnon communities become more sedentary and begin to slash and burn the Périgord's forests in order to cultivate plants and trees that produce edible grains, fruits, and vegetables.

In addition to substantially altering the natural environment of this region, Cro-Magnon man will change the human face of this area as well. Bereft of the more sophisticated tool kits, clothing, and communication strategies of their neighbors, Neanderthal bands will watch in dismay as the megafauna on which they depend for survival are hunted into extinction. Like the Indian tribes of 19th century North America, many of these folks will leave the Périgord in search of new hunting grounds only to find themselves confronting the same situation in other areas of Europe. Those that attempt to stay in this territory, or resist the invaders, will be wiped out. Indeed, by the end of the Pleistocene, modern man will have erased *Homo neanderthalensis* from the face of the earth.

This Cro-Magnon exercise in environmental and social engineering is carried out ruthlessly and without remorse. The natural world is treated as an enemy to be defeated, tamed, and exploited for the benefit of the new kids on the block, *Homo sapiens*. Similar treatment is meted out to the neighborhood's Neanderthals whose different physical appearance, unfamiliar language, crude clothing, simple tools, and seeming lack of any kind of cohesive society or culture quickly identify them as something not quite human and therefore a threat to be eliminated.

In both their treatment of the natural environment and the Neanderthals, our ancestors were engaged in what scholar and theologian Bruce Malina refers to in this section's opening epigraph as "line drawing." That is, they are defining the non-human world, and another group of hominids living within it, as "other" or alien from themselves. More importantly, at least for the purpose of this study, these first "wise men and women" of modern humanity identify and represent this difference in stories, songs, dances, and art as something dangerous, life-threatening, and wicked. Indeed, in many respects, this judgment is the first chapter in the history of villainy.

What follows addresses this sense of the villain as an "other," i.e., as *something* or *someone* that poses a real and present danger to the well-being of the human communities that settled in and around the Mediterranean, as well as Europe and the Americas. In the first chapter, the reader is introduced to the origins and development of the longstanding animus between Westerners and the natural world. It begins by taking a look at the many dangers confronting early humans during the Paleolithic period, and how the struggles of these individuals for survival against a hostile environment gives rise to a sense of nature as a dark, terrible, and chaotic place. This prehistoric prelude is then followed by an examination of how nature's villainous reputation is further enshrined within the storytelling traditions of pagan and later Christian civilizations, and then reinforced and strengthened by such developments as the new science and the industrial revolutions of the modern period.

The second chapter examines in some detail how and why Western civilizations from the Greeks to the present have villainized particular societies and social groups by labeling them "barbaric." Beginning as a moniker to describe peoples that simply do not speak Greek, barbarian becomes a largely negative catchword that is used over time to describe nomadic tribesmen, non–Christians, non–Westerners, impoverished, uneducated, and unwashed folk in general, and the modern social welfare state. This section concludes with some reflections on the ways in which the barbarian is rehabilitated in the modern world—a development that is a contributing factor to the wars and other crimes against humanity characteristic of the 20th century—as well as on what the continuing popularity of this villainous type tells us about popular attitudes towards the contemporary mass societies of the West.

It should be noted here in closing that this section does not address the ways in which different minorities, e.g., Jews, Sinti Roma, African-Americans, homosexuals, have been cast into the role of villainous "others" by various groups—anti-Semites, racists, homophobes—in Western history. While considerable energy has been expended, particularly in the modern period, on efforts aimed at portraying these groups in the worst possible light, their villainy has rested largely on who they are rather than on anything they have actually done to threaten the lives and well-being of the majority populations among whom they live and work. Concurrently, there already exist a great many reputable and exhaustive studies that address the many ways in which these peoples have been unjustly stereotyped, maligned, and persecuted.

1

"Red in tooth and claw"
The Villain as Nature

Wilderness is precisely what man has been fighting against since he began his painful, awkward climb to civilization. It is the dark, the formless, the terrible, the old chaos which our fathers pushed back.... It is held at bay by constant vigilance, and when the vigilance slackens it swoops down for a melodramatic revenge.
—Robert Wermick

The whole forest was peopled with frightful sounds,—the creaking of the trees, the howling of wild beasts, and the yell of Indians; while sometimes the wind tolled like a distant church-bell, and sometimes gave a broad roar around the traveler, as if all Nature were laughing him to scorn.
—Nathaniel Hawthorne, *Young Goodman Brown*

The wild is perhaps the very possibility of being eaten by a mountain lion.
—Gary Snyder

Just when you thought it was safe to go back in the water.
—*Jaws* tagline

In 1998, a film entitled *The Blair Witch Project* opened in movie theaters across the United States. Pieced together from amateur audio and video material shot in real time, the movie ostensibly relates the true story of three independent film students who disappeared somewhere in the woods near Burkittsville, Maryland, while shooting a documentary about a local legend known as the Blair Witch. Viewers of the *Project* were told they were watching footage recovered a year later that was produced by these young people prior to their disappearance.

Over the course of the film's running time of 86 minutes, the audience watches the movie's producers—Heather Donahue, Joshua Leonard, and

Michael C. Williams—interview locals about the nearby wood. These discussions reveal that this forest has been the site of a number of ritual killings and child murders, and is also believed to be haunted by the spirit of a witch who was hanged there in the 18th century. Later footage shows our intrepid filmmakers entering the woods, stumbling onto an old cemetery with some human-like stick figures hanging from trees, getting hopelessly lost, hearing lots of frightful sounds, becoming separated, panicking, and finally ending up in an abandoned house once owned by the murderer of seven children. The movie ends in the house's basement with a lot of screaming and Heather falling to the floor with her camera. The fact that these three are never seen again leads the viewer to the inexorable conclusion that the Burkittsville forest has claimed three more victims.

While there is a very real air of authenticity about *The Blair Witch Project*—the footage is choppy, grainy, and amateurishly shot, the audio track is chaotic, and the three students do appear to be a truly hapless lot who have, quite literally, lost their way—it is actually a cleverly crafted horror "mockumentary." Produced by a group of highly talented amateurs on a shoestring budget of about $35,000, the film was originally intended for cable television rather than theatrical release. However, a favorable response from critics at the 1999 Sundance Film Festival led to its acquisition by Artisan Studios, which decided to market the movie over the internet—an advertising first at the time—as a record of real events.

Despite the fact that *The Blair Witch Project* turned out to be the stuff of fiction rather than fact, the film was one of the blockbuster hits of 1999. It was well-received by both filmmakers and critics, winning both a Global Film Critics Award for Best Screenplay and the Independent Spirit John Cassavetes Award. And audiences flocked to the movie, allowing it to gross over $248 million worldwide.

This critical and box office success is not altogether surprising when one considers that menacing woods are a venerable and highly popular trope in the oral, literary, and performing arts traditions of the West. These forbidding forests are found in folk tales like *Hansel and Gretel* and *Little Red Riding Hood*, medieval quest literature, the modern short stories and novels of such authors as Nathaniel Hawthorne, Bram Stoker, J. R. R. Tolkien, and James Dickey, the musical scores of Stravinsky and Prokofiev, and films as varied as Werner Herzog's *Aguirre: The Wrath of God* and John MacTiernan's *Predator*. Indeed, for centuries, if not millennia, Westerners have been narrating, singing, writing, and enacting a vast compendium of stories that highlight the idea that the forest is essentially a repository of malicious forces—monsters, ghosts, carnivorous beasts, diseases, savages, cannibals, and killers—lying in wait to wreak havoc on humanity.

Nor is this animus limited only to woodlands. Western culture is also awash with stories of oceans infested with leviathans, killer whales and man-eating sharks; mountains that house grizzlies, pumas, trolls, nefarious dwarves, and deadly dragons; and desert wastelands inhabited by venomous serpents, scorpions, marauders, demons, and evil jinn. With the exception of romantic poetry—much of which is fixated on the "sublime" or awe inspiring *horror* of nature—and the narratives of assorted 19th and 20th century naturalists and ecological activists, the non-human natural environment has been routinely portrayed in the West as a villainous place that tests, torments, and, more often than not, terminates any unwary soul who enters into its environs.

The following pages argue that this animosity towards nature is a persistent and pervasive motif of Western civilization that originates in the Paleolithic Age when the first bands of *Homo sapiens* confronted a natural environment replete with toxic flora, fearsome fauna, challenging climatic conditions, and species extinguishing eco-catastrophes. In the face of these extraordinary challenges to their survival, early human societies developed a sense of the non-human world as a dark, terrible, chaotic place populated by hostile forces that needed to be kept at bay and, where possible, subdued. This antagonistic stance was further strengthened by the development of primal technologies and information exchange systems—stone tools and weapons, trade, art, storytelling—that served to distinguish human beings as markedly different from other animals.

The advent of agriculture, and the urban societies made possible by this development, only fortified this early human hostility towards the natural world. Threatened by periodic and devastating floods, droughts, and earthquakes, and often surrounded by mountains and forests populated by wild beasts and warlike hill folk, the early Mesopotamian kingdoms and empires—Sumerian, Babylonian, Canaanite, Hittite, Assyrian—all embraced a view of nature as a divine punishment visited on humanity by a race of cruel and capricious gods. This sense of the non-human environment as a cursed place was also adopted by the inhabitants of the Persian and later Greco-Roman civilizations that supplanted the Mesopotamians in the Near East and the Mediterranean basin. Indeed, even where one finds praise in these cultures for the "fields, crops and joyous vineyards" of pastoral life, this "tamed" nature is always distinguished from its more savage counterparts in the wild areas that border civilization.

Christianity does little to assuage Western anxieties regarding the dangers inherent in a state of nature. While there are theologians and saints, the most notable being Francis of Assisi, who view the natural world as a divine gift entrusted to the care and stewardship of humanity, the vast majority of Christians continue to view it through the lenses of their pagan and Jewish forebears, i.e., as an accursed wilderness created by God to punish the wicked and test the faithful. Consequently, from late antiquity through the Middle Ages, Christian literature is replete with stories of anchorites, maidens, pilgrims, and knights who are tempted and tormented in dark woods, miasmic marshes, and withered wastelands by the assorted demons and dragons that call these places home.

Even the "new science" and romanticism of the modern period, with its movements which embrace and in some cases worship the natural environment, only help further the idea of nature as a less than hospitable place for human beings. For example, while scientists successfully explore the wild places of Earth and put to rest all manner of misperceptions about them, they also bring to the fore evolutionary theories that portray the natural world as a savage state of being characterized by bitter and unequal struggles for survival and mastery. This portrayal of nature's realm as a place "red in tooth and claw" is further buttressed by self-styled romantic artists who generate poetry, prose, painting, and music depicting and celebrating powerful predators, fierce storms, tragedies at sea, and sublime vistas. All of which is merely a prelude to the disaster films—*Earthquake, Volcano, Day After Tomorrow*—television dramas—*Survivor, Lost, Shark Week*—and *Blair Witch* projects of the contemporary period.

The foregoing précis on nature and its detractors highlights the principal points that are addressed in greater depth below. In the sections that follow, we examine the origins of nature's villainous reputation in the Paleolithic period, how this ill-fame was reinforced and strengthened in the myths, legends, and folklore of pagan and later Christian civilizations, and why the advent of modernity has done so little to ameliorate the notion of nature as a place naturally disposed to wickedness, evildoing, crime, and human suffering. And this exploration begins in the savannas of east Africa.

"Lions and tigers, and bears, oh my!": *Modern Humanity's First Encounters* *with Nature*

The above-quoted expression of dismay uttered by Dorothy Gale and her companions upon entering a dark forest on the way to Oz was one with which our primeval ancestors could have easily identified. For their world was also a place full of forbidding woods and wastes populated with lions, tigers, bears and a great many other predatory animals. And for small bipedal creatures such as themselves—bereft of great strength, speed, or heightened senses—any encounters with such predators was, more likely than not, a sentence of death usually accompanied by grisly dismemberment. "Oh my" indeed!

In fact, it is hard to imagine a less hospitable moment for modern humanity to make its debut on the stage of history than the middle and upper periods of the Old Stone Age, i.e., the time span stretching from roughly

300,000 to 11,000 years before the Common Era. During this period, both eastern Africa, where our ancestors emerged some 200,000 to 100,000 years ago, and the Eurasian and Asian continents to which they migrated, were subject to radical variations in climate. On the African continent, for example, human bands experienced devastating mega- droughts that reduced the areas in which they hunted and gathered to arid, windswept, and often treeless landscapes. Their compatriots in Europe and northwestern Asia, on the other hand, confronted an environment that was often covered by vast sheets of ice brought on by long severe winters and subzero temperatures of the last great ice age, an event that lasted from 115,000 to 15,000 BCE. Suffice it to say that in the face of such climatic extremes, it must have been terribly difficult, if not at times impossible, for our forebears to locate such basics of survival as potable water, edible plants, and animal protein.[1]

Compounding these difficulties was the supereruption of the Toba volcano in Indonesia some 74,000 years ago. Rated an 8 on the Volcanic Explosivity Index—a number that represents a "mega-colossal explosion"—this blast leveled a mountain, unleashed lava flows that covered over 7,700 square miles, ejected something in the neighborhood of one trillion cubic meters of dust, ash, pumice, and other kinds of material into the atmosphere, and produced a cloud column that was over 32.5 kilometers (20 miles) high. It is believed that the fallout from this eruption covered the entirety of south Asia, the South China Sea, the Arabian Sea, and the Indian Ocean, and very likely brought on a global volcanic winter. A number of scholars also conjecture that this eco-catastrophe wiped out most if not all of the human bands in the Near East and Asia, decimated many of the plants and animals on which early humanity was dependent, and reduced the total human population to somewhere in the neighborhood of three thousand to ten thousand individuals, the vast majority of whom were in Africa. In short, this was a moment in time when *Homo sapiens* came perilously close to extinction.[2]

In addition to these droughts, glaciers, and environment altering mega-colossal explosions, early modern humans also had to compete for food on African plains and in Eurasian forests with some truly fearsome creatures. These included the more run-of-the mill predators alluded to above, as well as megafauna, or "large animals," such as mammoths, mastodons, wooly rhinos, aurochs, saber-tooths, and giant cave bears. And it bears repeating that these critters were not only imposing in size, but also stronger, faster, and equipped with far keener senses than their human counterparts.[3]

Confronted with life-threatening climates, cataclysms, and creatures, it is hardly surprising that early modern humans came to see nature as an adversary bent on their destruction. Indeed, many of the traits that define us as a distinctive species appear to have been adaptive responses to this hostile environment. The willingness of our early ancestors to band together and collaborate with one another afforded them an effective means of protecting themselves and their young from predators. Skill in fashioning weapons and other kinds of tools from fine-grained stone further enhanced the security of these bands, as well as their ability to acquire food. And the development of a "knowledge sense," as some anthropologists have described the human capacity for language and culture, provided *Homo sapiens* with a decisive advantage over their natural adversaries by allowing them to transmit information within and between human beings at different points in space and time.[4] Taken together, all of these behaviors allowed Stone Age humanity to "ride out the punches of rapid climate change and brutal temperatures, occasional hunger, and catastrophic hunting accidents."[5]

These patterns of behavior also reinforced a sense among humans that they were opposed to and distinctive from the surrounding natural environment. While other animals cooperate opportunistically in the search for food and are also capable of using rudimentary tools, only modern humans developed complex syntactical languages and other forms of symbolic communication such as chanting, dancing, drawing, painting, ceremonies, and rituals. These various signifiers of meaning not only allowed our ancestors to preserve and communicate information about technological innovations, sources of nourishment, predatory behavior, and climatic conditions, but they also afforded human bands with a means of identifying and differentiating themselves from one another and, most importantly, from the non-human world. Indeed, whatever the purpose or rationale of such early modern artifacts as shell necklaces, Venus figurines, or cave paintings of megafauna, they all highlight the ways in which humanity was coming to see itself as something of a distinctive, even alien presence within the state of nature. And, as we will see in the next section, this feeling of otherness became more entrenched as hunters and gatherers settled down into the first urban communities.[6]

"Cursed is the ground for thy sake; in sorrow thou shalt eat of it all the days of thy life": Nature as Divine Punishment

At first glance, the domestication of plants and animals during the New Stone Age, which encompassed the time period between 11,000 and 4,000 BCE, should have ushered in a rapprochement of sorts between early humanity and the natural world. The discovery that certain kinds of flora and fauna could be reproduced, harvested, stored, and herded allowed human bands to settle down in certain territories for most of the year and also reproduce at a more rapid rate. On the non-human side of the equation, intensive cultivation of certain seeds, and the selective breeding of assorted animals, favored genetic variations that made it possible for these crops and creatures to both survive and thrive.

Sedentarization, however, and the rapid population growth that accompanied this development, presented humanity with a whole new set of problems. Prolonged settlement, for example, coupled with the need to feed more mouths, led to an increase in hunting and gathering activities that decimated the non-domesticated food sources of the areas humans now called home. Bereft of the nourishment once provided by these wild plant and animal populations, human bands were increasingly compelled to adopt both a more restricted diet and the agricultural routines that made this dietary regimen possible. What had been simple gardening and herding operations aimed at providing supplementary forms of nourishment now became the central all-encompassing activity of human life.

And this new agricultural and pastoral lifestyle was anything but leisurely. Indeed, as farmers and herders from almost any period in human history could attest, their occupations entailed yearlong, dawn till dusk activities that were arduous and exhausting. Soil needed to be turned and seeded and the sown fields had to be constantly monitored lest weeds, birds, and various other pests destroy the crops. Domesticated animal stock—goats, sheep, cattle—required pasturage and around the clock protection from predators. Everything harvested from these plants and animals, whether grain, tubers, vegetables, fur, meat, or milk, required additional labor to preserve, secure, and transform it into a state where it could be eaten and/or worn. No gods or prophets were necessary to remind either our early ancestors or their later descendants that life on the land was literally living by the sweat of one's brow.

Cultivated crops and domesticated livestock also required considerable amounts of water and so humanity began to settle in ever increasing numbers along the banks of assorted rivers. Settled life next to these streams brought human communities into contact with assorted dangers such as venomous serpents, man-eating reptiles (crocodiles), and insect-borne diseases (malaria). River settlements also had to contend with the periodic tendency of these tributaries to overflow their banks and inundate the surrounding countryside. And these floods, which were usually sudden and without warning, were incredibly destructive events that washed away crops, tools, housing, and countless lives.

Finally, while the adoption of a settled way of life based on agriculture and pastoralism makes possible larger populations and the first urban civilizations, it also results in a situation where humanity finds itself increasingly dependent on a limited number of grain crops and animal by-products. When the weather is fair, the soil rich, and water plentiful, this dependency is a matter of little concern because these conditions make possible surpluses of food, which, for the first time in human history, allow hunger to be easily assuaged.

Unfortunately, as we have seen in our discussion of early modern humanity, the earth's climate is a dynamic system in which dramatic shifts of temperature and rainfall are commonplace. Too much or too little rain, in tandem with excessive heat or cold, can devastate both sown fields and the pasturage on which farm animals live. Couple these natural catastrophes with the tendency of human communities to exhaust the soil through slash and burn farming, or salt buildup from long term irrigation, and drought, famine, pestilence, and death are not far behind.[7]

In addition to these difficulties with "tamed" nature, early agricultural communities were not that far removed from natural environments that were still quite wild. On either side of the settled Nile River valley were wide expanses of waterless desert populated by asps, scorpions, and marauding Bedouin tribes. To the north, east and west of the Fertile Crescent, i.e., the land in and around the Tigris and Euphrates rivers, were formidable and forested mountain chains inhabited by savage animals and inhospitable nomadic communities. And in northern and central Europe, tribes practicing simple slash and burn agriculture lived cheek by jowl with dense dark woods teeming with fearsome boars, bears, and wolf packs. Folks in these areas did not have to wander far to find themselves back in the state of nature from which their ancestors had emerged in an older Stone Age. Suffice it to say that the continuing dangers posed to man by an untamed world that was still very much at his doorstep, as well as the periodic disasters attendant on a sedentary agricultural way of life, served to reinforce what was already a longstanding hostility to nature.

This ancient enmity was further reinforced by the storytelling traditions—written and oral, sacred and secular—of the urban civilizations made possible by Neolithic agriculture. In the first recorded story of the West, the *Epic of Gilgamesh*, the natural world was unequivocally associated with savagery and death. This was made clear at the very beginning of the tale, when the soon-to-be friend, lover, and companion-at-arms of the story's protagonist is created and described in the following way:

> She [the goddess Aruru] created a primitive man, Enkidu the warrior: offspring of silence, sky-bolt of Ninurta. His whole body was shaggy with hair, he was furnished with tresses like a woman, his locks of hair grew luxuriant like grain. He knew neither people nor country; he was dressed as cattle are. With gazelles he eats vegetation, with cattle he quenches his thirst at the watering place. With wild beasts he presses forward for water.[8]

When this "wild man" wreaks havoc in the countryside around the Sumerian city of Uruk, a prostitute is sent out to seduce and then persuade him to adopt a more civilized way of life. Enkidu is quite taken with this harlot, succumbs quickly to her sexual wiles, is tamed, and ultimately agrees to embrace big city life. Soon thereafter, the former primitive hooks up with Uruk's king,

Gilgamesh, and the two go off together on adventures that take them into an untamed natural world populated by fearsome monsters.

The first of these forays brings the tale's protagonists to a dense dark pine forest guarded by a ferocious creature called Humbaba, "whose shout is the flood-weapon, whose utterance is Fire and whose breath is Death."[9] After slaying this monster and cutting down his forest's trees to service Uruk's construction industry, the epic's intrepid heroes next find themselves contending with the goddess Ishtar, who is furious with Gilgamesh for spurning her amorous advances. As will be the case in countless other stories of this sort, the jilted divinity responds to such mortal impudence by unleashing a force of nature against the young king's subjects, i.e., a savage Bull of Heaven whose snorting generates earthquakes. Though the story's dynamic duo also slay this creature, its death visits doom on Enkidu and sends Gilgamesh off in search of immortality.

During his quest, Gilgamesh learns that the gods of his people once attempted to eradicate humankind—in some accounts because they were too noisy—with yet another natural disaster, a great flood. Not only does this effort fail, but the resulting deluge threatens even the deities who unleashed it, and so they resolve in the future to punish humanity more sparingly in the following ways:

> Instead of your imposing a flood, let a lion come up and diminish the people.
> Instead of your imposing a flood, let a wolf come up and diminish the people.
> Instead of your imposing a flood, let famine be imposed and lessen the land.
> Instead of your imposing a flood, let Erra[10] rise up and savage the people.[11]

Perhaps what is most striking about this passage is the way in which the non-human natural world is portrayed as a weapon forged by cruel and capricious gods for the express purpose of visiting misfortune on humankind. And this characterization, the first of its kind in recorded literature, becomes one of the enduring tropes in the storytelling traditions of the West. Indeed, nature as heaven's tool of choice when tormenting humanity recurs in a wide variety of pre-Christian tales scattered throughout the Near East, the Mediterranean basin, and the forests of northern Europe.

Among these texts, the Hebrew Testament was particularly unforgiving in its treatment of the natural world. Composed by the "children of Israel," a collection of pastoral tribes who inhabited an extremely arid stretch of the Near East, this holy book makes clear in its opening pages:

> Because you [Adam] listened to your wife [Eve] and ate from the tree of which I had forbidden you to eat, cursed be the ground because of you! In toil shall you eat its yield all the days of your life. Thorns and thistles shall it bring forth to you, as you eat of the plants of the field. By the sweat of your face shall you get bread to eat.[12]

If damning his chosen people to a precarious existence of subsistence farming and herding was not bad enough, Yahweh, the Hebrew deity that utters the abovementioned curse, continues to use natural disasters and the "wilderness"—as opposed to the blessed lands that support crops and herds—throughout the Hebrew books of the Bible as weapons to test and punish both the children of Israel and whoever else happens to displease him. Early in Genesis, for example, he follows the lead of his Mesopotamian predecessors in Sumer and unleashes a great flood that, with the exception of Noah and his family, exterminates the human race. Soon thereafter, in the same book, he also takes offense at the wicked city ways of the folks living in Sodom and Gomorrah and directs a sulfurous fire at them that transforms their lands into a desert of salt pits and brush. And in Exodus and Deuteronomy, he compels Moses and the 12 tribes to wander the Sinai Peninsula, "the vast and terrible desert with its seraph serpents and scorpions, its parched and waterless ground,"[13] for some 40 years.

Not surprisingly, these experiences, as well as Yahweh's repeated pronouncements through various prophets that he "will lay waste mountains and hills," "turn the rivers into marshes" (and dry those up), and "command the clouds not to send rain upon [the vineyards of Judah],"[14] cause the Israelites to view the natural environment as a scourge employed by their god to test and train his chosen people. As Roderick Nash notes in his own work on the roots of Western hostility to nature, this

> identification of the arid wasteland with God's curse led to the conviction that wilderness was the environment of evil, a kind of hell. There were several consequences. Like that of other cultures, the Hebraic folk imagination made the wilderness the abode of demons and devils. Among them were the howling dragon or tan, the winged female monster of the night called the *ilith*, and the familiar man-goat, *seirim*. Presiding over all was the *Azazel*, the arch-devil of the wilderness.[15]

Greco-Roman literature painted an equally unforgiving portrait of the natural world. As in the verses of Sumer and Israel, Archaic Greek poetry also reiterated the idea that the forces of nature were essentially a kind of anti-personnel ordnance routinely deployed by deities—Olympian ones in this case—intent on punishing any and all human infractions of their prerogatives and cult protocols. In Book 12 of Homer's *Iliad*, for example, a great wall built by the Greek host to protect their ships during the Trojan War deeply offends Poseidon because it was constructed without any assistance, or request for assistance, from the gods, and, as such, raised the prospect that "the fame of this will last as long as dawnlight is scattered, and men will forget that wall which I [Poseidon] and Phoibos Apollo built with our hard work for the hero Laomedon's city."[16] In retribution for this act of hubris, Zeus allowed his sibling to destroy this manmade earthwork after

1. "Red in tooth and claw"   21

the sack of Troy by unleashing the full strength of the Troad rivers against it.

> When in the tenth year the city of Priam was taken and the Argives gone in their ships to the beloved land of their fathers, then at last Poseidon and Apollo took counsel to wreck the wall, letting loose the strength of rivers upon it, all the rivers that run to the sea from the mountains of Ida, Rhesos and Heptaporos, Karesos and Rhodios, Grenikos and Aisepos, and immortal Skamandros, and Simoeis....
> Phoibos Apollo turned the mouths of these waters together and nine days long threw the flood against the wall, and Zeus rained incessantly, to break the wall faster and wash it seaward. And the shaker of the earth himself holding in his hands the trident guided them, and hurled into the waves all the bastions' strengthening of logs and stones the toiling Achaians had set in position.[17]

The non-human environment likewise serves as a vehicle of divine retribution in Homer's *Odyssey*. When Odysseus sings to his Phaikian hosts regarding his efforts to return home after the fall of Troy, he details how his impious acts and those of his crew were punished by fierce storm tossed seas and torments at the hands of monstrous inhuman creatures such as the Cyclops, Scylla, Charybdis, and the Laestrygonians. Indeed, despite his cunning, courage, and skill at arms, Ithaca's heroic king is ultimately forced to acknowledge that before nature "of all creatures that breathe and walk on the earth there is nothing more helpless than a man."[18]

Greece's classical period did little to dispel this assessment. Indeed, despite the pronouncements of a Protagoras that man was the measure of all things, as well as the appearance of philosophers who regarded Earth as a godless realm governed by clearly discernable laws, playwrights and poets continued to view nature as a place to be feared. Exemplary of this tendency were dramas such as Aeschylus' *The Eumenides*, Sophocles' *Philoctetes*, and Euripides' *Bacchae* in which protagonists contended with a natural world that was elemental, hard, savage, and a clear threat to the laws, rationality, art, and leisure characteristic of the Greek *polis*. And the pastoral poetry of this time, as well as that of later Hellenic and Roman writers, only helped to underscore this view by presenting audiences with images of an idealized rustic environment that was quite distinct from the wild areas of the world outside the sway of civilization.[19]

The Celtic and Germanic tribes of northern and western Europe shared their Mediterranean neighbors' disdain for the natural environment. This is evident in the word the early Teutonic and Norse languages came up with to describe the uncultivated and uninhabited places of the earth, i.e., *wilddēoren* (or as it ends up in English "wilderness"). Connoting both a state of disorder and confusion (or "wildness"), as well as untamed savage animals (*dēoren*), this term conveyed the idea of nature as a place bereft of civilization, a place where only wild beasts dwelled and where human beings were likely to become lost, disordered, and "wild."

Like their Sumerian brethren of an earlier time, northern Europeans also enshrined this notion of wilderness as an evil place, dismal in appearance and populated with dangerous creatures, in their epic poetry. In the Anglo-Saxon classic *Beowulf*, for example, the champion after whom the poem is named offers his assistance to a king whose country is plagued by a savage bloodthirsty pair of monsters, i.e., Grendel and his mother. We are told by the teller of the tale that these fiends

> hold to the secret land, the wolf-slopes, the windy headlands, the dangerous fen-paths where the mountain stream goes down under the darkness of the hills, the flood under the earth. It is not far from here [Hrothgar's hall Heorot], measured in miles, that the mere stands; over it hang frost-covered woods, trees fast of root close over the water. There each night may be seen fire on the flood, a fearful wonder. Of the sons of men there lives none, old of wisdom, who knows the bottom.[20]

After mortally injuring Grendel in a battle at his royal employer Hrothgar's mead hall—a manmade dwelling filled with light, liquor, victuals, and song—Beowulf bravely ventures into this wilderness in search of the creature's even more fearsome mother. Tracking her to a "joyless wood" with water that was "bloody and troubled," our champion descends into a place of "serpents and wild beasts" where he finally confronts the monstrous matriarch and slays her after a frenzied battle.[21] Yet another victory in mankind's struggle with the dark, terrible and chaotic forces of the natural world.

The advent of monotheistic Christianity does little to challenge these pagan conceptions of nature as a source of evil in the world. Not only did Jesus of Nazareth have little to say on this subject, but his initial followers, who were largely Jewish, continued to subscribe to their parent religion's longstanding conviction that the natural environment was an "abode of demons and devils." And this sentiment was only strengthened by the account in the gospels of Matthew, Mark and Luke of Christ's temptation by Satan during his 40-day sojourn in the wilderness.

Indeed, in the first centuries of the Christian era there were a great many accounts of Christians encountering the Lord of Lies and/or his lieutenants in the uninhabited places of the world. Of these encounters, the most famous—by dint of the fact that it became the stuff of countless icons, paintings, and literary works—was that which was reported by St. Anthony the Great (251–356 CE). An early Church father, Anthony lived the life of an anchorite on the edge of Egypt's western desert for some 13 years. During this time, we are told by Anthony's hagiographer, Athanasius the Bishop of Alexandria, that the blessed hermit was repeatedly tempted and even savagely beaten by the devil. Athanasius' account also reports that these diabolic attacks on Anthony reached their crescendo when he was assaulted by phantoms that took, appropriately enough for the wilderness setting of this drama, the form of wolves, lions, venomous serpents, and scorpions.[22] Of course, as in the case of the savior whose life he was emulating, none of these satanic acts were able to shake Anthony's religious convictions. Nevertheless, the fact that these temptations and torments were visited on this man of faith in one of the wild places of the earth, and that they took the form of creatures who inhabited these places, underscored in an unequivocal way for the adherents of Christianity that nature was the realm of Lucifer, and its inhabitants were his to command. And this prejudice was further confirmed by the accounts of countless other anchorites and monks who would follow in Anthony's footsteps, as well as by Christian missionaries who confronted and expelled assorted pagan deities and demons from their woodland shrines throughout northern Europe in the first centuries of the Middle Ages.

Aside from doing battle with Satan and his minions in the outbacks of the world, early Church fathers, such as Origen and Augustine of Hippo, were also busy at this time arguing that the natural world was not part of God's kingdom. They reasoned that because nature was material, finite and fallen, it could have no place in a divine realm that was spiritual, eternal, and free of sin. Further, because the human soul was immortal and could now be cleansed of Adam's original sin by dint of Christ's death on the cross, humanity was also apart from, as well as superior to, the non-human environment. While Augustine and company acknowledged that Earth was a divine creation endowed with beauty and a certain utility—where else would mankind find the stuff necessary to feed and clothe its decadent and corrupt corporeal bodies—they also argued that Christians should maintain a distance from all earthly things lest they be distracted from the critical business of attaining salvation.[23]

The exception to this Christian antagonism towards nature was of course the man who has become something of a symbol for the modern environmental movement, St. Francis of Assisi. Admired and loved for his voluntary poverty, fraternal charity, penance, preaching, and proselytizing, Francis was also renowned as a lover and defender of the non-human world. He penned canticles to the sun and the creatures in which he expressed his love of all God's creations great and small. He also talked to birds, tamed a savage wolf, and preached to, and in some accounts actually converted, the wild animals that were his neighbors in the mountains around Assisi where he lived out his final years in solitary prayer and meditation. Legend has it that the donkey which carried him throughout his life wept at the moment of his death.

Nevertheless, beloved as Francis of Assisi was both in his lifetime and ours, his efforts to convert birds, wolves, and other wild creatures were probably viewed by his contemporaries as eccentric behavior at best and borderline heresy at worst. While the Church accepted the idea that all living things had animating spirits of one sort or another, only angels and humans enjoyed what St. Thomas Aquinas identified as rational souls that were independent of the body and immortal in nature. Add to this notion the fact that most Christians viewed Genesis 1:28[24] as a clear and unequivocal affirmation by God of human domination over the earth, and the case of St. Francis turns out to be little more than "the exception that proves the rule."[25]

Of course the vast majority of Christians during Antiquity and the Middle Ages did not need their Church to warn them about the dangers lurking in the wild places of the world. Popular folk tales—*Red Riding Hood, Hansel and Gretel, Snow White*—and knightly romances—*Lancelot, The Quest for the Holy Grail, Yvain*—were replete with accounts of woods and wastes inhabited by wild animals, outlaws, malevolent spirits, trolls, ogres, and witches. And given the fact that well into the 19th century wilderness was indeed the refuge of bandits, "uncivilized" folk, and feral beasts, these stories were not far off the mark. As the late French historian Eugen Weber noted, the forests one finds in these narratives

> are places through which one wends one's way uneasily, especially if one is alone, most especially if woman or child, not knowing what to expect from the dark solitude. The sounds of forest or waste are not part of the villager's familiar symphony; their dwellers do not participate in the net of relations that makes one feel secure.[26]

Whatever the narrative—origin myth, epic poem, hagiography, folk tale—for five millennia Westerners have been told stories in which the natural environment was portrayed as a dangerous disorderly place where normal human relations and sentiments do not hold sway. This storyline, which probably owes its provenance to humanity's very real struggles for survival from the Pleistocene to the present, has not only been persistent, it has also been pervasive and privileged. Indeed, the notion that nature is a villain has figured prominently in the written, visual, plastic, and performing arts—popular and patrician, sacred and secular—of all Western cultures. In the following section, we will see how this ancient, widespread, and highly popular prejudice has fared in an enlightened age filled with folks who fancied themselves friends of the earth.

A Struggle for Survival: Nature in an Age of Enlightenment and Science

If there was a period in human history when nature's villainous reputation might have been rehabilitated, it was most certainly the so-called Age of Enlightenment that spanned the 17th and 18th centuries of the Common Era. Not only was this movement in European arts and letters dedicated to the eradication of ignorance and superstition in Western life, but it was also centered on a "new science" that was profoundly skeptical of all received knowledge. Rather than accept prior prejudices, assumptions, and shibboleths about the natural world, "enlightened" men and women approached the non-human environment as a phenomenon that could be objectively studied, explained and ultimately harnessed for the benefit of humanity. And out of this dispassionate inquiry emerged a view of nature as a place that was both free of supernatural forces and largely indifferent to *Homo sapiens*.

This scientifically neutral view of the natural environment, however, did not necessarily mean that humanity was ready to abandon its longstanding antagonism towards nature. While 18th and early 19th century accounts of scientific expeditions to the unmapped corners of Earth did much to dispel the notion that wilderness was the haunt of demons and dragons, they nevertheless highlighted how difficult, inhospitable, and dangerous these places could be. Indeed, the Enlightenment savants who embarked on these journeys, men like Pierre-Louis Moreau de Maupertius and Alexander von Humboldt, labeled themselves "explorers"—a term normally associated with soldiers who conducted highly risky reconnaissance in unfamiliar territory—to underscore the fact that encounters with the wild places of the world required not only the erudition of the scholar, but also the stamina and fortitude of the warrior.

This portrayal of nature as a battlefield was further reinforced in the 19th and early 20th centuries by a whole new wave of explorers—Sir Richard Francis Burton, David Livingston, Roald Amundsen, Robert F. Peary—who traveled to uncharted areas of Africa, as well as to the north and south poles. As with their counterparts during the 18th century, these latter day Argonauts also penned accounts of their travels and sold them to a public eager for stories of unknown lands and the hardships attendant on exploring them. Unlike their Enlightenment colleagues, these individuals were also accompanied on their journeys into the wilderness by the representatives of a sensationalist mass press.

Recognizing early on that exploration sells newspapers, large urban dailies often underwrote the expeditions of this time and assigned reporters—Henry Morton Stanley, William Henry Gibbs, Joseph Pulitzer, among others—to cover them. These journalists in turn acted as something akin to heralds, writing columns that accented the challenges and dangers of these journeys and played up the heroic features of the latter-day knights errant who led them. In their accounts of these trips, these newspapermen underscored the sublime and exotic features of the territories through which the scientists they were covering traveled, and highlighted the discomforts and dangers—dense jungles, frozen tundra, stifling heat, bone chilling cold, swarms of insects, wild animals, poisonous snakes, hostile tribes, altitude sickness—they endured. Not only did these news stories demonstrate that their subjects had what Tom Wolfe would later term "the right stuff"—great strength, courage, fearlessness, daring—but they also reinforced within the public mind the age old sentiment of nature as a perilous place with which mankind was in constant conflict.[27]

This sense of nature as a dark and dangerous realm was further strengthened by the appearance of the *Origin of the Species* and *Descent of Man* by Charles Darwin. *The* foundational works of evolutionary biology, these texts posit the idea that human development and behavior are governed neither by God nor sweet reason, but by processes of natural selection rooted in primordial, seemingly irrational and often vicious struggles for survival among the species. According to this schema, humanity is little more than one life form among many struggling to live in and master a limited number of niches in a natural environment that one of Darwin's contemporaries, England's poet laureate Alfred Lord Tennyson, famously described as "red in tooth and claw."

Suffice it to say that this portrayal of existence as a godless, essentially meaningless affair, in which organisms of varying complexity struggle for life, was deeply disturbing to folks who liked to see human civilization as something other than a collection of adaptive strategies adopted over time to address primal urges, needs, and fears. Rather than embrace the idea that humanity and its works are part and parcel of a greater "circle of life" that also includes non-human actors, the vast majority of Westerners at the end of the 19th century instead used the discoveries and theories of the new science to reaffirm the longstanding belief that humans were distinct from and in conflict with the natural world. Writing about this phenomenon in his *Nature's Economy*, Daniel Worster notes:

> Civilization in this view, is a declaration of independence from the natural world, when man "assumes an aggressive attitude, and thenceforward strives to subject to his control and subject to his uses, all her productive and all her motive powers." ... So familiar is this distinction today that it generally seems a truism, as it soon became for the Victorians. Their ideal of civilization almost always depended vitally on the vigorous conquest of nature by science and technology.[28]

It should also be noted here that this idea of man as a civilized being separate from and superior to fallen nature was not limited to critics of evolutionary theory. No less a figure than Thomas Huxley, one of the most notable scientists of the 19th century and Darwin's staunchest defender, also embraced the notion that the natural world is a base place that humanity needs to combat and transform into something better. In 1863, Huxley went so far as to declare:

1. "Red in tooth and claw"

> No one is more strongly convinced than I am of the vastness of the gulf between civilized man and the brutes, or is more certain that whether from them or not, he is assuredly not of them. The power of knowledge—the conscience of good and evil—the pitiful tenderness of human affections, raise us out of all real fellowship with the brutes, however closely they may seem to approximate us.[29]

This assertion by Huxley and others of his ilk that humanity is forever alienated from brutish nature was not without its critics. Many poets, painters, and musicians of the 18th and 19th centuries were highly critical of the Enlightenment assumption that the whole of experience could be understood and explained through reason and science. While not hostile to either rationality or scientific inquiry, these "romantics" were convinced that authentic knowledge and beauty were best found through explorations of the "unclassifiable" in human existence, i.e., through intuition, emotion, imagination, mystery, exoticism, and, most importantly, sublime nature. For these individuals, the natural world is not a phenomenon to be studied and exploited, but rather an organic living being imbued with divine energy that needs to be celebrated and embraced. And from the latter half of the 18th century to roughly 1848, romantic artists did just that.[30]

During this time, poets and writers, such as Johann Wolfgang von Goethe, William Wordsworth, George Gordon Lord Byron, Percy Bysshe Shelley, John Keats, Mary Wollstonecraft Shelley, Georges Sand, and Alexander Pushkin, treated their readers to a literature that was personal, passionate, and peopled with nature worshipping rebels. Their counterparts in the visual arts—Caspar David Friedrich, Eugène Delacroix, Joseph Turner—filled their canvases with color, remote and exotic subjects, and scenes depicting nature's power, terror, and mystery. In music, a generation of composers including, among others, Frédéric Chopin, Franz Liszt, and Ludwig van Beethoven, tripled the size of their orchestras and used percussion, wind instruments, strings, brass, and contrasting tones and themes to recreate for their audiences the splendor of the *Sturm und Drang*, the "storm and stress" of the natural world.[31]

All of this artistic activity generated a more favorable attitude towards nature in the West. While the unexplored and undeveloped reaches of Earth continued to be described as places that are mysterious, chaotic, and dangerous, these characteristics were transformed by romanticism into qualities that were also regarded as aesthetically pleasing, sublime, and "picturesque." Indeed, by the end of the 19th century it was increasingly common for not only artists, but explorers, scientists, intellectuals, and the traveling public-at-large to describe their encounters with mountains, deserts, oceans, storms, and predators as moments of exaltation, awe and delight, rather than as occasions for fear and horror.[32]

Another impetus for this romanticized view of nature was the industrial revolutions that were reshaping the West. While these events generated new products, jobs, and wealth, they were also responsible for pollution, environmental degradation, teeming urban slums, and mass movements of social and political unrest. In the face of these ills, many of the writers, philosophers, naturalists, and politicians of this period espoused what was essentially a romantic view of the natural environment as a refuge from and an alternative to the steam, steel, and strife of modern Western civilization. For these folks, the key to humanity's future health and happiness lay in a return to a simpler more primitive existence in which human beings would once again derive their living from the land, small rural communities would replace modern metropolises, and the surrounding non-human world would be left as a wild place for "rest, inspiration and prayers."[33]

This romantically inspired "primitivist" prescription for the various woes of the industrialized world enjoyed considerable support during the late 19th and early 20th centuries. Youth movements, such as Germany's *Wandervögel* and Britain and America's Boy Scouts, eschewed urban living in favor of hiking and camping in the unspoiled mountains and forests of their respective countries. Arts and crafts activists such as John Ruskin, William Morris, and A. H. Mackmurdo condemned the mechanical in all aspects of craftsmanship, calling instead for textiles, furniture, ceramics, metal ware, and buildings that were handmade and designed in accordance with the sinuous and structural principles found in the flowers, plant forms, and minerals of the natural world. Various nationalist groups in central and eastern Europe popularized the idea that every people, or "folk," was rooted in and shaped by the organic natural surroundings within which their history had unfolded. And "preservationists" such as Henry David Thoreau, John Muir, and Teddy Roosevelt used their pens and bully pulpits to win support for preserving enormous tracts of North American wilderness from development.

All of these efforts helped advance the idea that nature was more friend than foe of humanity, and they also laid the groundwork for both the "back to the land" and environmental movements of the latter half of the 20th century. This said, however, it should also be noted that for most moderns the natural world remained a forbidding presence, and the romantic fixation on sublime landscapes, storms and predators probably did little to change this reality. Indeed, while some might view the misty moonlit mountains and woods of a Caspar David Friedrich painting as sanctuaries of "rest, inspiration, and prayers," a great many others still saw them as disagreeable and dangerous places where humans got lost, went mad, and died horribly.

Art to the side, the romantic take on nature also suffered from the fact that the adherents of romanticism were by and large urban folk. The natural world for these individuals was largely a conceptual, semi-magical place to which they could retire for a weekend or a holiday in order to sip spirits around a camp fire, tell stories or read poems, and express delight at the sight of wild animals (usually at a safe distance), spectacular sunsets, and night skies thick with stars. And while these people might wax eloquent about the joys of living in the outbacks and Walden Ponds of the world, most of their waxing was usually done in a warm apartment or atelier with easy access to the bright lights and creature comforts of a big city.

For those actually living off the land—and until the 1920s most Westerners lived in rural rather than urban areas—nature remained very much an adversary. Whether farmer, fisherman, hunter, trapper, logger, or miner, the natural world was first and foremost a place from which you wrested a living, more often than not with great difficulty and danger. More to the point, for the vast majority of these people, mountains, forests, and bodies of water were ecosystems to be exploited, predators were pesky critters best exterminated, and wind, rain, and lighting were natural phenomena to be endured rather than admired. While romantics and their ilk pined for a return to a simpler way of life boundered by unspoiled wilderness, their far more numerous counterparts in the countryside dreamed of an urbanized (or suburbanized) existence for themselves and their children, which would be supported by a thoroughly tamed and quiescent nature.

In the years following the Second World War, this dream became a reality as the overwhelming majority of Westerners fled what Marx derisively referred to as "the idiocy of rural life" for new occupations and homes in the cities and suburbs of Europe and the Americas. Once ensconced in these urban habitats, very few of these new city dwellers evinced much interest in returning to the hard scrabble existence of hunting, fishing and farming for a living. Insofar as nature impinged on their lives at all, it was largely in the form of well manicured lawns or, if living in an apartment building, flower boxes on a balcony. As for the untamed areas of the natural world, they remained for most folks distant potentially dangerous places that, as Robert Wermick reminds us in the epigraph which opens this chapter, needed "to be held at bay by constant vigilance."

Indeed, what is most striking here is that despite advances in our scientific understanding of the natural world, as well as widespread extremely influential nature worshipping cultural movements, Western attitudes towards the non-human environment have remained remarkably consistent over the last four centuries (if not the last five millennia). In the end, whatever the affectations of modernity, nature continues to be conceived of much as it was in the Pleistocene, i.e., as a rancorous realm to be minded and managed.

As the French are so fond of reminding us *plus ça change, plus c'est la même chose.*

Nature as an Ecology of Fear

In his *Ecology of Fear: Los Angeles and the Imagination of Disaster*, social commentator and urban theorist Mike Davis notes that successive waves of immigrants from America and abroad have wended their way to LA in search of sun, sand, sea, and the promise that "no place on Earth offers greater security to life and greater freedom from natural disaster than Southern California."[34] Once settled in this metropolitan area, however, these folks soon discover that while there is much that is paradisaical about their new home, it is also a place that is privy to flash floods, fires, landslides, earthquakes, droughts, insect infestations, coyotes, and cougars. Not surprisingly, this discovery, which is often accompanied by an actual experience with one or more of these phenomena, has led a great many Angelinos to conclude over the last half century that their local environment is not so much Eden as a capricious, malevolent, and dangerous landscape, which is far from free of natural disasters.

As Davis makes clear in his work, this popular perception that the natural environment of the Los Angeles basin is somehow out to get its human population is ludicrous. Rather, Southern California's ecology, like that of all other ecologies, is a complex system of weather patterns, water sheds, and tectonic activities that determine to a large degree the flora and fauna that inhabit the area. If there is considerable seismic activity in the region, it is because California is part of a Pacific-wide "Ring of Fire" in which earthquakes and volcanic eruptions are commonplace. If there are periodic droughts accompanied by fires, flashfloods, and landslides, it is due to the fact that the regional climate is "Mediterranean" and therefore characterized by hot, dry summers and mild, sometimes wet winters. And if there are pesky critters about such as rattle snakes, skunks, coyotes, and cougars, this is because metropolitan LA is bordered by 657 square miles of mountains and deserts teeming with wild life.

Indeed, if there is a villain at work in Davis' *Ecology of Fear*, it is not nature but man. Commenting on the many ways in which human rather than natural activity is responsible for the region's many disasters, Davis points out:

> Paranoia about nature, of course, distracts attention from the obvious fact that Los Angeles has deliberately put itself in harm's way. For generations, market-driven urbanization has transgressed environmental common sense. Historic wildfire corridors have been turned into view-lot suburbs, wetland liquefaction zones into marinas, and floodplains into industrial districts and housing tracts.... As a result, Southern California has reaped flood, fire, and earthquake tragedies that were as avoidable, as unnatural, as the beating of Rodney King and the ensuing explosion in the streets.... But the social construction of

"natural" disaster is largely hidden from view by a way of thinking that simultaneously imposes false expectations on the environment and then explains the inevitable disappointments as proof of a malign and hostile nature.[35]

I have gone on at such length about Mike Davis' treatment of the Southern California environment because his observations regarding how that ecosystem has been transformed in the popular imagination into an "ecology of fear" are directly pertinent to our foregoing discussion regarding the human tendency to villainize nature. Just as the tectonic plates, water, weather, flora and fauna of Southern California have not behaved in a consciously "malign and hostile" manner towards the human population of the Los Angeles basin, the various ecosystems within which humanity has operated over the last five millennia have been equally guiltless of any malice aforethought towards our species. The non-human world behaves in the way that it does *not* out of any animus against mankind, but because of the various laws that govern physical and biological life on this planet. Unfortunately, as Gary Snyder reminds us, these natural operations sometimes involve "the possibility" that we might be "eaten by a mountain lion."

This unlikely scenario to the side, it appears that, as Davis suggests, we have made nature into a villain because we impose expectations on it that are inappropriate to anything in the natural world save human beings. Because *Homo sapiens* are sentient and remarkably free of the instinctual hard wiring that governs the behavior of most of the other life forms on this planet, our species has, for much of its existence, assumed that the non-human environment also operates at a level of consciousness comparable to our own. Thus, when the earth moves, lighting strikes, and cougars kill, we believe that they do so in a purposeful manner and with malevolent intent. As science reveals, however, this assumption is actually a projection of humanity's fears, vulnerabilities, and insecurities onto a realm that is not governed by the sensibilities of our species. Insofar as nature is villainous, it is a state of being that exists only in the human imagination.

This is not to say that mankind's relationship with Earth and its wild places is not fraught with hardship and danger. Natural disasters such as Hurricane Katrina, the eruption of Mount Saint Helens, and the recent Miyagi earthquake and tsunami off the coast of Japan continue to remind us that Odysseus is correct when he observed that before nature "of all creatures that breathe and walk on the earth there is nothing more helpless than a man." And it is equally unrealistic to expect folks who actually struggle with Earth for a living to feel fuzzy and warm about a natural environment that often injures and sometimes kills them.

These considerations to the side, however, humanity does appear to have arrived at a moment in its history when it is no longer feasible to continue viewing nature as an adversary to be combated and conquered. Such a stance has led to the extinction of whole species of plant and animal life, the exhaustion and erosion of the soil that makes possible the crops and livestock that feed us, depleted fisheries, lifeless swathes of ocean, strip-mined mountains, blighted wilderness, and urban centers erected in areas prone to fires, floods, and earthquakes. Indeed, it has become painfully apparent that the civilization which has made us the crown of creation on this planet is inextricably linked to the non-human environment on whose back it has been built. If this civilization is to survive, in the future we will need to begin the work of reimagining the natural world as less a villain than a kind of quirky, gun toting neighbor whose property lines and behavioral idiosyncrasies should be respected and, where possible, given a wide berth.

2

Sybarites and Savages
The Villain as Barbarian

How sweet is the air here! I can breathe here! Within there are Jews from Jerusalem who are tearing each other in pieces over their foolish ceremonies, and barbarians who drink and drink and spill their wine on the pavement, and Greeks from Smyrna with painted eyes and painted cheeks, and frizzed hair curled in columns, and Egyptians silent and subtle, with long nails of jade and russet cloaks, and Romans brutal and coarse, with their uncouth jargon. Ah! How I loathe the Romans! They are rough and common, and they give themselves the airs of noble lords.

—Oscar Wilde, Salome

They [the Huns] are certainly in the shape of men, however uncouth, but are so hardy that they neither require fire nor well-flavoured food, but live on the roots of such herbs as they get in the fields, or on the half-raw flesh of any animal, which they merely warm rapidly by placing it between their own thighs and the backs of their horses.

—Ammianus Marcellinus, History

You call me uneducated, a barbarian. Yes, we are barbarians, it is what we want to be. It's a title of honour. We are the ones who will rejuvenate the world. This world has reached its end.

—Adolf Hitler, Political Conversations

Tell me whom you call a barbarian and I will tell you who you are.

—Arno Borst, Medieval Worlds

Like many boys, my adolescent reading material was heavily weighted towards sci-fi and fantasy fiction. In particular, I was fond of pulp writers, such as Edgar Rice Burroughs, Robert E. Howard, Jack Vance, and John Norman, whose paperback novels invariably featured lurid covers sporting well-muscled men, usually wielding assorted scimitars and sabers, and their scantily clad, big breasted female companions. Indeed, I spent many a summer in my youth following the adventures of the manly protagonists in these books—John Carter of Mars, Carson Napier of Venus, Conan the Barbarian, Tarl Cabot of Gor—as they made their way across exotic alien landscapes, usually in search of their bosomy beloveds who had fallen into the hands of assorted antagonists that were often described as "barbarians."

These barbaric foes are, to put it mildly, a varied lot. Some of them hail from venerable, albeit dying, city states and empires that are repositories of ancient knowledge and sophisticated science. However, while the technology of these alien urbanites is often superior to that of Earth, their moral character leaves a great deal to be desired. Not only do they live in hierarchically organized slavocracies, usually governed by sinister and tyrannical potentates, but they are also quite fond of blood sports—normally of a gladiatorial variety—luxurious living, and a level of libidinous behavior that would have made the inhabitants of Sodom and Gomorrah blush.

Closely related to these extraterrestrial sybarites are the adherents of assorted cults, usually located in decadent kingdoms or dismal keeps, which are dedicated to dark gods and equally dark magic. These groups are usually led by an elite priesthood privy to assorted arcane mysteries and powers, and presided over by some messianic figure—sorcerer, shaman, messenger, or Mahdi—who claims either godhood or ready access to it. Like many a religious movement, these alien acolytes are fanatical, intolerant, and eager to engage in holy wars aimed at slaughtering, enslaving, and/or forcibly converting unbelievers. And it goes without saying, that the grisly blood sacrifice of scantily clad maidens—especially those associated with the protagonists of these stories—is simply *de rigueur*.

Finally, there are always a host of savage, often inhuman, barbarian tribes in these books. These include sharp clawed predatory Kurii, giant multi-limbed Tharks, and ferocious Zangans (man-beasts) who tend to be nomadic, unclean, ill clad, and unlettered. Loosely organized and governed by whatever warrior or band of warriors have proven themselves strongest in battle, these groups exist for one reason and one reason alone and that is to wage war on their neighbors; an exercise that usually entails a great deal of pillaging and plundering. Beastly as these folks are, however, they often prove to be loyal, capable, and trustworthy allies in the struggles of each novel's hero against the power mad monarchs and messiahs of their respective planets.

At the same time that I was becoming acquainted with alien barbarians, the Ursuline nuns responsible for the first eight years of my education were also familiarizing me with their non-fictional Terran counterparts. In religious instruction and Western history classes, these good sisters introduced

2. Sybarites and Savages

me and my classmates to the heroic struggles of early Christians with a whole range of "barbaric" pagans, heretics, and infidels. Among these fallen folk, considerable time was given over to the study of the decadent ways of Rome's idol-worshipping citizens and their besotted, often mad, emperors. Through readings from the lives of holy martyrs and reproductions of paintings and sculptures by Jean-Léon Gérôme—*Pollice Verso (Thumbs Down), Last Prayers of the Christian Martyrs, Departure of the Cats from the Circus, The Gladiators*—we were treated to a view of the Roman Empire as a tyrannical slavocracy in which ostensibly civilized men and women wiled away their hours attending chariot races, gladiatorial combats, orgiastic banquets, and events where the adherents of Jesus were either fed to wild animals or used as fuel to light up imperial gardens. And this sense of the Greco-Roman world as a cruel and barbarous place was further heightened by a whole slew of sword and sandal films—*Quo Vadis, Demetrius and the Gladiators, Ben-Hur, Spartacus*—that lit up the big screens of American drive-in movie theaters throughout the 1950s and 1960s.

Similar treatment was also meted out to the other barbaric foes of the early Church, i.e., the Goths, Germans, Huns, Vandals, Magyars, and Vikings that sacked and slaughtered their way across Europe during late antiquity and the first half of the Middle Ages. Unlike their pagan Greco-Roman counterparts, however, who lived in cities, knew their letters, were ruled by laws, bathed regularly, and cooked their food, these peoples were presented to us as nomadic, illiterate, and lawless raiders who knew nothing about either hygiene or the culinary arts. Through the commentaries of both the Christian missionaries who ministered to these peoples and those of assorted communities they terrorized, we were also treated to a picture of these folks as violent blood thirsty butchers who were inordinately fond of horses (or, if Norsemen, long boats), clothes made out of fur pelts, horned helmets of one sort or another, heavy axes and long swords, dark gods with a penchant for blood sacrifice, great gobbets of roasted flesh, and fraternity style drinking parties. As with the Romans, these stereotypes were also reinforced by such B movie releases as *Sword of the Conqueror, Sign of the Pagan, Prince Valiant*, and *The Vikings*.

Nevertheless, while all of these barbaric peoples and behaviors were regarded as reprehensible by our Ursuline mentors, they were ultimately forgiven their past transgressions by dint of the fact that they eventually converted to Christianity and, on more than one occasion, saved it from the depredations of heretics and infidels. Indeed, of all the barbarians we were introduced to at this time, it was the proponents of unorthodox Christianity and, even worse, Islam, that the good sisters found most fearsome. Not only did these individuals follow creeds and messengers that were capable of leading Christians into spiritual error and subsequent damnation, but at different points in Western history they were seen as having posed an actual existential threat to Christian Europe itself. This was especially the case with the assorted Arab, Saracen, Mongol, and Turkish adherents of the Islamic faith who had invaded and occupied Spain, Russia, Greece and the Balkans, and remained a very real threat to European Catholic countries until the defeat of the Ottoman fleet by Philip II (of Spanish Armada fame) at Lepanto in 1571. As for that prolonged period of Christian aggression in the Near East known as "the Crusades," suffice it to say, it was presented to us as nothing more than a noble effort by bands of highly chivalrous knights to liberate the Holy Land. A view that was also upheld in such popular movies as Cecil B. DeMille's *The Crusades* and David Butler's *King Richard and the Crusades*.

What did I take away from these Catholic sponsored lessons in the history of Western barbarism? First, it was apparent to me that my favorite pulp writers had essentially based their barbaric races on the assorted Romans, pagans, infidels, and migratory tribes that had made life difficult for Western Christians from Antiquity to the early modern period. Secondly, I was struck by how markedly different these folks were from the law abiding, hardworking, church going, and extremely hygienic suburbanites who raised me. Some of these differences were readily apparent, e.g., we did not live on horses and long boats (though we did spend an inordinate amount of time in cars); most of us could read; all of us used cutlery at meals and bathed regularly; our technology was considerably more advanced; and theft, murder and rape were capital crimes punishable, in some cases, by death. Other dissimilarities were more subtle, i.e., while city dwelling barbarians were more like us in terms of being settled, literate, more technologically savvy, and reasonably clean, they also appeared to be every bit as brutal, sadistic, drunken, gluttonous, and sex crazed as their horse riding, sea faring brethren. Add to these distinctions the fact that all of these communities spoke foreign languages, worshipped heathen gods, and were the bondsmen and slaves of tyrants, and there was no other conclusion possible but that these were very bad people.

This said, I was also secretly in love with these villains. In part this was due to an adolescent desire to be free of the rules and regulations of the adult world—broccoli, baths, boring books related to school, and regular bedtime. Preferable by far was the idea of sailing the seas with piratical marauders like the Vikings, attending the Circus Maximus in the time of the Caesars, or donning—à la Peter O'Toole in *Lawrence of Arabia*—the robes of an Arab sheik and riding into battle on camelback. This "Peter Pan complex" to the side, however, it also did not escape my notice that we (my teachers, classmates, and I) were the descendants of these barbarians (no one could grow up in the Ohio Valley, with its many German, Irish, and Scottish families, and not know that our ancestors were on the other side of the many walls the Romans built to maintain their vaunted *Pax Romana*), and that much of what we Americans tout as "Western civilization"—Greco Roman literature, law, and architecture; representative democracy; trial by jury; Romance, Germanic, and Slavic languages; Ikea—was their gift to us.

Nor does it appear that I was alone in my admiration for these villainous characters. Indeed, in the years that have elapsed since my graduation from a Catholic junior high school, the heroic protagonists in much of the historical, sci-fi and fantasy fiction and film that fills our cinemas, bookstores, and internet sites are themselves identified as barbarians, or at least folks not that far removed from a former state of barbarism, e.g., the Fremen of Frank Herbert's *Dune* saga; the outlaws aboard Joss Whedon's *Serenity* or Jack Sparrow's *Black Pearl*; Buliwf's Vikings in the *13th Warrior*; the Cheyenne of Thomas Berger's *Little Big Man*; and Mad Max, the Road Warrior of the Australian wastes. Figuring out how and why these hitherto "uncivilized" individuals and groups—once associated with all manner of murder, mayhem and megalomania—got rehabilitated is of course one of the key questions to be considered in what follows.

Prior to addressing this query, however, we must first examine how a term that was initially used to simply signify someone who did not speak Greek became a rubric with all kinds of negative political, social, and cultural connotations. To answer that question, we will survey the evolution of the word "barbarian" from its first use in Homer as a descriptor for the language of a foreign people to its adoption as an honorific by assorted fascists, communists, teenage boys, and members of the Society for Creative Anachronism. Following this brief history of what medieval historian Arno Borst has labeled "a European catchword," we will then conduct a much more in-depth exploration of the two most common facets of this villainous type, i.e., the slavish, sensual sybarite and the simple sadistic savage. Finally, we will conclude our discussion with a look at the remarkable popularity barbarians have attained in the modern world.

From Baby to Bad Boy: Barbarian and the Western Lexicon

In his work *The New Testament World*, theologian Bruce Malina asks his readers to imagine Earth as a boundless desert lacking any distinguishing features such as trees, streams, rocks, or mountains. He then introduces human beings into this setting and asks us to consider the following scene:

> With their hands in the supple sand, they start making lines to indicate to each other that this side is "my side," that side is "your side." Another group comes along, makes a line, and declares that this side is "our side," that side is

"your side." The wind comes and covers over the explicit lines, yet all continue to act as though they were still there, implicit in the sand. What happens in such line drawing? Etymologically, the words "define" and "delimit" refer to the process of drawing lines, setting up boundaries between inside and outside, hence between insiders and outsiders.[1]

"Barbarian" is one of those line drawing words that Malina is referring to when he speaks of the human propensity for "setting up boundaries." Indeed, the word's earliest use by Homer in Book Two of the *Iliad* is intended to underscore the fact that the Carians, an ally of the Trojans, are distinct from the Greek-speaking combatants in the conflict due to their "outland speech."[2] Because the Carian language is incomprehensible to the Argives, Homer labeled it *barbarous*, which is an expression normally associated with the meaningless babble of a baby. In using this word, the *Iliad's* author intended no insult to its speakers, whom he praised in the same passage as "shining sons" of brave warriors.

The same cannot be said, however, of the Greek storytellers who succeeded Homer. During the Greco-Persian Wars, i.e., the conflicts between the Hellenic city states and the Persian Achaemenid dynasty from 499 to 449 BCE, both the playwright Aeschylus and the historian Herodotus added a highly political and derogatory meaning to *barbarous*. In their works on this 50 year contest, both men labeled the Persians "barbarians" because their language was said to resemble that of horses, and their political and cultural arrangements were regarded as markedly inferior to those of the Greeks. This judgment was based on these authors' perception of the European Hellenes as a hard self-sufficient people ruled by laws, while their barbaric counterparts in Asia were a soft amalgam of enslaved peoples cowering under the whip of a lawless luxury loving tyrant. Indeed, as we will see in considerably more detail in the section that follows, this distinction between civilized Europeans and barbaric Asiatics continues to some degree down to the present day.[3]

This idea of the barbarian as an "other" who speaks differently and hails from a society lacking in certain characteristics regarded as "civilized" is adopted in turn by the Romans. However, because of their centuries long conflicts with the Celtic and Germanic tribes of northern Italy, Spain, Gaul, Britain, and Germany, as well as their shared culture with the Greek speaking communities of the east, the Latin term *barbarus* was largely applied to warlike, non-urban, nomadic, loosely organized, illiterate, and "uncultivated" peoples, i.e., societies that did not live in the urbane manner of Greeks and Romans. The sack of Rome by the Visigoth king Alaric—who is usually represented on horseback in bear skins—in 410 CE, and the subsequent invasion and dismemberment of the Western Roman Empire by assorted tribes from northern, central, and eastern Europe, further cemented this sense of the barbarian as a kind of ignorant, footloose, and violent vagrant.

It should be noted here, however, that the Romans were also aware that the cruel, inhumane, often animal-like behavior they deemed barbaric was not just limited to peoples living in non-urban unlettered communities that were often on the move. Philosophers and historians as diverse as Cicero, Seneca, and Tacitus all acknowledged that so-called "wild peoples" bereft of cities, scholarship, and formal systems of governance could be civilized insofar as they were guided by social and ethical codes of conduct, which stressed the importance of hospitality to friends and strangers, honesty in public and private affairs, respect of elders, gods, and traditions, and loyalty to one's immediate and extended families. As such, it was possible to speak favorably of foreign peoples often at odds with Rome—something that Tacitus does in his *Germania*—while also castigating members of one's own community for behaving in a barbarous manner—a stance taken by more than one chronicler of the follies and foibles of the empire's many Caesars.

When Europe falls under the management of the Roman Catholic Church in late antiquity and the Middle Ages, barbarian becomes a word that is also associated with folks who are pagans and infidels. These include the abovementioned tribes responsible for the destruction of the Western Roman Empire, the Norsemen and Magyars who terrorized the continent in the 9th and 10th centuries, and the various adherents of Islam—Arabs, Berbers, Mongols, and Turks—that invaded and for a time actually occupied Spain, Russia, and the Balkans. Because these communities are considered to be strangers to the true God, and are also associated with the other kinds of barbaric behaviors described above—nomadism, lawlessness, violence, raiding, licentiousness—the Church portrays them as alien, almost inhuman peoples worthy of little more than extirpation. Indeed, joining assorted Crusades whose purpose is the destruction of "godless" barbarians becomes something akin to a Christian duty.

The implication of labeling non-Christians barbarians proves to be far-reaching, especially during the European voyages of discovery in the 15th and 16th centuries. Though many of the societies that Europeans stumble onto at this time are as old and, in some cases, every bit as sophisticated as those found in the West, they are regarded by their discoverers as barbaric by dint of their fondness for "heathen gods." Add to this the fact that they also speak incomprehensible non-Western languages—a sign of barbarism in the West since the time of the ancient Greeks—and live and behave in ways that often challenge Christian conventions, and you have the grounds for what will be a five-century-long campaign by Europe's colonial powers to conquer, convert, enslave, and exploit assorted peoples—Arabs, Africans, Amerindians, Asians, Aborigines—throughout the world.

Not everyone in the West was enamored with this so-called "civilizing mission" to bring the light of Christianity, as well as European ways of living and thinking, to the benighted barbarians of the non–Western world. Indeed, there were a great many missionaries, administrators, and intellectuals who viewed the atrocities—massacres, rapes, forced labor, theft of native lands and resources—that were visited on the indigenous populations of the new Western colonies, as evidence that barbarism was alive and well in their own cultures. These individuals also tended to view the newly colonized peoples in much the same way that Tacitus viewed his German neighbors, i.e., as folks who were in many respects more virtuous and civilized than their conquerors.

This idea that the tribal peoples of the non–Western world are more "noble savages" than barbarians enjoyed considerable popularity among both the enlightened savants of the 17th and 18th centuries and the romantic artists and litterateurs of the 19th century. Not only did these individuals regard "primitive" populations to be closer to a state of nature, which is blessedly free of the inequities, materialism, hypocrisy, and empty refinements of modern Western civilization, but they also believed that the inhabitants of these societies possessed a kind of vitality that made them more potent and creative than their civilized Western counterparts. As we will see below, this talk of vital noble savages leads almost inexorably to a glorification of the barbarian as a necessary and desirable agent of change—usually in his less savory guise as a cruel animal-like beast of prey.

Nevertheless, while there have been numerous permutations in the meaning of the word "barbarian," it is a term Westerners have used to define and delimit themselves from others. As we have seen, initially, this delineation process is a relatively benign exercise aimed at identifying the speakers of languages that were incomprehensible to the Greeks. Over time, however, both the Greek *barbarous* and the Latin *barbarus* are deployed increasingly as expressions of opprobrium directed at individuals and groups that are regarded as

- accursed "others" with different languages, customs, ethics, and forms of governance;
- hard "wild peoples" living in nomadic, illiterate, subsistence societies on the frontiers of soft urban civilizations with literacy and a high level of material culture;
- vandals and/or raiders fond of violence and mindless destruction;
- pagans and infidels;
- ignorant, superstitious, irrational folk living in an "unrefined" manner; and
- any of the indigenous non–Western civilizations and tribes subjugated and exploited by the West's colonial powers.

Having established some sense of the genealogy of this remarkable catchword, we will now turn our attention to its first manifestation in the history of villainy, i.e., as the luxury loving, effeminate, sexually aberrant, and decadent despotisms of the "East."

"We shall bring all mankind under our yoke": The Barbarian as Sybarite

In Zack Snyder's film adaptation of Frank Miller's graphic novel *300*, audiences are treated to a visually stunning, highly exaggerated, and historically inaccurate recreation of the battle at Thermopylae between an outnumbered Greek force under the command of the Spartan King Leonidas and the much larger army of the Persian King Xerxes. In keeping with many of the Greek sources on which the movie is loosely based—Aeschylus, Herodotus, Diodorus—the Persians are portrayed in the worst possible light. They are guilty of impiety (the bribing of the Spartan Ephors with gold and concubines), the violent and inhumane treatment of civilian populations (one scene depicts the gruesome crucifixion on a rather large tree of an entire community), tyranny, overweening pride and arrogance, slavish effeminate behavior, and dalliance with dark magic. There are even moments in the movie—the appearance of a gigantic, heavily pierced and chain clad Xerxes looking like a Mr. Leather contestant at a gay circuit party gone bad, and the attack on the Greeks by the Persian king's monstrous Immortals—that call into question the very humanity of both Persia's "god king" and the people who serve him.

Almost all of this is preposterous and can only be characterized as an exercise in "historical fantasy fiction." In point of fact, there were actually some 4000 Greeks at Thermopylae, not just 300 Spartans, and both military experts and historians agree that there is simply no possible way that the Persian Empire could have fielded an army of one million men during the fifth century BCE. Further, while the Persians were certainly guilty of sacking Athens and putting it to the torch, there are no accounts of hapless civilians being nailed to trees. And while Xerxes was a self-styled "Great King" who lived in considerable luxury and exercised unquestioned authority over his empire, to the best of our knowledge he neither suffered from overgrowth syndrome nor affected a fondness for piercings and sadomasochistic leather gear.

While there is much about Snyder's film that is wrong, he nonetheless alludes, albeit in an exaggerated way, to those aspects of the Persian Empire that are considered barbaric by their Greek foes. Key among these are the way in which the Persians and their many subject peoples are governed. Whereas the Greeks reckoned themselves the free citizens of city states ruled by laws, their Persian counterparts are regarded as little more than the slaves of a Great King who is free to dispose of their lives in whatever ways he deems appropriate. This dichotomy is highlighted in Book Seven of Herodotus' *Persian Wars* in a conversation between Xerxes and the former Spartan king Demaratus, who has joined the war against the Hellenes in the hopes of regaining his throne. When Demaratus assures the king that his countrymen will oppose his invasion, Xerxes dismisses such resistance as futile, both because of the numbers that he commands and the fact that they are not governed by one leader such as himself.

> If, indeed, like our troops, they had a single master, their fear of him might make them courageous beyond their natural bent, or they might be urged by lashes against an enemy which far outnumbered them. But left to their own free choice, assuredly they will act differently.[4]

Demaratus responds:

> For though they be free men, they are not in all respects free, Law is the master whom they own, and this master they fear more than your subjects fear you. Whatever it commands they do; and its commandment is always the same: it forbids them to flee in battle, whatever the number of their foes, and requires them to stand firm, and either to conquer or die.[5]

The lawless tyranny of Xerxes also ensures that he and his people will fall prey to what might be called the trifecta of bad behavior in Greek culture, i.e., *koros* (insatiable appetite), *atē* (excessive violence), and *hubris* (delusional thinking).[6] One can see all three of these less than desirable traits on display in the following passage from Book Seven of Herodotus' history, when the Great King discusses his war aims with the Persian nobility:

> Once let us subdue this people [the Greeks], and those neighbours of theirs who hold the land of Pelops the Phrygian, and we shall extend the Persian territory as far as God's heaven reaches. The sun will then shine on no land beyond our borders; for I will pass through Europe from one end to the other, and with your aid make of all the lands which it contains one country.... The nations whereof I have spoken, once swept away, there is no city, no country left in all the world, which will venture so much as to withstand us in arms. By this course then we shall bring all mankind under our yoke, alike those who are guilty and those who are innocent of doing us wrong.[7]

Not content to rule what is already one of the greatest empires in human history, Xerxes reveals to the reader his hunger for yet more territory and subjects, an ambition that apparently knows no bounds. And to achieve this dream of worldwide dominion, Persia's Great King also makes it quite clear that he is willing to visit on mankind whatever violence is necessary to "yoke" its disparate peoples to his imperium.

Aside from the fact that they are the slaves of a violent megalomaniac, the Persians are also considered barbaric because they are what classicist

James M. Redfield labels a "soft" people. That is, they love luxury; their society is complex and bounded by a great many customs and laws; they engage in commercial activities; and they treat their women as mere chattels to be bought and sold. Worst of all, the Persian Empire is a seductive feminine culture that confuses, emasculates, and assimilates "hard" folks like the Greeks who are simple, tough, and fierce; favor gift giving and theft over trade and womanish bargaining; live in loosely organized societies comprised of free citizens; and treat their women with respect. Indeed, what is particularly horrifying to Herodotus is that the Persians start out as a hard people but upon conquering softer civilizations—money loving Lydians, pleasure obsessed Babylonians, decadent Egyptians—become corrupt, and, like the other empires before them, prone to tyranny, *koros*, *atē*, and *hubris*.[8]

It is important to keep these barbaric traits in mind as they tend to loom large in the history of Western villainy. As we will see, not only do they define the barbarian as someone who is a sybarite and a slave, but they also serve as useful indicators of a great many other villainous types as well. Indeed, whether one is speaking of tyrants or traitors, Mengele or Magneto, all of these characters tend to have an insatiable appetite for something—power, wealth, sex, suffering—which generates delusional thinking that leads, almost inexorably, to violence of one form or another against others.

Returning to the subject at hand, however, the Greek commentators on the Persian Wars essentially create a model of the sybaritic barbarian that will loom large in the Western imagination. Like the Persians and their subject peoples who originate in Asia, this person will, from Herodotus to the present, be associated with what literary theorist Edward Said has described as an "imaginative geography" that encompasses the near and far eastern reaches of "the Orient."[9] Also like Xerxes and his minions, this Asiatic "other" will be identified as someone who speaks, writes, and worships in a non–Occidental fashion; indulges in luxury, vice, and sexual promiscuity; and slavishly serves the whims of a tyrant.

Perhaps the best example of how this Greek conception of "Eastern " barbarism plays out in the ancient world is Rome's entanglement with Ptolemaic Egypt during the last century of the Roman Republic. Though the Ptolemies are a Hellenic dynasty established by one of Alexander the Great's generals, Ptolemy Lagides, and their kingdom is one of the most venerable and materially sophisticated civilizations in the Mediterranean basin, the Romans regard both the Egyptian ruling family and its subjects as barbarous. In part, this judgment is based on the fact that Egypt's rulers are "god kings and queens" exercising absolute authority over the lives and possessions of their subjects. For the free citizens of a republican city state such as Rome, this exemplifies Asiatic tyranny at its worst, i.e., unchecked lawless monarchs ruling in a rough shod manner over an enslaved people.

There is also much about Egyptian culture Rome finds disconcerting and dangerous. Both the native language and its hieroglyphic script are completely unlike either Latin or Greek. Egypt's deities are fashioned after animals—birds, jackals, hippos, cows, crocodiles, cats—rather than in the familiar human guises of the Olympian sky gods. Alexandria, the Ptolemaic capital, is a cosmopolitan city noted for its exotic inhabitants, mysterious cults, intellectual circles, rich cuisine, thriving night life, and busy brothels. And, perhaps most problematic of all for anyone raised in a Greco-Roman context, the women of the two lands enjoy both occupational mobility and the freedom to manage their own affairs.

Finally, it was not lost on the Romans that the Ptolemies were at one time part of a Macedonian culture that valued hardiness and living simply, virtues that were held in high esteem in Rome. Nevertheless, once ensconced in a wealthy "Eastern " land fond of luxury and license, they had become soft, effeminate and barbaric in their lifestyles. Brothers and sisters mated and married one another; parricide and fratricide became commonplace; Egyptian gods were placed on an equal footing with the residents of Olympus; rulership was reduced to the pursuit of spectacle and indulgence; and the actual affairs of state became the province of eunuchs.

Rome's unease with Egypt and its barbaric ways only increased during the protracted struggle between Octavian Caesar and Mark Antony for mastery of the Roman world in the last half of the first century BCE (43–30 BCE). As is well known, during this time, Antony entered into a long-standing political alliance and romantic relationship with Egypt's last Ptolemaic ruler, Cleopatra VII. While there were certainly solid strategic reasons for this union, Antony's association with what Virgil would later describe in the *Aeneid* as his shameful "Egyptian consort" proved to be his downfall.[10]

Playing on Roman fears of decadent Eastern despotisms, Octavian waged an unrelenting propaganda campaign aimed at elevating Egypt's queen and her barbarous country to the level of a major threat against Rome's independence and empire. In speeches, he claimed that Cleopatra had vowed to dispense laws on the Capitoline, make Romans her personal bodyguards, and compel them to worship her animal-like gods.[11] Worst yet, she and her countrymen had also emasculated Mark Antony by indulging his gross appetites for wine, food, wanton sex, and luxurious living; a charge that was borne out by reports of the Roman consul shopping with Cleopatra in the Alexandrian marketplace, dressing in Eastern clothes, carrying a Persian dagger, and holding court seated on a gilded chair.[12] Indeed, this line of attack was so effective that when war finally commenced between the two men, Octavian was able to have his supporters in the Roman Senate declare it against the barbarians of Egypt rather than Antony:

2. Sybarites and Savages

> Let no one consider Antony a Roman, but rather an Egyptian; let no one call him Antony, but rather Serapion [an Egyptian version of Zeus in the form of a bull]; let no one believe that he was ever a consul or commander, but rather a gymnasiarch [a magistrate in charge of training young athletes].... Divesting himself of all the respectable titles of his homeland, he has become a cymbal-player of Canopus.... It is not possible for someone living in royal luxury and being treated like a woman to think or act like a man.... As a result, if this were a contest of dancing foolishly or of comic buffoonery and one of us had to compete against him, our man would surely lose, for Antony is the expert in these skills.... What could anyone fear from him? The fitness of his body? He's old and completely effeminate. His mental powers? He has the mind of a woman and the physical desires of one too. His respect for our gods? He fights against them as he does against our homeland.[13]

In the aftermath of Octavian's victory at Actium, these aspersions against Antony and Cleopatra became the largely uncontested facts of a grand narrative in which the civilized West, with its traditions of representative democracy, law, reason, restraint, and manly vigor, triumphed over a barbaric East characterized by despotism, unrestrained passion, profligance, and soft effeminacy. This despite the fact that the vanquished Eastern "barbarians" were largely Hellenes who shared a common culture with their Roman conquerors, and the Principate of Octavian (later Augustus Caesar) was little more than a monarchy in republican clothing; one which, it should be noted, would make possible such rational, restrained rulers as Caligula, Nero, Domitian, and Heliogabalus. This demurral to the side, however, Rome's triumph over Egypt, like Persia's defeat at the hands of the Greeks, makes possible some three centuries of Western supremacy and sets in stone the idea of the Orient as a repository of uncivilized sybaritic barbarism. Further, as historian Michael Grant notes, because "the countries of western Europe, and the United States of America, are the direct heirs of the occidental victor of Actium," this is a tradition that we continue to embrace down to the present day.[14]

Indeed, it is striking how this barbaric type continues to play out in the present "war on terror." Despite the fact that Arabs created a civilization between the seventh and 11th centuries of the Common Era, which was regarded with envy by their Christian counterparts, as well as evidence that, no less than in the West, the overwhelming majority of Muslims yearn for democracy, and also consider Al-Qaeda to be a criminal gang of terrorists, the Arab in particular and followers of Islam in general continue to be regarded by considerable numbers of Westerners as barbarians. And the reasons that are often given for this prejudice are strikingly like those that were mouthed by our ancient predecessors with regard to their Eastern adversaries.

The first of these is the fact that most of the peoples in the Middle East are governed by despotic regimes. That these governments were often established and supported by various Western powers is usually overlooked. Secondly, just as the Zoroastrianism of Xerxes and the "animal gods" of Egypt were regarded with disdain by their Greek and Roman detractors, Islam continues to be viewed by a majority of devout Christians throughout the West as either a completely false religion or one that is merely derivative of older and more respectable Jewish and Christian traditions. Thirdly, like the playwrights and poets of Greece and Rome who filled their work with images of licentious, soft, effeminate, and savage Easterners, latter day Western storytellers generate novels, plays, films, and television programming that portray Muslims as an irrational, lecherous, bloodthirsty, and treacherous folk. As Edward Said notes, they are cast as

> slave trader, camel driver, moneychanger, colorful scoundrel: these are some traditional Arab roles in the cinema. The Arab leader (of marauders, pirates, "native" insurgents) can often be seen snarling at the captured Western hero and the blond girl (both of them steeped in wholesomeness), "My men are going to kill you, but—they like to amuse themselves before." ... In newsreels or newsphotos, the Arab is always shown in large numbers. No individuality, no personal characteristics or experiences. Most of the pictures represent mass rage and misery, or irrational (hence hopelessly eccentric) gestures.[15]

Whether the current "Arab Spring," i.e., the wave of protests and demonstrations that have toppled despotic regimes in Egypt, Tunisia, Libya, and Yemen, and plunged Syria into civil war, cause Westerners to re-consider these stereotypes, remains to be seen. For the moment, however, it is probably safe to say that the West's longstanding belief that its way of life is threatened by villainous Eastern sybarites is alive and well.

"They came like locusts": The Barbarian as Savage

Since 2009, the Capital One company has been running a series of highly amusing commercials for its credit cards that feature barbarians in modern-day situations. The actors appear to be dressed in a Viking fashion—horned helmets, furs, leggings—they are hirsute (even the children sport beards), and are heavily armed with assorted axes, swords, spears, and long bows. Whatever the setting in which we find them—ski lodges, grocery stores, banks—they make a mess of things, e.g., shooting Christmas reindeer decorations with arrows; beheading snow men; sacking the homes of folks who do not use Capital One credit cards; chasing after extras clad as Roman soldiers in a Hollywood studio back lot; putting their goats on skis, and their pigs in motorcycle side cars. They are, quite simply, lovable savages.

2. Sybarites and Savages

As with Zack Snyder's historical fantasy film, these ads highlight in an exaggerated and comical fashion some of the principal traits associated with the savage barbarians that we are addressing in this section. Because many of these peoples hailed from harsh climates, furs and leggings were not uncommon garb, and long hair and beards were equally commonplace. Most of these folks were nomadic and, because they were often fleeing aggressors seeking to kill and/or enslave them, they tended to be heavily armed and accompanied by livestock, which included, as in the commercials, both pigs and goats. Whenever they entered into the territories of their more settled "civilized" neighbors, trouble usually ensued, albeit of a much less amusing sort than found in these ads. Indeed, lovable is never a word used by the chroniclers of the past to describe these individuals.

Capital One caricatures to the side, who are these villainous "wild people" that are feared and loathed by so many ancient and medieval communities? For Greek commentators such as Herodotus, they are the antithesis of the sybaritic barbarians of the East, and are best exemplified by the Scythian tribes that hailed from the Caucasus region in modern-day Russia. Unlike the soft, decadent and tyrannized Persians who are addressed in the preceding section, Scythians are portrayed as a hardy, relatively free folk ruled by many kings who are actually no more than "firsts among equals" within their respective communities. And while Eastern sybarites—as well as their Greek foes—dwelled in cities with monumental architecture; engaged in agriculture and trade; worshipped assorted gods served by organized priesthoods; boasted a measure of literacy; enjoyed a refined cuisine; imbibed a variety of potent potables; and were fond of regular bathing; their Scythian counterparts lived on horses and in wagons; constructed no permanent urban settlements; were pastoralists; honored only one set of gods served by shamans; had no written language; ate boiled flesh, mare's milk, and cheese; drank wine neat; and never washed. Finally, while all barbarians, soft or hard, were inordinately fond of war, Scythians were particularly good at raiding their enemies, and fending off would be conquerors.[16]

As already mentioned in the section addressing the lexicography of the word barbarian, when Romans used this expression, they are most often referring to the wild men and women living on the western, northern, and southeastern frontiers of their European empire, i.e., the Celts, Germans, Pannonians, and, later in the Common Era, the Goths (who are themselves probably just another collection of Germanic tribes). By and large, these peoples are not unlike the Scythians described by Herodotus in his *Histories*. That is, they are illiterate, non-urban, semi-nomadic, and extremely warlike pastoralists living in loosely organized tribal confederacies governed by assorted "kings" or chieftains who are largely concerned with military affairs and intertribal relations. They are also reputed to be an unwashed, immodest lot, overly fond of heavy drinking—usually beer, mead and undiluted wine—tall tales, gambling, and unorthodox sex (Gallic men in particular are singled out by the Roman commentator, Diodorus Siculus, for their bisexuality and fondness for same-sex orgies).[17]

While there are questions concerning the accuracy of Roman accounts of their northern neighbors' vices—as classicist J. B. Rives notes, these works are based on "a welter of sources that varied greatly in focus, reliability and date,"[18] and they all repeated certain ethnographic stereotypes intended to underscore the stark differences between Romans and their barbaric counterparts—there is no doubt that these tribes posed a very real and present danger to the Roman Empire throughout its thousand year history. During the early days of the Republic (391–390 BCE), for example, a Celtic host routed the main levy of the Roman army, occupied Rome, and plundered the city for some seven months before accepting a ransom of gold and retiring to the north. Celtic tribes in northern Italy, or Cisalpine Gaul, continued to contest Roman control of that region up until the second century BCE when they were finally subdued in a series of hard fought campaigns that stretched from 197 to 191. Outside of Italy proper, Celts in Far Spain, Gaul, and Britain resisted Roman rule throughout the first century before the Common Era, and were never brought to heel in either Ireland or Scotland.

Troublesome as the Celts were, however, it was the Germans that Rome feared most. Noted for their great height—a trait every size-challenged Roman commentator feels it necessary to underscore—and physical strength, these folks had

> no taste for peace; renown is more easily won among perils, and you cannot maintain a large body of companions except by violence and war. For the companions make demands on the generosity of their leaders, asking for "that war horse" or "that bloody and victorious spear." As for the feasts, with their abundant if homely fare, these count simply as pay. Such open-handedness needs war and plunder to feed it. You would also find it harder to persuade them to plough the land and await its annual produce than to challenge a foe and earn the prize of wounds; indeed, they think it spiritless and slack to gain by sweat what they can buy with blood.[19]

And blood there was aplenty from Rome's first encounter with the Germanic Cimbri and Teutones at the end of the second century BCE to the final collapse of the Western empire in 476 CE. During these six centuries, German migrations and invasions into the territory of Rome and its allies in northern and northeastern Europe wreaked havoc. Farms, villages, and towns were pillaged and plundered, their inhabitants were murdered, raped, and enslaved, and both civic life and commerce were disrupted over large swathes of territory for extended periods of time. While largely successful in repelling these attacks, Roman arms were defeated on more than one occasion by these

2. Sybarites and Savages

invaders, and they were never successful in subduing them. As Tacitus noted in 98 CE, some 210 years after Rome's first run-in with these folks,

> Neither the Samnites nor the Carthaginians, neither Hispania nor Gaul, not even the Parthians have taught us more painful lessons. The freedom of Germania is a deadlier enemy than the despotism of Arsaces [founder of the Parthian Empire in what is now modern-day Iran].... The Germans routed or captured Carbo, Cassius, Scaurus Aurelius, Servilius Caepio and Mallius Maximus [Roman consuls and generals], robbing the Roman people at almost a single stroke of five consular armies; even from Caesar [Augustus Caesar] they stole Varus and his three legions. Nor was it without painful loss that C. Marius smote the Germans in Italy, that Divus Julius smote them in Gaul, that Drusus, Nero and Germanicus smote them in their own lands.[20]

While Greco-Roman attitudes towards these peoples are largely negative, there are aspects of their behavior that their more civilized counterparts find admirable. Herodotus may have considered Scythians and Thracians to be savages, but, unlike the Persians and the other sybarites of the east, they are free and unconquerable. Concurrently, Roman commentators on the Celts and Germans are quick to note that in addition to their impressive size and strength, these barbarians are also pious towards their gods and elders, care for their families, take their marriages seriously, treat their women with respect, eschew materialism, are often skilled craftsmen, and enjoy considerable personal freedom. Indeed, in situations where they are confronted by common foes, e.g., Parthians and Huns, Greeks and Romans were even known to consider their barbaric neighbors as something akin to "bitter friends."[21]

This was certainly not the case with regard to the various peoples that pillaged and plundered their way across Europe during late antiquity and the early Middle Ages. Accounts of these invaders—Goths, Huns, Vandals, Magyars, Vikings—are unremittingly negative, and helped ensure that "barbarian" would be most commonly associated with people who both lived in an uncivilized manner, and behaved in a cruel, destructive, and inhumane fashion. Exemplary of this tendency is the second epigraph that opens this chapter wherein the Roman historian, Ammianus Marcellinus (c. 330–391 CE), describes the Hunnish people, a Central Asian tribe that appeared out of nowhere in the late fourth century, and, like a swarm of locusts, sacked and razed cities, towns, villages, and farm holdings throughout the Roman Empire for 60 years. In Marcellinus' account, as well as those of later commentators, these invaders are described as more animal-like than human. In appearance they are portrayed as short, squat, ugly, and hairless. And their lifestyle is equally repellent, i.e., they live on horseback, eat half-raw meat (warmed between their thighs and the backs of their horses), drink mare's milk, never bathe, and wear garments made of the skins of field mice. Certainly not the kind of people you would invite to a dinner party.[22]

Several centuries later, similar kinds of accounts are written by both Christian and Muslim chroniclers about yet another "scourge of God," i.e., the Norsemen. Unlike the Huns, these Scandinavian raiders are regarded as "perfect physical specimens, tall as date palms, blond and ruddy."[23] However, while their features may have been more fair to gaze upon than those of their Central Asian counterparts, their personal habits also left a lot to be desired:

> Every day they must wash their faces and heads and this they do in the dirtiest and filthiest fashion possible; to wit, every morning a girl servant brings a great basin of water; she offers this to her master and he washed his hands and face and his hair—he washed it and combs it out with a comb in the water; then he blows his nose and spits into the basin. When he has finished, the servant carries the basin to the next person, who does likewise. She carries the basin thus to all the household in turn, and each blows his nose, spits, and washes his face and hair in it.[24]

In addition to this unhygienic grooming exercise, these folks are fond of heavy drinking, public group sex, gang rape, and a form of suttee that involves the murder of slave girls to be burned alongside their dead Viking masters.

Their personal appearance and funeral arrangements to the side, the very mention of these Norsemen struck terror in the hearts of peoples throughout Europe for over a hundred years. From the ninth until well into the 11th century of the Common Era, Norse longboats raided communities in Britain, France, Spain, northern Africa, Italy, the Balkans, and Russia. Throughout this period, entries such as the following are commonplace:

> AD 843: Pirates of the Northmen's race came to Nantes, killed the bishop and many of the clergy and laymen, both men and women, and pillaged the city.
>
> AD 859: The Danish pirates have made a long sea-voyage ... entered the Rhone, where they pillaged many cities and monasteries and established themselves on the island called Carmargue. They devastated everything before them as far as the city of Valence [150 miles from the coast].... Thence they went on toward Italy, capturing and plundering Pisa and other cities.
>
> AD 994: Then they got horses and afterwards took control of East Anglia, and plundered and burned the countryside for four months—they even went as far as the wild fens and killed men and beasts and set fires throughout the fens, and burned down Thetford and Cambridge and then turned south to the Thames.[25]

Suffice it to say that by the end of this reign of terror, Norseman or Viking had become synonymous throughout Europe with theft, rape, murder, and indiscriminate violence of all kinds.

More to the point, the depredations of these assorted groups help fix in the Western mind an image of the barbarian as a remorseless, amoral savage bent on wonton destruction for both personal gain and a perverse sense of pleasure in the suffering of others. Indeed, when motorcycle gangs take on monikers such as the "Vandals" or the "Mongols," films feature antagonists like the Joker or Bain, and assorted prophets of cultural despair paint apocalyptic landscapes peopled with roaming rapacious hordes, they are all paying homage to the assorted tribes, bands, and thuggish marauders that bedeviled Rome and its heirs from late antiquity to the high Middle Ages.

"What daring! What outrageousness! What insolence! What arrogance! ... I salute you": The Barbarian as Savior

With the exception of the Ottoman expansion into southeastern Europe from the 15th through the 17th centuries, the great migrations and invasions addressed in the previous section ended by the beginning of the early modern period. More to the point, the migrants and marauders associated with these earlier incursions converted to Christianity, took up the plough, settled in villages, towns, and cities, and began the business of constructing new national cultures with written languages, literature, art, and music. While "barbarian" continues to be used to describe nomadic, pastoral tribal societies, such as the ones Europeans are now encountering in Africa, Asia, and the Americas, the word is more commonly employed as a less than endearing moniker for anyone who behaves in a fashion regarded as "uncivilized."

As to what constitutes civilized behavior at this time, Europe's aristocrats and their factotums in the continent's middling classes largely subscribe to the thinking of their classical predecessors on this subject. That is, a civil person is someone who is urban, literate, rational, well-mannered (particularly while eating), respectful of other people's property, and, above all, clean (or at least well-scented). Unfortunately, the ability to live in such an urbane manner is limited to an extremely small part of the continent's population, which means that the vast majority of the West's impoverished, illiterate, superstitious, not terribly well mannered, and largely unwashed city and country folk are regarded as barbarians.

Reversing this sad state of affairs becomes a matter of great import for the philosophes and savants of that movement in European arts, letters, and science known as the Enlightenment. Believing that superstitions, creeds, dogmas, and ancient prejudices are at the root of human ignorance, and that natural philosophy could both enlighten mankind and harness the power of nature to improve the lot of humanity, these individuals and their publics set into motion a series of revolutions that effectively created modern Western civilization. Indeed, by the end of the 19th century, both courtiers and commoners could look back on almost three centuries of unparalleled progress in every area of human endeavor.

Natural scientists in Europe and America had made groundbreaking discoveries and technological breakthroughs in engineering, metallurgy, optics, chemistry, electricity, and biology. Enterprising entrepreneurs and industrialists on both continents had exploited this scientific work and launched two industrial revolutions, which generated a wide array of new products, industries, markets, transportation systems, and jobs. These scientific and industrial advances also meant more manufactured goods, better diets, longer life spans, increasing literacy, and some measure of formal schooling for Westerners of all nationalities and classes. And in the political realm, peasants, Jews, ethnic minorities, skilled and unskilled laborers, and even women were enjoying more freedom and control over their lives as the institutions and practices of bourgeois liberalism—parliamentary democracy, the right to petition and assemble, religious toleration, and a free press—took root throughout Europe. Indeed, taken together, all of these achievements in science, industry, society, and politics appeared to point to a future free of the stuff of barbarism, i.e., ignorance, poverty, disease, tyranny, and war.

Despite these impressive achievements, however, somewhere along the line, barbarians and barbarous behavior not only resurfaced, but actually became wildly popular. In large part, this development was the result of the Romantic Movement addressed in the previous chapter. Not only were the adherents of this celebration of "emotional exuberance, unrestrained imagination, and spontaneity in both art and personal life"[26] highly critical of Enlightenment assumptions regarding human nature and creativity, but they were also very enamored with individuals and groups who were at odds with the status quo of their time, e.g., historical outlaws, rebels, knightly freebooters, and wild tribesmen. Rather than see these figures as opponents of order and civilized life, romantics imagined them as champions of individual freedom in revolt against the tyranny of centralized authority.

This tendency to heroize individuals and groups once considered beyond the pale of civilization was also furthered by the spread of another romantic cause célèbre, nationalism. Fueled by a belief that every people sharing a common language, culture and history should enjoy both self-determination and a national territory of its own, this movement came to the fore in the 19th century and enjoyed widespread support among the peoples of already well-established nation states such as Britain, France, and the U.S., as well as those aspiring to nations of their own, e.g., Germans and Italians. Unlike the past, when most of these peoples sought to associate themselves with a common Greco-Roman heritage that distinguished them as "civilized," as opposed to barbaric, these same groups now embraced as symbols of their nationhood assorted barbarian chieftains that had resisted their ancestors' assimilation into Rome's empire. In France, this involved erecting statues of the leader of the last great Gallic revolt against Rome, Vergingetorix. Across the channel, the British dedicated a statue on the banks of the Thames to the Iceni queen, Boudica, who, ironically enough, had burned London to the ground during her uprising against the Roman Empire in the first century of the Common Era. And in the freshly minted Second Reich of Bismarck, the landscape was dotted with grandiose sculptures to either Ariovistus, the German king defeated by Julius Caesar in 58 BCE, or Arminius (aka Hermann the Barbarian), the Cherusci chieftain who defeated a Roman army at the Battle of the Teutoburg Forest in 9 CE.

This rehabilitation of the barbarian also receives further impetus from a heroic ideology that came to the fore in the West during the late 19th and early 20th centuries. Often called "heroic vitalism," this philosophy of heroism is an odd amalgam of illiberal politics, romanticism, violence, and utopian reveries. Its proponents—a motley crew of hero worshipping crackpots, dreamers, madmen, artists, revolutionaries, and dictators—believed that Western civilization was morally bankrupt, disintegrating, and drifting towards degeneration, war, and chaos. These heroic vitalists also believed that they could reverse this dire state of affairs by sweeping away the liberal bourgeois capitalist societies of the West and replacing them with a "new order" created and governed by a "race" or, if of a more leftwing political persuasion, "cadre" of energetic, gifted, willful, amoral, and merciless heroes. Unhindered by Judeo-Christian ethical qualms, interest group party politics, or the capitalist preoccupation with profits, vitalists believed this heroic elite would restore order, win worlds and build empires, divine what is necessary for the common good, and initiate policies aimed at creating new "human types" capable of rising "to the heights of an Aristotle, a Goethe, or a Marx."[27]

While spokesmen for this vitalist perspective—Thomas Carlyle, Friedrich Nietzsche, *völkish* ideologues Paul LaGarde, Julius Langbehn, Moeller van den Bruck, and assorted Russian revolutionaries like Nikolai Chernyshevsky and Alexander Bogdanov—usually cited men such as Alexander the Great, Julius Caesar, Caesare Borgia, Napoleon Bonaparte, Leonardo Da Vinci, and Michelangelo as their heroic models, any individual who was "vital," i.e., willful, creative, ruthless, cruel, and, most importantly, hard, was an acceptable paradigm for the generation of super men and women these people envisioned. Given these parameters, it is not surprising, as the quote by Adolf Hitler at the beginning of this chapter attests, that the barbarians of antiquity and the Middle Ages are often cited with approval by these folks. Not only are they what Nietzsche would have admiringly termed *preparatory men* who lived dangerously, sailed ships into uncharted seas, warred with their peers and themselves, and acted as robbers and conquerors, but their savagery showed them to be the kind of "violent, domineering, undismayed, cruel" "beasts of prey" that Europe's fascists and communists alike envisioned as the leaders of their respective new world orders.[28]

As I have noted elsewhere, under normal circumstances, all of these musings about vital barbarians, supermen, and new human types would have been little more than grist for the mills of lunatics, poets, and science fiction writers. The outbreak of World War I in 1914, however, catapulted this vitalist creed from the fringe to the mainstream of Western culture, society, and politics. The horrors of the First World War coupled with the chaos that ensued in the period following it, undermined the widespread belief at the turn of the century that the West was progressing towards a more rational, benign and prosperous future. Fearful of another world war and weary of the chronic political instability and economic uncertainty of the 1920s and 1930s, increasing numbers of Europeans abandoned the liberal credo of democratic government and free market capitalism and turned instead to the movements of demagogic self-styled *Übermenschen* who promised order, reliable train schedules, full bellies, secure jobs, peace, and a future filled with heroic deeds. Some of these "supermen" actually came to power in a number of European countries during the first half of the 20th century and established dictatorships that were bent on realizing the vitalist vision of a "stronger, wiser, and subtler" humanity led by amoral, willful, and ruthless heroes.

The results of this totalitarian effort to translate a fanciful philosophy of hero worship and human engineering into the stuff of modern statecraft were nothing short of catastrophic. Millions lost their lives in government sponsored programs of social improvement and racial purification. Much of Europe and Asia were laid waste in a second world war launched by dictators intent on being counted among history's heroic conquerors. And the very idea of heroism was degraded by the acts of SS "black angels" and Communist "new men" whose only claim to distinction was their extraordinary capacity for cruelty and barbarism.

Nevertheless, while the idea of the hero was besmirched by the actions of these new barbarians, the savage, violent, unrefined, and often amoral figures after which they modeled themselves remain popular in contemporary Western culture. Indeed, as mentioned in the introduction, movies, television shows, fiction, and video games continue to feature both the sybarites and savages addressed in this chapter. More often than not, however, the "good guy or gal" in these stories is a barbarian—usually of the gruffer, fur clad, sword wielding type—noted for their strong moral code, loyalty to friends, and hearts of gold.

To what do we attribute this remarkable turnabout in the reputation of what was once one of the most feared villainous types in Western history?

2. Sybarites and Savages 55

Part of the answer to that question may lie in the fact that there is always a measure of ambiguity in how barbarians are viewed in the West. While ancient chroniclers such as Herodotus and Tacitus highlight the customs and behaviors that they found repellent and/or uncivilized about these folks, there is also much about them that they regard as admirable. More to the point, there is always a not so subtle hint in these accounts that we all start out as "hard" barbarians and, over time, become "soft" ones. Add to this the fact that our own sanitized, deodorized, luxury loving civilization is itself the product of peoples once regarded as savage, soiled, and smelly, and the allure of the barbarian for both vitalists and gamers alike is not so difficult to understand.

Concurrently, the Enlightenment that made possible a new science, which markedly improved the lives of billions, and, for some two centuries, held out the promise of a paradise on Earth, also produced the state systems and technologies that made possible the 20th century's totalitarian regimes, world wars, concentration camps, mass murder programs, and nuclear strategies of "mutual assured destruction." All of these unfortunate developments led a great many people in the Cold War period (1945–1991) to conclude that barbarism is an endemic feature of the human condition that can be checked (with great difficulty), but never completely eradicated. Perhaps no work captures this attitude better than William Golding's *Lord of the Flies*, an allegorical tale recounting the descent into mindless savagery of a group of British boys who find themselves marooned on a deserted island following the outbreak of World War III. Two-thirds of the way into the story, Simon, an adolescent epileptic who is also representative of reason and civilization, has a hallucination in which a pig's head on a stick—left as a sacrificial offering to an imaginary monster on the island—shares the following rather depressing observation on human nature:

> "Fancy thinking the Beast was something you could hunt and kill!" said the head. For a moment or two the forest and all the other dimly appreciated places echoed with the parody of laughter. "You knew, didn't you? I'm part of you? Close, close, close! I'm the reason why it's no go? Why things are what they are?"

This notion that the barbarian is both the hated "other" on the frontiers of our civilization and the fearsome id-monster within us is certainly nothing new. A great many Western thinkers—Zeno, Epictetus, Cicero, Hobbes, Freud—argue that we are all innately irrational, inhumane, and savage, and become civilized only through a long process of coerced cultivation and education. Nevertheless, after some two centuries of very real progress in so many areas of human existence, it is disconcerting to be told that we must embrace our inner barbarian (or at the very least subscribe to a Capital One credit card).

"If they take the ship, they'll rape us to death, eat our flesh, and sew our skins into their clothing—and if we're very very lucky, they'll do it in that order."

The line quoted above is from the first episode of Joss Whedon's science fiction series *Firefly*, which first aired in 2002. It refers to a savage animalistic group of humans known as the Reavers who live a nomadic existence on the fringes of civilized space, and spend most of their time raiding adjoining human colonies for captives that they torture, rape, mutilate, and eat (not necessarily in that order). These folks also practice a form of ritual scarification; sport a rather eclectic wardrobe comprised of furs, leggings, boots, and body armor; and, though they can operate sophisticated space ships and advanced weaponry, possess no spoken or written language.

Ranged against these savages is the Union of Allied Planets (UAP), a centralized authoritarian empire that controls most of human space. This society is settled, urbanized, literate, highly refined, and governed by a Parliament, which is served by a vast and shadowy security apparatus. Over the course of this series' story-arc (and a 2005 motion picture), we learn that this Alliance is intent on exercising complete control over its system's inner and outer worlds and their populations. Indeed, in order to achieve this end, the UAP has forcibly subjugated the independent frontier planets, and conducted secret experiments aimed at suppressing humanity's violent tendencies on the unsuspecting population of a planet called Miranda (ironically, it is this very experiment that gives birth to the fearsome Reavers).

In opposition to both the Reavers and the Alliance is the plucky crew of *Serenity*, a "fire-fly class" space ship. These individuals are scruffy independent outworlders, as well as veterans of that region's war of independence against the UAP. They drink, gamble, smuggle, purloin other people's property, rob banks, and assist, where possible, the enemies of the inner worlds. Among themselves, they treat each other as equals, take their relationships seriously, honor their pledges, and do whatever is necessary to protect one another from the depredations of the outside world.

I go into such detail about Whedon's imaginary universe because it demonstrates how the different facets of the barbarian addressed in the foregoing sections continue to influence our thinking about this villainous type in the new millennium. Indeed, according to the criteria of the various commentators addressed up to this point, all of these fictitious social groupings are considered barbaric for one reason or another. The savage, nomadic, illiterate, badly clothed, and doubtless foul smelling Reavers, for example, would be all too familiar to an Ammianus Marcellinus or Ibn Fadlan. Herodotus would doubtless have noted similarities between the *koros, atē,* and *hubris* of the sybaritic Alliance and the Persian barbarians of his own time. And Tacitus would have found much that was admirable about the uncivilized marauders of the star ship *Serenity.*

Perhaps what is most striking about this film, however, is the fact that while all of the major players in the movie can be regarded as barbaric for one reason or another, the villain of the piece is unquestionably the über civilized United Alliance of Planets. This is made clear in the movie's opening scene where a young girl informs her teacher that the reason the Alliance is disliked by so many people, particularly those on the outer worlds, is because

> people don't like to be meddled with. We tell them what to do, what to think, don't run, don't walk. We're in their homes and in their heads and we haven't the right. We're meddlesome.[29]

The truth of this observation is then borne out in succeeding scenes that reveal to the viewer a society that thinks nothing of conducting secret experiments on its citizens, using covert operatives to terrorize and assassinate folks deemed security threats, and committing mass murder on a planetary scale.

While it is obvious that Whedon is playing to the libertarian sympathies and fondness for conspiracy theories of his largely American audience, he is also critiquing a modern civilization that often engages in actions that violate and/or endanger what the West regards as the hallmarks of a civilized society, i.e., freedom, rule of law, representative government, civility, modesty, and rationality. Nor is he alone in this critique. From Voltaire's *Candide* to Suzanne Collins' *Hunger Games,* Westerners are regaled with stories regarding the many ways in which our latter day social arrangements and institutions often engage in the kinds of barbaric behavior—wars of aggression, wanton destruction, genocide, tyranny, torture, terror, theft—they are created to curtail. Indeed, it is terribly tragic that at the end of five millennia of the Western civilizing process, a great many people regard our urbane civil societies as *the* villainous other, *the* barbarian extraordinaire.

Of course, as the current wave of nativism and xenophobia that is currently sweeping the United States, the European Union and Russia demonstrates, there remain non–Western peoples, as well as sizable pockets of impoverished ill-educated Westerners, that a great many Europeans and Americans (both North and South) continue to regard as barbaric. In fact, much of the behavior being critiqued in films such as Whedon's is related to the fallacious belief that these often dispossessed "others" pose an existential threat to the West's way of life that must be eliminated at any cost. Aside from the damage that this kind of thinking does to the ideals and principles of Western civilization, it also displays an astonishing absence of historical memory.

After all, it is not so long ago that the very populations calling for electrified border fences and stricter immigration controls were themselves regarded as little more than a pack of uncivilized, unwashed, illiterate, and disease ridden barbarians. That their fear of the other is also helping to create the kind of "meddlesome" nanny state they regard as public enemy number one is really too ironic for words.

As Arno Borst reminds us, "Tell me whom you call a barbarian and I will tell you who you are."

PART TWO

Tyrants, Traitors and Tramps
The Villain as Agent of Discord and Disorder

Things fall apart, the centre cannot hold;
Mere anarchy is loosed upon the world,
The blood-dimmed tide is loosed, and everywhere
The ceremony of innocence is drowned;
The best lack all conviction, while the worst
Are full of passionate intensity.
Surely some revelation is at hand;
Surely the Second Coming is at hand....
And what rough beast, its hour come round at last,
Slouches towards Bethlehem to be born?

—William Butler Yeats

Trust and loyalty are fundamental facets of cultures. When they fail, chaos follows.

—Nachman Ben-Yehuda

The Master of the Universe has bestowed upon them [women] the empire of seduction; all men, weak or strong, are subjected to a weakness for the love of woman. Through woman we have society or dispersion, sojourn or emigration.

—Mohammed al-Nefzawi

In the preceding part, we examined how notions of villainy are used to distinguish the human from the non-human world and insiders from outsiders. The following chapters continue to investigate this process of delineation by considering how certain villainous types are used to identify political, social, economic, and cultural behaviors that are believed to constitute a threat to the order, harmony, and well-being of society itself. Specifically, they look at how the actions of the tyrant, traitor, and so-called femme fatale have both challenged and reinforced Western thinking with regard to legitimate governance, loyalty to one's people, and proper male/female roles and relationships.

Of these villainous types, none has been more problematic in the history of the West than the tyrant. Starting as a rubric for the ruler of a Greek city state who was not a *basileus*, or king, this term became associated with usurpers who governed without regard to existing law and tradition, despots who abused the powers of their offices to further their own personal ambitions, and ruthless dictators intent on reshaping every aspect of their peoples' lives. At the beginning of the 21st century, it is an expression associated with any individual—anointed monarch, elected official, caudillo, commissar, bully—who exercises authority over others in a cruel and oppressive manner.

As the following makes clear, this was not always the case. The first Greek tyrants were often seen as liberators and guarantors of order, stability, and prosperity. The despots that followed them were not only legitimate rulers, but, in certain cases, had the cognomen "Great" affixed to their names because the policies they pursued fundamentally altered, in both positive and negative ways, the countries and peoples they governed. Even the dictators of the modern period were regarded, at least initially, as heroic figures. As Yeats reminds us, for a great many Westerners, these rulers were messiah-like "rough beasts" whose hour come round at last were making their way to Bethlehem (via Athens, Rome, Paris, Berlin, and Moscow) to be born.

Unfortunately, the rule of these figures was also associated with repression, murder, coercion, disregard for legal, social, and cultural norms, and war. Whether we are speaking of Greek *tyrannoi*, or Soviet General Secretaries, all of these rulers feared opposition and often suppressed it with great brutality. Their agendas were also pursued with scant regard for the needs, traditions, or desires of those they governed. Exemplary of this were the reigns of such "enlightened despots" as Louis XIV of France and Peter I of Russia—both regarded as "Great" in their lifetimes. In order to realize their dreams of glory and empire, these two men thought nothing of plunging their respective countries into lengthy, destructive, and fiscally irresponsible conflicts with their neighbors. They also regarded their subjects as raw material to be used, abused, and disposed of as they saw fit. Indeed, thousands of French and Russian peasants were dragooned, beaten and starved to satisfy the desire of their monarchs for palatial residences, new cities, and professional armies.

The rise of representative democracy, two world wars, a Holocaust, and the collapse of the Soviet Union, has insured that most Westerners are now free of the tyrannies that were once rather commonplace in Europe and Latin America. This said, the continuing popularity of biographies, documentaries, docudramas, plays, and other treatments of tyrants past and present underscores how many of us continue to be fascinated by these figures and their actions. As political scientist Roger Boesche notes, "However terrifying and odious, they also excite. We watch them like we watch a fire."

To paraphrase *The Who*, let's hope we don't get burned again.

While there is a certain *frisson* associated with the tyrant, there is only fear and loathing for the traitor. In large part, this is because we live in societies that are predicated on the notion that we can believe in the good faith and credit of our friends, neighbors, and countrymen. When a person, group, or institution betrays this assumption, they undermine the trust that makes possible everything from marriage and family life, to religion, politics, law, commerce, and diplomacy. Indeed, as sociologist Nachman Ben-Yehuda observes in this part's second epigraph, "trust and loyalty are fundamental.... When they fail, chaos follows."

Traitors also arouse considerable antipathy because betrayal is the one form of villainy most of us experience over the course of our lives. This usually entails a violation of some trust by people we know, or thought we knew, and, as anyone who has ever been lied to, cuckolded, or defrauded can attest, such acts of falsehood and disloyalty are both disillusioning and terribly painful. Not only do the memories of these betrayals remain with us, but they also arouse feelings of anger, suspicion, and fear that make it difficult—for some impossible—to enter into future partnerships, business ventures, and public service.

While all breaches of mutual obligation and trust are regarded as repugnant and deleterious to the social order, those that entail treason are considered especially egregious because they involve actions aimed at overthrowing one's duly constituted government, and/or aiding and abetting the enemies of one's people. Not only does such activity endanger the very existence of a society, but its perpetrators are also guilty of violating sacred oaths, and breaking faith with family, friends, and fellow countrymen. Indeed, treasonous acts are regarded as so villainous in nature that their commission usually entails a death penalty.

This section examines this particular group of traitors in some detail, and also underscores what a varied lot they are. The perpetrators of this crime can be men or women, hail from every social class and income group, live in villages, towns, and cities, and are mal- and well-adjusted. Nor do these people betray their governments and peoples for the same reason. Some seek enrichment; others suffer from wounded egos; many are the partisans of an ideology or cause; and not a few are the hapless victims of "honeytraps," or other compromising situations. Concurrently, while all of these individuals are regarded as criminals by their respective countrymen, they do not all share the same pride of place in the annals of villainy. Understanding why this is so is one of the questions addressed below.

Of all the villainous types covered in this section, perhaps the most controversial are those females who are willing to use their arms, legs, style, sidestep, fingers, and imagination (to paraphrase the lyrics of *The Pretenders* song "Brass in Pocket") to capture the attention of men and bend them to their will. Throughout most of Western history, "good girls" do not do this sort of thing. Instead, they passively accept both the notice and the authority of their male counterparts, be they fathers, brothers, lovers, or husbands. Those ladies who choose to do otherwise end up associated with the demi-monde and get labeled "femme fatales," or fatal women.

As the last chapter in this section makes clear, these deadly females are quite varied. Some, like Cleopatra, are ladies of power and wealth that command kingdoms and interact with men of their rank on an equal basis. Many are seductresses in the mold of Lola Montez, an exotic dancer who consciously set out to use her smoldering good looks and sexual allure to ensnare and exploit various male benefactors. Others fall into the category of emancipated women, such as the feminist artist and activist Isadora Duncan, who repudiated all traditional male and female roles in favor of an open society in which both sexes were free to live their lives as they pleased.

Whether *Machtweiber* (power woman), seductress, or feminist, all of these women were regarded as deadly to both men and traditional society at large. The very idea that a woman might be free to live and partner with whomever she wished, without recourse to male authority and supervision, was deeply disturbing to societies predicated on the notion that a woman's lot was to keep a man's home, bear and raise his children, prepare meals, and gather wool. Should females behave differently, there was a very real fear that marriages, families, and households would collapse and with them society itself.

Added to this concern for social stability, there was also the widespread and widely accepted belief that women were weak willed, overly emotional, sexually promiscuous, and extremely devious. Left to their own devices, it was assumed that they would be easily duped; take lovers other than their husbands; harm others in fits of pique; and lie, cheat, and steal in order to get their own way. Given all of these purported flaws in their characters, it is hardly surprising that men, and not a few women, considered the female of the species ill-suited to govern the day-to-day details of their own lives, much less those of men and nations.

This idea that women were frail, licentious, easily angered, and often deceitful creatures was also affirmed—indeed, enshrined—in the myths, legends, religious writings, and histories of the West. Greco-Roman and Hebrew creation stories placed the blame for all human misery on the overly curious, simple minded, and easily swayed Pandora and Eve. The ancient goddesses of the Mesopotamian and Hellenic pantheons were bitchy shrews, sexually crazed man-eaters, or virgin tom boys. Their nobly born sisters in the Norse and Germanic sagas were quick to anger, and willing to engage in every crime or unnatural act deemed necessary to redress any dishonor they felt had been visited upon them. Even in the modern era with its many movements for women's emancipation, novels, plays, movies, and soap operas continue to be awash in dangerous female characters who use their sexual charms to lure men to their doom.

Nevertheless, while some people still regard independent sexually active women who exercise authority as a threat to the moral and social order of the West, most of us do not. Indeed, despite lingering inequities in pay and professional advancement, at the beginning of the 21st century, females routinely receive educations, work outside the home, head businesses, and serve in government. They also enter into relationships of their own choice, and, when they cavort with men, it is usually for no more sinister reason than having a good time. Indeed, one of the key questions this section poses is whether it is time to rehabilitate all of those ladies who in the past were routinely labeled "fatal women," and consigned to the history of villainy.

3

"One who rules without law"
The Villain as Tyrant

Tyrants fill our history books and our headlines as they both repel us and intrigue us. They seem unconstrained and unconcerned about our persistent questions of morality; they seem powerful in a world in which most of us feel powerless; they seem to act, while we seem to drift; they do not seem bent over by the winds of history, but rather they stand firm, stand out from history, and sometimes change history. However terrifying and odious, they also excite. We watch them like we watch a fire.

—Roger Boesche, *Theories of Tyranny*

To robbery, butchery, and rapine, they give the lying name of "government"; they create a desolation and call it peace.

—Tacitus, *Dialogue on Oratory*

A prince ... cannot observe all those things which are considered good in men, being often obliged, in order to maintain the state, to act against faith, against charity, against humanity, and against religion.

—Machiavelli, *The Prince*

His power cannot, without his consent, be transferred to another: he cannot forfeit it: he cannot be accused by any of his subjects of injury; he cannot be punished by them: he is judge of what is necessary for peace; and judge of doctrines: he is sole legislator; and supreme judge of controversies; and of the times and occasions of war, and peace: to him it belongeth to choose, magistrates, counselors, commanders, and all other officers, and ministers; and to determine of rewards, and punishments, honour, and order.

—Hobbes, *Leviathan*

3. "One who rules without law" 65

My father was a decorated veteran of World War II who survived the D-Day landing at Omaha Beach, the Battle of the Bulge and the invasion of western Germany. He was also part of the joint Franco-American force that entered Paris on August 26, 1944, and he was assigned to the army company that liberated the Nazi concentration camp at Dachau on April 29, 1945—an event that haunted him for the rest of his life. If the Japanese had not surrendered in August 1945, he would most likely have seen military action in the Pacific as well.

These wartime experiences deeply affected my father, as they did the other men of his generation who experienced combat. As a child, not only did I hear more than a few stories about "dubya dubya two," but I was also fed a steady diet of World War II film fare throughout my youth. This included movies—*The Enemy Below*, *The Bridge on the River Kwai*, *The Guns of Navarone*, *The Longest Day*, *The Dirty Dozen*—television shows—*Combat*, *The Rat Patrol*, *12'O'Clock High*, *Garrison's Gorillas*, *Hogan's Heroes*—documentaries—*The 20th Century* (narrated by Walter Cronkite), Erwin Leiser's *Mein Kampf*, David Wolper's small screen précis of William L. Scheirer's *The Rise and Fall of the Third Reich*—and the film series that built the History (or Hitler) Channel, *The World at War*.

I was often disturbed while watching these films and television shows by the fact that I found the "bad guys," i.e., the assorted Fascists, Nazis, and militarists against whom my father had fought, to be more interesting, and in some cases more exciting, than the Allies. Their uniforms, military insignia, and weaponry were well designed and highly memorable. They put on fabulous shows—marches, rallies, openings, dedications, sporting events— that were beautifully staged and full of pomp and pageantry. And, with the exception of Colonel Klink and Sergeant Schultz, their officers and soldiers appeared to be models of loyalty, dedication, and efficiency.

I also found the leadership responsible for all these fancy dress uniforms and splashy fascist festivals to be more colorful and charismatic than their counterparts in the Western democracies. While it was made clear to me by family, teachers, and the various screenwriters of the abovementioned movies and TV series that Hitler, Mussolini, and their assorted imitators were indisputably wicked, when they appeared on screen I still found it impossible to come to any conclusion other than these were extraordinary men destined to rule. Not only was this feeling reinforced by their striking military regalia and the assorted (and quite colorful) national and party symbols with which they associated themselves, but also by the ways in which they moved, postured, and spoke. Indeed, whether they were reviewing an army march, speaking to their partisans, negotiating with their opponents, or just striking a pose for the camera, everything in their manner communicated a sense of certainty, confidence, and control.

Further contributing to this aura of authority was the "rags to riches" success stories of these dictators, perhaps best exemplified by the life of Adolf Hitler. As Walter Cronkite, Richard Basehart and other commentators of the time noted, despite the fact that he lacked social connections, higher education, administrative experience, or even German citizenship, Hitler managed to rise from Munich beer hall rabble-rouser to leader of Germany's most powerful political party, chancellor and dictator of the German Reich, and master of Europe in less than 20 years. By any standards, these achievements set him apart from not only ordinary people, but also from most of the politicians, leaders, and statesmen with whom he interacted—and usually bested—during this time.

Added to the remarkable life trajectory of these individuals, there was also their initial success—attested to by film footage of their adoring publics—in addressing the various crises that helped propel them to power. Returning to the example of Hitler, all the documentaries about his dictatorship attest to the fact that in the 1930s the overwhelming majority of Germans regarded their Führer as a heroic figure. Not only had he rescued Germany from political and economic chaos, but he had erased the shame of Versailles, and restored their fatherland to its rightful place as a great European power.

Obviously, as Roger Boesche points out in the epigraph that opens this chapter, there was something about these early 20th century tyrants that was both repelling and intriguing. On the one hand, the knowledge that their actions nearly cost my father his life, and were also responsible for the corpse filled concentration camp that haunted his dreams, made them "terrifying and odious" to me. On the other hand, the fact that they came seemingly out of nowhere and, for a moment, made the whole world hold its breath, excited me.

I would later learn that this youthful *frisson* was far from unusual. Almost 70 years after the end of World War II, documentaries and films chronicling this period's various dictatorial regimes and their assorted crimes continue to be big box office draws. New biographies of Hitler, Mussolini, and Stalin appear almost annually and are eagerly snapped up by a reading public hungry for new tidbits about their lives (and especially their loves) that were not revealed in prior accounts. Contemporary novels, television programs, comics, video games, songs, and even Broadway award-winning musicals (*The Producers*) are often centered on these tyrants and their lieutenants. And college classes—including several I have offered over the years at UCLA—addressing the Nazi dictatorship, Fascist Italy, the Holocaust, and the Stalin-era are always fully subscribed.

At first glance, this mania for what the History Channel has referred to as "the mad men of the twentieth century" is somewhat puzzling. After all, as citizens of contemporary Western democracies that celebrate representative government and the inalienable right of every human being to life, liberty, and the pursuit of happiness, the kind of tyrannical absolutism represented by these dictators—and justified in this chapter's opening epigraphs by Machiavelli and Hobbes—should elicit fear rather than fascination. This reaction would seem even more likely when one considers the very real "desolation" these despots, and their historical confreres—Sulla, Caesar, Attila the Hun, Genghis Kahn, Tamerlane, Louis XIV, Napoleon Bonaparte—visited on the folks that either fell under their control or ran afoul of their ambitions.

Nevertheless, as Boesche notes above, there is a glamour about these tyrants. When they emerge on the stage of history—usually in times of turmoil and chaos—they act decisively with a certainty and conviction notably lacking among their compatriots. Further, for good or ill, their actions often reshape, sometimes radically, the contours of the world within which they operate. Julius Caesar, for example, destroys the oldest republic of the ancient era, but in doing so lays the groundwork for a Roman Empire that future generations will hale as comprehending "the fairest part of the earth, and the most civilized portion of mankind." Centuries later, one of his admirers, Louis XIV, implements policies that spark worldwide wars, bankrupt his country, and force thousands of innocent Protestants to flee France. This same king, however, also makes possible the French Academy of Sciences, a flowering of Gallic literature and art, and the Versailles palace. In our own time, Joseph Stalin, an ostensible opponent of empire builders and their imitators, rules the Soviet Union as a kind of Red Tsar, murders and enslaves millions of Russians, and crushes movements of self-determination throughout the USSR. Despite these crimes, a majority of his countrymen still regard him as a heroic figure that transformed Russia into a modern industrialized superpower capable of defeating Hitler and, for a time, dominating the post-war Eurasian continent. Whatever one's opinion of these individuals, their behavior and achievements command our attention. To paraphrase Boesche once again, we are drawn to them like moths to a flame.

What follows is an attempt to arrive at both an understanding of the meaning and practice of Western tyranny, and the factors that make tyrants both repellent and also highly attractive figures. This inquiry begins with the Greeks who first coined the word *tyrannos* to describe a particular kind of political regime that came to prominence in the city-states of Archaic and Classical Greece. Using the works of Plato, Aristotle and the Attic dramatists, as well as the case of the Pisistratid tyranny in Athens, we will try to arrive at an understanding of how the term tyrant goes from being a neutral, even benign signifier for a certain kind of ruler, to a rubric associated with lawlessness and terror.

After this brief history of the origins and early practice of *tyrannos*, we will then consider how this regime and its practitioners adapted to changing historical conditions by taking a look at two tyrants associated with regimes identified by past and present commentators alike as despotic, absolutist, or totalitarian. First up in this tour of tyranny is that paragon of 17th century absolutism and "enlightened despotism," Tsar Peter the Great, Emperor and Autocrat of all the Russias. Following this examination of tyranny during the Enlightenment, we will fast forward to the 20th century and consider once again the case of Adolf Hitler, unquestioned leader of the Third Reich, and quite possibly the most villainous tyrant in Western history.

This survey of what has been labeled "an ever-recurring and very frightful melody"[1] in our past concludes with some reflections on what a tyrannical tune might look like in the future. Specifically, the final pages of this chapter take a look at certain prognostications put forward over the last two centuries by a number of political thinkers—de Tocqueville, Marx, Weber—and speculative fiction writers—Huxley, Heinlein, Orwell, Bradbury—regarding the possibility of a "tyranny without a tyrant." By using the speculations of these individuals as a launching off point, readers will be asked to consider two distinct, albeit related, questions: (1) Are both tyrants and their opponents (aristocratic, republican, or democratic) irrelevant in a world that is increasingly governed by ever more sophisticated systems of bureaucratic oversight and control; and (2) Are people truly free in mass societies where public and private agencies provide all necessities, tranquilize all anxieties, and amuse all boredom?

Before we engage in this futurist exercise, however, we will first need to consider how a word that initially connoted nothing more than a ruler of a community became a byword for a cruel and oppressive despot. As with so much else in Western civilization, finding the answer to that question will require us to pay a visit to ancient Greece.

Overture: Setting the Stage

The word from which tyrant is derived, *tyrannos*, makes its first appearance in a poem penned by a seventh century Greek named Archilochus. The passage reads as follows:

> I do not care about the wealth of Gyges, there is no envy in me, I am not jealous of the works of the gods, nor do I desire to be a great tyrant.[2]

The Gyges referred to in these lines was a seventh century military officer in the service of King Candaules, ruler of Lydia. Around 685 BCE, Gyges assembled an armed force of foreign mercenaries, seized the Lydian capital of Sardis, murdered his royal employer, and married his wife. For reasons that are not completely clear, he refrained from assuming the symbols or titles of his predecessor, and was instead referred to as *tyrannos* by his subjects and their Greek neighbors.

What *tyrannos* actually meant to the folks who applied the term to Gyges is not known (the word is not an Indo-European expression). It is possible that tyrant was merely another Lydian name for "king," though Gyges' successors were usually identified as *basileis* (kings) by their Greek neighbors, rather than as tyrants.[3] A number of scholars have also posited the idea that the rubric was likely employed by both Lydians and Greeks as a way of underscoring the fact that Gyges lacked a legitimate claim to the throne he had seized, i.e., he was not a member of the reigning dynastic family; could claim no descent from a god or goddess (Candaules on the other hand could trace his lineage back to Heracles); and did not enjoy the special favor of any tutelary deity (though this state of affairs would later change when Gyges began making liberal donations to the Delphic oracle). Rather than acclaim him king—a position for which he lacked any constitutional credentials—his people instead opted for a rubric that underscored the fact that he was a usurper whose claim to rulership was based on military might.[4]

Tyrant also does not appear to have carried with it any negative connotations at this time. Indeed, Gyges quickly consolidates his rule, carries out an aggressive foreign policy, which brings much of the Ionian and Aeolian coast of Asia Minor under Lydian control, acquires great wealth for himself and his people, lives lavishly, and makes rich gifts of gold and silver to the temple of Apollo at Delphi. In fact, his rule proves to be so popular that when he falls in battle against an invading Cimmerian army around 652, his son Ardys II is acclaimed king of Lydia, a title that Gyges' descendants hold for the next five generations.[5]

Whatever the origins or meaning of the word, tyrant is a title bestowed on several men that seize power in a number of Greek city-states during the seventh and sixth centuries BCE. These individuals—Pheidon of Argos, Cypselus and his son Periander of Corinth, Orthagoras and his successors in Sicyon, Pittacus of Mytilene, and the Pisistratids of Athens—share much in common. Like Gyges, they are all professional soldiers who either hold military office in their respective cities, or have experience raising and leading armies. They are also among the first Greek commanders to extensively employ the new hoplite formations of heavily armed infantry that replace the individualized combat celebrated in the Homeric epics.[6]

In addition to their military experience, these tyrants are members of the noble families that dominate their city-states. While they may not belong to the most wealthy and influential echelons of aristocratic households, these individuals are well born, extremely ambitious, eager for power and prestige, and open to shaking up the status quo. Towards this end, they also prove themselves to be extremely adept at putting together winning coalitions of fellow aristocrats, smaller landholders, well-to-do merchants and craftsmen, and urban laborers who share their disaffection with the social, economic, and political arrangements found in most Greek *poleis* during the Archaic period.[7]

These men also attain power in their city-states through armed coup d'états that are accompanied by purges—often bloody—of their opponents. Key figures in the former regimes are frequently murdered, their families and clientele banished, and their property confiscated. Even opposition households that accede to their rule are usually required to provide family members as hostages to ensure their loyalty and good behavior.[8]

Once ensconced in power, Archaic Greek tyrants tend to pursue policies of "whip and sugar" to keep opposition in check and win over the populace-at-large. Individuals suspected of trying to undermine the new regimes are either killed or exiled and their holdings are confiscated. The appropriated property of these opponents is either redistributed to the supporters of the tyrannies, or sold to raise the funds needed to finance various projects aimed at solidifying public support. These include pursuing foreign policies aimed at establishing colonies in Thrace, the lands surrounding the Aegean and Black Seas, and the island of Sicily; encouraging mining, manufacturing, and trade; underwriting the construction of roads, harbors, aqueducts, fountains, and public buildings, specifically temples; and patronizing various religious practices, such as mystery cults, play and poetry contests, and athletic competitions (e.g., Athens' Panathenaea Games).[9]

These first tyrants also tend to refrain from tampering with the constitutional arrangements of their city-states. Assemblies continue to meet, elections of officers proceed, and justice is dispensed. While some of these rulers arrange to be appointed to certain key posts that legitimize their personal regimes, most tend to merely hold on to the military titles they held prior to their tyrannies. Rather than govern directly, these individuals elect instead to fill the governing offices of their *poleis* with supporters and/or members of their families.[10]

Taken together, all of these arrangements make these men extremely popular figures. Their ability to raise and command armies and fleets helps them secure their respective homelands from foreign invasion, and also establish satellite colonies in other parts of the Mediterranean. The revolutions they launch tend to sweep away entrenched and ossified aristocratic cabals, end factionalism and its accompanying strife, and open executive and judicial offices to new men of ability in trade and commerce. Their public works projects also employ large numbers of people, improve the infrastructure of their respective cities, and instill a sense of civic identity and pride. Indeed, at least during the seventh and sixth centuries, these tyrannies are seen as guarantors of order, stability, and prosperity.

3. *"One who rules without law"* 71

The one area that proves highly problematic for the early Greek tyrants is the whole question of succession. Though these men try to assure the continued ascendancy of their families in the political life of their cities, the sons and/or lieutenants that succeed them seldom retain the popular support they enjoyed. Whether this stems from a lack of ability and acumen on the part of the tyrant's successors, or a widespread sense among the governed that conditions no longer necessitate one-man rule, the individuals who succeed these first *tyrannoi* tend to face increased opposition to their rule. And in the face of this opposition, these individuals often resort to the kinds of terror and torture that increasingly become synonymous with the idea and practice of tyranny.

The case of Pisistratus, the tyrant of Athens during the latter half of the sixth century BCE, provides us with an excellent example of how these early tyrannies, rose, ruled, and were ultimately replaced by other forms of government. Both a nobleman and a military commander (*polemarch*), Pisistratus made a mark for himself in 565 by capturing the port of Megara, a neighboring city-state with whom Athens was at war. In addition to his success on the field of battle, both Herodotus and Aristotle tell us that he was a major player in Athenian politics at this time, heading up the so-called "men of the hills," one of the three parties—the other two being "the men of the plain" and "the men of the coast"—that were vying for control of Athens. While we are not sure what these party labels actually meant to the individuals using them, there is evidence that they referred to the geographical regions of the Attic peninsula from which their leaders haled. In the case of Pisistratus, this explanation makes sense as he was born and raised in an ancient aristocratic family from Brauron, a northeastern town beyond the Hymettus, Pentelikos, and Parnes mountain ranges. As such, he was not only "of the hills," but very likely the representative of that part of the Attic nobility that resented the disproportionate influence exercised over Athens' political life by the great families of the plains and coast who were resident in or near the city itself.[11]

Whatever the significance of these party labels, Pisistratus seized power in Athens on three separate occasions. In 560, claiming that he had been assaulted by his enemies and wounded (injuries that Herodotus and Aristotle claim were self-inflicted), Pisistratus prevailed upon the Athenian assembly to provide him with an armed bodyguard, which he then used to occupy the Acropolis and install himself as tyrant. This first attempt failed when the adherents of the two other parties closed ranks against him and drove him from the city. Some five years later, this time in alliance with the head of "the men of the coast," and accompanied by a six-foot-tall woman attired in a suit of armor as the goddess Athena, Pisistratus re-entered Athens and was restored to his former authority by public acclaim. His tenure on this occasion also proved brief when he was once again forced into exile after his erstwhile ally opted to betray him in favor of an alliance with the "men of the plain." Finally, after a ten year period in which he acquired silver-mining interests in Thrace, cultivated alliances with a number of city states such as Thebes, Argos and Eretria, and raised an army of mercenaries, Pisistratus returned to Athens in 545, defeated the army of his enemies at the battle of Pallene, and re-established his tyranny.[12]

Once in power, Pisistratus moved quickly to consolidate his position. The aristocrats who had openly opposed or betrayed him during his 20-year struggle to attain power were either killed or fled into exile. Those opponents who did not flee were required to send their sons as hostages to Naxos, an island city-state controlled by a tyrant who owed his position to Pisistratus. As for the lands and movable wealth of these individuals, it is highly likely that it was confiscated and redistributed to members of the Pisistratid party throughout Attica.[13]

Pisistratus also left intact the reforms of his predecessor and friend, Solon, the great Athenian lawgiver. Solon's laws and constitutional arrangements, which had freed Athens' small farmers from crushing debt and opened the city's magistracies and assemblies to all citizens of property, enjoyed considerable popular support. By allowing his friend's legislation to remain in effect, Pisistratus was able to position himself as both a foe of aristocratic privilege and a defender of the economic and political rights of the city's peasantry, craftsmen, manufacturers, and merchants. Upholding the Solonian settlement also had the advantage of assuaging any anxiety Athenians may have had with regard to Pisistratus' extraconstitutional position as tyrant.

Leaving Solon's constitution in place, however, did not mean that Pisistratus actually allowed any meaningful opposition to his rule. Rather, he manipulated his friend's reforms to further strengthen and legitimize his position. Specifically, he took steps to insure that members of his family or faction were always elected to the nine yearly archonships, the principal executive magistracies of Athens. And because these archons automatically entered into the city's Council of the Aereopagus, i.e., the city's assembly of elders, it was not long before he enjoyed majority support in that body as well.[14]

Once secure in his position, Pisistratus launched an ambitious program of reform aimed at strengthening both Athens and his popular support. To insure the continuing good will of the city's small landholders, he created a new class of judges who traveled to rural districts to inspect conditions, resolve disputes, and make recommendations for agricultural improvements. Like an Athenian version of Hārūn ar-Rashid, he also toured the countryside personally to check on the work of his justices and to give the peasantry the opportunity to speak to him directly. During these tours, Pisistratus would also dispense loans with easy terms of repayment to peasants he found in need of assistance.[15]

Within Athens proper, Pisistratus instituted a wide range of public works that employed a great many laborers, craftsmen, sculptors, and architects. These included construction of the temple of Athena Parthenos on the Acropolis, later destroyed by the Persians in 480; the first structures of what would become the great temple to Olympian Zeus; the Telesterion, or initiation hall, at Eleusis; and a complete water and drainage system for the city called the Enneakrounos, or the Nine Springs. In tandem with these building projects, Pisistratus also took measures aimed at turning Athens into the religious center of Attic Greece. These included the erection of the aforementioned temples to Athena and Zeus; bringing the Eleusinian Mysteries of the goddess Demeter under Athenian control; cultivating the celebration of Theseus as Athens great "national hero"; transforming the Panathenaea into one of the most prestigious athletic contests in the Mediterranean; and establishing a yearly festival to the god Dionysus replete with the dramatic contests that would eventually give birth to the Athenian tragedy of the fifth century. All of these activities enriched the city and its inhabitants, cultivated civic pride, and fostered unity.[16]

On the foreign front, Pisistratus kept the peace. He remained on friendly terms with his neighbors, and used his connections and alliances with other tyrants and aristocratic families throughout Greece to open up new markets for his country's crafts, particularly Attic black-figure pottery. He also established Athenian settlements on both sides of the Hellespont (the present-day Dardanelles in Turkey), which made possible trade with the city-states and kingdoms of the Black Sea region. Not only did this development guarantee a rich market for Athenian goods (especially oil and pottery), but it also made possible the importation of plentiful and cheap grain (always in short supply in thirsty Greece) from southern Russia.[17]

When Pisistratus died in 528, Athenians could look back on almost 20 years of uninterrupted peace and prosperity. Indeed, his rule was such a success that his eldest son Hippias was able to assume his position as tyrant and also rule peacefully until 514. In that year, Hippias' brother, Hipparchus, was murdered by two men, Harmodius and Aristogeiton, in what appears to have been a lovers quarrel. Though these assassins were both slain, their association with some of the Athenian aristocratic families that had opposed Pisistratus aroused a suspicion in Hippias that his father's old foes were plotting against him. Over the next three years, this apprehension found expression in a series of increasingly oppressive measures that involved the execution, banishment, and confiscation of the property of various nobles suspected of conspiring against the Pisistratid tyranny.

Unfortunately for Hippias, these repressive actions did little more than spark a full-blown rebellion against his rule. Aristocratic families injured by his acts joined together in a common front against his regime, raised armies, and launched several attacks against the city. When these sorties were repulsed, the rebels appealed to Sparta's King Cleomenes I for help, and he replied by bringing a Spartan army to their assistance. Though Cleomenes first expedition to Athens was defeated, he returned in 510 and, with the assistance of his Athenian allies, expelled Hippias and his supporters from Attica.[18]

The fall of Hippias proved to be a significant event in the history of Western villainy because it is from this moment on that "tyrant" becomes increasingly associated in the popular mind with lawlessness, oppression, and murder. In part, the term picks up these negative connotations because Athens' post–Pisistratid rulers moved quickly to defame their predecessors in power. Though both Pisistratus and his son's tyrannical rule had been popular and highly successful in promoting Attic peace and prosperity for over 35 years, their enemies now portrayed them as lawless men who had seized power, usurped the Solonian constitution, and governed the *polis* solely for their own benefit. They were also accused of a decades long reign of terror that was so odious it had driven patriotic nobles like Harmodius and Aristogeiton to become "tyrannicides" (the fact that the murder of Hippias' brother by these two men was actually an act of passion rather than politics was conveniently ignored). Indeed, in the following century, these assassins were actually lauded as champions of the *demos* (the people), immortalized with a group statue in the Athenian agora, and granted an official hero cult.[19]

Hippias' opponents were also assisted in their vilification of the Pisistratids by his decision to join with other deposed tyrants and make common cause with the Persian Empire in the hope that its "Great Kings" might restore him to power. When the Greco-Persian Wars commenced in 499, these former rulers accompanied and advised the armies that first Darius and later Xerxes sent against their countrymen. Hippias in particular played a major role in Persia's first invasion of Greece (492–490 BCE). He assisted the Persian commander Mardonius in conquering Thrace and Macedon, took part in the sacking and burning of Eretria, a city not far from Athens, and directed the landing of the Persian army that was defeated by the Athenians at Marathon in 490. Given these acts, it is not terribly surprising that Hippias' fellow Athenians opted to heroize the murderers of his brother.[20]

Suffice it to say that it was not lost on the former subjects of either Hippias or the other tyrants with whom he was allied that these men were working hand-in-hand with foreign "barbarians" who were not only intent on enslaving Greece, but on pillaging and plundering any and all city-states that opposed them. As a consequence of this collaboration, these men, who had once been regarded as guarantors of order and security, were now seen as agents of discord and strife willing to go to any lengths to attain untrammeled power and self-aggrandizement. And one result of this sea change in public opinion was that by the end of the Greco-Persian conflict, if not before, the title of tyrant, which Hippias and his colleagues had sported so proudly in their heyday, had gone from being a neutral expression for the ruler of a *polis* to a negative descriptor used to identify a usurper who ruled a community without regard for law, custom, or the general welfare of its people.

This judgment also found expression in the literature of mid to late fifth century Athens. In his histories of the Persian Wars, for example, Herodotus focused on certain alleged actions and statements of Xerxes for the purpose of demonstrating the insatiable appetites (*koros*), delusional thinking (*hubris*), and propensity for violence (*atē*) that are characteristic of tyrants. These same tyrannical traits were also highlighted in dramas from this period, most notably in *The Persians* by Aeschylus and Sophocles' *Antigone*. In the former play, Greek audiences were again treated to a portrayal of Xerxes—this time responding to the news of his fleet's defeat at Salamis—which showed him to be a deluded and unrestrained autocrat ruling over an empire of slaves. *Antigone*, on the other hand, introduced audiences to the character of King Creon, a haughty and self-righteous Theban ruler who was so convinced that "the city *is* the king's" that he commits acts of impiety and cruelty, actions that forever mark him as one of Western literature's *tyrannoi* par excellent.[21]

While these fifth century political and cultural developments played an important role in transforming tyrant from a relatively benign word into one of odium, it was the work of the fourth century philosophers Plato and Aristotle that guaranteed this term, and those associated with it, would be forever inscribed in the lexicon of villainy. In tracts such as the *Republic*, *Laws*, and *Gorgias*, Plato associated tyranny with disease, describing it as a kind of pathology that strikes the body politic in tumultuous times and causes its members to behave in a manner that is neither just nor virtuous. The outward manifestation of this disorder is the *tyrannos*, a kind of fallen philosopher king who takes advantage of his community's disharmony to acquire power for the purpose of realizing certain base desires. Like a virus, this figure eliminates all who oppose him and then takes control of every aspect of a *polis*' life; a process that involves restricting the political activities of its citizens, fostering class division, encouraging the pursuit of private wealth over public service, and gratifying the appetites of the *demos* for pleasure.[22]

In his *Politics* and *The Athenian Constitution*, Plato's student, Aristotle, reiterated many of his teacher's objections to tyrants and their rule. Specifically, he noted that these men

- utilize terror to seize and hold power in contravention of the constitutions and customs of the *polis*;

- maintain an appearance of legality and tradition, while violating both in practice;
- cater to the base appetites of the population by providing them with lavish entertainments; and
- promote economic policies and public works programs that depoliticize the citizenry by focusing their energies and attention on pursuits of profit and private pleasure.

Unlike Plato, however, who compared *tyrannia* to a disease, Aristotle categorized tyranny in his classification of different kinds of government—monarchy, oligarchy, democracy—as an unnatural form of governance, a perversion of monarchy. Specifically, he argued that unlike a monarch who rules in the general interest, a tyrant governs only to satisfy his selfish desires. Thus,

> tyranny is just that arbitrary power of an individual that is responsible to no one, and governs all alike, whether equals or better, with a view to its own advantage, not to that of its subjects, and therefor against their will. No freeman willingly endures such a government.[23]

Whether viewed as pathology or perversion of the natural political order, by the end of the fourth century BCE, tyranny and its practitioners were not held in terribly high regard. To be sure, individuals and families continued to establish tyrannical regimes in a number of Greek city states, but none of them proved particularly stable or long-lived. Indeed, by the time Greece falls under the control of Macedon in 338 BCE, tyrants were no longer a significant factor in Greece's political life.

Before turning our attention to later variations on the "frightful tune" of tyranny, it might be beneficial at this point in our inquiry to consider why tyrants arose in Archaic Greece during the seventh and sixth centuries before the Common Era. One school of thought on this matter argues, as did Aristotle, that these early *tyrannoi* were essentially demagogues who gave voice to the anger of the people, or *demos*, against a dominant class of arrogant and abusive landed aristocrats. According to this argument, prior to 700 BCE, surpluses of land and livestock had afforded a select group of nobles the leisure and wherewithal to develop the skills necessary to fight, à la Homer, as independent warriors against the equally noble men-at-arms of other cities. Because these warrior princes owned most of a community's "non-movable wealth," and bore the brunt of its defense, they regarded it as their right to dominate the political and economic life of their respective city-states.

The rise of so-called "movable wealth," i.e., wealth based on manufacturing and the trade of commodities, in tandem with a new form of warfare centered on formations of men fighting with spears and shields (the so-called hoplites), altered this traditional social arrangement by dramatically expanding the numbers of citizens who were now both men-of-means and -arms. By the middle of the seventh century, these newly empowered "commoners" began to agitate for access to the political and judicial offices long dominated by the traditional nobility. When the aristocracy refused to share power, certain disgruntled nobles and hoplite commanders—Pheidon, Cypselus, Pisistratus, among others—were able to harness popular discontent, direct it against the status quo, seize control of the state, and establish personal regimes.

Though this socio-economic explanation of Archaic Greek tyranny is a compelling one, some historians believe that it smacks too much of modern concerns about class, capitalism, and mass politics. They remind us that this is a period when people were first and foremost members of families, clans, and tribes; conceptions of wealth and well being remained very much rooted in ownership of land and livestock; and the word *demos* often referred only to the propertied members of a community. These scholars also point to the fact that a great many of the early tyrannies were located in the Peloponnese, a part of Greece where non-Dorian Greeks were subject to repressive Dorian rule; the most noteworthy example being that of the Spartans and their helots. Noting that a number of the Peloponnesian tyrants—Cypselus, Orthagoras, Cleisthenes, Pantaleon—were non-Dorians, this "racial" school of thought argues that these men may very well have played on widespread resentment of the Dorians in order to organize a series of non-Dorian revolutions in their home cities. Indeed, the need to resist any Dorian counterrevolutions would have justified the establishment of regimes that were clearly outside of the normal political order.[24]

While it is likely that some combination of social, economic, and political conditions contributed to the rise of tyranny in Archaic Greece, the sheer paucity of primary source material makes it impossible to isolate any single factor, or group of factors, which created the conditions that made tyrants possible. Perhaps the most promising explanation for this phenomenon is the one proffered by Robert Drews in his article on the first tyrants in Greece:

> The direct "cause" of tyranny was something far more obvious to both ancients and moderns: the desire for power and prestige, or philotimia. And not so much the philotimia of the middle class farmers, the nouveaux riches merchants, or the non-Dorians, but rather the philotimia of the individual who aspired to tyranny.[25]

Indeed, whatever the nature of the environment within which tyranny arose, we do know that it comes to the fore at a time in Greek history when there appears to have been considerable tumult and turmoil. As Drews notes, notwithstanding the causes of this state of disorder, certain individuals—usually schooled in war, and always desirous of power—find ways of manipulating the situation to their advantage. These may include attaining military office, forming a popular faction, acquiring wealth, purchasing the services of mercenaries, and/or fomenting tensions between different groups. Regardless of the tack they take, these men also have an eye for the opportunities Fortuna sends their way, and, at the most opportune moment, they demonstrate a willingness to take whatever actions—murder, rebellion, treason—they deemed necessary to seize and hold power.

Once in control of a city-state, these individuals, these "tyrants," also pursue remarkably similar policies. They suppress their opposition, restore order, observe the letter (if not the spirit) of the law, and act to legitimize their rule and secure their legacy through public works, patronage of the arts, and often, though not always, acts of aggression against their neighbors. Either because those who follow them are incompetent, or the exigencies that brought them to power have passed, the efforts of these men to secure their succession are usually for naught. Indeed, these folks tend to enter and exit the stage of history on what we might call a discordant note.

This said, as Herodotus notes, "tyranny is a fickle mistress and many are her lovers," and it is to one of them in the Tsardom of Muscovy that we will now turn our attention.

Vivace Grandioso: The Tyrant as Despot

From a modern perspective, there would appear to be precious little difference between "tyrant" and "despot." Both terms describe rulers of territories who enjoy near absolute power, which they employ to achieve ends that are not always compatible with the welfare of their subjects. The two words are also associated with regimes that are undemocratic, oppressive, cruel, and overly fond of war. And those who get labeled as either tyrants or despots are usually regarded as so odious they are deemed worthy of deposition and/or death.

Earlier commentators on the subject of tyranny, however, would have taken issue with this modern tendency to conflate these two words. Indeed, for thinkers such as William of Ockham, Marsilius of Padua, Bodin, and Montesquieu, while a despot might be a tyrant, a tyrant could never be a despot. In making this distinction, these men were following in the footsteps of that great taxonomist of Western thought, Aristotle, who argued that tyranny and despotism were very different offshoots of constitutional monarchy. While the tyrant was little more than a usurper who was responsible to no one and governed solely for his own advantage, his despotic counterpart was a legally designated ruler—usually the scion of an established dynastic family with a long history of rulership over a given territory and people—who was pledged to observe and defend the established and longstanding laws and customs of the community he governed.

Despite the fact that a despot governed in accordance with the law and by public assent, Aristotle also noted that such a person could easily become corrupted by pursuing policies that were not in the common interest. When such a situation occurred, what had been a free partnership between ruler and ruled became instead an Asiatic (specifically Persian) form of governance, i.e., a bonafied tyranny in which the monarch reduces his subjects to the status of slaves to be used and disposed of as he sees fit. Though such rulership is technically legal because the despot occupies a lawful office and rules a quiescent public, it is nonetheless associated with a violation of custom, tradition, and public trust that one only expects from a tyrant.[26]

Some three centuries after his death, one finds Aristotle's distinction between tyrannical despotism and constitutional monarchy clearly on display in the works of Publius Cornelius Tacitus, a first century Common Era Roman statesman and historian who chronicled Rome's transition from republic to empire. In his history the *Annals of Imperial Rome*, Tacitus discusses how, in the years following his final victory over Marc Antony, Octavian Caesar was able to establish a so-called *principate* in which he and his successors were acknowledged to be "first" among both senators and citizens (*princeps senatus/princeps civitatis*). This Augustan settlement established what could be described as a quasi-constitutional monarchy that kept certain republican institutions and offices—Senate, tribunes, consuls—in place, while at the same time allowing for the concentration of both legislative and executive power in the hands of whomever was designated the "first man" or *princeps* of Rome.

Moreover, because he was writing his histories almost a century after the establishment of this *principatus*, Tacitus was also in a position to distinguish between good and bad emperors, or as Aristotle would frame it, constitutional versus despotic monarchs. The former included men such as Augustus, Nerva, and Trajan who governed in collaboration with the Senate, respected the legal rights of the people to be secure in their persons and property, upheld traditional values, kept the peace, and maintained order. The latter were individuals like Caligula, Nero, and Domitian who behaved as *dominii* (despots) that ruled without restraint, regarded the empire as their personal property, and reduced the citizenry to a state of servitude through acts of terror, free grain, and lavish entertainments.

Tacitus' histories of the early Augustan *principate* and its assorted bad eggs, in tandem with Aristotle's earlier political taxonomies, make "despot" rather than "tyrant" the term of choice for powerful princes who exercise their authority in a selfish, unrestrained, and abusive manner. In part, this distinction reflects the powerful intellectual influence that these classical authors exercise on succeeding generations of political thinkers in the West.

Of greater importance, however, is the simple fact that most of Europe, as well as all of the later European colonies in North and South America, are under the control of assorted autocrats from late antiquity to the end of the 19th century. Even the successful American and French Revolutions of the late 18th century do little to change this overall picture (and in the case of France both its first and second republics are quickly followed by an assortment of emperors and kings). Indeed, it is not until the shattering experience of the First World War that most Westerners find themselves living under something other than *ancien regimes* presided over by anointed monarchs who hail from hereditary dynasties that rule by the grace of God and/or the will of the people.[27]

Another reason that despot becomes such a keyword in Western political lexicology at this time is the absence of any effective checks on the power of these princes. That is, with the exception of England's parliament, most of Europe's monarchs are constrained in what they do vis-à-vis their subjects by their understanding of, and willingness to comply with, various religious strictures, traditions and customs, accepted legal precedents, and laws ostensibly originating in nature, e.g., human beings are essentially rational and seek to insure the common good; both individuals and groups require a measure of security in order to live and prosper; everyone enjoys a natural right to life, liberty, and property. Taken together these assorted rights and responsibilities form what might be called the unwritten constitution of a ruler's realm, and his willingness to abide by this "common law" determined whether he was regarded as either benevolent or despotic.

Not surprisingly, few rulers wanted to be regarded as despots. Such a designation identified its bearer as a tyrant who governed in an arbitrary and abusive manner; and it also invited unrest and even open rebellion. Indeed, much of Western history has been concerned with the assorted uprisings, Frondes, and wars of succession that were launched by various groups against princes that were regarded as tyrannical rulers. This said, there were also monarchs, particularly in the modern period, who opted to rule in a despotic fashion so as to achieve ends they deemed necessary both for personal glory and the general welfare of the peoples they governed. Moreover, though these individuals were regarded both in their own time and ours as tyrants, their accomplishments were such that succeeding generations affixed the cognomen "Great" to their names.

Among these notable despots, perhaps none better captures the multifaceted nature of this particular face of tyranny than Peter I, the Great, of Russia. Statesman, warrior, organizer, and reformer, Pyotr Alekseyevice Romanov was proclaimed tsar in 1682 at the age of ten. Over the next 14 years he acquired absolute power over his country's destiny in several stages, all of which involved considerable intrigue, skullduggery, and violence.[28]

3. "One who rules without law"

The first of these phases revolved around the struggle for power of two Russian noble families, i.e., the Naryshkins, the clan of Peter's mother, Natalya, and the Miloslavskys, the family of Mariya, the first wife of Peter's father Alexis. Though the Naryshkins were initially successful in elevating Peter to the throne, the Miloslavsky party led by Peter's half-sister Sophia quickly supplanted them by raising a rebellion of the Moscow militia, or *streltsy*. Though Peter survived this coup, he was compelled to witness the murders of leading members of his mother's family, including Natalya's former guardian and his beloved tutor, Artamon Matveyev. Doubtless, this violence made an impression on the young tsar's mind and explains to some degree his later actions against the fomenters of this revolt.

Before that could come to pass, however, Peter had to spend the next seven years under the thumb of his half-sister, Sophia. Following the purge of the Naryshkins, she installed her chronically ill and mentally deficient younger brother, Ivan V, as Peter's co-tsar, and had herself proclaimed regent during the minority of both boys. In this capacity, Sophia was able to take control of the government, rule the country in the name of her bothers, and, with the exception of major state occasions when his presence was required in the capital, keep Peter out of the public eye in a small village on the outskirts of Moscow named Preobrazhenskoye.

By all accounts, Peter appears to have made good use of his time away from the Kremlin. Gifted with great stamina and energy, physically strong (at his full height he would be six feet, eight inches [2 meters] tall), and blessed with an insatiable curiosity, the young tsar devoured everything he could find on military matters, while also learning carpentry, joinery, blacksmith's work, printing, ship building, and sailing. It was also during this period that Peter discovered Moscow's German quarter where Europeans of various nationalities resided. During his frequent visits to this area, he became acquainted with a variety of experts in different fields who taught him what he wanted to know about such topics as mathematics, fortification, and navigation. The most impressive aspect of this period, however, was that he put into practice what he learned by actually forming and drilling a couple of guards regiments (that would later become the nucleus of his new army), constructing a model fortress, and building a number of small sailing vessels.

In 1689, in response to news that his half-sister was planning to depose him and his brother and install herself as sole ruler, Peter mobilized the regiments he had raised and trained and rallied key elements of Moscow's population to his cause. He then removed Sophia from power, banished her to a convent, executed a number of her key aides, and exiled several other officers and nobles who were part of her faction. Though Ivan V was allowed to remain co-tsar, power was now effectively in the hands of Peter's mother and her kinsmen, the Naryshkins. When she died in 1694, and Ivan in 1696, Peter was finally able to assume unchecked control of the Russian state at the age of 24.

The next 29 years of Peter's reign would be, to put it mildly, remarkable. Concerned about what he perceived to be his country's backwardness and weakness, Peter set out to westernize and modernize every aspect of Russian government, society, life, and culture. Towards this end, he led a "Grand Embassy" of 250 advisers and colleagues abroad from 1697 to 1998 to western Europe with the aim of familiarizing himself with the international situation, studying nautical matters, and gathering information on the economic and cultural life of his more advanced neighbors. During his travels, he engaged in diplomatic talks with his counterparts in Prussia, Holland, England, and the Austrian Empire; talked with politicians and business people about ways of introducing their administrative and technological methods into Russia; served as a carpenter in the shipyards of the Dutch East India Company; worked in the English Royal Navy's dockyard; and visited workshops, mines, arsenals, forts, hospitals, schools, museums, and even a session of Parliament. He also recruited over 750 foreign experts in different fields to assist him in his reform efforts back home.

Upon his return to Russia in 1698, Peter signaled his intent to radically reconstruct Russian society by dealing savagely with a conspiracy on the part of the ever-troublesome *streltsy* to overthrow him and return Sophia to power. After disbanding their corps, Peter arrested over a thousand of these musketeers and had them brutally tortured. They were then executed and their mangled bodies put on public display as a lesson to all other would-be rebels. As for Sophia, she was expelled from the royal family and compelled to become a nun.

This purge was then followed by a slew of initiatives—some superficial others quite substantive—that were aimed at remaking Russia into a European country. To give his court a more Western appearance, Peter issued a *ukase* (decree) requiring his nobles to shave off their beards and wear Western clothes. He also required them to build European style homes in his new capital (more on this below), hosted special parties to teach them proper manners, and prepared a Russian etiquette book with instructions on how they should

> not spit on the floor, scratch themselves, or gnaw bones at dinner ... [but] mix socially with women, take off their hats, converse pleasantly, and look at people while talking.[29]

More meaty measures included changing the Russian calendar so that time would be reckoned from the birth of Christ rather than the creation of the world; reforming the administration of the country; subsidizing industry, particularly mining and manufacturing; requiring state service of the nobility, and compulsory education for their children; opening the aristocracy to men of merit; and establishing an Academy of Sciences.

To show both his contempt for the old Russia he had inherited and further wean his country from its Muscovite past, Peter established a new capital at the mouth of the Neva River on the Baltic Sea in 1703, which he named, appropriately enough, St. Petersburg. Constructed by the slave labor of tens of thousands of state peasants—a great many of whom perished from malnutrition, exposure, disease, and brutal treatment—this city was Western in design and decoration, and built in stone according to plans drawn up by foreign architects. Indeed, it was intended to be Russia's "window on the West," a modern metropolis in the style of Venice, Paris, and London that was faced towards Europe and away from the backward Asiatic culture Peter associated with Moscow.

All of these reforms, however, paled before Peter's efforts to create an army and navy that could both defend his country and expand its territorial boundaries. Indeed, over the course of his reign, Peter directed all of Russia's vast resources to the arming, training, feeding, clothing, and housing of a military establishment that, at his death, would number 210,000 regular troops, 100,000 Cossacks, 48 major warships, 787 minor and auxiliary craft, and 28,000 naval support personnel.[30] To service this war machine, he essentially militarized Russian society by requiring everyone in it, save the clergy and certain members of the merchant guilds, to perform some kind of martial service, usually for life. This entailed the conscription and forcible separation from families and occupations of hundreds of thousands of serfs, state peasants, and townspeople, and the commissioning of the nation's nobility to serve as permanent officers in his new infantry and navy.

Nor did Peter transform Russia into an armed camp for show. Believing that his country was backward because it was landlocked and isolated from the West, the young tsar set himself the goal of acquiring warm water seaports on the Baltic and Black Seas. As these ports resided in territories under the control of his neighbors, Turkey and Sweden, Peter spent most of his reign in a constant state of warfare with these nations. Though his wars with the Turks were sporadic and ultimately unsuccessful in winning him a berth on the Black Sea, Peter's conflict with the Swedish king Charles XII—the so-called "Great Northern War"—was a protracted ten year affair (1701–1721) that won him control of considerable Baltic real estate, warm-water outlets, and a new capital.

Suffice it to say that these wars were extremely costly in blood and treasure. Indeed, these conflicts in tandem with building a new army, government, educational system, and capital city all required enormous amounts of capital, which was very scarce in Russia at the time. To pay for his many projects,

Peter essentially imposed taxes on everything—"heads, as poll taxes; land; inns; mills, hats, leather, cellars, and coffins; on the right to marry, sell meat, wear a beard, or be an Old Believer."[31] Not surprisingly, most of this tax burden fell on the country's peasantry and to insure they paid these levies, Peter restricted their mobility and made them the property of the nobles to whom they owed service as serfs, a de facto system of slavery that would last until Alexander II's Emancipation Act of 1861.

It should be noted here that Peter also regarded the owners and employers of this enserfed peasant population as little more than personal servants at his beck and call. As we have already noted, he believed himself entitled to legislate their grooming, dress, table manners, and place of residence. By the end of his reign, he was telling them what service they were expected to render his state, as well as how they should run their farms, manage their enterprises, and invest their capital.

A great many, probably most, Russians deeply resented Peter's efforts to westernize their country. Rebellions were not uncommon during his reign, the Russian Orthodox Church opposed much of his modernization program, and his own son Alexis declared that he would undo his father's work and return Russia to its former customs and traditions when he ascended the throne. True to form, Peter responded to this resistance in a direct and ruthless fashion. All popular risings were brutally crushed, Russia's churchmen were placed under the rule of a tsar-appointed procurator, and he had his son and successor arrested, striped of his title, and tortured to death.

Without question, Peter I was a despotic ruler. Though the legitimate heir to the Russian throne and the anointed and crowned Tsar Autocrat of All the Russias, he ruled with scant regard for established customs, traditions, or laws. Indeed, as the preceding illustrates, his overriding ambition was to completely uproot the old Russia he had inherited and make it over completely in his own fashion. Nor would it be an exaggeration to say that he treated the entire country and its peoples as his personal patrimony to be disposed of as he saw fit (and hundreds of thousands were quite literally disposed of in order to realize his reforms).

Nevertheless, in 1721, three years before his death and at the conclusion of his "Great Northern War" against Sweden, Peter was given the titles of "Great," "Father of the Fatherland," and "Emperor" by Russia's Governing Senate (yet another Petrine institution that was set up to supervise all of the country's judicial, financial, and administrative affairs). While it would be easy to dismiss these accolades as the base flattery of sycophants eager to curry favor with their *Vozd* (boss), the fact remains that almost three centuries after they were pronounced a majority of Russians would probably agree that Peter was indeed a great ruler, who fathered imperial Russia and made it into a formidable Western power. Why this is so is perhaps best captured in the following lengthy excerpt from the writings of one of Peter's 19th century admirers, the Russian historian Mikhail Pogodin:

> Yes, Peter the Great did much for Russia. One looks and one does not believe it, one keeps adding and one cannot reach the sum. We cannot open our eyes, cannot make a move, cannot turn in any direction without encountering him everywhere, at home, in the streets, in church, in school, in court, in the regiment, at a promenade—it is always he, always he, every day, every minute, at every step!
>
> We wake up. What day is it today? January 1, 1841—Peter the Great ordered us to count years from the birth of Christ; Peter the Great ordered us to count the months from January.
>
> It is time to dress—our clothing is made according to the fashion established by Peter the First, our uniform according to his model. The cloth is woven in a factory which he created; the wool is shorn from the sheep which he started to raise.
>
> A book strikes our eyes—Peter the Great introduced this script and himself cut out the letters. You begin to read it—this language became a written language, a literary language, at the time of Peter the First, superseding the earlier church language.
>
> Newspapers are brought in—Peter the Great introduced them.
>
> You must buy different things—they all, from the silk neckerchief to the sole of your shoe, will remind you of Peter the Great; some were ordered by him, others were brought into use or improved by him, carried on his ships, into his harbors, on his canals, on his roads.
>
> At dinner, all the courses, from salted herring, through potatoes which he ordered grown, to wine made from grapes which he began to cultivate, will speak to you of Peter the Great.
>
> After dinner you drive out for a visit—this is an assemblé of Peter the Great. You meet the ladies there—they were admitted into masculine company by order of Peter the Great.
>
> Let us go to the university—the first secular school was founded by Peter the Great.
>
> You receive a rank—according to Peter the Great's Table of Ranks.
>
> The rank gives me gentry status—Peter the Great so arranged it.
>
> I must file a complaint—Peter the Great prescribed its form. It will be received—in front of Peter the Great's mirror of justice. It will be acted upon – on the basis of the General Reglament
>
> You decide to travel abroad—following the example of Peter the Great; you will be received well—Peter the Great placed Russia among the European states and began to instill respect for her; and so on, and so on, and so on.[32]

Clearly with Peter I and other autocrats of his ilk—Louis XIV, Frederick II, Catherine II, Napoleon I—we find ourselves dealing with a completely different kind of tyrant in Western history. To be sure, there are similarities between these monarchs and their earlier predecessors in ancient Greece and Rome. They all tend to come to power in times of great stress and strife. They also deal ruthlessly with their opposition; demonstrate considerable military acumen; invest heavily in public works; embrace wars of aggression; treat their subjects as if they were personal servants (or slaves); and struggle with problems of succession.

This said, there is a grandiosity, indeed a monumental hubris, about these figures that is markedly different from the tyrants of the ancient world. Whereas the latter were largely concerned about maintaining their power, currying favor with the populace, and keeping their opponents in check, the "enlightened despots" of the 17th, 18th, and 19th centuries viewed themselves as the living embodiment of an unchecked state power to which everyone and everything was subject. As such, they believed themselves justified, even required, to legislate and execute policies that intruded into every aspect of their subjects' lives—how they should make a living; what careers they might pursue; the education they should receive; what they were allowed to read, write, and speak; whether or not they could travel; how much of what they produced and/or earned they could keep; where and how they should live; what creeds they might embrace; and in what wars they would be sent to kill or be killed.

Further, to realize the visions they entertained about themselves and their nations, these despots created mechanisms of control that augmented their authority and that of their successors. These included more specialized and centralized bureaucracies charged with the oversight of justice, finance, and administration; the appointment of regional governors, intendants, or viceroys answerable only to the monarch; state monopolies and trading companies; mandatory primary education taught by state subsidized teachers; royal universities and scientific academies; internal security services (aka secret police); and permanent standing armies and navies. In short, Peter, and the others deemed "Great" from this period, lay the groundwork—and serve as the models—for the totalitarian systems of tyranny addressed in our next section.

These autocratic despots also foreshadow the tyrannical Duces, Führers, and party General Secretaries of the future in their complete indifference to the widespread suffering and violence that accompanies their efforts to centralize power, acquire territory, and refashion the peoples under their control. Indeed, between the ascent of Louis XIV to the French throne in 1643 and the final defeat of Napoleon Bonaparte at Waterloo in 1815, millions of lives are lost in the unceasing wars these "enlightened" monarchs wage in pursuit of empire and personal glory. Millions more are immiserated by the royal taxes, rents, corvées, and assorted requisitions of grain, livestock, and fuel these rulers levy to pay for the military adventures, urban developments, palaces, and colonies they believe necessary to aggrandize both themselves and their nations.

Nevertheless, despite their overweening ambition, insatiable appetite for power, and willingness to employ whatever violence and terror they deem necessary to attain their aims, these despotic tyrants are often regarded as heroic figures by the very people whose ancestors they exploited and terrorized. To some degree, as Pogodin's paean to Peter the Great demonstrates, this is a response to the simple fact that these despots initiate institutions, laws, and manners that shape future generations. For example, whatever a present-day French citizen may think of the ambitions and wars of Napoleon, he or she cannot deny that everything from the *département* in which they reside to the basic laws under which they and their children live bear his imprint. As Roger Boesche notes in this chapter's opening epigraph, these figures do indeed "stand out from history, and sometimes change history."

More to the point, the historical changes these despots implement while they are alive endure long after they pass from the scene. In part, this is due to the fact that, unlike their Greek predecessors, most of these individuals are the scions of established dynasties that directly benefit from their actions and have every incentive to defend and promote their handiwork. Returning to the example of Peter I, his successors do not repudiate his reforms because such an action would have left them both in a weakened position vis-à-vis church and nobility, and bereft of a military establishment that secured them from enemies both foreign and domestic. Concurrently, measures taken by these individuals to rationalize administration and finance, create a common law code, establish a judiciary, promote industry, foster commerce, educate the public, and defend the nation do prove to be beneficial to their respective societies. Even the reactionary Bourbons who supplant Napoleon I in 1815 recognize the soundness of his measures in all of the aforementioned areas and opt to leave them in place.

Finally, the intellectuals and historians tasked with judging these despots are often conflicted about them. Indeed, because they see the period preceding these rulers as essentially a lawless, disorderly time characterized by knightly violence, dynastic civil war, inquisition, ignorance, superstition, disease, and hunger, thinkers such as Hobbes, Voltaire, Kant, Hegel, Carlyle, and Nietzsche actually welcome the advent of these autocrats as a positive development in the history of the West. For these philosophers, the efforts of a Louis XIV, Peter I, or Frederick II to centralize authority, rationalize administration, control religion, and foster learning and science are seen as not only laudable, but actually essential to securing the safety and freedom of humanity.

For others among the Western intelligentsia of the 17th, 18th, and 19th centuries, there were also considerations of class and patronage, which inclined them to look favorably on despotic rule. For example, with the exception of self-made men like Joseph Priestly and Benjamin Franklin, most of the 18th century's scientific celebrities were the scions of well-too-do families, many of whom belonged to the lower ranks of the European aristocracy. For scientists like Pierre-Louis Moreau de Maupertius, Alexander von Humboldt, Joseph Louis Lagrange, and Jean le Rond d'Alembert, Louis XIV and company were not only "family," but also the principal patrons of the academies and associations that financed their experiments and expeditions.

In the end, all of these considerations—the impact of absolutist reforms on future generations; dynastic self-interest; the benefits of more rational administrative, economic and social policies; the approbation and cooptation of Western scholars and literati—work together to create the paradox of the "enlightened despot," i.e., a ruler who is both an oppressive tyrant and a heroic champion of reason, science, art, literature, learning, and sound government. As we will see in what follows, this successful, and often much lauded, association of what was essentially lawless rule with policies aimed at refashioning the human landscape will provide fodder to a number of profoundly chiliastic and anti-democratic movements in the 20th century. One of them is National Socialism.

Prestissimo con Fuoco: The Tyrant as Dictator

There is a confluence of events and ideas during the 19th and early 20th centuries that lead a great many people to embrace the tyrant as a heroic archetype. Perhaps the most important element in this mix is the simple fact that the policies pursued by the great autocrats of the Enlightenment prove largely successful in winning for their countries considerable power and influence in the modern period. Further, as Pogodin's remarks regarding Peter the Great demonstrate, this achievement is embraced and celebrated by later generations of their countrymen who either turn a blind eye to, or find ways to justify, the many wars, repressive measures, and onerous exactions of these regimes.

The success of these despots in aggrandizing themselves and their nations is also not lost on the statesmen and rulers of the 19th century. All of the major players of this period—Talleyrand, Metternich, Disraeli, Napoleon III, Cavour, Bismarck—are avid practitioners of the kind of *Realpolitik* that was the trademark of Peter and his fellow Greats during the 17th and 18th centuries. As such, these individuals are willing to employ any means necessary—repression, skullduggery, bribery, espionage, blood, iron—to achieve what they believe to be in the best interests of their respective dynasties and states. Indeed, this is a century in which Piedmont-Sardinia's Camillo Benso, Count of Cavour, and Prussia's Otto von Bismarck feel perfectly justified in launching several coolly calculated wars of aggression to unify Italy and Germany; while their colleagues in the other European capitals just as cold-bloodedly set out to conquer and ruthlessly exploit colonial empires in Africa and Asia.

3. *"One who rules without law"*

These 19th century power brokers are also operating in an intellectual environment that both legitimizes and lauds the self-centered, ruthless, and amoral actions of "great men" (and the occasional "great woman"). As we have already noted in the preceding chapters, the 19th century is the high water mark of Romanticism, a movement that celebrated not only "sublime" nature, lawless bandits, and noble savages, but also self-made "world historical" personalities like Napoleon Bonaparte, i.e., individuals who exhibit emotional intensity, genius, creativity, and disdain for any social stricture or convention not of their own making. Nor are the Romantics alone in their fondness for extraordinary history-making men and women. There are also heroic vitalists, such as Thomas Carlyle and Friedrich Nietzsche, who embrace the notion that human progress results from the actions of certain willful, creative, "vital" individuals such as Alexander of Macedon, Julius Caesar, and Caesare Borgia, individuals who, in the words of Niccolo Machiavelli, often feel compelled to act "against faith, against charity, against humanity, and against religion" in order to realize their aims. Not surprisingly, all of these hero worshippers tend to view the despots treated in the preceding section in a favorable light, and are fond of characterizing their reigns as veritable "ages" in which Western humanity progressed to new levels of power, sophistication, and accomplishment.

Finally, the principal schools of science and philosophy at this time also appear to make a case for the historical necessity of tyrants and tyranny. Materialism, evolutionary biology, social determinism, existentialism, and Marxism all tend to view existence as a godless amoral affair characterized by an ongoing, brutal, and unequal struggle for survival and mastery. In this scenario, the human being counts as merely one life form among many struggling to live in and master its surroundings. As for human civilizations, their social arrangements, cultures, moralities, and states are seen not as evidence of mankind's divinely ordained place in an orderly chain of being, but rather as adaptive strategies adopted by human beings over time to address primal urges, needs, and fears, all of which are part and parcel of our struggle to survive. Many of the adherents of this "war of all against all" storyline believe it to be self-evident that extraordinary men and women, notable for their strength and intellect, and capable of acting in a decisive, hard, and sometimes ruthless manner, are key to both human survival and development. For these folks, archaic Greek tyrants and enlightened despots who had acquired power in tumultuous times, and then used it to restore the fortunes of their respective peoples, were a case in point.

Despite the fact that all of these developments help to make tyrants and their tyrannies appear more benign, the 19th and early 20th centuries also witness the dramatic expansion of the institutions and practices of bourgeois liberalism—written constitutions, parliamentary democracy, the right to petition and assemble, religious toleration, and a free press. Even those countries that had been ruled by the great despots of the preceding centuries—France, Prussia, Russia—sport constitutional governments with legislative assemblies, suffrage (in Germany universal), charters stipulating citizen rights, judicial oversight, and occupational mobility. Indeed, this political progress appears to point to a future in which all manner of authoritarian and absolutist rule will be consigned to the dustbin of history.

Unfortunately, as recounted in the preceding chapter, this hope proves chimerical. The horrors of the First World War coupled with the chaos of the period following it, undermines the widespread belief at the end of the 19th century that the West is progressing towards a more rational, benign, and prosperous future. Fears of another world war and weariness with the chronic political instability and economic uncertainty of the 1920s and 30s also lead a great many Europeans to question and then abandon both democratic government and free market capitalism. Both of these developments work in favor of mass movements on the right and left—Fascism, National Socialism, Bolshevism—that are led by individuals who openly admire the despots of the past, and are well-steeped in the abovementioned vitalist reveries and pseudo-scientific theories so widespread in Europe at the turn of the century.

When these movements and their leaders actually come to power in a number of European countries, they establish dictatorships that are not atypical of the ancient tyrannies addressed at the beginning of this chapter. That is, following their usurpation of power, they snuff out democratic government (while often maintaining its forms), incarcerate and/or murder political opponents, underwrite massive public works programs, and pursue aggressive foreign policies. Also like their Greek predecessors, the dictators running these regimes are essentially "new men" who struggle with the whole question of how to secure their handiwork after they pass from the scene.

In other respects, however these tyrannical dictatorships are more like the despotic states examined in the last section, albeit on steroids. Like their Enlightenment predecessors, the respective Duces, Führers, and General Secretaries of the 1920s and 30s also believe themselves entitled, either by providence or the laws of history, to promulgate and pursue any policies necessary to refashion their respective countries and peoples. The reformation these men have in mind though is far more radical and far-reaching than anything attempted by the despots of the 17th and 18th centuries. Indeed, the efforts of these men to establish totalitarian "command" societies populated by new "human types" result in millions of deaths in wars and government-sponsored programs of social improvement and racial purification.

One can get some sense of how these dictatorial regimes were both a continuation of and a radical departure from the tyrannies of the past by considering the career of Adolf Hitler. As noted in the introduction to this chapter, Hitler was admired by a great many people because of his remarkable rags to riches success story. Born into a lower middle-class Austrian family, Hitler's childhood and youth were completely uneventful and gave no indication that he would one day be a significant historical figure. Upon finishing secondary school, he fancied himself an artist and something of an architect, but he failed twice to gain admission to the Academy of Graphic Arts in Vienna. For five years after this rejection, he was an aimless drifter doing odd jobs, immersing himself in *völkish* tracts, and leading a bohemian existence in the Austrian imperial capital. In 1913, he moved to Munich to escape conscription in the Austro-Hungarian army and enlisted in the German military as an infantryman at the outbreak of the First World War. He distinguished himself during this conflict, winning the Iron Cross first class for bravery, but he failed to win promotion because his superiors felt he lacked leadership qualities. Indeed, for 32 years of his life there was nothing about Adolf Hitler that distinguished him from his peers or indicated he was destined for anything save a fringe existence.[33]

As mentioned earlier, however, from 1921 on, Hitler's life trajectory was extraordinary. Starting out as a beer-hall rabble-rouser and leader of a right-wing fringe party comprised largely of anti–Semitic cranks, he managed in 12 years to become chancellor and dictator of the German Reich. While much of this extraordinary success was owed to historical circumstances outside of Hitler's control—Germany's humiliation at Versailles; the instability of the Weimar Republic; the Great Depression; the complicity of the German ruling class; Europe's war weary populations; and the lackluster leadership of Great Britain and France—there were a number of personality traits that allowed Hitler to capitalize on the many opportunities that came his way in the years before Stalingrad. His remarkable speaking ability, as well as his unshakeable belief that he was a messiah tapped by Providence to realize the *völkish* ideal of a racially pure Pan-German empire, conferred on Hitler a charismatic quality completely lacking in the colorless career politicians he competed with in his rise to the chancellorship. His willingness to take whatever steps necessary, no matter how ruthless, to gain untrammeled personal power made it easy for him to dispose of anyone—friend or foe—who opposed him. His abiding faith in his gut instincts, coupled with a willingness to gamble recklessly, also freed him to consider courses of action—the remilitarization of the Rhineland; the annexation of Austria and Czechoslovakia; an armored thrust through the Ardennes during the campaign against France—that his more rational and cautious advisors and generals would never have entertained. And a complete lack of morals made it possible for Hitler to engage in conduct—breaking promises; violating treaties; ignoring the rules of war; terrorizing civilian populations; enslavement and mass murder—that his counterparts in other countries found shameful and criminal.

Further assisting Hitler in his rise to and consolidation of power was his masterful use of propaganda to promote the idea that his Nazi dictatorship was not a radical departure from German history, but merely its fulfillment. Perhaps the best example of this kind of messaging was Hitler's decision, soon after his accession to the chancellorship, to inaugurate the newly elected Reichstag—the very one that would grant him full dictatorial powers—on March 21, 1933, in Potsdam's Garrison Church. The date was significant because it coincided with the anniversary of the opening of the first Reichstag of Bismarck's Second Empire (March 21, 1871), and the setting was of great symbolic importance because it was the site of both the palace (*Sans Souci*) and burial place (the aforesaid Garrison Church) of that prominent representative of 18th century enlightened despotism, Frederick II, the Great, of Prussia. By associating himself with both the *Kaiserreich* of Bismarck and the despotic regime of Frederick, Hitler was signaling that his own brand of absolutist rule would be on a par with his aristocratic predecessors. While this would prove to be patently false—indeed, Hitler's dictatorship would make the Hohenzollerns look like democrats—it did have the advantage of assuaging both domestic and foreign anxieties about his new regime.

Whatever the personality traits and propaganda tricks that allowed Hitler to take and hold on to power, from 1933 to 1941 he enjoyed a remarkable string of successes, most of them relatively bloodless. As he promised throughout the 1920s and early 1930s, he renounced the Versailles Treaty and, through policies of rearmament and heavy state spending on public works such as the autobahn, ended the depression in Germany and brought the country to full employment. He then proceeded, without a shot being fired, to remilitarize the Rhineland, annex Austria, and occupy Czechoslovakia. Even with the outbreak of World War II—an event for which Hitler bears full blame—the German Führer really did appear blessed by Providence as his armies rolled over Poland, Denmark, Norway, the Benelux countries, France, Yugoslavia, and Greece with surprisingly light casualties in less than two years.

As with so many of the tyrants of the past, however, Hitler's rapacious appetite for power and overweening hubris led him to acts of violence and savagery that proved to be his undoing. Indeed, his extraordinary successes from 1933 to 1941 convinced him that it was his divinely ordained duty to fully realize the National Socialist agenda. This included cleansing Europe of Jews, Sinti Roma, and all those he designated "unworthy of life" (*Lebensunwert*); carving out a vast German empire in Russia served by a semi-literate population of Slav slaves whose cultures and cities had been completely obliterated; and breeding a new eugenically engineered race of Aryan *Übermenschen*. To achieve these goals, Hitler, and those many Germans and Europeans who were enthusiastically "working towards their Führer," embarked on ever more radical courses of action that included a euthanasia program, which killed more than 70,000 mentally ill and deformed patients in German asylums; ethnic cleansing operations in Poland resulting in the deaths of some two to three million non–Jewish Poles; a "war of extermination" against the Soviet Union responsible for some nine million military and 13 million civilian deaths; and a "final solution of the Jewish question" that led to the mass murder of five to six million European Jews.[34]

Aside from the fact that these actions represented a complete repudiation of every ideal, every principle of civilized behavior that had held sway in the West for almost two millennia, Hitler's drive to refashion Germany and Europe into a racially pure Aryan paradise was ultimately self-defeating. The arrogant and often brutal treatment of occupied populations—ethnic cleansing operations, mass arrests and mistreatment of individuals and groups regarded as security threats, reprisal killings of innocent civilians, forcible conscription of slave labor, illicit seizure of property, foodstuffs, and raw materials—generated ever increasing levels of partisan resistance throughout Europe. The Soviet Union, with its vast expanses of territory, brutal winters, Ural based industrial centers, considerable army reserves, and large patriotic population, proved impossible to conquer. And the implementation of a European-wide Judeocide not only diverted considerable resources and manpower from the German war effort, but also helped to discredit anti–Semitism and generate international support for the establishment of a Jewish state in Palestine in the post-war period.

In the end, Hitler's dreams and delusions saddled his country with a war on three fronts against an international coalition that included Great Britain, the United States, and the USSR. From 1942 to 1945, these allies reclaimed the territories the German army had so easily conquered between 1938 and 1941, invaded Germany, and laid siege to Berlin. On April 30, 1945, with the Russians closing in on his Führerbunker and his thousand-year Reich in ruins, Adolf Hitler put a bullet through his brain thus ending one of the most infamous tyrannies in world history.

Looking over the trajectory of Hitler's career, one can certainly see similarities between his dictatorship and the despotisms of the earlier modern period. Like his aristocratic predecessors, his position as head of state was both legal and legitimate. Whatever the unscrupulous backroom machinations that led Paul von Hindenburg, Germany's aging and increasingly senile president, to appoint him chancellor in 1933, Hitler was perfectly within his rights to demand this office as the head of the Reichstag's largest democratically elected political party. It was also an Enabling Act approved by a two-thirds majority of the Reichstag that granted him the near absolute power he enjoyed; and his position as the country's supreme leader was acceded to by his conservative dominated cabinet, the military establishment, and a popular plebiscite. Indeed, though Hitler had only contempt for the rule of law, the Weimar constitution, the country's traditional governing elites, and the German bureaucracy, he left most of the pre–Nazi political framework in place, governing instead through decrees, Nazi party factotums, and special Reich "plenipotentiaries."

No less than Peter and his peers, Hitler also sought to radically reconstruct his country and treated the people under his control as little more than the raw materials he required to realize his aims. As such, he felt no qualms about regulating how Germans were to be raised, what they might read, watch, and listen to, how they were to make a living, what they should produce and purchase, and who they might marry. As we have already noted, he also believed himself fully justified in promulgating often murderous policies that were aimed at eliminating Germany's internal and external "race enemies."

Finally, as with most of the tyrants examined up to this point, Hitler was inordinately fond of war. Believing it to be Germany's mission to dominate Central Europe and rule over a Russian colonial empire, and convinced that only he had the requisite "will" to realize this destiny, Hitler remilitarized German society in the 30s and pursued an aggressive foreign policy aimed at the defeat of the Western democracies, the destruction of Bolshevik Russia, and the extirpation of world Jewry. Attempting to attain these aims required him to spend over half of his 12-year dictatorship waging a worldwide war.

Whatever Hitler's similarities with his tyrannical predecessors, he and his fellow dictators were also markedly different from the tyrants of the past. Perhaps the most novel thing about these individuals was their conviction that they were the propagators and executors of some all-encompassing "idea," which they believed would summon forth a completely new humanity. For Hitler, this was the notion that he was called by Providence to lead a superior Aryan race in its struggle for survival against racially inferior, culture destroying "Jewish Bolsheviks."

Winning this racial war was Hitler's *raison d'être*, and to achieve this end he was willing to pay any price and endure any sacrifice, including, if necessary, the destruction of his own people (something he actually countenanced in the final months of World War II). While Hitler's counterparts on the left were motivated in their actions by a very different ideology—specifically, the belief that they were waging a class war aimed at ushering in a stateless workers' paradise—they too were equally apocalyptic in their thinking and extreme in their actions.[35]

By way of contrast, however ruthless and aggressive the tyrants of the past were, none of them subscribed to ideas or policies promoting the refashioning of every aspect of human life at any cost. The Greek *tyrannoi* acted as they did out of a desire to acquire and retain power in their respective communities. As long as their authority was respected, their fellow citizens were

3. "One who rules without law"

largely free to behave as they pleased. Much the same can be said of Augustus and his successors. That is, with the notable exception of a Caligula or Nero, most of these "first and best men" of Rome contented themselves with maintaining the internal and external security of their longstanding multi-cultural empire. Even the absolutist monarchs of the Enlightenment, who were intent on modernizing their peoples and waging wars to reach the "natural boundaries" of their nations, largely respected the *ancien regime* on which their claim to rule was based.

Such restraint was notably lacking among the ideologically driven dictators of the 20th century. Because these men saw themselves as Nietzschean-style "preparatory men" who were laying the groundwork for history-ending new orders, they showed little interest in preserving much, if anything, from the past. Indeed, Hitler welcomed the leveling of German cities by Allied bombers because it would make it easier for him to rebuild them after the war along National Socialist lines, and his counterpart in the Soviet Union felt much the same way. Before the war, Stalin approved the wholesale destruction of historical landmarks and neighborhoods in Moscow to construct a new subway system for his capital. Afterwards, he covered the rubble of the USSR's bombed out cities with colorless concrete high rises and ornate monumental public buildings that were often referred to as "Stalin's wedding cakes."

Whatever the architectural tastes of these dictators, the great irony of their forward-looking regimes was the fact that they were built on the legacies of both the enlightened despots and democrats that preceded them. However much Hitler and company may have despised the constitutions, elections, parties, assemblies, mass media, plebiscites, and parliaments of bourgeois liberalism, it was these instruments and practices of representative democracy that made it possible for them to win mass followings, form dictatorial governments, and later pass themselves off as representatives of the popular will. Similarly, while they might rail against the bureaucracies, judicial tribunals, policemen, prisons, and professional military establishments of the modern state, they were quick to use the same or similar kinds of institutions to suppress dissent, eliminate so-called class and race enemies, and wage large-scale wars of aggression. Finally, whatever their ideological predilections, these tyrants also found their predecessors' cities, factories, cartels, and schools to be both excellent sources of capital, research and development, and trained labor, as well as ideal vehicles for the regulation and regimentation of their respective populations.

Indeed, the key role that the modern industrial nation state played in the rise and consolidation of the 20th century's dictatorships, and the fact that it also helped provide these regimes with the wherewithal to wage worldwide warfare, murder millions of innocents, and develop weapons of mass destruction, gave a great many people pause at the end of World War II. Just as this conflict and the one immediately before it had called into question human rationality and morality, it now drove home how easily the handiwork of the Enlightenment—strong centralized states, political economies, representative governments, urbanization, cartelization, mass production and marketing—could be reprogrammed to achieve extremely irrational and immoral ends. Increasingly, one began to hear warnings about a possible future in which all human beings might find themselves enslaved to the very systems that feed, clothe, house, educate, and employ them; and it is to this prospect of a "tyranny without a tyrant" that we now turn.

Coda: "An ever-recurring and very frightful melody"

The carnage and cost of the Second World War—60 to 85 million deaths (most of them civilian), large swathes of Europe and Asia in ruins, two radioactive cities in Japan—lowered the curtain on the late 19th and early 20th century love affair with tyrants and tyranny. A great many of the architects and factotums of the defeated National Socialist, Fascist, and militarist regimes were arrested and/or apprehended, placed on trial, and either hanged or imprisoned. The tyrannical governments these criminals established were dissolved, their laws abrogated, and their parties and movements banned. Even the dictatorship of Joseph Stalin, one of the victors of World War II, was discredited when, following his death in 1953, his henchmen and successors released hundreds of thousands of political prisoners, condemned the Stalinist "cult of personality," and exposed the many crimes against both the Communist party and the peoples of the Soviet Union that were committed by this self-styled "Father of All the Nations" and "Driver of the Locomotive of History."

The latter half of the 20th century also witnessed the slow but steady triumph of electoral democracy throughout the West. Democratic rule was restored in northern, central, and southern Europe during the postwar period, major advances in minority civil rights were achieved in the United States, and, as Cold War tensions declined, civilian governments replaced military dictatorships throughout Latin America. The years between 1989 and 1991 also witnessed the breaching of the Berlin Wall, the collapse of Eastern Europe's authoritarian Communist regimes, and the replacement of the Soviet Union by a more democratic Russian Federation. As this is being written, an "Arab Spring" continues to rock entrenched despotisms across northern Africa and the Middle East.

3. "One who rules without law" 97

Despite these advances, however, there remains a widespread and deep-seated fear that, like a virus, the "very frightful melody" of tyranny will mutate and recur in some new form. As noted in the preceding section, much of this unease revolves around the various instrumentalities of control—centralized governments, bureaucracies, military establishments, mass electoral parties and politics, print and electronic media, corporations and multinationals—that made it possible for the assorted dictators of the 20th century to acquire and exploit power. Not only do these institutions and practices remain fixtures of modern life, but the fact that they have become even more established, sophisticated and intrusive makes it possible for many to imagine how, under the right conditions, authoritarian movements might once again use the apparatus of the modern state and economy to suppress freedom, eradicate undesirable "others," and wage wars of aggression. Indeed, there is a considerable body of post–World-War I and II literature and film—*We, Metropolis, 1984, Fahrenheit 451, THX 1138, The Handmaid's Tale, Brazil, V for Vendetta, The Hunger Games*—that postulates just such a future.

Of these works, the most influential has been, without question, George Orwell's classic *1984*. Completed in 1948 (the title is an inversion of the year in which it was finished), and very much influenced by actual events and practices in Stalinist Russia, this novel revolves around the travails of two lovers—Winston Smith and Julia—who live in a dreary totalitarian state named Oceania, which is ruled by an omnipresent "Party" that is organized around the cult of Big Brother, a quasi-divine leader who may or may not exist. Subjected to constant electronic surveillance, propaganda campaigns, censored news, "revised" history, spies, secret police, periodic purges, unending wars (with two other totalitarian states), and chronic shortages of everything save synthetic foodstuffs, and "Victory" gin and cigarettes, Winston and Julia attempt to maintain their individuality, foster their love, and resist the tyrannical system within which they are enmeshed. In the end, however, they are betrayed, arrested for "thought crime," brutally tortured, broken in body and spirit, and returned to society as devoted, loyal, and fanatical followers of BB (Big Brother) and the Party. While undergoing his "rehabilitation," the Inner Party functionary responsible for breaking Winston offers him what has to be one of the most chilling visions of a future tyranny ever penned:

> There will be no loyalty, except loyalty toward the Party. There will be no love, except the love of Big Brother. There will no laughter, except the laugh of triumph over a defeated enemy. There will be no art, no literature, no science. When we are omnipotent we shall have no more need of science. There will be no distinction between beauty and ugliness. There will be no curiosity, no enjoyment of the process of life. All competing pleasures will be destroyed. But always—do not forget this, Winston—always there will be the intoxication of power, constantly increasing and constantly growing subtler. Always, at every moment, there will be the thrill of victory, the sensation of trampling on

an enemy who is helpless. If you want a picture of the future, imagine a boot stamping on a human face—forever.[36]

While such a totalitarian society remains a distinct possibility, the fall of the Communist dictatorships that inspired Orwell's dystopia, and the entrenchment of democratic regimes throughout the West, make such a development seem increasingly remote. Of greater concern perhaps is an idea put forward by a number of political commentators—de Tocqueville, Weber, Marx—to the effect that we are moving toward, indeed, may already be living in, a tyranny without any visible tyrant. Essentially, these individuals argued that because capitalist societies need disciplined producers and dependable consumers of their goods and services, over time all the organizational components of modern Western society—state bureaucracies, corporations, unions, police, hospitals, schools—will work together to transform us into "cogs" whose sole purpose in existence is to serve that part of the machinery of modern civilization in which we are placed. Further, because human beings need and, most importantly, desire security, comfort, and a full belly, we will gladly take up residence in our little corner of this "iron cage."

Nor will this process entail doing away with what de Tocqueville labeled "the theatrical representation" of democracy. Elections will continue to take place and various parties, which do not disagree on matters of any real substance, will continue to vie for the attention and support of a population that is largely concerned with the pursuit of its private pleasures and investments. Real power, however, will rest in the hands of assorted specialists who are themselves trained to keep the trains running and the consumer goods flowing. In this world of "bureaucratic domination" (to use a phrase coined by Max Weber) there will be no need for tyrants, spies, paramilitary forces, or terror. Instead, we will find ourselves in

> a despotism without an identifiable despot, a web in which each individual is caught without anyone precisely doing the catching. In it we find only a centralized administration, a bureaucratic structure, that thinks it is providing for the common good, and decent people who do not recognize that they are both experiencing and extending tyranny as they work day by day.[37]

This notion of a world in which we are all essentially "masterless slaves" has also found expression in such 20th century dystopias as *Brave New World*, *Logan's Run*, *Rollerball*, *Gattaca*, and *Minority Report*. Unlike their Orwellian counterparts, the protagonists in these stories live in socially and/or genetically engineered "paradises" where all needs are satisfied, all boredom is amused, all anxieties tranquilized. Wars are a thing of the past, crime is non-existent, eugenics and euthanasia have made disease redundant, and the maintenance of order no longer relies on the threat of terror and torture. Of course, as some of the characters living in these societies make clear to us over the course of their narratives, utopian living also requires the individual to surrender all control over his or her destiny, and with that surrender goes much of the joy in life, as well as any incentive to produce great art, music, and thought.

What is disturbing about this particular dystopian take on our future is how much of it has already been realized. Most Westerners live in modern mass societies with market economies and representative governments. From childhood we are disciplined and educated to abide by certain pre-arranged norms of thought and behavior. A considerable part of our youth is dedicated to finding an area of specialization in which we are trained and for which we will labor until retirement or death. When not working, we are expected to consume ever-increasing amounts of food, drink, clothing, accessories, cosmetics, cars, homes, and vacations. Our boredom is assuaged by "reality shows," 24/7 sports events, soap operas, and online pornography. Any anxiety and/or despair that we experience can be treated with a wide variety of somatic substances—liquor, cigarettes, tranquilizers, anti-depressants, marijuana, LSD, cocaine, meth amphetamine. Outside of the private sphere of our lives is a political process that most choose to ignore out of a conviction that voting changes nothing except the faces of the men and women representing the "special interests" that are really running things. Surveillance is omnipresent, and genetic engineering is no longer the stuff of fiction.

Of course, one can also look on all of the above as examples of what might just as easily be called the tyranny of existence. There is nothing particularly modern or tyrannical about human societies indoctrinating their young, equipping them with vocations, and expecting them to work. Consumption, even on a mindless scale, hardly equates to slavery; and seeking relief from the tedium of daily life through entertainment, sports, and a few belts from a bottle probably works to keep most of us calm and reasonably sane. There is also nothing terribly disturbing about the idea that most of us spend a considerable part of our lives within the private sphere of family, friends, and personal pastimes. And whatever the problems of our representative democracies, as this chapter demonstrates, the alternative is much, much worse.

In the end, the price of being human in a reasonably civilized and open society is acceptance of the fact that we are indeed enmeshed within a web of relationships from which there is no escape. Even Thoreau, a man who espoused a simple hermit-like existence, eventually felt compelled to leave Walden Pond and return to the "iron cage" of life in Concord, Massachusetts, with the family of Ralph Waldo Emerson. Indeed, rather than rail against the bonds that bind us together and make our lives possible, we should instead remain wary of those that seek to either rend those ties or turn them into chains.

This is particularly important to bear in mind when thinking about the villain we name tyrant. For whatever guise these figures assume—rebel strongman, benevolent despot, supreme leader—they always seem to arise at those moments in history when the gossamer-like threads that hold society together appear to be unraveling. Whether this dissolution takes the form of ethnic conflict, class warfare, political gridlock, aggression from abroad, economic collapse—or all of the above—these individuals arrive on the scene as saviors equipped with some special dispensation and/or vision that will set matters aright and restore the body politic to health. In addition to this sense of destiny, these men and women are utterly ruthless and bring formidable gifts—wide-ranging curiosity, great intelligence, an enormous capacity for work, military ability, administrative acumen, charm, charisma—to the task at hand. Once in power, they recognize few limits to the exercise of their wills, regard state, economy, and culture as extensions of themselves, and often attempt the refashioning of society in their own image and likeness.

Initially, these tyrants are successful in their efforts to restore stability and a semblance of dynamism to their respective societies. Factions are suppressed, order is restored, government appears to operate smoothly, generous state spending brings forth prosperity, opportunities for social advancement abound, and new territories are acquired. Invariably, however, as in a Greek tragedy, these tyrannical victories tend to be followed by Hubris, and in the wake of great pride always comes Nemesis and the fall. Unfortunately, for those subject to such a regime, this fall from grace is often accompanied by the very kinds of societal dissolution and disorder the tyrant promised to make a thing of the past.

Is it possible to curb or even cure this particular form of villainy in the future? If history is any indicator, the immediate answer to such a question is "highly unlikely." There are a great many individuals—many of them borderline personalities (a topic to be addressed in a later chapter)—who harbor great ambitions, have enormous appetites, and entertain certain megalomaniacal fantasies. As Robert Drewes notes in his discussion of the early Greek tyrants, these folks suffer from *philotimia*, or a desire for great honor, fame and power, and this condition is seldom assuaged in social systems that require their leaders to behave in a collaborative, selfless, and democratic manner. Concurrently, these individuals also move and operate in human societies that are subject to periodic paroxysms—political polarization, economic recessions, social divisions, environmental crises—during which anxious and frightened populations are all too easily tempted by the allure of *tyrannoi* who offer them security, order, and three meals a day.

Of course, as Robert Boesche reminds us:

> Just as there is tyranny, so is there opposition to tyranny, so if there is indeed a frightful melody, there is also the powerful and hopeful song of human freedom and excellence.[38]

Let us hope that this song is never lost.

4

"Et tu, Brute?"
The Villain as Traitor

Trust and loyalty are fundamental facets of cultures. When they fail, chaos follows.
—Nachman Ben-Yehuda

Then one of the twelve, called Judas Iscariot, went to the chief priests and said, "What are you willing to give me if I deliver Him [Jesus] to you?" And they counted out to him thirty pieces of silver.
—Gospel of Matthew 26:14

This was the noblest Roman of them all: All the conspirators save only he did that they did in envy of great Caesar; he only, in a general honest thought and common good to all, made one of them. His life was gentle, and the elements so mix'd in him that Nature might stand up and say to all the world 'This was a man!'
—Shakespeare, *Julius Caesar*

Men worshipped her like a goddess, only to be betrayed by a kiss!
—tagline for the film *Mata Hari*

Treason doth never prosper; what's the reason? Why, if it prosper, none dare call it treason.
—Sir John Harrington

In Dante's *Inferno*, hell is a vast gulag divided into nine circles. While the first of these—Limbo—is essentially a comfortable holding cell for the unbaptized and assorted virtuous pagans, the other eight are places of eternal torment for those guilty of different sins. As with penal systems in the real world, each of these incarceration zones houses a distinct population of offenders and features specific kinds of punishment tailored to the severity of their inmates' transgressions. Lusty folks, for example, find themselves assigned to hell's second circle—an Alcatraz-like minimum-security setup—where they are tormented by relentless winds and storms that are intended to remind them of how their carnal appetites hurled them from one unquenchable desire to another. Bad tempered types given to anger and violence, on the other hand, get hurled into the noisome bowels of level seven where they live in either rivers of boiling blood or stretches of scorching sand, and are tormented around the clock by vicious centaurs and harpies.

The worst that hell has to offer, however, is reserved for those guilty of treachery. Circle nine of the *Inferno* is a frozen, lifeless waste in which those found culpable of betraying family, community, guests, and liege lords are entombed at different levels and degrees of discomfort in an icy lake. Because he has betrayed both his creator and god, Satan—a hideous three-faced monster with six eyes that weep tears "mixed with bloody froth and pus"—is at the center of this infernal Siberia, ensnared from the waist down in an impenetrable sheet of ice that is kept in place by the freezing winds that are generated when he flaps his bat like wings in a futile attempt to fly free of his arctic prison. Next up for punishment are three traitors whose treason Dante considered so egregious he condemned them to "eternal pain" by placing them in the mouths of hell's lord to serve as his "eternal dinner."

> "That soul that suffers most," explained my Guide
> "is Judas Iscariot, he who kicks his legs
> On the fiery chin and has his head inside.
>
> Of the other two, who have their heads thrust forward,
> The one who dangles down from the black face
> Is Brutus: note how he writhes without a word.
>
> And there, with the huge and sinewy arms, is the soul
> Of Cassius."[1]

Other than some extreme winter sports enthusiasts, most would agree that an eternity spent trapped in a lifeless arctic tundra would constitute a fairly horrendous punishment. Add to this the prospect of being repeatedly chewed, shredded, digested, and regurgitated, and we have entered the world of snuff films like *Nightmare on Elm Street* or *Saw*. Nevertheless, while Dante's ninth circle of hell is certainly a gruesome place for those incarcerated within it, there still remains the question of why the poet reserved his *Inferno*'s most painful punishment for those guilty of treachery. For while most would agree that the breaking of a trust is indeed an egregious act, individuals who engage in such actions are not always regarded as villains. Indeed, as Sir John Harrington notes in the last of this chapter's epigraphs, certain circumstances and considerations can work together in such a way as to allow treason "to prosper" and traitors to become heroes. And nothing exemplifies this dynamic better than the four figures Dante condemns to hell's cruelest torments.

4. "Et tu, Brute?"

Take the devil that dwells at the heart of Dante's ninth circle. Depending on your myth, Satan is originally a god or angel whose original name, Lucifer, means "the shining one, the morning star." Not content with his place in the heavens, this golden boy attempts a hostile takeover of the celestial sphere in an effort to make himself its chief executive. Though this power grab fails, and Lucifer finds himself and his supporters consigned to the less desirable nether regions of the earth, his refusal to accept the status quo—perhaps best captured in Milton's *Paradise Lost* when the fallen Arch Angel asserts that it is better "to reign in Hell, than serve in Heav'n"—ultimately makes him a symbol of heroic rebellion for generations of Western romantics and revolutionaries. Concurrently, there are also Hebrew and Sufi Muslim stories (*The Book of Job*, the *Hazār hikāyat-i sūfiyān* of the poet Farid ud-Din Attār) in which the so-called Prince of Evil is actually a trusted agent of the Lord who has been charged by his heavenly employer to test the faithful and winnow out the wicked.

Much the same can be said about the hapless fellows Dante condemns to Satan's maws. As with the devil, from the Gnostics to the present, there are narratives regarding Judas Iscariot's actions that run counter to those found in the canonical Gospels (all of which disagree with one another on different details). In these stories, Judas is a devoted follower of Jesus who betrays his master only at his bidding so as to bring about the "Passion of the Christ," which is necessary for the redemption of humankind. As for Brutus and Cassius, not only was the former celebrated by Shakespeare as "the noblest Roman of them all," but if the battle at Philippi had gone differently, both men would likely have been regaled as tyrannicides both in their own time and ours.

Despite the relativism that often surrounds judgments about treachery and betrayal—even for the likes of Satan and Judas—one suspects Dante reserved his final circle of hell for traitors because he accepted sociologist Nachman Ben-Yehuda's observation that without trust and loyalty human society would fall into chaos. Indeed, of all the "pre-contractual" social elements that are necessary for communities to come together and cohere over time, none is probably more important than the belief that the people with whom you abide not only share a set of common values, but can be expected to honor them in their daily lives. In the absence of such faith, there can be no marriage, family life, religion, politics, law, commerce, or diplomacy. Instead, we would find ourselves in a world not altogether different from that of Dante's arctic wasteland, i.e., a place where no one could move with any degree of certainty and where everything would tend toward inertia, entropy, and death.

Nor does one need Dante's magnum opus to drive home the repellent nature of treachery. Indeed, of all acts of villainy addressed in this work, betrayal is the one most humans experience at some point in their lives, usually in the form of being lied to, shortchanged, cuckolded, stung, or defrauded in some manner. These violations of trust are also often by people we know, or thought we knew, and they invariably arouse feelings of dismay, distress, and anger that make it difficult—for some impossible—to enter into new partnerships, business ventures, and civic engagements.

This said, there remains the paradox that while all breaches of mutual obligation and trust may be deemed acts of betrayal, some of these actions are regarded as acceptable while others merit a death sentence. For example, practices, such as surgical procedures, makeup, or articles of dress aimed at changing one's actual appearance, are regarded as harmless acts of personal vanity. Similarly, lying to a loved one about the seriousness of an illness or a terminal disease is considered an act of kindness, even mercy. And infidelities, which, with the exception of France, are regarded almost everywhere with disapproval, and often lead to serious repercussions within the affected relationships, marriages, and families, are commonplace in the West and consigned largely to the realm of couples therapists, talk show hosts, and divorce courts.

Acts of betrayal, however, which are aimed at actually injuring society itself, i.e., treason, are regarded in an entirely different light, and it is these actions and the individuals who perpetrate them that are the subject of this chapter. In what follows, we will address how treason has been defined in the West from the Greeks through the Cold War of the 20th century with an eye aimed at answering some of the following questions:

- Why is this particular form of betrayal so egregious?
- What motivates someone to betray their country?
- Are certain forms of treason considered more villainous than others?

In order to isolate and further study distinctive types of traitorous behavior, this chapter also relies heavily on British journalist Chapman Pincher's contention that all acts of treason can ultimately be attributed to considerations of money, ideology, compromise, and ego (or MICE for short).[2] Specifically, different sections will consider case studies of individuals who betrayed their friends and country for reasons of greed—Ephialtes, Judas Iscariot, John Anthony Walker—egoism—Coriolanus, Benedict Arnold—ideology—Rose O'Neal Greenhow, Kim Philby of the Cambridge spy ring—and passion—the Samson of Delilah fame and John Vassall.

Hopefully, by the end of this analysis, the reader will have not only a better understanding of why traitors rate special attention in the annals of villainy and the verse of Dante, but also a clearer sense of who these people are and what motivates them to such grave acts of betrayal and treachery.

"For there to be betrayal, there would have to have been trust first": Betrayal and Treason in the West

The quote opening this section is from author Suzanne Collins' *Hunger Games* trilogy, a series of young adult novels that detail the efforts of two adolescents, Katniss Everdeen and Peeta Mellark, to survive an annual event in which 12 couples are compelled to enter an outdoor arena and engage in mortal combat for the viewing pleasure of a television audience. Because only one of the 24 contestants is allowed to leave alive, the game favors those players who are especially ruthless, deceitful, and disloyal. While partnerships and alliances between the game's contenders are not unusual, they are temporary, highly mercenary arrangements subject to betrayal at any given moment.

With the exception of folks with anti-social personalities, few of us would want to live in the world of the *Hunger Games*. Indeed, the inability to trust others of your kind to do anything other than deceive and betray would undermine all the moral and legal norms that bind societies together. It would make it impossible to enter into intimate relationships, live in security with one's neighbors, create a stable polity, engage in commerce, practice a profession (other than grifting), or even do science. We would in short find ourselves in a Hobbesian *bellum omnium contra omnes,* or "war of all against all."

Because trust is the very thread out of which all social relationships are woven, it's not surprising that violations of it—spouses who betray the pledged troth of a marriage by taking other lovers; business partners who embezzle a company's assets; bankers that bilk their clients of their savings; politicians that work against the interests of their party; friends who fail to watch the backs of their buddies—are harshly judged and vilified. Indeed, we are subjected to this vilification process on a daily basis. Tabloids, gossip columnists, TV talk show hosts, and prying paparazzi revel in the business of disclosing the romantic indiscretions of the celebrity class. Radio shock jocks savage political leaders and representatives who sway too far from the party line. Press, pundits, and politicians routinely pillory Wall Street for the misdeeds of its financiers. Writers, playwrights, and directors often sing for their supper by treating their audiences to titillating tales of betrayal—*Le Mort d'Arthur, The Count of Monte Cristo, Madame Bovary, Faust, Miss Julie, The Descendants, The Good Wife, Nashville, Survivor,* and all the installments of the Iron Man franchise.

As noted in the introduction, however, violations of trust are not all treated equally and those culpable do not always find themselves consigned to the rogues' galleries of their respective societies. The abovementioned examples of betrayal are cases in point. Though once regarded as a clear and present danger to society worthy of death by stoning, in the present-day West, adulterers face disdain and pity, rather than life threatening projectiles. Party stalwarts may fuss and fume at the fecklessness of politicians, but a degree of prevarication, as well as a willingness to compromise on core principles, are the prerequisites of electoral democracy. Market economies encourage a wide range of financial shenanigans, the legality of which are sometimes unclear. And without lying, cheating hearts, there would likely be a marked decline in the reading and viewing public, as well as an increase in the numbers of unemployed and destitute storytellers.

Whereas these violations are often tolerated as the price of living and doing business in an established and lawful society, those that entail treason elicit a much harsher response. Commonly defined as actions that are aimed at overthrowing one's duly constituted government, and/or aiding and abetting a foreign entity in making war on, or injuring one's parent nation, this particular form of betrayal is regarded as so heinous a crime, it is normally punishable by death. Indeed, in the not too distant past, traitors were so despised it was common practice to hang, draw and quarter them if they were men, and draw and burn them at the stake if they were women.

Though universally detested, however, what passes for treason often relies, as with other forms of betrayal, on one's point of view. Tyrants, for example, regard all who resist their rule as traitors, while opponents of tyrannical regimes consider the actions of their rulers to be a violation of their fundamental rights to life, liberty, and happiness. Even in the case of individuals and groups that are essentially seeking to acquire or regain power in their respective homelands—Chapter Three's Pisistratus and his son Hippias being two such examples—the determination as to whether or not their actions are treasonous ultimately relies on whether or not their efforts "prosper." For if they do, as John Harrington reminds us, "none dare call it treason."

One consequence of this relativism is that a considerable amount of attention has been paid in the annals of Western jurisprudence to the whole question of what constitutes traitorous behavior on the part of an individual. Among the ancient Greeks, the answer to this query was relatively simple, i.e., whoever governed the city state was the living embodiment of the *polis* and therefore any act aimed at undermining or injuring said party (or parties) was an act of violence against the entire community and therefore treasonable.[3] Greece's Latin neighbors in Italy, on the other hand, were much more nuanced in their thinking on this subject. Because the *res publica* (the "public thing/affair") of Rome was distinct from any one individual or faction within the general body politic, treason had to take the form of a hostile, violent act against either the Roman state or its duly appointed magistrates. Consequently, there were actually two officially designated forms of treasonous activity during Rome's republican and imperial periods, *Perduellio* and *Maiestas*.

The former of these, *Perduellio*, was essentially defined as an act of hostility by a citizen against the Roman people and their *res publica*. This included such actions as desertion from the army in times of war; delivery of Roman property and citizens to an enemy (*Proditio*); providing aid and comfort to Rome's enemies in the form of intelligence, weapons, and food; inciting foreigners—allies or aliens—to make war on Rome; and giving assistance to a citizen that had been exiled for crimes against the Roman people and Senate.

Maiestas, on the other hand, encompassed injuries—verbal or physical—visited on the "majesty of the Roman people" via offenses of one sort or another against their magistrates. This latter take on treason is believed to have originated in the struggles of the plebeians in the early centuries of the Republic to protect their tribunes from harm, and it came to encompass such actions as injuring a magistrate or the emperor; undermining the Roman constitution (as the Gracchi brothers were accused of doing in their efforts to push through land reform legislation in the late second century BCE); official maladministration; and violations of civic religious duties that could give offense to the gods and bring down their wrath on Rome.

Of these two forms of treason, *Maiestas* was the one most commonly invoked and abused, particularly during the late republic and Empire. Indeed, during the last one hundred years of the republic, almost everyone of any prominence in the senatorial class—Marius, Sulla, Cicero, Catiline, Caesar, Pompey, Gabinius, Brutus, Cassius, Antony—was declared a traitor by their colleagues for violating in one fashion or another the majesty of the Roman people and state. Concurrently, in the imperial era, even jokes about the reigning emperor could be construed as injurious acts against Rome because they were directed at her principal magistrate whose person was regarded as sacred and inviolable. If the emperor happened to be one of those deified by the Senate after their death (or in the case of Caligula, while still alive), a slip of the tongue might find one charged with crimes of sacrilege as well.[4]

Among Rome's Germanic neighbors, treason was largely regarded as the breach of a faith or troth (*Treubruch*) that one person had voluntarily assumed vis-a-vis others in their tribe. This offense could take the form of a broken pledge made by a subordinate to a superior, or an action, such as aiding and abetting an enemy, which could result in harm befalling the community-at-large. The Germans also practiced a form of *Maiestas*, or *Lese Majeste*, that regarded the injuring of a tribe's chief or king, particularly in a time of war, as a form of traitorous behavior. This said, German tribes also reserved to themselves the right to take action against chieftains and kings who were adjudged guilty of crimes against the land and *Volk* (people).[5]

This Germanic notion of treason as the breaking of a troth or obligation to provide some kind of duty or service to another is passed down into English Common Law and is eventually codified in the Treason Act of 1351. Under the terms of this statute, a distinction was made between petty and high treason. The former entailed the murder of a husband by his wife, a prelate by his clergyman, or a master or mistress by their servant. These crimes were differentiated from ordinary murder because they were regarded as a betrayal of oaths and arrangements that were considered the very foundations of Western social and religious life. High treason, on the other hand, was specifically aimed at those actions deemed injurious of the state, i.e., waging war against one's country; attempting to overthrow the government or do harm to its duly constituted sovereign; and aiding and abetting the government and military of a hostile foreign nation. Both of these forms of treason commanded the death penalty for those found guilty of them.

Though petty treason ceases to be a crime distinct from murder in all common law countries by the 19th century, its counterpart remains very much alive and well in Western jurisprudence. To the present day, the betrayal of one's country, by acts aimed at aiding and abetting its enemies, overthrowing its government, or injuring its magistrates, remains one of the most heinous forms of villainy. Indeed, it is so serious an offense that it is the only crime, other than impeachable "high crimes and misdemeanors," actually addressed in the American constitution, itself the handiwork of men who were regarded by the English crown as traitors most foul.

While we have arrived at a reasonably clear idea as to what constitutes treasonous behavior from a historical and legal point of view, we are still unsure as to why certain individuals opt to betray their homelands, an act that puts not only their fellow countrymen in danger, but their friends and families as well. Some psychologists have proffered the idea that traitors tend to be "anti-social" personalities. That is, for reasons that are still not completely clear to us, these persons have an underdeveloped moral sensibility, a stunted conscience if you will, that makes it possible for them to disregard or violate the rights of their peers. It is not unusual for those who are afflicted with this personality disorder to commit crimes, engage in deception, harm others, fail to meet various social and financial obligations, and, if deemed a desirable outcome, sell out one's country.[6]

While this is a compelling theory, it is not without problems. Perhaps the greatest of these is the fact that most "anti-social" personalities—grifters, gangsters, gunmen—do not betray their countries even when it might be profitable to do so. A case in point is the collaboration of the American Mafia with the U.S. government during World War II. Not only did mob boss Lucky

Luciano agree to provide intelligence to the military about fascist attempts to sabotage shipping on the eastern coast of the United States during the war, but his associates in the dockworker unions used their muscle and influence to prevent strikes during the duration of the conflict. Concurrently, another Mafia don, Vito Genovese, served as an interpreter and advisor to the U.S. Army during the invasion of Italy, and also found members of the Sicilian *Cosa Nostra* to draw up maps of the Italian coastline, as well as provide information on German troop dispositions and movements. While there were certainly elements of self-interest in these arrangements—Luciano, for one, was freed from prison after the war—patriotism also figured into the decision by various mobsters to join the fight against fascism.[7]

Further, as many of the cases cited in this chapter will demonstrate, most traitors do not appear to suffer from anti-social personality disorder. Coriolanus, Benedict Arnold, and Kim Philby of the Cambridge spy ring, for example, all appear to have been conscientious men who were highly regarded by their peers and often enjoyed healthy, personally satisfying emotional attachments with others. While their treasonous actions may have deviated from the accepted social norms of their respective societies, in all other respects they appear to have been perfectly normal men.

Sociologists addressing this problem have posed the possibility that there might be something about Western society itself that encourages treason. Drawing on elements found in the works of Durkheim, Weber, and Marx, this argument unfolds along the following lines. During the 18th and 19th centuries, a series of political, economic, and social revolutions weakened the traditional bonds of faith and trust that were characteristic of rural communities of the past. This occurred because people residing in small agrarian enclaves, with centuries old traditions of loyalty and duty to family and community, are transplanted to large cities characterized by anonymous multicultural populations, impersonal forms of bureaucratic control, and capitalist economies that encourage endless novelty and selfish consumption. Once settled in these crowded cosmopolitan urban centers, these country folk find themselves bereft of the customs and practices that underscored for them in the past what constituted ethical as opposed to unethical behavior. And one consequence of this state of *anomie*, or "normlessness," is that it becomes progressively easier for these individuals and their descendants to betray others in order to advance their own personal agendas.[8]

Perhaps the best examples of treason as a species of modern *anomia* are the careers of the American military and computer intelligence specialists Bradley Manning and Edward Snowden. Arguing for the right of the global community to know what their governments are up to in the name of national security, these two men hacked into the military and diplomatic data bases of the United States government, downloaded a great many sensitive files, and released them to the press and public-at-large. Suffice it to say, such actions violate a veritable slew of laws and regulations, as well as the oaths both men took to safeguard the secrecy of their work. These acts are also regarded as treasonable because the released information could be accessed by America's enemies and used to uncover the identities of secret American operatives in the war against terror. None of these considerations, however, deterred these men because they essentially regarded themselves as something akin to autonomous "world citizens," and, as such, exempt from the "norms" and laws of their native country.

The major problem with this particular take on treasonous behavior is the simple fact that individuals have been betraying their respective homelands and/or engaging in activity aimed at overthrowing their governments long before the advent of the modern period. In fact, some of history's most infamous acts of betrayal—Ephialtes' sellout of his countrymen at Thermopylae, Judas Iscariot's delivery of Jesus into the hands of his enemies, the assassination of Julius Caesar by Brutus and Cassius—all occur well before the advent of nation states, capitalism, mass societies, or the self-actualization movement. Nor is there any compelling evidence that membership in a cosmopolitan society encourages a higher degree of traitorous behavior than what one finds in more provincial settings.

For the present at least, there appear to be no satisfactory "nature or nurture" theories that adequately explain the who and why of treason. Traitors can be men or women. They include in their ranks personalities that are both mal- and well-adjusted. One finds them in villages, towns and cities, and they can also be found in every societal class, income bracket, and profession. Further, these persons also appear to betray their countrymen for a variety of reasons; the most common of which are those summarized by Chapman Pincher's acronym MICE, i.e., Money, Ideology, Compromise, and Ego.

Of these four motives for treason, the one most commonly cited as grounds for betraying one's homeland is greed. Indeed, whether one is talking of Judas Iscariot in the first century of the Common Era or the John Walker spy ring at the end of the 20th, traitors have often been individuals for whom lucre is more important than loyalty. And because this motive is so mercenary in nature, involving as it does the literal "selling out" of one's friends, family and neighbors for what can aptly be described as "blood money," it ranks as a particularly egregious kind of treasonous behavior.

Equally loathed are those individuals who betray their land and people out of a sense of wounded pride. Unlike the abovementioned mercenaries, this particular class of traitors is usually comprised of men and women who have a highly developed sense of loyalty to their respective countries and causes. In fact, if not for their egoism, a Coriolanus or a Benedict Arnold would normally be candidates for heroization. Unfortunately, the tendency on the part of these persons to see themselves as superior to others, coupled with an aversion to any kind of criticism or oversight, often brings them into open conflict with their peers who, for reasons of either envy or genuine concern, seek to curtail whatever powers and privileges they enjoy. Rather than seeing such acts as the normal give and take of political life, these prideful people interpret them instead as expressions of ingratitude, disloyalty, and treachery, a form of "shaming" if you will, that requires an equally extreme response. Ultimately, it is a desire for revenge, rather than profit, that motivates egoists to aid and abet the enemies of their countries.

More problematic are those traitors who act against their countrymen for reasons of ideology. As with the egoist, these individuals are often consummate insiders, i.e., members of families and professions with long records of service to their peoples and governments. For varied reasons, these persons become alienated from the political, social, and/or economic arrangements of their societies, and embrace instead doctrines and movements aimed at altering the status quo. However, rather than work through legal channels to effect such change, these folks opt to take such treasonous actions as providing intelligence to a foreign power, engaging in acts of terror and sabotage, and actively making war on one's country. Insofar as these activities fail to generate the desired outcome, these men and women are regarded as traitors most foul. Should their works "prosper," on the other hand, they sometimes become "founding fathers and mothers."

The final group on Pincher's list of traitors, and certainly the most problematic, are those who betray their homelands because they find themselves compromised in one way or another. This includes individuals who are susceptible to blackmail either by way of so-called "honeytraps," i.e., compromising sexual situations, or threats to the physical well-being of family members and friends. Though these persons do indeed commit treasonous actions aimed at protecting their reputations and/or loved ones, and are punished accordingly when apprehended, there is some question as to whether or not it would be more apt to describe them as innocent victims rather than treacherous villains.

Before turning to a more thorough examination of the traitorous types addressed above, it should be noted that there are a number of other factors that figure into how an act of betrayal is regarded. That is, even though individuals who commit treason are routinely reviled regardless of whether they are motivated by considerations of money, ideology, ego, or because they are compromised in some way, the severity of the judgment to which they are subjected by history ultimately rests on two things, i.e., the degree of secrecy and deceit that was involved in their actions, as well as the amount of harm that was caused by their treachery.[9] What singles out the case studies that now follow is that in all of them the traitors involved were secretive in their actions, violated the trust placed in them by their friends and confederates, and caused injury, often considerable, to others. With this in mind, let us now turn our attention to those treasonous persons who acted out of greed.

Thirty Pieces of Silver: The Traitor as Mercenary

The first recorded instance in the West of a person who betrays his countrymen in order to enrich himself takes place during the Battle of Thermopylae in 480 BCE. By way of background, this clash occurred during the second Greco-Persian War pitting King Leonidas of Sparta, the 300 warriors of his royal retinue, and roughly 7,000 allied Greeks against a much larger Persian host numbering some 100,000 to 150,000 men commanded by Xerxes I, the Great King of the Persian Empire. It took place at the narrow coastal pass of Thermopylae (thus the battle's name), located in eastern central Greece on the Malian Gulf.

This battle occurred because of the strategic importance of the Thermopylae pass, which allowed for the easy movement of traffic from northern to southern Greece. Aware of the fact that Xerxes needed to traverse this passage in order to invade Attica and the Peloponnesus, Leonidas and his men occupied and fortified it prior to the arrival of the Persian army. Though outnumbered over four to one, from September 8 through the 10th, the Greeks managed to hold off repeated attacks against their position by Xerxes' forces.

Though this pass was highly defensible and could be easily held against a superior army, there was a mountain path that led across the highlands parallel to Thermopylae, which could be used to outflank the Greek lines. While the Spartan king was aware of this tactical weakness, and in fact posted a rear guard to prevent just such a development from occurring, he was also confident that the Persians were unlikely to take advantage of this trail because awareness of it was largely limited to communities living in and around the Malian strait. Unfortunately for Leonidas and his allies, not everyone among the local population was trustworthy.

As Herodotus notes in Book VII of his *Persian Wars*:

> Now, as the king [Xerxes] was at a loss, and knew not how he should deal with the emergency, Ephialtes, the son of Eurydemus, a man of Malis, came to him and was admitted to a conference. Stirred by the hope of receiving a rich reward at the king's hands, he had come to tell him of the pathway which led across the mountain to Thermopylae; by which disclosure he brought destruction on the band of Greeks who had there withstood the barbarians.[10]

4. "Et tu, Brute?"

The consequences of Ephialtes' betrayal were indeed severe. With Leonidas and his army out of the way, the Persians were able to invade and occupy Boeotia and Attica, as well as sack and burn the cities of Plataea, Thespiae, and Athens. Only the Greek naval victory at Salamis prevented a similar fate from befalling the peoples of the Peloponnesus.

As for the author of all this suffering and death, Herodotus tells us that in the aftermath of the Persian defeat at Plataea, Ephialtes flees "from fear of the Lacedaemonians" into Thessaly, where he lives in exile with a price on his head. Though he is eventually slain, his killer, a fellow named Athenades from Trachis, kills him for reasons unrelated to his treason (what those are we never learn). So, with the exception of his betrayal of Leonidas and company, and his eventual demise a long time after that event, we know next to nothing about Ephialtes' life or even the circumstances surrounding his death.[11] This said, his name lives on in Greek as a byword for traitor in much the same way that Judas, Benedict Arnold, and Quisling convey the same idea in English.

Outside of Greece, it is interesting to note that latter day portrayals of Ephialtes tend to play down the mercenary nature of his treason. Perhaps the best examples of this tendency are the two films that were produced about the Battle of Thermopylae, i.e., the 1962 Cinemascope production *The 300 Spartans*, and Zach Snyder's 2007 comic-to-screen fantasy action adventure movie *300* (already referenced in the chapter addressing the barbarian). In the former, the audience is treated to a portrayal of Ephialtes as a lonely goat herder who is enamored of a young Spartan woman pledged to one of Leonidas' companions. A desire of the heart, rather than greed, motivates his decision to betray his countrymen to Xerxes. In the Snyder production of Frank Miller's graphic novel of the same name, Ephialtes is presented as a somewhat sympathetic figure. We are told that his parents were Spartans who opted to live in exile rather than commit infanticide due to the fact that he was born deformed. Though he matures into a hideously malformed hunchback (made even more grotesque by computer enhanced effects), he yearns to prove his worth by fighting alongside Leonidas; a desire that is thwarted by the fact that his disability makes it impossible for him to hold his shield properly. In this case, it is wounded pride, rather than a love of lucre, that moves him to betray to the Persians the secret way around the Greek lines.

Why these storytellers feel it necessary to ascribe motives other than greed to explain Ephialtes' treachery provides us with some sense of how loathed the traitor-for-hire is in Western culture. Indeed, despite the fact that our principal primary source on this incident notes quite clearly that the Malian acted as he did out of "the hope of receiving a rich reward," selling out one's countrymen for money is held to be so abhorrent that later commentators feel compelled to find other less objectionable grounds for doing it. As we will see in what follows, treason for reasons of pride, principle, or passion is always regarded as less objectionable than the same crime committed out of a desire for profit. Why this is so is not completely clear, but it may have something to do with our next case study in paid treachery, i.e., Judas Iscariot.

As with Ephialtes, we know little if anything about the man Dante singled out to satisfy the eternal hunger of Satan. That Judas was one of Jesus' 12 apostles is attested to in the Gospels. Other than this, we have no idea where he was born, who his parents were (there is mention of a father named Simon in the Gospel of John), what he did for a living prior to his calling to follow Jesus, and whether or not he was married or had children. Even his surname, "Iscariot," raises more questions about him than it answers. Some conjecture this cognomen identifies him as "a man of Kerioth," a village in southern Judea. Others hold it was an epithet, a corruption of the Latin *sicarius* ("murderer" or "assassin"), which was used to highlight the fact that he was a member of the Sicarii, a radical Jewish sect that engaged in acts of terror against the Romans. There are also theories that Judas' last name is meant to signify that he was a liar, a red head, a deliverer, or someone who choked to death. In the end, the etymological significance of this moniker remains as mysterious as the man with whom it is associated.[12]

Everything else we know about Judas comes from the synoptic Gospels (Matthew, Mark, and Luke), the Gospel of John, and the Acts of the Apostles. In John 12:6, we are told that he acted as the treasurer, or keeper of the "money box," of the disciples, and that he took this job rather seriously. Indeed, other than his infamous act of betrayal, the only other action of Judas attested to in the Christian testament is his annoyance with Mary, the sister of Martha, when she anoints the feet of Jesus with an expensive ointment made of spikenard. "Why," Judas asks, "was not this perfume sold? It could have brought three hundred silver pieces, and the money have been given to the poor."[13] Though this seems a perfectly reasonable objection coming from someone charged with managing the finances of a movement dedicated to serving, among others, the needy, it elicits an aside from John to the effect that it was not heartfelt because the speaker is a thief—as well as a rebuke from Jesus, who, foreshadowing his doom, tells Judas: "Leave her alone. Let her keep it against the day they prepare me for burial. The poor you always have with you, but me you will not always have."[14]

Other than being an apostolic accountant, Judas is best known for his betrayal of Jesus. However, though all of the sources agree that he is the one who delivered his friend and teacher into the hands of his enemies, there remains some question as to why he engaged in this act of treachery. The most subscribed to explanation is that which is offered in Matthew 26:14:

> Then one of the twelve, called Judas Iscariot, went to the chief priests and said, "What are you willing to give me if I deliver Him [Jesus] to you?" And they counted out to him thirty pieces of silver.

The mercenary nature of Judas' act is further substantiated by both Luke (22:4–6) and Mark (14:10) who also note that he was promised some kind of monetary reward from Caiaphas and his fellow priests for delivering Jesus into their power.

This said, there remains some question as to just how culpable Judas actually was in betraying Jesus. Both Luke (22:3) and John (13:27–29), for example, point out that while the priests offer Judas remuneration for his treachery, he acts as he does because Satan has taken possession of him. Further muddying the waters, in John (6:64, 13:27–28) and Matthew (26:25), we have evidence that Jesus is aware of Judas' impending act of betrayal and encourages him to carry it out because the fulfillment of his destiny requires his suffering and death on the cross. Later Gnostic texts, such as the *Gospel of Judas*, go a step further in this direction by suggesting that the two men were actually in league with one another and that Jesus ordered his disciple to betray him. Whether greed, demonic possession, or some kind of Passover plot lay behind Judas' decision to betray Jesus, things do not end well for him. According to Matthew (27:3–10), he repents his act of treachery, tries to return the blood money paid out to him by the priests, and hangs himself. Because of the tainted nature of Judas' ill-gotten wages, the authorities opt to use his 30 pieces of silver to buy a potter's field—the so-called "Field of Blood"—in which they inter his body. One other biblical account, Acts 1:18–19, differs from Matthew's account in that it tells us the accursed apostle actually purchased this field himself and then proceeded to fall headfirst into it with the result that he "burst asunder in the midst, and all his bowels gushed out." As with everything else to do with Judas, the actual particulars of his demise remain a mystery.[15]

Whatever the questions surrounding Judas' life and death, his betrayal of the man who would come to be revered by roughly 33 percent of the world's population as the Christ, or Messiah, has guaranteed him a special place in the annals of villainy. His betrayal of a person believed by many to be the Son of God, guaranteed that Judas would figure prominently in Western art, literature, and performance as a veritable archetype of treachery.[16] And this cultural prominence has not only made his name a synonym for traitor in a great many languages of the world, but it has also insured that people who betray others in order to enrich themselves are regarded in a more severe light than their counterparts who commit the same transgression for reasons of ego, ideology, or extortion.

Within a modern context, some of the worst traitors-for-hire have been individuals who acted as spies for one, or in the case of double agents, both of the opposing sides in the Cold War that was waged between the United States and the Soviet Union from1947–1991. Unlike the two men we have examined up to this point, this particular group of mercenaries counted among its membership key figures in the diplomatic and security establishments of their respective countries. As such, they were not only a particularly deceitful lot, but the consequences of their treasonous actions, which often involved the transfer of militarily sensitive information, left their homelands, and the world for that matter, vulnerable to nuclear annihilation.

One of the most notorious members of this cohort was an American naval intelligence officer by the name of John Anthony Walker, Jr., a fellow who is credited with organizing and operating "the most damaging Soviet spy ring in history."[17] Born into a somewhat dysfunctional middle class Pennsylvania family in 1937, Walker spent his early years engaged in acts of vandalism, theft, and armed robbery. These crimes included breaking the windows of the local Catholic Church, stealing coins from assorted church poor boxes, burglarizing local businesses, and holding up a bus. Though he was apprehended and sentenced in 1954 to serve time in a state correctional institution, he managed to avoid prison by agreeing to join the U.S. Navy.[18]

From 1955 to 1959, Walker served on a destroyer and an aircraft carrier, and also married Barbara Crowley, a woman with whom he would have three daughters and a son. In 1960, he was approved for submarine duty and, following a stint at the submarine school in New London, Connecticut, received a series of favorable fitness reports that led to seven promotions in nine years. Among these advancements was a decision by the Navy at the end of 1964—ostensibly after a background investigation of his life and character—to clear him for work with top secret and cryptographic materials.[19]

This clearance made it possible for Walker to become a radioman aboard nuclear-powered submarines with access to the highly sensitive "keylists" that were used to decipher the messages received by the code machines American subs used to communicate with each other during the Cold War. In this capacity, he received top secret ciphers from naval surface vessels, spy satellites, shore stations, and other submarines, decoded this material, and then relayed its contents to his superior officers. Suffice it to say that all of this intelligence was critical to U.S. national security. Indeed, possession of the aforementioned keylists alone could provide an enemy with the wherewithal to read the messages sent to the various decoding devices that were in wide use at this time by the United States armed forces and the State Department. In short, Walker found himself in the perfect job for someone who might be inclined to be a spy-for-hire.[20]

Such an inclination came to the fore in 1967 when Walker invested heavily in a bar that went belly up soon after it opened. Saddled with debt and struggling to support a family with four children, he paid a visit to the Soviet embassy in Washington, D.C., and offered to sell them classified U.S. government intelligence information. To demonstrate his bona fides, he produced a stolen keylist and offered to provide more of the same for a weekly salary of $500 to $1,000. When asked by the embassy's KGB operative why he was engaging in such clearly treasonous activity, Walker is reputed to have said that his motives were "purely financial. I need the money."[21] As far as his Russian interlocutors were concerned, this was a satisfactory response and they proceeded to hire him on the spot, giving him $1,000 for the purloined keylist and promising him more for additional such decoding materials. Thus was born one of the most damaging spy operations in American history.

Over the next 17 years, Walker would put together an espionage ring that included his wife, Barbara, older brother Arthur, son Michael, and a Navy Senior Chief Petty Officer and Senior Chief Radioman named Jerry Whitworth. In exchange for something in the neighborhood of one million dollars, this group provided the Soviet Union with "a blizzard of technical manuals, key cards, keylists, and rotor readings for such systems as the KWR-37, Adonis, and KW-26."[22] Walker alone was able to provide the Russians with enough intelligence data during his three years (1971–1974) aboard the supply ship the *Niagara Falls* that they were able to read U.S. Navy secret messages as easily as the American naval personnel receiving them.

How damaging was all of this? As journalist Richard Sale notes in his work on Walker:

> In war or peace, security of a country's secret communications is everything. As a U.S. intelligence official once said, to have the enemy be able to read your communications is like playing poker with someone who already knows what you have in your hand.[23]

By the time that Walker and his accomplices were apprehended in 1985, the information they had provided to the Soviet Union had made it possible for the Russians "to read 1.2 million classified U.S. military messages."[24] This in turn allowed our Cold War enemies to know the exact location of every American nuclear submarine on the planet, as well as their probable strategic operations in the event of a war. As one high ranking KGB defector, Vitaly Yurchenko, noted to the FBI in the same year that the members of the Walker spy ring were arrested, if warfare had broken out between the United States and the U.S.S.R. in the early 80s, "the U.S. Navy would have been 'annihilated,' thanks to the edge given Moscow's military by Walker and Whitworth."[25]

In the end, Walker and his colleagues were themselves betrayed by his wife Barbara. Though the two had divorced in 1975, Walker's lapses in alimony payments, coupled with his refusal to provide her with any additional money, led to Barbara's decision to get back at her former husband by revealing his spying activities to the FBI. Her revelations received further confirmation from her daughter Laura, who revealed to federal agents that her father had also tried to recruit her into his spy ring. Following a lengthy investigation that involved extensive wire taps and tailing operations, John, Arthur, and Michael Walker, as well as Jerry Whitworth, were taken into custody. In a rare display of selflessness, John Walker agreed to accept a life sentence, provide a full disclosure of his espionage activities, and testify against his partner Whitworth, in exchange for a more lenient sentence for his son. Following a series of plea bargains and trials, all of the members of his spy ring were found guilty of espionage and conspiracy and, save for Michael Walker, sentenced to life imprisonment and hefty fines on their ill-gotten wealth.

John Walker, Jr., is currently dying of stage IV throat cancer in the Butner Federal Correctional Complex in North Carolina. During his 68 years of incarceration, he has never exhibited any remorse for his crimes against his country. As he explained to his Soviet handlers in 1967, he needed money, and to satisfy that greed he was willing to cross the Judas line.

"Pride goeth before destruction, and a haughty spirit before a fall": The Traitor as Egoist

The individuals treated in this section should have ended their lives as heroes rather than villains. They were well-born, comely in appearance, strong, intelligent, gifted with extraordinary abilities, ambitious, and eager to excel in whatever they did. Over the course of their careers, they also rendered valuable service to their peoples, and were honored accordingly with encomiums, high office, and material rewards. Indeed, their lives were the very stuff of a classic heroic biography.

Like many a character in an Attic tragedy, however, these persons were also guilty of the kind of extreme pridefulness and arrogance the Greeks labeled *hubris*. They believed themselves superior beings, and openly shared this conviction with those they regarded as their inferiors. The actions they took on behalf of their homelands were less about selfless service than self-aggrandizement. And in return for the assistance they rendered their respective peoples, they expected praise, promotion, deference, and immunity from criticism or reproach.

As *Proverbs* reminds us, such "pride goeth before destruction," and this was certainly the case with Coriolanus and Benedict Arnold, the "haughty" spirits addressed below. These two men were egoists of the first order and their self-love was fed by the fact that they were brilliant military commanders with a string of impressive successes on the battlefield against the enemies of their peoples. The fact that these achievements were greeted with praise and honor from a great many of their contemporaries only strengthened their sense of being among the *aristoi*, or "best men," of their times.

Not everyone, however, was enamored with these fellows. Many of their countrymen were offended by their arrogance and complete lack of humility. Others were jealous of their ability and success. Some simply feared that individuals who were so openly contemptuous of their fellow citizens might pose a threat to the civic order. Whatever their reasons for opposing them, the critics and enemies of Coriolanus and Arnold were ultimately successful in curbing their ambitions, a state of affairs that did not sit well with either of these men.

Because they viewed themselves as both infallible and above reproach, any resistance to their initiatives was seen as both foolhardy and malicious. Nor were they swayed to think otherwise by the fact that many of their peers were either in agreement with their critics, or at least willing to acknowledge some merit to their arguments. Instead, they chose to regard the actions that were directed against them as gross ingratitude for the many services they had rendered their countrymen, as well as an injury to their personal honor. Rather than seek redress of their grievances in the manner prescribed by the constitutions of their respective countries, they chose to make war on them; an action that would ensure their inclusion in the annals of villainy.

The first recorded case in the West of treason rooted in pride is that of Gaius Marcius Coriolanus. Born in the late sixth century BCE into the house of the Marcii, a patrician Roman family, we are told by Plutarch that young Gaius Marcius demonstrated a fondness for war from his earliest years. In boyhood he learned to handle all manner of arms and "trained his body so thoroughly for every type of combat that he acquired not only the speed of an athlete, but also such muscular strength for wrestling and close combat that few opponents could escape his grasp."[26] While still an adolescent, he also participated in the war against the deposed King of Rome, Tarquinius Superbus, and won a civic crown, a garland of oak leaves, for saving the life of a fellow citizen during the Battle of Lake Regillus in 498 BCE.[27]

As a young man, Marcius took part in the war against the Volscians, an ancient Italic people whose territory was to the south of Rome. It was during this conflict that he earned his surname for the singular bravery he displayed at the Volscian town of Corioli, which was under siege by the Roman army. According to both Livy and Plutarch, at a critical moment when the Romans were facing the prospect of a rout at the hands of a Volscian relief force, Marcius collected a small band of men and led them in an attack that beat back the enemy and seized one of Corioli's gates, a maneuver that made it possible for the Roman commander to capture the city. In the aftermath of the battle, his fellow soldiers acclaimed him "Coriolanus."

If Marcius had restricted himself to purely military matters, it is likely that we would not be reading about him here. That he was a formidable warrior, a gifted commander, and a veritable scourge of Rome's Italic enemies was never in question. Unfortunately, republican Roman politics made it almost impossible for a patrician citizen who had covered himself in glory on the field of battle not to participate in the civic life of his city. Indeed, it was expected that such men would take their place in the Senate, as well as pursue the highest and most prestigious of the republic's elected magistracies, i.e., the consulship.

This was in fact what Marcius decided to do upon his return from the Volscian wars. Because of his noble birth and military background, he was very much a man of the Roman elite with a pronounced disdain for Rome's populist politicians and their supporters among the city's plebeian class. Not surprisingly, he soon found himself the leader of a reactionary faction of the city's patrician party opposed to the reforms that allowed for the election of plebeian tribunes who could veto the actions of the Senate and propose legislation directly to the popular assemblies. When he urged his senatorial colleagues to force the commons to accede to the abolition of the tribunate in return for the distribution of free grain during a time of food scarcity and hunger in Rome, the public reacted violently and fights broke out among the magistrates. In the end, cooler heads in the Senate prevailed, Marcius' proposal was rejected, and corn flowed freely to the people.[28]

Rome's popular party, however, did not forget or forgive either Marcius' words or actions. He had aroused their enmity, as well as their "fear that if a man who wielded so much influence among the patricians and was so intensely aristocratic in his sympathies should ever hold the chief office of state, he might deprive the people of every liberty that they possessed."[29] These concerns were also shared by a great many patrician senators who did not relish the prospect of more civic unrest in the Forum. Consequently, when Marcius made his bid for the consulship, he was denied the office by an unlikely coalition of aristocrats and plebeians.

In addition to this electoral setback, efforts were made by the tribunes to convict Marcius of treasonable actions against the republic, specifically his efforts to incite the Senate to set aside the constitution and abolish the privileges of the people. Rather than seek a rapprochement with his accusers, Marcius appeared in the Forum and

> began to speak with an offensive bluntness, which soon developed into an outright attack upon the commons. At the same time both the tone of his voice and the expression on his face conveyed a fearlessness which betokened a total disdain and contempt for his audience, and at this the people lost all patience and began to show their mounting indignation and anger at his words.[30]

These remarks elicited a sentence of death from the tribunes, which was to be carried out by flinging Marcius from the Tarpeian Rock, the traditional penalty for Roman traitors. Only the insistence of Marcius' patrician supporters and senatorial colleagues on a trial decided by a vote of the people prevented this penalty from being carried out.

At Marcius' second trial, the tribunes largely ignored the treason charges, which were not only difficult to prove, but also carried with them a punishment viewed as too extreme to impose on a man of Coriolanus' reputation and accomplishments. Rather, they brought forward new trumped up charges concerning the general's distribution of spoils that were taken by him when he captured the Volscian town of Antium. Though Marcius' had mounted this campaign at his own expense and distributed what was captured to his soldiers in payment for their efforts, he was accused of misappropriating funds that should have been paid into the public treasury. While this charge was completely unjustified given the private nature of the military action, the commons voted in favor of finding Marcius guilty and sentenced him to perpetual banishment.[31]

Suffice it to say that Marcius did not take well to these trials or his sentence of exile. He viewed himself as having been unjustifiably dishonored and disgraced, and he saw the actions taken against him as evidence of the gross ingratitude of the Roman people. After a few days stay at a country estate, "he decided to incite one of the neighboring countries to wage a destructive war against them, and the people whom he chose to approach first were the Volscians."[32]

Specifically, Marcius approached a Volscian nobleman, Tullus Aufidius, with whom he had fought during his campaigns against the Volsci. The two men agreed to make common cause against Rome, and then persuaded the Volscians to break a two year truce they had entered into with the Roman people. They then mobilized a large army, with Aufidius agreeing to remain behind to defend Volscian cities and towns while his new found ally carried the war to his former countrymen.

This Marcius did with great resolve and impressive success. He invaded and ravaged the territory of Rome's Latin allies, taking several large cities, enslaving their inhabitants, and plundering their property. When the Roman Senate failed to field an army against the invaders, many other allied towns and cities sued for peace and came over to the Volscian side. Free of any threats to his rear or flanks, Marcius then marched on Rome itself and camped his army outside its walls.

Two delegations were sent by the Senate to entreat Marcius to declare a truce, and mediate a peace agreement with the Volsci. One of these was comprised of his partisans within the city and the other was made up of the entire Roman priesthood. To both he turned a deaf ear, and demanded instead that

Rome surrender cities and territory previously seized from the Volscians and grant them the same rights as those enjoyed by Rome's Latin allies. Neither of these terms were acceptable to the Senate and both sides girded themselves for a protracted siege.[33]

It was at this precarious moment that Marcius' mother, Volumnia, and his wife, Vergilia, with their children in tow, led the women of Rome to the Volscian camp. Plutarch tells us that Volumnia castigated her son for his pride, and damned him for the untenable situation in which he had placed his family.

> Now you must know that we who have come to you here are the unhappiest women alive, for Fate has made that sight which should have been the most joyful into the most terrible of all, when Volumnia is compelled to see her son and Vergilia her husband turning his arms against the walls of his native city. And even to pray to the gods, which others may find a comfort in their misfortunes, has become impossible for us, since we cannot ask them in the same breath to make our country victorious and to keep you safe. When we pray for you, we are calling down a curse upon Rome, such as the bitterest of enemies could desire, and your wife and children are compelled to sacrifice either their native land or yourself.[34]

Nor does she leave Marcius in any doubt as to what choice she is prepared to make in the face of his treason:

> As for me, I shall not wait for the war to decide this issue for me. If I cannot prevail upon you to prefer friendship and harmony to enmity and strife, and thus become the benefactor of both countries rather than the scourge of one of them, then you must know—and let there be no doubt of this—that you shall never attack Rome unless you trample first upon the dead body of the mother who bore you. I do not choose to wait for the day when I shall be forced to watch my son either led in triumph by his fellow-citizens or triumphing over them.[35]

Following this diatribe, Marcius' mother, wife and children reputedly threw themselves at his feet in supplication, an act that moved him to relent from his course of vengeance and withdraw the Volscian army from Roman territory.

Suffice it to say that Coriolanus' Volscian allies were none too pleased with his decision to call an end to a war that had been going so well for them. Indeed, the Roman commander had not only betrayed his own people, but his adopted countrymen as well. Consequently, on his return to Antium, Marcius was charged with treason, put on trial, and, during the proceedings, assassinated by an angry mob at the behest of his former co-conspirator, Tullus Aufidius. Tradition has it that despite his ignominious end, the Volscians did accord Marcius an honorable burial. As for his countrymen, they opted to neither honor nor condemn him, though they did give his family permission to wear mourning on his behalf for ten months. Certainly the least they could do for the women who had saved Rome from Western history's first egoist turned traitor.[36]

Within a modern context, perhaps the most infamous example of someone who betrayed his country out of wounded pride is the American traitor, Benedict Arnold. Born in 1741 in what was then the colony of Connecticut, Arnold was, like Coriolanus, the scion of a patrician family. Though his father grew up in rather poor straits and was a cooper, or barrel maker, by trade, his great-grandfather had been the governor of Rhode Island. On his maternal side, Arnold's mother belonged to a very wealthy family, which ensured that he attended private schools as a child and moved in the upper echelons of colonial society.

Also like his Roman counterpart, Arnold demonstrated at a very young age both considerable courage and "the drive of an imperious will to succeed."[37] When his family fell on hard times as a result of his father's bad investments and heavy drinking, he apprenticed at age 13 with two of his mother's cousins who were in the colony's apothecary and general merchandising trades. During this apprenticeship, he demonstrated that he "was a tremendously hard worker, energetic, prompt, conspicuously efficient, full of purpose and drive, and possessed of a great power to compete."[38] Indeed, his relatives were so impressed by him that they made him a junior partner at age 20. Three years later, he had his own business with three ships and lucrative trading arrangements in Canada and the West Indies.

When the American Revolution broke out in 1775, Arnold was elected a captain in Connecticut's militia. From that point on, his military career was nothing short of meteoric. In the early years of the war, he participated in the capture of Fort Ticonderoga, invaded Canada, laid siege to Quebec City, and delayed a British advance down Lake Champlain that threatened Washington's army. In 1777, he inflicted a crushing defeat on the army of General Johnny Burgoyne at the Battle of Saratoga, a victory that helped convince France to ally itself with the colonial cause. Because of these achievements, as well as the severe wounds he suffered in these battles, he was promoted by the Continental Congress to the rank of Major General.

In addition to this office of high command, Arnold's exploits won him the friendship and admiration of such central figures in the American Revolution as Philip Schuyler, Horatio Gates, and George Washington. Unfortunately, these triumphs also made him quite a few enemies among lower-level officers who were envious of his battlefield successes, as well as congressmen who feared that his military abilities betokened a would-be Caesar. Even worse, these antagonists hounded Arnold throughout the war by printing up scurrilous handbills that impugned his character, and initiating congressional inquiries that called into question his financial probity.

Such attacks infuriated Arnold. Aside from the fact that there was no basis to the charges his enemies leveled at him other than animus, Arnold was extremely sensitive to any and all criticism of his character and conduct. Like Coriolanus, he viewed his opponents' critical remarks and efforts to censure him as both a personal affront and an expression of gross ingratitude for the many services and wounds he had rendered and received on behalf of his country. As the war wore on, and the efforts of his critics to discredit him continued, Arnold began to cast about for a way of obtaining some measure of satisfaction against them.

This desire for retribution became even more pronounced when Washington appointed him military governor of Philadelphia in 1779. In this position, Arnold believed it was his just due to live well and to recoup some of the personal fortune he had spent on behalf of the revolution raising, arming, and clothing the armies under his command. Consequently, he moved into a mansion, where liveried servants waited on him, drove about the city in a well-appointed carriage, and lavished money on furniture, fine wine, and haute cuisine. He also paid for this lifestyle by making wholesale purchases of goods on behalf of the Continental Army, and then selling some of this merchandise on the side as compensation for himself.

While Arnold's love of luxury and his business practices were questionable, particularly in a time of war, they were not illegal. They did, however, afford his enemies in Congress with the wherewithal to issue an eight-point indictment of his governorship that alleged he was engaged in illegal economic activities for personal gain, as well as behaving in an unpatriotic manner. These allegations deeply angered Arnold and he responded to them by demanding the convening of a court martial where he might clear himself of any wrongdoing. This request was granted, a tribunal was convened in 1779, and at the end of that year its judges exonerated him of all charges made against him save two minor infractions, for which he was mildly and reluctantly reprimanded by George Washington.

Even this proved too much for Arnold, who was further riled by a Congressional inquiry into his expenditures that concluded he owed the government a thousand pounds for expenses he incurred during his invasion of Quebec. Believing himself the victim of unjust persecution by a country that owed him so much, he resigned his command, and entered into secret negotiations with the British to change sides. He was assisted in this by his new wife, Peggy Shippen, the daughter of a Loyalist sympathizer, who acted as Arnold's intermediary with the enemy by carrying correspondence back and forth between him and Major John André, a young man who had courted her during the British occupation of Philadelphia.

From the spring of 1779 through the fall of 1780, Arnold provided the British with information regarding American troop movements, supply depots, and the status of French reinforcements. When Washington named him commander of West Point, and gave him authority over military operations from Albany to New York City, he offered to surrender the fort, and with it control of the entire Hudson River Valley, to the British general Sir Henry Clinton. In return, he asked for £20,000 and a commission in the royal army, terms to which Clinton readily agreed.

Unfortunately for Arnold, his treason was revealed when his courier, Major André, was captured by an American patrol. Papers detailing Arnold's plot were found on the British officer and sent to Washington, who ordered his lieutenant's immediate arrest. Arnold was tipped off, however, about André's capture and fled before he could be taken into custody. Making his way to a British ship, the HMS *Vulture*, which was anchored not far from West Point, he was taken to safety in British controlled New York City. His English intermediary was not nearly so fortunate. He was placed on trial before a military tribunal, found guilty of spying, and hanged on October 2.

Arnold received £6,315 for his efforts on behalf of the British at West Point, the rank of brigadier general in the British Army, with a pension of £360 per annum, and the command of a Loyalist American regiment. Despite this commission, he continued to feel underappreciated and ill-used. Though he rendered his new employers commendable service by conducting successful operations against American forces, forts, and foundries in Virginia and Connecticut, his new allies did not conceal their disdain for him, and his advice, though militarily sound, was largely ignored.

Peace found him in the unenviable position of being unpopular with both his former countrymen and a great many Englishmen. In the newly independent United States, the name Benedict Arnold became a by-word for traitor. One of his American biographers at this time, the military surgeon James Thatcher, accused him of "treason, avarice, hypocrisy, ingratitude, barbarity, falsehood, deception, peculation and robbery." Thatcher also told his readers:

> He aimed to plunge a dagger into the bosom of his country, which had raised him from the obscurity in which he was born, to honours which never could have been the object even of his hopes.[39]

Among many of his new British compatriots, Arnold was also damned for being a traitor. No less a figure than Edmund Burke rose in Parliament and demanded that the Crown not give Arnold a command in the British army "lest the sentiments of true honour, which every British officer holds dearer than life, should be afflicted."[40] Similar remarks were also forthcoming from other parliamentarians, lords, and the English press. In the end, despite the fact that he enjoyed the favor of George III, as well as many members of the Tory party, Arnold found himself unable to find a position within the military, government, or the East India Company.

Deprived of the opportunity to serve in the public sphere, Arnold returned with some success to private business. He moved to Canada and reconstituted his old shipping business with the West Indies. He also received 13,400 acres in Upper Canada after complaining to the Crown that "there is no other man in England, who has made so great sacrifices as I have done of property, rank, prospects, &c., in support of government, and no man who has received less in return."[41] Though this grant was far less than the 50,000 acres he believed his due, it nonetheless allowed the Arnold family to settle in Canada where a great many of his descendants live to the present day.

As for the country he betrayed, though he continues to be regarded by most Americans as a traitor most foul, his contributions to the American war of independence have not gone unnoted. There is a memorial in the Saratoga National Historical Park that, while not bearing Arnold's name, does commemorate his courage and the key role he played in winning that battle. It reads as follows:

> In memory of the most brilliant soldier of the Continental Army who was desperately wounded on this spot ... winning for his countrymen the Decisive Battle of the American Revolution and for himself the rank of Major General.[42]

One reads these words with not a little sadness because they attest so clearly to the fact that, if not for his great pride and destructive egoism, Benedict Arnold would likely have been regaled as a heroic founding father rather than as one of his country's greatest villains.

"To betray, you must first belong": The Traitor as Ideologue

On March 15, 44 BCE, Roman consul and dictator for life, Julius Caesar, was assassinated by a group of senators in the vestibule of a theater erected by his former son-in-law and later rival for power, Pompey the Great. Caesar's assassins were part of a larger senatorial conspiracy organized and led by two patrician members of the Senate, Marcus Junius Brutus and his brother-in-law Gaius Cassius Longinus. These conspirators styled themselves *Liberatores* (Liberators), and justified their act of treason by claiming that Caesar was intent on replacing the Roman Republic with a monarchy headed by himself.

Though it is highly unlikely that Julius Caesar desired, much less planned, to be made king of Rome, his victory over the Senate during the civil war between himself and Pompey (49–45 BCE) resulted in a marked decrease in the power and authority of Rome's senatorial oligarchy. This situation, in tandem with Caesar's accumulation of unprecedented honors, titles, and authority, was simply unacceptable for the senators who entered into a conspiracy to assassinate him in 44 BCE. Though Shakespeare was doubtless correct in his assertion that envy played some role in the decision by these men to murder Caesar, it is far more likely that they acted as they did out of a sense of duty and republican fervor. These were, after all, individuals who hailed from families that had created and sustained Rome's republic for five centuries. Indeed, from birth, they had been raised to resist anyone who appeared to threaten the institutions and prerogatives of the *res publica*.

Initially, Caesar's assassins were pardoned by the Senate and accorded the political offices to which they had been appointed by the late dictator. This course of action, however, proved unacceptable for Caesar's partisans, who rallied to the standards of his nephew, Gaius Octavius, and his friend and military lieutenant, Mark Antony. Civil war ensued, the Liberators and their sympathizers were proscribed, and Brutus and Cassius met defeat and death at the Battle of Philippi in October 42 BCE. Ironically, the assassination that was meant to save the republic proved to be the event that guaranteed its demise. In its aftermath, emperors who styled themselves Caesars would rule Rome, and Brutus and Cassius would make their way into the maws of Dante's Satan.[43]

Mention is made of the conspiracy against Julius Caesar because it is perhaps one of the earliest examples of the kind of treason that is the subject of this section. The men who murdered Caesar did so not out of greed or solely for reasons of ego, but because of their commitment to "the time-honoured conviction [among Romans] that anyone who strives for tyranny must be killed."[44] For Brutus, Cassius and their co-conspirators, the idea of a *res publica*, of a constitutionally bound state governed by laws and collectively administered by the Senate and People of Rome, was paramount, and any threat to this set of arrangements had to be resisted by any means necessary, even if this entailed the treasonous killing of Rome's legally designated chief magistrate. If these so-called Liberators had been successful in their efforts, history would likely have named them heroes. Instead, their failure in the civil war that followed the murder of Caesar insured their status as villains.

The traitors treated below share a great many things in common with the abovementioned assassins. First of all, they "belonged," in every sense of that word, to the social and political elites of their homelands. They hailed from good families, went to prestigious schools, moved in the right circles, were privy to important and often sensitive national security information, and enjoyed the trust of their superiors and confidants. In addition to being well-heeled, they were a prideful lot with a much-vaulted sense of their own self-importance. Indeed, like the Liberators, these individuals considered themselves to be the caretakers and guardians of their societies, and it was this custodial sensibility that made it possible for them to contemplate and then commit treason. Finally, as with Brutus and Cassius, if the respective causes these persons served had been victorious, they would not now be included in the annals of villainy.

The first of the two ideological traitors to be considered here is Rose O'Neal Greenhow, one of the Confederacy's most successful spies during the American Civil War. Born circa 1815 into a slave holding planter family in Maryland, Maria Rosatta O'Neal and her older sister, Elizabeth, were sent at an early age to live with an aunt who ran a boarding house in Washington, D.C. This establishment was the favored residence of a great many antebellum congressmen and politicians, including the foremost champion of states rights, John C. Calhoun of South Carolina. Living among such distinguished clientele helped insure that Rose and her sister acquired the kind of education, refinement, and connections, which would make them two of the capital's great hostesses.

Rose's status as a doyen of Washington society was only strengthened when she wed Dr. Robert Greenhow in 1835, a Virginia gentleman from an old Richmond family, who was also an official in the State Department. Through her husband, as well as her sister Elizabeth, who married the nephew of a former First Lady, Dolly Madison, Greenhow was able to move in the highest circles of the capital. She counted among her close friends and confidants in the years before the Civil War that great triumvirate of American politics, Daniel Webster, Henry Clay, and the already mentioned Calhoun, as well as such lesser lights as senators Jefferson Davis of Mississippi, William Seward of New York, and the chairman of the Senate's Military Affairs Committee, Henry Wilson of Massachusetts. One of her greatest devotees at this time was James Buchanan, the Senator of Pennsylvania elected President of the United States in 1856. Though Greenhow enjoyed the company of influential friends from both the North and South, she was strongly pro-slavery and very much in favor of the states rights arguments advanced by antebellum southern politicians. Indeed, as a self-described "southern woman, born with revolutionary blood in my veins,"[45] she fully supported the formation of the Confederate States of America in the aftermath of Abraham Lincoln's election to the presidency in 1860. Rather than leave Washington, however, for points further south, Greenhow elected to remain in the U.S. capital and join a pro–Confederate espionage network organized by a Virginia officer, Colonel Thomas Jordan.

In her capacity as a spy for the Confederacy, Greenhow used her contacts in Congress and the State Department to obtain crucial military intelligence, which she passed on to Richmond, Virginia, the Confederate capital. Her greatest achievement was in 1861 when she used secret couriers to smuggle ciphered messages out of Washington containing information about Union troop movements before the First Battle of Bull Run (June 21, 1861). In her dispatches, Greenhow alerted the Confederate army to the marching orders, numbers of troops, and quantity of artillery of the opposing Army of the Potomac, information that helped secure a southern victory. In a letter to her afterwards, Jordan wrote: "Our President [Jefferson Davis] and our General [P.T. Beauregard] direct me to thank you. We rely upon you for further information. The Confederacy owes you a debt."[46]

In August 1861, Allan Pinkerton, the head of the newly formed Union Intelligence Service, placed Greenhow under house arrest on suspicion of spying for the enemy. A search of her residence turned up plans of the fortifications around Washington, as well as information about Union troop strength and movements in the vicinity of the capital. Rather than deny the charges against her, Greenhow justified her intelligence gathering activities in terms of her constitutional rights:

> In the careful analysis of my papers I deny the existence of a line I had not a perfect right to have written, or to have received. Freedom of speech and of opinion is the birthright of Americans, guaranteed to us by our Charter of Liberty, the Constitution of the United States. I have exercised my prerogative, and have openly avowed my sentiments.[47]

Though the Lincoln administration had a fairly clear cut case against her, it was wary about charging her with treason and putting her on trial. In part, this was because Greenhow's sources of military intelligence included Union officers and prominent politicians such as the Chair of the Senate's Military Affairs Committee, Henry Wilson (a number of his love letters to Mrs. Greenhow were found in Pinkerton's search of her residence). There was also the fact that the Southern press was scoring quite a propaganda coup with articles decrying the cruel and ungallant treatment to which Greenhow and other "Secesh dames" in the District of Columbia were being subjected.

Faced with a trial that would embarrass the administration and result in the hanging of a prominent Washington hostess with friends in high places on both sides of the conflict, Lincoln's cabinet opted in 1862 to exchange Greenhow and another "Secesh" dame, a certain Mrs. Baxley, for two Pinkerton agents in Confederate hands. With her young daughter, "Little Rose," in tow, Greenhow made her way south to Richmond where she was afforded a hero's welcome by no less a figure than the President of the Confederacy, Jefferson Davis. Soon thereafter, she was pressed into service by the rebel government as an unofficial ambassador to England and France.

Sailing out of Wilmington, North Carolina, on a blockade-runner in August of 1863, Greenhow made her way first to Paris where Emperor Napoleon III received her, and then to London where she enjoyed a private audience with Queen Victoria. In addition to being able to plead the Confederate cause to these monarchs, Greenhow made a number of influential friends among the aristocrats of both countries, and the memoir she penned at this time, *My Imprisonment and The First Year of Abolition Rule at Washington*, was a best seller among well-heeled circles in Britain. Despite these impressive personal successes, however, Greenhow's diplomatic mission was a failure. Aside from the fact that there was considerable opposition among the British and French populations-at-large to slavery, by the end of 1863, it was quite clear that the Confederacy was not likely to win the war.

In 1864, Greenhow opted to leave Europe and return home on another blockade-runner, the *Condor*. She carried with her dispatches for Jefferson Davis, as well as gold from the sale of her book that she was going to donate to the Confederate treasury. Her ship ran aground at the mouth of the Cape Fear River near Wilmington, North Carolina, while attempting to evade a Union gunboat. Fearing capture and imprisonment, Greenhow attempted to reach shore in a small rowboat that was capsized by a wave. Because the royalty money she carried in a purse around her neck, and had also sewn into her underclothes, weighed her down, she drowned.

Greenhow's body was recovered and taken to Wilmington where it was accorded a full military funeral with honor guard and volleys of gun and cannon fire. In 1888, a Confederate memorial association erected a white stone surmounted by a cross over her grave with the following inscription:

> Mrs. Rose O'N. Greenhow
> A Bearer of Dispatches
> To the Confederate Government
> Drowned Off Fort Fisher,
> From the Steamer Condor,
> While Attempting to Run the Blockade
> Sept. 30, 1864.[48]

To this day, she remains a heroine to those Americans who continue to regard the Civil War as the lost cause of Southern independence.[49]

Our second case study in ideological treason is the British "mole," Harold Adrian Russell "Kim" Philby. The "third man" of the so-called "Cambridge Five" spy ring—the other four men being Donald Maclean, Guy Burgess, Anthony Blunt, and John Cairncross—Philby passed highly sensitive diplomatic and national security intelligence to the KGB from World War II until his flight to Moscow in 1963. Indeed, his service to the USSR was such that he was awarded the Order of Lenin and the Order of the Red Banner, and when he died in 1988 he was given a state funeral. The Communist government also issued a commemorative stamp that identified him as one of the heroes of the Soviet Union in 1990.

As with the other ideologues examined up to this point, Philby was the

4. "Et tu, Brute?"

scion of a distinguished upper middle-class family. Dora Johnston, his mother, was a wealthy and well-connected London socialite. His father, Hillary "Harry" St. John Bridger Philby, was a noted scholar, Orientalist, and civil servant who ostensibly worked on behalf of British interests in India and Mesopotamia. "Ostensibly" because Philby *père* was also a rather unorthodox fellow who embraced socialism, agitated for Indian independence, converted to Islam, married an Arab woman (after divorcing Dora), and served as a special adviser to the King of Saudi Arabia, Ibn Sa'ud. In this latter role, the senior Philby was often at odds with his superiors in Britain. He opposed the establishment of a Jewish state in Palestine, was openly sympathetic to the Nazi government in Berlin, disclosed secret military intelligence to the Saudi king, and won concessions for American oil companies at the expense of their British counterparts. As the old idiom goes "like father, like son."

Whatever the idiosyncrasies of the senior Philby, Kim, nicknamed, ironically enough, after the young British spy in the Rudyard Kipling novel of the same name, attended his father's public school in England and won a scholarship to Trinity College, Cambridge, where he read history and economics in the early 1930s. While at Cambridge; Philby was tutored by a number of Fellows with strong Marxist leanings, the most influential of whom was Maurice Dodd, a Communist sympathizer who recruited him to do work on behalf of anti–Nazi refugees in Vienna, Austria. It was while living and working in the Austrian capital in 1933 that Philby made contact with the Comintern and became an agent of the Soviet government.

What followed was a highly successful career as a spy. After a stint as a journalist covering the Spanish Civil War, during which he forwarded to Moscow information regarding German weaponry being used by the Nationalist side, Philby became an agent of MI6, the British security service in charge of espionage and foreign intelligence. In this capacity, he supplied the Soviet Union with all the information his office unearthed with regard to Nazi war plans and operations during World War II. After the war, he became the British government's chief intelligence officer in Washington, D.C., a post that allowed him to share a considerable amount of top-secret information with his Soviet handlers about Anglo-American military plans and counterintelligence measures in eastern Europe and Russia.

The flight and defection of Donald Maclean and Guy Burgess, two members of the Cambridge Five spy ring, in 1951, cast considerable suspicion on Philby. Soon thereafter, he was recalled to London, interrogated, and forced to leave the British intelligence service. Subsequent interrogations failed to elicit a confession from Philby, and in 1955 he was officially cleared of all espionage charges by the British foreign secretary, Harold Macmillan, who stated, "While in government service he carried out his duties ably and conscientiously, and I have no reason to conclude that Mr. Philby has at any time betrayed the interest of his country, or to identify him with the so-called 'Third Man,' if indeed there was one."⁵⁰

Following his clearance, Philby made his way to Lebanon where he served as the Middle East correspondent for *The Economist* and *The Observer*. Ironically, this was a cover arranged for him by his old employers at MI6, for whom he continued to work as an intelligence operative. Suffice it to say that everything he was forwarding to London also found its way to Moscow. This idyllic arrangement lasted until 1963 when a KGB defector, Major Anatoly Golitsyn, revealed to the British Secret Intelligence Service what was up with their man in Beirut. When confronted with Golitsyn's charges, Philby confessed to being a spy, but rather than return to Britain to make a full confession in return for immunity, he boarded a Soviet freighter headed for Russia where, as mentioned earlier, he was feted as a hero of the Soviet Union.

How does one assess a man like Kim Philby? Much has been made of the fact that following his official defection he smoked and drank heavily and engaged in a series of tempestuous marriages and affairs (one with the wife of his fellow spy, Donald Maclean). His last wife, Rufina Ivanova, also tells us that he was lonely, depressed, and suicidal during his years in Moscow. These revelations in turn have led some commentators to conclude that Philby regretted his actions against his country, and was disillusioned with the ideology he had served throughout his life. One of Philby's detractors, spy novelist John le Carré, has gone so far as to assert:

> Philby has no home, no women, no faith. Behind the inbred upper-class arrogance, the taste for adventure, lies the self-hate of a vain misfit for whom nothing will ever be worthy of his loyalty. In the last instance, Philby is driven by the incurable drug of deceit itself.⁵¹

Whatever Philby's personal habits and tastes, and as any fan of Ian Fleming's James Bond series knows, a taste for fast living appears to go hand in hand with the intelligence trade, he does not appear to have regretted his life as a double agent for the Soviet Union. Indeed, in his memoir *My Silent War*, as well as in interviews conducted with him before his death, Philby expressed no remorse whatsoever for his actions, arguing that "to betray, one must first belong" to one's established society, and in his case he asserted that "I never belonged." He also wrote:

> It cannot be very surprising that I adopted a Communist viewpoint in the Thirties; so many of my contemporaries made the same choice. But many of those who made their choice in those days changed sides when some of the worst features of Stalinism became apparent. I stayed the course.⁵²

Nor is Philby without his admirers. One of these is noted novelist Graham Greene, who worked with Philby in the British Secret Intelligence Service during World War II. He had this to say about his former colleague in the introduction that he wrote for Philby's memoir in 1968:

> He betrayed his country—yes, perhaps he did, but who among us has not committed treason to something or someone more important than a country? In Philby's eyes he was working for a shape of things to come from which his country would benefit.[53]

Though a completely moot question, it is intriguing to consider whether or not Philby would have maintained his commitment to the Communist ideal following the breakup of the state he served so loyally and well throughout his life. As matters stand, he remains one of those spies that never came in from the cold.[54]

Compromising Positions: The Traitor as Cuckold

Frank Herbert's epic space opera *Dune* envisions a future in which a human inhabited universe is structured along the lines of medieval Europe during the Holy Roman Empire. Emperors, noble houses, space faring guilds, and religious orders maintain an uneasy balance of power, while vying with each other to control and shape human destiny. All of these players are, in turn, served by various individuals hailing from a variety of schools and professional orders—mentats (humans with the cognitive and analytical abilities of computers), swordmasters, assassins, Bene Teilaxu (genetic engineers), and an assortment of medical practitioners, the most prominent of which are the graduates of the so-called Suk School.

What makes the aforementioned Suk doctors so special in the Dune universe is the fact that they undergo a kind of conditioning that makes it impossible for them to inflict harm on another human being. As such, they are considered to be the perfect physicians and advisers to the assorted emperors, dukes, and mother superiors who make Herbert's imperium hum. For if these Suks are incapable of harming their human employers, then they should be equally impervious to treasonous activities that might lead to the death or injury of those in their care.

Or so matters stand until one of these physicians, Wellington Yueh, actually does betray his liege lord, Duke Leto I Atreides, one of the principal protagonists of Herbert's story. As matters turn out, the Harkonnens (rivals and archenemies of the Atreides) find a way to compromise the hapless Yueh and thus bend him to their will. Specifically, they abduct his wife and threaten to subject her to unspeakable tortures unless he complies with their demands. This threat, in tandem with a promise to release her, works to undermine the doctor's conditioning, thus allowing him to betray the family of the Great House that he serves.

I have gone into such detail about this fictitious traitor because he exemplifies those hapless individuals treated in this section, i.e., persons who feel compelled for one reason or another to betray the interests of their homelands and countrymen. Or as the Harkonnen henchman responsible for turning Yueh explains to his employer in *Dune*:

> It's assumed that ultimate conditioning cannot be removed without killing the subject. However, as someone once observed, given the right lever you can move a planet. We found the lever that moved the doctor.[55]

As already mentioned, this lever took the form of a threat of violence against a loved one that could only be averted through a gross act of betrayal. As we will see in what follows, there are other such fulcra that can be used to pry someone loose from their allegiances. One of these involves threatening to disclose information that will bring disgrace or ruin onto a person, i.e., blackmail. Another entails seduction, lust, and the promise of true love.

Perhaps the earliest known example of someone betraying everything—God, countrymen, and self—for both lust and love is the Israelite Judge, Samson. As recounted in Judges, Chapters 13-16 of the Bible's Old Testament, Samson appears on the scene during one of the many times in which the Hebrew god, Yahweh, is displaying his displeasure with his Chosen People by delivering them into the hands of their enemies. In this case, the enemy in question is the Philistines, a seafaring people who conquered the coastline of southern Canaan and settled in five cities—Gaza, Ashkelon, Ashdod, Ekron, and Gath—sometime around the 12th century BCE.

Samson's biblical account tells us that he was the gift of the Angel of the Lord to an older couple—Manoah and an unnamed wife—that were unable to conceive. In return for this boon, Yahweh informs the new parents-to-be that they must raise their son as a Nazirite, i.e., as someone consecrated to God from birth. This condition, which entails Samson renouncing alcohol and remaining hirsute for life, is necessary because the Lord intends the boy to be one of his deliverers of the Jewish people from the yoke of the Philistines.

Samson grows up to be a sober, ill-groomed beefcake with an eye for the ladies and a fondness for riddles. At some point in his early manhood, he makes his way to the cities of the Philistines and falls in love with one of their fetching Shiksas. A marriage proposal leads to a wedding banquet at which Samson enters into a wager with a group of Philistine bravos that have been chosen to be his groomsmen. Under the terms of the bet, the aforesaid men of honor are given seven days to come up with the answer to a riddle that references an encounter between Samson and a lion whose remains have become a repository for bees and their honey (for full details see Judges14:8–14). The loser of this contest is required to pay the winner or winners 30 linen tunics and 30 sets of garments (a hefty haul even by modern standards).

Suffice it to say, Samson's groomsmen are unable to come up with the answer to his riddle and pressure his fiancé to find the answer, or else they threaten to burn down the family house with her in it. After much whining, which is a foreshadowing of what is to come later in the story, Samson tells her the solution to the puzzle and she in turn promptly shares the answer with her countrymen. What follows is not pretty.

Enraged by his fiancé's betrayal, not to mention the fact that he has to come up with 60 sets of clothes for 30 men, Samson begins what will be a 20-year one-man war against the Philistines. He burns their fields, slaughters their kinsmen "hip and thigh," massacres one of their armies with the jawbone of an ass, and tears down the gates of Gaza, one of the Philistine city states. In retaliation, his enemies carry out their threat to murder his bride-to-be and her father by burning them alive in their home.

True to form, Samson falls in love again with yet another Philistine woman named Delilah. Her countrymen get wind of the affair and make her an offer that she cannot refuse, i.e., a fortune in silver if she manages to uncover the secret of her paramour's extraordinary strength. After considerable wheedling—three times she asks Samson why he is so mighty and three times he gives her a false answer—the Israelite champion betrays his trust with God and reveals that his prowess is linked to his hair. After lulling him to sleep on her lap, Delilah has a servant give Samson a trim and then summons her employers to take him into custody.

This the Philistines do with a vengeance by gouging out Samson's eyes and chaining him to a grindstone in Gaza. However, in what has to be one of the great oversights of history, they foolishly neglect to keep their captive's hair cut. Consequently, when Samson is brought out for the amusement of the local populace during a festival honoring the pagan god, Dagon, he finds his way to the supporting pillars of the Philistine temple and brings down the house, so to speak. Everyone present is killed. As for the other traitor in this story, the mercenary Delilah, she appears to have lived happily ever after with her ill-gotten fortune.

Mysterious are the ways of God.

The last traitor to be treated in these pages was the victim of a classic Cold War "honeytrap." Unlike the other British moles examined in the preceding section, William John Christopher Vassall was most assuredly not an "insider." The only child of an Anglican chaplain and his nurse wife, Vassall attended a respectable boarding school in his youth, but failed to gain admission to Oxford. During World War II, he worked for the Royal Air Force as a photographer, and at the end of that war secured a job as a clerk in the

British Admiralty. He was also a homosexual at a time when such proclivities were illegal and could be punished with incarceration.

If not for a posting to the staff of the Naval Attaché at the British embassy in Moscow in 1952, it is likely that John Vassall would have lived an unremarkable, albeit closeted, life in Britain. Instead, he found himself alone, isolated, and depressed in a diplomatic service that regarded him as a social inferior, and in a foreign capital where homosexuality was also illegal. Unfortunately for Vassall, the KGB was aware of his plight and arranged for him to make the acquaintance of Sigmund Mikhailsky, an interpreter on the embassy's staff who was one of their operatives.

The two men became lovers and Mikhailsky introduced Vassall to Moscow's gay underground. Three months into their affair, Vassall's lover arranged for him to attend an intimate dinner party with a number of male friends. After being plied with a considerable amount of liquor, Vassall was coaxed into a sexual orgy, which was photographed in its entirety by the KGB. Afterwards, Soviet intelligence threatened to release these photographs to the press, and then use them to have him stripped of diplomatic immunity so that he could be tried in Moscow for sexual deviancy (conviction of which entailed a lengthy sentence in the Gulag).

Terrified of what would happen to him should these incriminating pictures come to light, Vassall agreed to work as a spy for the Soviet Union. Consequently, from 1954 when the Soviets snared him in their honeytrap, until 1962 when he was finally apprehended by Britain's Secret Intelligence Service, Vassall passed on to his KGB handlers thousands of classified documents on British radar, torpedoes, and anti-submarine equipment that came his way while he was working first in the Naval Intelligence Division in London, and later as a secretary to Thomas Galbraith, a peer of the realm and Civil Lord of the Admiralty. The two KGB defectors, Anatoly Golitsyn and Yuri Nosenko, who exposed Vassall's espionage activities in 1961, stated that though he was a low-level functionary, the information he provided to the USSR was invaluable in its efforts to expand and modernize the Red Navy.

Once he was arrested and charged with espionage, Vassall made a full confession and also revealed the whereabouts of cameras and film he had used in his work on behalf of the Soviet Union. He was sentenced to 18 years in prison, where he was regarded as an exemplary prisoner (he is reported to have become quite religious). In 1972, after ten years behind bars, he was paroled. He penned a memoir in 1975, entitled appropriately enough, *Vassall: the autobiography of a spy*. Following this publishing foray, Vassall changed his name to Phillips, lived a quiet life, and worked as an administrator for the British Records Association and a firm of lawyers. He died on a London bus in 1996 of a heart attack.[56]

While Vassall did indeed betray his country, he did not do so for reasons of greed, wounded pride, or ideology. Instead, he was the hapless victim of a carefully arranged blackmail scheme that was only possible because of the prevailing homophobia of his time. Revelation of his sexuality would not only have spelled the end of his civil service career, but would likely have led, as it did for computer scientist Alan Turing in 1952, to a choice between imprisonment or chemical castration.

It should also be noted, as it was during the investigations surrounding Vassall's espionage activity, that the British government violated its own protocols by assigning an unmarried man to a staff position in the highly sensitive Moscow embassy. Prior to Vassall, only married men were placed in these jobs due to the very high likelihood that a single man, whether a hetero- or homosexual, would be a likely target for a Soviet honeytrap. Vassall was appointed in violation of this policy because the Home Office was seeking to minimize the expense of finding accommodations for two people rather than one.

Given these extenuating circumstances, many people have concluded that John Vassall was less a villain than a hapless dupe. One might also say the same thing for Vassall's biblical confrere, Samson. After all, as Judges notes, God gifted his Israelite strongman with roaming eyes because he knew his affairs with wicked Philistine city women would lead to conflict with their countrymen. In light of the compromised positions their superiors—secular and divine—placed them in, it is not completely surprising that these men behaved in the way that they did. This being so, it is possible to see in these two cases examples of what might be called villainy by default.

"Now filthy traitor, say no more!": Treason and Villainy

As with my earlier book on the heroic ideal in the West, the present treatment of villainy arises out of an undergraduate seminar on Western villainous types that I offered at UCLA. I was struck in one iteration of this class by the remark of a student that while the notion of what it means to be a hero has dramatically expanded over the last three millennia to include not only demi-gods and warriors, but rebels and reprobates, the idea of what constitutes a villain appears to be contracting. Nature is now something to be hugged, "otherness" is celebrated, tyrants are in short supply, bitches are successful business executives, and psychotics are just badly wired folks who are in need of an anti-depressant.

Whatever our changing views with regard to many of the villains addressed in this book, however, individuals who betray a trust remain universally detested. In part, this aversion stems from the pain that is visited on any person who discovers they have been deceived by someone they believed to be a friend, lover, or ally. Such deception makes the affected party feel foolish, vulnerable, and, especially in a case where harm is visited on others, deeply ashamed for having been, no matter how unwittingly, a party to deceit.

On a less personal level, as Nachman Ben-Yehuda notes, trust and loyalty are fundamental to the health of any social unit. Without the ability to believe that others around you are loyal to the same values and can be relied upon to abide by them, society would fall into chaos and disorder. Marriages, politics, economic arrangements, diplomacy, religious life, indeed every institution and relationship that requires some degree of trustworthiness, would become, quite literally, impossible. Given the corrosive nature of treachery on the ties that bind us together, it is not surprising that persons identified as "traitors" continue to rank high in the annals of villainy.

This said, we have also seen in the foregoing how problematic this label can be. Tyrants, for example, consider any who resist them to be traitors, and folks in the business of betraying others often do so for what they consider to be compelling reasons, e.g., defending freedom, ushering in a more just society, upholding the status quo, avoiding the gibbet. Indeed, distinguishing between heroism and treachery often relies on little more than the judgment of whichever party comes out on top in a given conflict, or, as Harrington reminds us, if a cause regarded as treasonous happens to prosper, "none dare call it treason."

This said, it would appear that there are forms of treachery that remain beyond the pale of acceptable behavior regardless of time or place. Individuals who betray others in order to enrich themselves take pride of place in this category, followed closely by those who commit treason for no other reason than pride and wounded ego. Indeed, these persons are considered to be so villainous that their very names—Ephialtes, Judas, Benedict Arnold—are synonymous with traitor in the worst sense of that term. Dante is certainly not alone in regarding such malefactors as worthy of hell's ninth circle.

5

"Her arms are wicked and her legs are long"
The Villain as Femme Fatale

No longer was she [Salome] merely the dancing girl who extorts a cry of lust and concupiscence from an old man by the lascivious contortions of her body; who breaks the will, masters the mind of a King by the spectacle of her quivering bosoms, heaving belly and tossing thighs; she was now revealed in a sense as the symbolic incarnation of world-old Vice, the goddess of immortal Hysteria, the Curse of Beauty supreme above all other beauties by the cataleptic spasm that stirs her flesh and steels her muscles,—a monstrous Beast of the Apocalypse, indifferent, irresponsible, insensible, poisoning.

—Joris-Karl Huysmans, *À rebours*

Where a woman reigneth ... there must needs Satan be president of the council.

—John Knox

JOEL: Wednesday, do you think that maybe someday you might want to get married and have kids?
WEDNESDAY: No.
JOEL: But what if you met the right man, who worshiped and adored you? Who'd do anything for you? Who'd be your devoted slave? Then what would you do?
WEDNESDAY: I'd pity him.

—*Adams Family Values*

In the 2006 film adaptation of Lauren Weisberger's 2003 novel *The Devil Wears Prada*, movie audiences were introduced to Miranda Priestly, the tough as nails editor-in-chief of *Runway* fashion magazine. Played with great brio by actress Meryl Streep, Miranda is a power player without peer in the world of haute couture. She has impeccable taste, considerable business acumen, and an unerring sense of what is "fashion forward." When she purses her lips in disapproval of a collection, its designer trembles and scurries back to the drawing board. When she deigns to smile at someone's work, a star is born. Indeed, when Miranda delivers her signature line, "That's all," on some matter pertaining to female clothing and style, it is understood that nothing more need be said.

Aside from being a mover and shaker in the world of fashion publishing, Miranda is also something of a temptress. This is especially evident in her relationship with the other principal character in the movie, Andrea "Andy" Sachs. When we first meet Andy, she is a callow, unkempt young lady who aspires to a career in "serious" journalism. She is blithely unconcerned about women's clothing, spends little time worrying about her figure—she actually consumes carbs—and regards couture concerns as frivolous at best.

Once ensnared in Miranda's web, however, Andy is compelled to make choices that literally transform her into a young fashionista whose life completely revolves around the needs and demands of *Runway*'s editor-in-chief. Though this transformation secures her a stunning wardrobe, a glamorous look, entrée to the salons and runways of New York and Paris, and the attentions of a handsome writer, it also comes at the expense of her career aspirations, her friends, and the young man with whom she is ostensibly in love. It is only at the end of the film, during the following exchange, that Andy finally realizes the extent to which she has sold her soul to a devil that wears Prada:

> MIRANDA: I never thought I would say this, Andrea, but I really, I see a great deal of myself in you. You can see beyond what people want, and what they need and you can choose for yourself.
> ANDY: I don't think I'm like that. I couldn't do what you did to Nigel, Miranda. I couldn't do something like that.
> MIRANDA: You already did. To Emily.
> MIRANDA: That's not what I ... no, that was different. I didn't have a choice.
> MIRANDA: No, no, you chose. You chose to get ahead. You want this life. Those choices are necessary.
> ANDY: But what if this isn't what I want? I mean what if I don't want to live the way you live?
> MIRANDA: Oh, don't be ridiculous, Andrea. Everybody wants this. Everybody wants to be us.

What exactly is the "this" that Miranda assures Andy everyone wants? Taking a cue from the title of the movie, it would appear to be the promise Miranda's predecessor made to Eve in the Garden of Eden, i.e., knowledge that will transform us into something akin to gods. Or in the case of *Runway*'s largely female readers, the inside dope on the kinds of clothing, jewelry, unguents, lotions, scents, diets, and exercise regimens guaranteed to transform young ladies into latter-day Aphrodites capable of shifting their shapes, gratifying their egos, ensnaring desirable mates, and securing the worship of men.

Miranda also offers to Andy and her audience the allure of becoming a "new woman" free of the family ties, romantic sentiments, and conventional morals that have bound women to hearth and home for the better part of Western history. Indeed, one could think of her as a kind of Nietzschean *Überfrau*, a great silver-haired "beast of prey"—smart, tough, completely ruthless—sidling down a runway towards Bethlehem to be born (and leaving in her wake a slew of emasculated men, terrorized employees, betrayed friends, and fatherless children).

I have gone on at such length about the character of Miranda Priestly because she exhibits three distinct, albeit related, aspects of this chapter's subject, the femme fatale. The German expression, *Machtweiber*, or "power woman," best sums up the first of these. As the editor-in-chief of a major publishing enterprise—an executive position normally reserved for males—Miranda is a member of that very select club of women in history, which, much to the chagrin of the men around them, have enjoyed both autonomy and unquestioned authority. In her second guise as the devil in Prada, she is the dreaded seductress, the direct descendant of all those female figures from Circe to Evita who use their glamour as a kind of charm to ensnare and enslave those around them. And as the modern career girl fixated on professional advancement, she evokes the dreaded "new woman" of the 19th and 20th centuries, the emancipated female whose unorthodox lifestyle undermines traditional notions of marriage, family life, work relations, and femininity itself.

In what follows, we will be looking at these different faces of the femme fatale through case studies of actual women who were regarded in their own times as "mad, bad and dangerous to know." These include that preeminent *Machtweiber* of the ancient world Cleopatra VII, last Ptolemaic Pharaoh of Egypt and consort of both Julius Caesar and Marc Anthony; Lola Montez, the great seductress of the 19th century, for whom a king abdicated his throne; and Isadora Duncan, an "emancipated woman" of the early 20th century, who scorned all traditional female roles in favor of a life dedicated to art and dance. While examining the careers of these remarkable women, we will attempt to arrive at an understanding as to why Cleopatra's political acumen, Montez's sexual allure, and Duncan's independent lifestyle made them villainous "fatal women" in the eyes of their contemporaries.

While this approach to the study of the femme fatale is intended to focus on specific aspects of female behavior long regarded as threatening to the political and social order of the West, it obviously does not do full justice to the multifaceted nature of the women selected for its case studies. Cleopatra, for example, was not only a formidable ruler and stateswoman, but also an intellectual, author, matron, and, when necessary, accomplished seductress. Concurrently, Lola Montez was a remarkable adventuress who, in addition to her sexual prowess, was noted for her intellect and political savvy (she largely governed Bavaria as Ludwig I's mistress). And while she was contemptuous of traditional female roles, Isadora Duncan was also a loving mother and a committed partner to the men in her life. In short, these ladies defy easy characterization.

Much the same can also be said about the overall subject of this chapter. The influx of women into the workplace during the modern period, their assumption of executive positions in industry, finance, the arts, and government, the emergence of a critical feminist scholarship, and the adoption by many women of the femme fatale as a symbol of female empowerment, all call into question the whole notion of the "fatal woman." Indeed, one of the matters to be addressed below is whether or not these figures should even continue to be thought of as villains.

Before turning to this question, however, we need first to address the origins of this villainous archetype in Western culture. To achieve this end, we will focus on what constituted a "fatal woman" in some of the principal myths, legends, and biblical stories of the West. This includes such figures as Gilgamesh's nemesis, the goddess Ishtar, the Olympian triumvirate of Hera, Athena, and Aphrodite, the bad girls of the Hebrew Testament—Delilah, Jezebel, Athaliah—and the women of the Völsung saga. Given the importance of this figure in modern letters and movies, we will also consider certain select figures in literature—John Keats' *La Belle Dame sans Merci* and Oscar Wilde's *Salome*—as well as film noir.

"A bitch's mind and a knavish nature": The Archetype of the Fatal Woman

The quote that introduces this section is from Hesiod's *Works and Days*, a didactic poem addressing such topics as agriculture, justice, the five ages of mankind, and the origins of human suffering. It is a reference to Pandora, the first woman created by the gods, who is credited with opening a certain jar and releasing from it all "the grievous sicknesses that are deadly to men." Though she is completely unaware of the container's contents, and actually manages to prevent the loss of hope, Hesiod uses the story of Pandora's mishap to drive home the idea that women are "a calamity for men who live by bread."[1]

Cheek by jowl with the Pandora myth is the account found in Genesis recounting how yet another divinely created first woman named Eve is duped by a crafty serpent into eating the forbidden fruit of a certain tree of knowledge in the Garden of Eden. At Eve's urging, her companion Adam also partakes of the prohibited morsel, which results in the two of them suddenly becoming aware of the fact that they are naked, and, in what may have been an early foreshadowing of Project Runway, trying to hide this fact with hastily improvised aprons made of fig leaves. Suffice it to say that neither their poaching activities nor their fashion sense please their creator who decides, as recounted in Chapter One, to condemn them and their descendants to a short, brutish, sweaty, and ill clad existence toiling for a living in a very hostile natural world.

Creation myths such as these have given rise in the West to all manner of prejudices about women. Key among these is the idea that the female descendants of Pandora and Eve are cursed with the curious and credulous natures of the first mothers. As such, they are believed to be easily tempted, weak willed, and likely to end up in dangerous situations.

Ironically, these same stories also get used to justify the notion of females as tricky seductresses intent on leading men to their doom. In the same *Works and Days* where Pandora is presented as "a calamity" for mankind, we are told that Zeus had Aphrodite "shower charm about her head," which would awaken "painful yearning and consuming obsession" among her male admirers.[2] Eve, on the other hand, actually gets blamed by both Adam and God for humanity's fall from grace, because it is she who sweet talks her gullible partner into partaking of the forbidden fruit.

These stereotypes made the lot of women in the West terribly difficult. Prior to the 20th century, with few exceptions, most Western societies sought to protect women from themselves and others by restricting their movements and their ability to make life choices without the guidance and approval of men. This entailed strict control of whom they could meet and interact with, whether or not they were educated, where they could work, what they might own, and who they could marry. Indeed, outside of certain elite and/or highly rarefied social circles, the idea of a strong, learned, sexually active woman operating independently of males both in private and public life was anathema in much of the Greco-Roman world, as well as in the Christian principalities that emerged after the fall of Rome.

This attitude was furthered by assorted stories of women whose sexual appetites and/or exercise of independent authority proved fatal to the men with whom they interact. Perhaps the earliest example of this fictional femme fatale is to found in that most venerable story of the Western canon, the Mesopotamian *Epic of Gilgamesh*. In the first half of this narrative, the reader finds the protagonist, a legendary warrior king of the Sumerian city of Uruk named Gilgamesh, in fine fettle. He has a steady boyfriend, a former wild man of the forest by the name of Enkidu, a wise and supportive mother, and the love of his subjects. He has also carried out a successful quest with his partner to procure a valuable cedar forest for his people by slaying its guardian, a fearsome monster named Humbaba.

Into this happy idyll steps Ishtar, a formidable female deity whose portfolio includes responsibility for matters of love, sex, fertility, and war. Enamored with Gilgamesh, she offers him not only her sexual favors, which are considerable, but also a golden chariot drawn by *ūmu-* demons, a lovely country home, the homage of kings and nobles, and herds of productive and extremely fertile livestock. Uruk's king, however, is unmoved by her promises of passion and prizes because he is all too aware of the fate that has befallen others who have caught her eye. Among these:

> Dumuzi the lover of your youth, you decreed that he should keep weeping year after year.
> You loved the colourful allalhu-bird, but you hit him and broke his wing. He stays in the woods crying "My wing!"
> You loved the lion, whose strength is complete, but you dug seven and seven pits for him.
> You loved the horse, so trustworthy in battle, but you decreed the whip, goad, and lash for him.
> You decreed that he should gallop seven leagues (non-stop), you decreed that he should be overwrought and thirsty.
> You decreed endless weeping for his mother Sililu.

In addition to these assorted animals, there is also a shepherd who gets turned into a wolf, which is then hunted down and torn to pieces by his own herdsmen and dogs, and a gardener that finds himself transformed into a toad. All of which leads Gilgamesh to exclaim, "And how about me? You will love me and then treat me just like them!"[3]

Ishtar is not fond of having her advances spurned and her fickle nature revealed. In response to Gilgamesh's rejection of her, she goes on a rampage that disturbs the peace of both heaven and earth. First she threatens her father, the creator god, Anu, with a zombie apocalypse unless he gives her control of a ferocious Bull of Heaven. When dad does so, she unleashes this creature on the hapless people of Uruk with great loss of life. Though Gilgamesh is able to slay this creature with the help of Enkidu, his partner's decision to slap the goddess across the face with the shoulder of the dead beast gets him executed by the gods for impiety.

Gilgamesh's portrayal of the trouble that follows in the wake of powerful, independent, and sexually active women was given further expression in the myths and legends of the Greeks, particularly those having to do with Hera, Aphrodite, and Athena. Deities of domestic life, love, wisdom and war respectively, these goddesses were quite literally the bane of anyone who dared to cross them. Indeed, in many respects they were the archetypal representatives of the three faces of the femme fatale addressed below, i.e., the *Machtweiber*, seductress, and emancipated woman.

5. "Her arms are wicked and her legs are long"

The first of these female divinities, Zeus' sister, consort, and queen, Hera, is a powerful and formidable goddess in her own right. Though her husband is lord of Olympus, he fears her biting tongue and shrewish behavior. In fact, the great "gatherer of the clouds" is so cowed by his wife that he feels it necessary to carry out his many amorous escapades with various mortal women disguised as assorted swans, bulls, bears, and golden showers. This of course does not fool his wife, who is infamous for her relentless harassment of her husband's paramours and their semi-divine offspring—Heracles and Dionysus being the most obvious examples.

Hera's jealous nature and capacity for cruelty are also very much on display in the accounts of Homer and Virgil regarding the Trojan War and its aftermath. As anyone familiar with this conflict is aware, its origins lie in a beauty contest in which Paris, a handsome and callow prince of Troy, is asked to judge the claim of three goddesses—Hera, Athena, and Aphrodite—to a golden apple that names its bearer "the fairest one." In return for this trophy and title, Olympus' queen offers the boy those things that she holds dear, i.e., great wealth and dominion over the kingdoms of the earth. When Paris spurns her offer in favor of Aphrodite's promise of the world's most beautiful woman, Hera vows vengeance, organizes an anti–Trojan coalition of gods and men, and keeps it together through a ten-year war that results in untold misery, countless deaths, the destruction of high-towered Ilium, and the slaughter and enslavement of the city's inhabitants. Even after the conflict is over, she makes it her business to pursue and persecute Troy's last remaining champion, Aeneas, as he seeks a new life for himself and the remnants of his people in Italy.

While Hera's stepdaughter, the lascivious Aphrodite, goddess of beauty, love, and lust, is more good-natured than her stepmother, she is equally troublesome to those mortals who happen to catch her eye. As already related, her appeal to Paris' prurient desire for the most beautiful woman in the world leads to the lad's abduction of the fair Helen, wife of Menelaus of Sparta, which is the *casus bellum* for the ensuing ten year war round the walls of Troy. Though she sides with the Trojans during this conflict, Aphrodite's glamor, and the powers of seduction associated with it, are no match for the power of Hera and the strategic martial skills of Athena.

Otherwise, Aphrodite is a walking compendium of the dangers attendant on the unrestrained female libido. Indeed, anyone—mortal or immortal—who offends her is rewarded with assorted punishments associated "with some terrible disorder of amour, including obsessive love, violent love, unrequited love, lost love, and taboo love."[4] Some of the more prominent examples of this include:

- When Calliope decrees that Aphrodite's lover, Adonis, must spend part of the year with Persephone, the goddess punishes her by driving

the women of Thrace into a frenzy of passion for her son Orpheus, which is so intense they end up dismembering him and tossing his head into a nearby river.
- To punish Poseidon's sons for not letting her land on the island of Rhodes, Aphrodite fills them with a lust so great for their mother that they rape her, an act of violence that causes the poor lady to leap into the sea.
- When Hippolytus, the scion of Theseus, incurs Aphrodite's wrath by expressing a preference for Artemis. The boy's mother, Phaedra, suddenly develops an unnatural affection for her son, which leads to her suicide and his murder at the behest of his father.
- After bedding Aphrodite's husband, Ares the god of war, Eos, the goddess of dawn, is cursed by love's mistress with an incurable case of nymphomania.[5]

As William Congreves observed, "Hell hath no fury like a woman scorned."

Aphrodite's stepsister, the goddess Athena, is without question the most fully realized member of the Olympian pantheon. Her portfolio includes not only warfare—in particular its strategic conduct—but also the wisdom and imagination that make possible civilization, law, justice, art, craft, and mathematics (areas for which she also bears responsibility). She is comfortable wielding weapons, weaving textiles, dispensing justice, engaging in spirited debate with her fellow deities, and mentoring headstrong, and often rash, human heroes, among them Perseus, Heracles, and Odysseus.

Athena's versatility stems in large part from the fact that she is not a traditional woman. From the moment she springs forth from her father's head, she eschews the clothing and manner of her sisters in favor of short haircuts, body armor, and battle cries. She also opts to remain single, avoids sexual and emotional entanglements with both men and women, maintains her virginity, and escapes motherhood. Indeed, this is a goddess who comes and goes as she pleases, pursues her own agendas both in Olympus and on earth, and enjoys the company of male rascals, who wisely agree to follow her lead and heed her career advice.

What makes Athena a problematic figure both by ancient and modern standards is the fact that she finds success in a man's world by essentially denying her own femininity and sexuality. When walking among mortals, she is almost always in the guise of a man, and because of her unnatural birth from the head of Zeus, she is able to claim, as Aeschylus has her do in *The Eumenides*, that "no mother gave me birth. I honor the male, in all things but marriage. Yes, with all my heart I am my Father's child."[6] In fact, she is so much daddy's daughter that she always sides with the men in any male-female conflicts to which she is a party in either Greek tragedy or epic.

5. *"Her arms are wicked and her legs are long"*

Consequently, whether one is speaking of classical or contemporary Western culture, to be "an Athena woman"—independent, accomplished, astute, efficient, successful—is also to be regarded as a female who is overly rational, incapable of feeling, undemonstrative, and largely sexless. While such a person enjoys a remarkable amount of freedom, she is also doomed to a life without love, romance, marriage, or family. Indeed, a world of Athena women would likely prove fatal for the future of humanity.[7]

The advent of monotheism does little to change popular prejudices with regard to women who operate outside of male control. We have already noted how one of the first two females of the Hebrew Testament, the naïve and highly gullible Eve, gets saddled with the blame for humanity's fall from grace, and finds herself and her descendants cursed to serve as brood mares and subordinates to their male companions. Eve's predecessor, the mysterious lady of Genesis 1:27 who was also created in God's image alongside Adam, mysteriously vanishes from the creation narrative, only to resurface later in Jewish folklore as Lilith, a nefarious demon, vampire, and succubus who kills babies and seduces men.

This less than promising beginning sets the stage for assorted laws, proverbs, prophecies, and historical accounts that severely restrict a woman's life choices in ancient Israel. As theological scholar Phyllis Bird notes:

> The picture of woman obtained from the Old Testament ... can be summarized in the first instance as that of a legal non person; where she does become visible it is as a dependent, and usually an inferior, in a male-centered and male-dominated society. The laws, by and large, do not address her; most do not even acknowledge her existence.... Where ranking occurs she is always inferior to the male. Only in her role as mother is she accorded status and honor equivalent to a man's. Nevertheless she is always subject to the authority of some male (father, husband or brother), except when widowed or divorced—an existentially precarious type of independence in Israel.[8]

As for those women who do achieve a measure of autonomy in the Promised Land, their freedom to act is usually associated with betrayal, idolatry, and murder. One prominent example of this tendency has already been addressed in the previous chapter on traitors, where we noted what happens to Samson when he runs afoul of Delilah, a courtesan who uses her sexual wiles to coax from him the secret of his great strength. While she makes off with a considerable fortune in Philistine silver, which likely enables her to spend a very comfortable retirement in some Canaanite resort town, he ends his days a blinded beast of burden chained to a millstone. Only Samson's willingness to commit suicide by bringing down the temple of Dagon on himself and his tormentors brings an end to his misery.

What befalls Samson in this story serves to remind its audience of the dangers posed to men by sexually independent women. Other biblical narratives address the disasters that befall the nation of Israel as a whole when females—particularly foreign ones—are allowed to exercise power in their own right. Of these cautionary tales, the two best known are those that relate the misdeeds of Jezebel and Athaliah.

The former of these two women is the daughter of Ethbaal, King of Tyre. Her father gives her in marriage to Ahab, a ninth century ruler of Israel, for the purpose of sealing an alliance between their two kingdoms. Once ensconced in her new husband's court, however, Jezebel makes it apparent that she has no intention of being a traditional Hebrew queen who avoids the public eye and tends to the needs of her family. Instead, she takes an active role in governing the country with her husband, and also wins him over to the worship of Baal and Asherah, two of the deities of her homeland. At her behest, Ahab erects shrines to these gods in his capital at Samaria, establishes a priesthood to serve their cults, venerates and worships them in place of Yahweh, and gives his wife leave to persecute and murder the prophets of the Lord.[9]

It goes without saying that these actions do not sit well with the God of Israel who is reported in the Book of Kings to be angrier with Ahab "than any of the kings of Israel before him."[10] Yahweh is so annoyed in fact that he sends forth one of his trusty prophets to be a thorn in Ahab's side and that of his pagan wife. This fellow is the legendary Elijah who spends a considerable amount of time confronting the royal couple and threatening the Lord's vengeance on them and their descendants for violating the first two commandments of the Decalogue.

When not excoriating Ahab and Jezebel, Elijah is busy arranging contests with the priests of Baal. One of these involves erecting two altars, one to the Canaanite deity, and the other to Yahweh. Bulls are sacrificed to each of these gods and then they are called upon to consume their respective offerings by fire. The Lord of Israel is the only one who bothers to reply, which enables his supporters to declare, "the Lord, he is the God," as well as to seize and execute the prophets of the other side. It goes without saying that this incident earns Elijah the undying enmity of Ahab's queen.

In addition to meddling in the religious life of her adopted country, Jezebel interferes in her husband's business dealings as well, sometimes with fatal consequences for the other party. As related in Chapter 21 of the Book of Kings, Ahab very much wants to get his hands on the vineyards of a Jezreelite named Naboth. Because this property had been in his family for several generations, Naboth is not interested in selling. The distress this refusal causes the king does not go unnoticed by Jezebel. In a move that might have made Lady Macbeth blush in shame, she fabricates false evidence of blasphemy against the hapless vintner and then arranges for him to be arrested and stoned to death. This execution then clears the way for Ahab to confiscate Naboth's property at no cost to himself.

5. "Her arms are wicked and her legs are long"   149

Yahweh is terribly angered by this crime because it is committed in his name. Consequently, he sends Elijah back to Ahab and Jezebel to give them notice that he not only knows what they did to Naboth, but that he intends to punish them by wiping out Ahab's posterity and insuring that "the dogs shall eat Jezebel by the wall of Jezreel."[11] Three years later, all of this comes to pass when Ahab dies in battle, and an officer in his army, a certain Jehu, seizes power and murders every member of the royal family. One of those killed is Jezebel, who, after powdering her nose, is seized by supposedly loyal eunuchs and tossed out a window. Jehu rides over her body, which, as prophesized, is left to be eaten by stray dogs.

Ahab and Jezebel have a daughter, Athaliah, who survives this massacre. Like her mother, she had been married off to a foreign prince, in this case, Jehoram the King of Judah, in order to seal an alliance between his country and Israel. Consequently, she was in Jerusalem when Jehu murdered the entire northern branch of her family.

From what little we know about her, Athaliah also appears to have shared her mother's strength of will, independence, ruthlessness, and lively interest in religion. She too won her husband over to the worship of Baal, and appears to have been the power behind both his throne and that of his successor, their son Ahaziah. When the latter dies at the hand of the same Jehu who murdered the rest of her relatives in Israel, Athaliah decides to rule Judah in her own right as Queen Mother. To strengthen her claim to the throne, she also takes the precaution of wiping out the entire Judean royal family, with the exception of a young boy named Joash, who is spirited out of the palace by Ahaziah's sister.

For the next six years Athaliah openly rules the Kingdom of Judah without a male consort. Her reign appears to have been successful, as we have no record of the usual round of wars, famines, and plagues that normally accompany those rulers who have incurred the wrath of Yahweh, his prophets, or the often fickle Hebrew population. This is even more surprising when one considers that the worship of Baal continues apace under royal protection in Jerusalem.

Unfortunately for Athaliah, the boy Joash becomes the linchpin in a conspiracy fomented by Jehoida, the high priest of Yahweh, and the captains of the various armed guards in Jerusalem. In Athaliah's seventh year of rule, these conspirators proclaim this child king. After anointing and crowning him in the temple, they arrest his grandmother and execute her outside of the palace. In the usual bloodbath that ensues, they also demolish the temple of her god Baal and murder his high priest. When informed of her demise, we are told "all the people of the land rejoiced and the city was quiet, now that Athaliah had been slain with the sword."[12]

While independent, strong and powerful queens may have been unwelcome in ancient Israel, they were a mainstay in the myths and legends of northern Europe. Indeed, the Norse *Völsunga* saga and *Nibelungenlied* feature such colorful female characters as Signy, the avenging daughter of King Völsung, Brynhild, a shield maiden and Valkyrie who defied Odin and was doomed to live a mortal life, Grimmhild, sorceress and queen of the Nibelungs, and Gudrun, wife of the hero Sigurd and later consort of Atli, King of the Huns. These women play a central role in these stories, often successfully manipulating the male characters in them to do their bidding.

This said, that bidding usually brings down doom on the assorted spouses and families of these ladies. Signy, for example, is married against her will to a treacherous king by the name of Siggeir, who later murders her father and all of her brothers save the youngest, Sigmund. In her quest for vengeance, she arranges to have her children by Siggeir murdered, while also committing incest with her remaining brother so as to give birth to a pure Völsung warrior. This champion, a fellow by the name of Sinfjötli, goes on to assist his father/uncle Sigmund in killing Signy's husband and his retainers.

Having avenged her family, Signy confesses her incest to Sigmund, sets fire to the royal palace, and immolates herself therein uttering the following:

> All is finished now. The vengeance is wrought and I have no more to keep me in life. The Volsung race lives on in you, my brother, and that is my joy. Not merrily did I wed King Siggeir and not merrily did I live with him, but merrily will I die with him now.[13]

Signy's other female companions in these stories are equally treacherous, vengeful and murderous. Grimmhild, the ambitious and scheming Queen of the Nibelungen, wishes to procure for her family the hoard of a dragon slain by the great hero Sigurd. To achieve this end, she feeds the boy a potion that makes him (1) forget the ex-Valkyrie, Brynhild, to whom he had pledged undying devotion and (2) fall in love with and marry her daughter, Gudrun. Both of these developments set in motion a series of events that leads to the extinction of both the Völsung and Nibelung lines.

This comes about because Sigurd, who no longer remembers his former flame, and is now a member of Grimmhild's family, feels duty bound to help his wife's brother, Gunnar, win the former shield maiden of Odin. This involves some tricky shapeshifting in which Sigurd assumes the appearance of his brother-in-law and faces the various obstacles that must be overcome—riding through a wall of fire, beating Brynhild in a fair fight—by anyone who would claim the ex-Valkyrie as his bride. Suffice it to say that when this proud woman discovers how she has been deceived, she vows vengeance. This comes about by conspiring with her husband and his brother, Hogni, to have one of their half-brothers murder the unsuspecting Sigurd (as blood brothers of the Völsung champion they had sworn oaths not to harm him). Following this act of treachery, Brynhild commits suicide by flinging herself onto Sigurd's funeral pyre.

Sigurd's widow, Gudrun, is none too pleased with this turn of events and decides to make her brothers pay for their treachery. This she achieves by marrying a certain Atli, King of the Huns, who desires the dragon hoard of her late husband Sigurd. When Gunnar and Hogni visit their sister, their new brother-in-law quickly dispatches them and the Völsung/Nibelung fortune finds itself under new management. Unfortunately for Atli, his wife now feels honor bound to punish him for murdering her kin. In a nice twist on Signy's revenge on Siggeir, she does this by killing their two sons, roasting their bodies, and feeding them to their father at a feast. Afterwards, she reveals her crime to him, wipes out his court by setting fire to the palace, and throws herself in the ocean.[14]

Clearly, the grand dames of these Norse legends are fatal to not only the men with whom they are involved, but to themselves as well. Unlike their Mediterranean counterparts, however, they are neither sex kittens nor females usurping male roles. Rather, they are all women who clearly see themselves as independent agents free to take whatever actions they deem necessary to advance and protect their own fortune and honor, as well as that of their respective families. That this conviction often leads them to acts of treachery, incest, prolicide (the killing of one's children), pyromania, mass murder, and suicide is of little matter as long as they are avenged on those who have wronged them and theirs. Woe betide the man (or woman) who crosses one of Northern Europe's highborn queens.

If we fast-forward to the modern period, we find that the femme fatale is increasingly associated in literature, art, and film with mysterious, highly erotic women who ensnare men with their sexual wiles and then lead them to destruction. Exemplary of this figure is the faery queen in John Keats' 19th century romantic poem, *La Belle Dame Sans Merci*. This woman is an ethereal figure with long hair, a light foot, and wild eyes who catches the attention of an itinerant knight. She then seduces and leaves him "haggard and woebegone" in a dreary lake country where birds no longer sing. After a long snooze, the young man awakens to the realization that he is now one of a slew of "pale" kings, princes, and warriors held in thrall by a beautiful woman without mercy.

Later in the century, Keats' fatal faery queen is supplanted by the figure of the exotic dancing girl, perhaps best exemplified in Oscar Wilde's play, *Salome*. As recounted in Mark 6:14–29 and Matthew 14:1–12, the title character of this drama was little more than the naïve daughter of Herodias, a Judean princess who had divorced Salome's father Herod II and remarried his brother Herod Antipater. Apparently, this match was regarded as incestuous and unlawful by many of Antipater's subjects, including that great curmudgeon of the New Testament, John the Baptist. Angered by the Baptist's pronouncements against her, Herodias prevailed upon her husband to have him arrested, chained, and imprisoned. She also wanted him executed, but Herod refused to take this action because John was regarded as "an upright and holy man."

An opportunity for Herodias to kill the Baptist, however, was not long in coming. On the occasion of Herod's birthday, she arranges for her daughter to dance for her husband. Salome must have been quite the hoofer because the evangelist Mark tells us that Herod was so pleased by his stepdaughter's performance that he unwisely promised to grant her "whatever you ask, even to half of my kingdom."[15] When the girl asks for her mother's advice as to what she should request, Herodias answers, "the head of John the Baptist."[16] The account goes on to tell us:

> At that the girl hurried back to the king's presence and made her request: "I want you to give, at once, the head of John the Baptizer on a platter." The king bitterly regretted the request; yet because of his oath and the presence of his guests, he did not want to refuse her. He promptly dispatched an executioner, ordering him to bring back the Baptizer's head. The man went and beheaded John in the prison. He brought in the head on a platter and gave it to the girl and the girl gave it to her mother.[17]

In Wilde's hands, this biblical account of a young girl being manipulated by her mother in order to carry off an ignoble murder gets turned on its head. The Salome of his play is a world weary, sybaritic seductress who is sexually attracted to the Baptist. When John spurns her advances, she is enraged and, like Ishtar in *Gilgamesh*, schemes to bring about the destruction of the New Testament prophet.

This Salome achieves by putting on a dance of the seven veils for her stepfather, who has promised her anything she desires in return for what is essentially an erotic striptease number. After completing her performance, she then demands that Herod behead the man who has rejected her, and though he is reluctant to do so, the hapless king feels compelled by his oath to give his stepdaughter what she wishes. Upon receiving John's severed head on a bloody dish, Salome shocks the Herodian court by kissing the Baptist's mouth and likening its bloody taste to that of love. Her father is so horrified by this unnatural deed and pronouncement that he declares his daughter monstrous and orders his guards to "kill that woman."[18]

Wilde's femme fatale generates a "Salome craze" that continues down to the present day. Operas, ballets, poems, songs, vaudeville acts, and at least 25 films have retold the story of this exotic princess whose erotic dance enslaves a king and slays a prophet. In part, the popularity of this figure stems from the prurience of men hungry for the "spectacle of her quivering bosoms, heaving belly and tossing thighs." That said, it should also be noted that a great many people, including a sizable number of women, are drawn to Herod's stepdaughter because

> Salome is subversive. She threatens the social order, civilized behavior, monogamy. She is every woman who has ever dreamed of stripping for a lover—or an audience—and she is every woman who has.[19]

This modern fixation on the fatal woman as a female character who uses her beauty and sexual allure to entice, entrap, and then lead men to their downfall and death is also a fixture of the American cinema. One sees this most vividly in the femme fatales of the so-called film-noir tradition, a loosely defined genre of darkly lit urban crime dramas populated by private eyes, police detectives, grifters, gangsters, and "bad girls." Among the latter are assorted women—Brigid O'Shaughnessy (*Maltese Falcon*); Phyllis Dietrichson (*Double Indemnity*); Dora (*The Postman Always Rings Twice*); Matty Walker (*Body Heat*); Catherine Tramell (*Basic Instinct*)—who use their feminine wiles to manipulate innocent men into committing murder, usually for financial gain.[20]

By this point in our examination of fictional femme fatales it should be evident that women who operate outside of male control have been regarded as dangerous, even deadly, for most of Western history. Of particular concern are those females who

- exercise political authority in their own right;
- use sex to ensnare and entrap men; and
- live in an independent, unsupervised manner.

Indeed, the message in all of the stories examined up to this point is quite clear, where women rule, rut, or roam freely, discord and disorder is not far behind. In what follows, we will examine this idea within the context of the lives and careers of three of history's most notable femme fatales. The first of these was the lady of the two lands, Cleopatra VII, last pharaoh of Egypt.

"No people who place a woman over their public affairs prosper": The Femme Fatale as Machtweiber

The quote beginning this section is attributed to the prophet Muhammad and it expresses a longstanding historical prejudice in the West with regard to women who govern in their own right. As many of the preceding stories demonstrate, this attitude is predicated on the notion that females are either too weak willed or too governed by their emotions to rule effectively without a man's guidance. Lacking strong wills, women are thought incapable of making the difficult decisions—eliminating opposition, suppressing rebellion, waging war—often required of one who governs. And on account of their overly emotional natures, they are also considered more likely to engage in the kinds of activities—illicit affairs, favoritism, ill-advised marriages—that can fatally compromise a ruler and those subject to her. That there might be ladies who were capable of being both hardheaded and hardhearted does not appear to have crossed the minds of the many male "experts" on this subject.

Cleopatra VII of Egypt was one such woman. During her lifetime, she demonstrated in no uncertain terms that a woman could govern ably, ruthlessly, and rationally. Indeed, from her birth in 69 BCE, until her death 30 years later, this remarkable lady survived various court intrigues, eliminated any and all factions opposed to her rule, bedded and wedded the two most powerful Romans of her day, and effectively managed, without recourse to male guidance or oversight, one of the largest and wealthiest kingdoms of her era. In all of these activities, she demonstrated what would later be called a Machiavellian appreciation for the practice of politics, and the often amoral acts necessary to acquire and exercise power.

Because the Ptolemies followed their Pharonic predecessors' custom of brother-sister marriage, or as historian F. E. Adcock styled it, the Egyptian practice of keeping "the business in the family by keeping the family in the business,"[21] Cleopatra was the third of four daughters born to Ptolemy XII and his sister-wife Cleopatra V Tryphaena. Her three sisters were, in order of birth, Cleopatra VI Tryphaena, Berenice IV, and, the youngest of the four girls, Arsinoe IV. She also had two younger brothers—Ptolemy XIII and XIV—who were the offspring of a second marriage that her father entered into at the death of his first wife.

Given her notoriety, it is surprising how very little we know about Cleopatra's appearance. Portraits of her that were made during her lifetime are extremely varied and appear to be aimed at different audiences. In Egyptian sculptures and reliefs, she is portrayed as a powerful pharaoh. The likenesses of her we find on coins from the period either emphasize the prominent, and not terribly flattering, Ptolemy nose, or make her look like Mark Antony. Certain busts associated with her, and it should be noted here that these may in fact be of someone else altogether, present her as a young, rather plain, Greek maiden. As we will discuss below, reports and representations of her as a great beauty come much later in history when chroniclers of her life were looking for a reason other than political aptitude to explain her overall effectiveness as a ruler.[22]

Indeed, Cleopatra's allure appears to have had less to do with her physical appearance than with her easy manner, ready wit, and wide erudition. Plutarch tells us:

5. "Her arms are wicked and her legs are long" 155

Her own beauty, so we are told, was not of that incomparable kind which instantly captivates the beholder. But the charm of her presence was irresistible, and there was an attraction in her person and her talk, together with a peculiar force of character, which pervaded her every word and action, and laid all who associated with her under its spell.[23]

Plutarch also reports that she could be as "broad and gross" in her humor as a soldier, match Mark Antony drink for drink, and speak nine languages fluently—including Egyptian, Hebrew and a little known dialect of Ethiopian called Troglodyte. Her learning also extended to "arithmetic, geometry, music, equitation, rhetoric, astronomy, medicine.... The epics of Homer, the poetry of Hesiod and Pindar, the dramas of Euripides and Menander and the histories of Herodotus and Thucydides."[24]

Much of this worldliness can be attributed to Cleopatra's father, who educated her in the same manner as his sons. Nicknamed "Auletes," or "flute-player," because of his delight in playing an oboe-like pipe called the *aulos*, Ptolemy XII appears to have been genuinely fond of his third daughter. Part of this may have stemmed from the fact that in 58 BCE, his two eldest children, the abovementioned Cleopatra VI and Berenice IV, made common cause with an Alexandrian mob and deposed him from the throne. When he sought asylum and assistance from patrons and allies in Rome, Cleopatra, aged 11, went with him.

Over the next four years, Cleopatra observed how a Ptolemy living in a Roman world played politics. The first thing she learned at this time was that murder is often integral to the game of statecraft. This was demonstrated in no uncertain way when her sisters sent envoys to argue against her father's restoration to the Egyptian throne, and Ptolemy XII had them assassinated.

Her second lesson was that the way to a Roman magnate's heart was through his purse. To win over Rome's principal power brokers, Caesar, Pompey, and Crassus, to his cause, Ptolemy XII offered them a bribe to the tune of ten thousand talents, a sum equal to over a year's worth of Egypt's total revenue. It was an offer these men could not refuse. Not only did they arrange to have the Senate declare Ptolemy Rome's good friend and ally in 55 BCE, but they also dispatched an army to restore him to power.

Upon their return to Alexandria, Ptolemy executed his daughter, Berenice IV, who had already deposed, and probably murdered, her sister and co-conspirator Cleopatra VI. He then made the surviving Cleopatra his co-ruler and married her to his son and her half-brother Ptolemy XIII. In a will that he dispatched to Rome for safekeeping, he designated these two as his heirs in the event of his death, an event that occurred in 51 BCE.

Though only 18, Cleopatra moved quickly to consolidate her position. To curry favor with her Egyptian subjects, she and her brother were crowned in the traditional garb of the pharaohs at Memphis, the spiritual capital of

Egypt. In the same year of her coronation, she also presided over the installation of a new Buchis bull, an animal regarded as the manifestation of the Egyptian war god Mentu, as well as Osiris and Ra. This event required her to travel upriver to Thebes, the old center of the New Kingdom, a trip that allowed her to introduce herself to the native population of her country as pharaoh, incarnation of the goddess Isis, and defender of Egypt's ancient traditions. The fact that, unlike her predecessors, she actually spoke Egyptian was not lost on the throngs that are reported to have followed her progress up the Nile.[25]

She also proved herself adept at dealing with Rome. When the Roman governor of Syria, Cornelius Bibulus, sent his two sons to Alexandria to bring back the army that had restored Cleopatra's father to his throne, they were met and murdered by mutinous soldiers who were unwilling to leave Egypt. Aware of her dependency on Rome, as well as the fact that this incident could be used to justify the invasion and annexation of her kingdom, Cleopatra arrested the guilty culprits and sent them in chains to the aggrieved father.

Not long after this incident the Roman world was riven by one of its periodic civil wars, in this case the conflict between Julius Caesar and his former colleague and son-in-law, Pompey the Great. When the son of the latter dynast, Gnaeus Pompey, arrived in Alexandria to demand assistance from Cleopatra for his father in this conflict, she quickly complied by lending him the Egyptian fleet. Plutarch also hints at a brief affair between her and the younger Pompey. If true, it was the first of a series of eventful trysts with notable Roman men.[26]

That same year, Egypt itself was plunged into civil war when Cleopatra's brother and co-ruler, Ptolemy XIII, drove her out of Alexandria. Actually, it would be more accurate to say that a cabal of the young king's advisers—Achillas, the general of his army, Pothinus, a eunuch in charge of his finances, and Theodotus, his tutor—staged a palace coup that forced Cleopatra to flee. Once rid of her, these three formed a regency council, which purportedly ruled in the name of her 13-year-old brother.

A remarkable confluence of events brought about the downfall of this coterie and the restoration of Cleopatra to her throne. In 48 BCE, Julius Caesar arrived unexpectedly in Egypt in search of his rival Pompey, whom he had defeated in Greece. Unbeknownst to Caesar, Pompey had gotten there ahead of him in search of support from what he thought were his Ptolemaic allies, only to be treacherously assassinated and beheaded by the boy king and his advisers. When presented with the grisly proof of Pompey's murder, Caesar is reputed to have been shocked and outraged. Aside from the fact that before they were foes this man had been his friend, ally, and son-in-law, he was also a consul of Rome. Such a figure was deserving of a demise other than being butchered by Egyptian barbarians.

5. "Her arms are wicked and her legs are long"

Caesar makes his displeasure known to his reluctant hosts, sets up house in the royal palace, and summons Cleopatra back from exile. Though an army stands between the young queen and Alexandria, she manages, with the assistance of a Sicilian attendant named Apollodoros, to sail a tiny two-oared boat down the Nile and into the Alexandrian harbor. Once docked, she then wraps herself into some kind of bedding, which is secured with a leather strap, and carried by Apollodoros to Caesar. When she steps forth from this sack—a scene made famous over the centuries in literature, art, and film—she captivates the most powerful Roman of her time.

The why of this captivation continues to be a subject of conjecture and discussion. Much is made of the fact that Caesar was an older man—52 at the time—with a noted weakness for the ladies. Later commentators would also play up Cleopatra's great beauty, as well as her wanton sexuality. While there is probably some truth to the idea that Caesar found the young princess sexually attractive, one suspects that he was also charmed by her daring and fearlessness. Add this to the fact that she was reputed to be an effective speaker with an easy laugh, an ancient lineage, and an awful lot of money, and Caesar's attraction to her makes perfect sense.[27]

It should also be noted here that these two needed each other. With the Egyptian army under the control of her brother's general, Cleopatra was very much dependent on the legions that were Caesar's to command. For his part, this young queen offered him the puppet ruler he needed to keep Egypt quiescent and its resources at Rome's disposal. There was also the not so small matter of money. The Roman dictator's tastes were expensive and his armies required payment. Cleopatra's father had left an outstanding debt to Caesar of many thousands of talents, which, if recovered, would go a long way towards making his financial problems disappear.

Whether for reasons of passion, self-interest, or both, Cleopatra and Caesar made common cause together in 48 BCE. She stayed by his side during the so-called Alexandrian War, a four-month campaign by her brother's allies to drive them from the city (in typical Ptolemy fashion, one of those arraigned against them was Cleopatra's youngest sister Arsinoe IV). Though hard-pressed at first, Caesar emerged victorious, Ptolemy XIII perished in battle, Arsinoe was taken captive, and Cleopatra was reinstated as Egypt's queen alongside her new husband, half-brother Ptolemy XIV. In celebration of his victory and her installation, the two lovers journeyed up the Nile in a luxurious floating palace on which they reputedly wiled away the days eating, drinking, and making love.

Not long thereafter, Caesar left Egypt in order to settle scores with one of the ever-troublesome kings of Pontus (the one of "I came, I saw, I conquered" fame), as well as to mop up the Pompeian opposition that had regrouped in what is now Tunisia. While he was attending to these military affairs, Cleopatra was giving birth to a child she claimed was his, a son she named Ptolemy XV Caesar. While we cannot know for certain if this boy, nicknamed Caesarion, or Little Caesar, by the Alexandrians, was actually Caesar's child, the fact that the Roman did nothing to deny Cleopatra's claim would seem to indicate that he believed the boy to be his own.

Having crushed his opposition on all fronts, Caesar returned to Rome in 46 and celebrated four triumphs. The second of these commemorated his victory in the Alexandrian War, and it is very possible Cleopatra was present to add luster to the event. Whether she was or not, we do know that later in the year she, her brother-husband Ptolemy XIV, and her son, Caesarion, were in the city to negotiate a new treaty of friendship with the Roman Senate.

Over the next two years, Caesar showed great favor to his Egyptian consort. When in Rome, she resided in one of his villas, which was directly across the Tiber from his own residence. In his capacity as dictator, he had the Senate ratify a treaty that confirmed the independence of Egypt and declared Cleopatra a friend and ally of the Roman people. When he built a temple to his ancestress, the goddess Venus, he placed alongside her statue a sculpture of Cleopatra in gilded bronze. Impressed by the many wonders of Alexandria, he surrounded himself with her advisers and came up with proposals that included a public library where Romans could access Greek and Latin literature, an official census of the city's population, the draining of the Pomptine marshes, a canal from the Adriatic to the Tiber, and a vast new harbor at Rome's principal port of Ostia. Indeed, working with Cleopatra's astronomer Sosigenes, Caesar replaced the inefficient and often out of sync Roman lunar calendar of 355 days with the Alexandrian solar calendar of 365.25 days, and then named it, appropriately enough, the Julian Calendar.

It also appears that Caesar attempted at this time, unsuccessfully, to pass a law that would have allowed him to formally marry Cleopatra and confer legitimacy on their child. Under the laws and customs of republican Rome, marriage was defined as a union between two Roman citizens. Marriages between Romans and foreigners, as well as any offspring that might ensue from those relationships, were simply not recognized. Caesar's proposed statute would have eliminated these strictures and allowed him to take multiple wives and marry whomever he wished. Children from these unions would also have been counted citizens. If passed, Caesar could have maintained his marriage to his Roman wife, Calpurnia, wedded Cleopatra legally, and given full citizenship rights, including those of inheritance, to his son Caesarion.[28]

All of these efforts in favor of his Egyptian mistress did not sit well with Caesar's fellow citizens. As already addressed in Chapter 2, Cleopatra and her people were regarded as sybaritic barbarians—soft, luxury loving, effeminate, sexually perverse, and tyranny loving. Whatever her status as a friend

5. "Her arms are wicked and her legs are long" 159

and ally of the Roman people, her presence in their capital was seen as an affront to the virtues that had made Rome strong and feared throughout the West. More to the point, there were increasing concerns that her influence on Caesar was moving him to embrace the trappings—triumphal robes, gilded chairs, laurel crowns, golden shoes, statues in temples, images on coins—and practices—securing the office of dictator for life, accumulating and exercising untrammeled power, acting in an increasingly authoritarian manner, disdaining republican tradition—of a despotic Oriental king.

In addition to being a barbarian, the other thing that made Egypt's queen problematic for the Romans was her independence, her freedom to act without male interference. Unlike the traditional Roman matron who was expected to marry someone selected for her by her family, Cleopatra had entered into her relationship with Julius Caesar freely and without interference from anyone, including her ostensible husbands, Ptolemy XIII and XIV. She also did not see her sex as limiting her to bearing children, tending the hearth, and working in wool. In fact, Caesar was likely attracted to Cleopatra because she

> handled matters no woman of his acquaintance had touched. He would have been hard pressed to find a woman in all of Rome who had raised an army, lent a fleet, controlled a currency. As incandescent as was her personality, Cleopatra was every bit Caesar's equal as a coolheaded, clear-eyed pragmatist.[29]

Unfortunately, as Cleopatra's latest biographer Stacy Shiff has noted, "what passed on his [Caesar's] part as strategy would be remembered on hers as manipulation."[30] Indeed, in accounts that followed her demise, Cleopatra's hold over Caesar (and later Antony) would be attributed not to her intellect and political acumen, but to magic, spells, and sexual seduction. Perhaps one of the best examples of this thinking is the following passage from the poet Lucan's *Civil War*:

> There [on the Nile cruise following the Alexandrian War] the monarchs reclined alongside Caesar, whose power exceeded theirs; and the queen, her dangerous beauty heightened by cosmetics, not satisfied with the power she and her brother had, was decked out in the spoils of the Red Sea. Her head and neck felt the weight of her jewels. Her alabaster breasts shone through fine Sidonian cloth, tightly woven by the Oriental shuttle, then loosened by the Egyptian needle that relaxes the taut threads.[31]

As the French would say, "Ooh la la."

Cleopatra's Roman idyll ended on the Ides of March in 44 BCE when Caesar was assassinated by a coterie of 60 senators in, ironically enough, the theater of his late rival Pompey the Great. In the ensuing disorder, Cleopatra fled the city and made her way back to Alexandria. She would never see Rome again.

This said, she was certainly not finished with Romans. Over the next two years, she executed a nimble dance between the Caesarians, led by the late dictator's chief military lieutenant, Mark Antony, and his grandnephew, Octavian Caesar, and the so-called "liberators" under the leadership of two of Caesar's principal assassins, Caius Longinus Cassius and Marcus Junius Brutus. Though she largely sat out the conflict, she did give some support to the Caesarian side, which ultimately triumphed over their republican foes at the Battle of Philippi in 42 BCE.

During this time, Cleopatra was busy consolidating her power in Egypt. This involved the cold-blooded murder of her husband-brother Ptolemy XIV, allegedly by poison, and the crowning of Ptolemy XV Caesar, as king and pharaoh, with his mother serving as co-ruler. To celebrate the new regime, Cleopatra engaged in a clever propaganda campaign in which the new mother-son team was featured on the walls of various temples up and down the Nile as Isis and Horus, the avenger of Osiris (and by proxy, Caesarion's father, Gaius Julius Caesar).

These were also years in which Cleopatra demonstrated that she was more than just a pretty face with a gift for seducing older men. To curry favor with Egypt's religious establishment, as well as benefit her country's various building and craft trades, she initiated the repair of existing holy sites and the construction of new ones throughout the kingdom. In Alexandria, she presided over an intellectual renaissance by patronizing and promoting the work of local artists, writers, and philosophers. And when the Nile failed to overflow its banks in 43 and 42, she distributed free wheat from the royal granaries and declared a tax holiday until the crisis passed. When Cleopatra left for Tarsus in 41 to meet with Mark Antony, she left behind her a largely contented Egypt.[32]

From this moment in Cleopatra's life until her suicide in 30 BCE, accounts of her actions very much reflect the version of events favored by the man who defeats her and Antony, i.e., Octavian, or as he styled himself at this time, Gaius Julius Caesar Otavianus. The gist of these histories and biographies is as follows. Mark Antony, a Roman of great ability with a pronounced weakness for drink, soft living, luxury, and strong women, meets the queen of Egypt, a bewitching beauty learned in spells and enchantments, who also shares many of Antony's appetites. From the moment he meets her on a great pleasure boat at Tarsus, where he is wined and dined and given a glimpse of the sybaritic existence that awaits him in Egypt, Antony is Cleopatra's slave. Indeed, he is so besotted with this Egyptian witch that he abandons his planned campaign against the Parthians and sails back with her to Alexandria, where they frolic for the better part of a year in the company of like-minded drunks and philanderers known as The Order of the Inimitable Life. During this time, Antony goes native, wearing Greek tunics rather than Roman togas,

5. "Her arms are wicked and her legs are long"

attending lectures and discussions, visiting temples, spending time in local gyms with Greek boys, and accompanying his mistress to the market walking behind her litter with her eunuchs. Even worse, he sires twins with her, Alexander Helios (the Sun) and Cleopatra Selene (the Moon).

When the Parthians invade Syria, an act that finally forces Antony to do something other than party with his Egyptian whore, he initially shows good sense by re-establishing his alliance with Octavian and, to seal the deal, marrying his sister, a good Roman girl by the name of Octavia. Unfortunately, when he finally begins his campaign against the Parthians in 37, he sends for Cleopatra and spends a debauched winter with her in Antioch. Afterwards, he commences a campaign against the Parthian Empire that proves an unmitigated disaster. Rather than return to Greece or Italy to regroup with Octavia at his side, he instead returns to Alexandria to find comfort in the bosom of his Eastern consort.

Things go steadily downhill from there. In 34 BCE, following a successful campaign in Armenia that culminates in the capture of that country's king through treachery, Antony shows where his true loyalties lie. He stages a Roman style triumph in Alexandria, presenting his captive and the spoils of his war to Cleopatra. A few days later, the two lovers stage a celebration that comes to be known as the Donations of Alexandria. At this event, Cleopatra and Antony present themselves to the Alexandrians as Isis and Osiris-Dionysus, and in this capacity they shower their children with titles and territories, many of them Roman. Caesarion, aged 13, is named the legitimate son of Caesar and proclaimed King of Kings. Six-year-old Alexander Helios is declared king of Armenia and overlord of Media and Parthia (neither of which are under Roman control), and his twin sister, Cleopatra Selene, is given Cyrenaica (northern Libya) and Crete. Their third and youngest son, two-year-old Ptolemy Philadelphus, receives Phoenicia, Syria, and Cilicia.

Suffice it to say, none of this is lost on Antony's rival in Rome. As demonstrated in Chapter 2, his actions at this time give Octavian license to castigate him as an effeminate buffoon with "the mind of a woman and the physical desires of one too." It also gives the young Caesar grounds to strip Antony of his offices and powers on the grounds that he is clearly bewitched by Cleopatra and not responsible for his own actions. Indeed, when war finally comes in 32 BCE, the Roman Senate declares it not against Mark Antony, but against his Egyptian consort, Cleopatra.

Everything comes to a head on September 2, 31 BCE at the Battle of Actium off the southern coast of Greece. Plutarch tells us that the decision to commit everything to a naval battle was done at Cleopatra's behest so that her navy could participate in what she assumed would be a glorious victory. Unfortunately for her and Antony, Octavian and his very capable admiral,

Agrippa, had the better fleet, and the hapless couple find themselves trapped and blockaded on a spit of land with little food and water. When Antony attempts to break through Octavian's ships, Cleopatra is said to have a panic attack—she is, after all, both a woman and an Egyptian—raises her sails and, literally, heads south. Abandoning the men under his command, Antony follows her:

> And it was now that Antony revealed to all the world that he was no longer guided by the motives of a commander nor of a brave man nor indeed by his own judgment at all; instead, he proved the truth of the saying which was once uttered as a jest, namely that a lover's soul dwells in the body of another, and he allowed himself to be dragged along after the woman, as if he had become a part of her flesh and must go wherever she led him. No sooner did he see her ships sailing away than every other consideration was blotted out of his mind, and he abandoned and betrayed the men who were fighting and dying for his cause. He got into a five-banked galley, and taking with him only Alexas the Syrian and Scellius, he hurried after the woman who had already ruined him and would soon complete his destruction.[33]

The two lovers return to Alexandria and, true to form, pass the time remaining to them in debauchery. Certain accounts tell us that the ever-devious Cleopatra entered into secret negotiations with Octavian and even entertained thoughts of seducing him as she had his grand uncle. None of this goes anywhere, however, and, as has been recounted in numerous tragedies, novels, films, and TV shows, the two lovers commit suicide, Antony first by falling on his sword, Cleopatra sometime later with poison (later transformed into a nasty little asp).

It is obvious looking over this account that the partisans of Octavian and his later successors were intent on delivering up to posterity what Stacy Shiff calls "the tabloid version of an Egyptian queen, insatiable, treacherous, bloodthirsty, power-crazed."[34] Indeed, this is a story that is meant to impart two very important lessons to its audiences. The first of these is that where women rule, trouble is not far behind. Because of Cleopatra's monstrous ambition, family members are murdered, great men are emasculated, wars are initiated, and her country's independence is snuffed out. The second revolves around the dangers associated with uncontrolled female sexuality. In contravention of what Romans, and their later Christian successors imagined to be the natural order of things, Cleopatra freely initiated and entered into relationships with the two most notable men of her era. Further, her sexual prowess was such that she was able to get these fellows to do her bidding. Though Caesar and Antony appear to have been well pleased with their relationships with the young lady, their later biographers felt it necessary to attribute much of the evil that befalls them as attributable in one way or another to their dalliance with this wanton woman of the East.

5. *"Her arms are wicked and her legs are long"*

Modern historians, at least those writing in the latter half of the 20th century and the beginning of the 21st, have treated the ancient accounts of Cleopatra with considerable skepticism. They note that for Antony to maintain his hold over the eastern half of the Roman empire, which was ceded to him by Octavian in the aftermath of Philippi, Egyptian gold and grain were imperative, and the way to these things was through that country's queen. As such, with or without a personal relationship, a close alliance with this lady was inevitable. Concurrently, Cleopatra needed no one to remind her that Rome was the arbiter of her world and the best way to maintain her position and Egypt's independence was to ingratiate herself with whomever happened to be the first man in Rome; and in 41 BCE Mark Antony was that fellow.

Their subsequent marriage and the decision to designate their children rulers of various territories in the East was also not without political merit. If these dynastic arrangements had materialized, areas that were often troublesome for Rome would have become client kingdoms bound personally to Antony, and through him the Roman Empire. France and Britain entered into very similar kinds of arrangements in this area of the world after World War I.

As for Actium, military historians largely concede that Antony and Cleopatra had no option but to try to break through Octavian's blockade and regroup in Asia. As such, her supposed flight was actually the successful culmination of a plan aimed at saving the Egyptian fleet and her gold for the purpose of fighting another day. Had Antony's legions remained loyal and followed his orders to rejoin him in Syria, Octavian would have found Egypt a much tougher nut to crack.

In the end, however, victors write the histories, and the history of Cleopatra became a morality play in which she was presented as the femme fatale twice over, i.e., as both mad queen and seductive witchy woman. Which is why, after some two millennia of patriarchal propaganda, it is refreshing to be able to end this all too brief and cursory treatment of one of the world's most impressive *Machtweibern* with the following lines from Stacy Schiff's biography of Egypt's last pharaoh:

> Two thousand years of bad press and overheated prose, of film and opera, cannot conceal the fact that Cleopatra was a remarkably capable queen, canny and opportunistic in the extreme, a strategist of the first rank. Her career began with one brazen act of defiance and ended with another. "What woman, what ancient succession of men, was so great?" demands the anonymous author of a fragmentary Latin poem, which positions her as the principal player of the age. Boldly and bodily, she inserted herself into world politics, with wide-reaching consequences.... From our first glimpse of her to the last, she dazzles for her ability to set the scene. To the end she was mistress of herself, astute, spirited, inconceivably rich, pampered yet ambitious.[35]

"She went through men like cordwood": The Femme Fatale as Seductress

One of the most controversial films of Hollywood's pre-code era is a 1933 71-minute black and white movie entitled *Baby Face*. It recounts the story of a young woman named Lily Powers (played with great verve by a very young Barbara Stanwyck) who uses her sexual charms to advance herself socially and financially. Or, as the movie tag line suggests, "She had *it* and made *it* pay!"

As the film's opening scenes make clear, Lily learns what *it* is early in life when her father, a Pennsylvania speakeasy owner, pimps her out to various customers in exchange for assorted favors. When the old man dies in an accident involving an exploding still, his sexually aware and very experienced daughter is counseled by a friendly cobbler—who also happens to be a devotee of Nietzsche—to move to the big city and use her sexual wiles to become both an *Überfrau* and a mistress of men. She takes this latter day Zarathustra's advice, hops a freight train to New York with her best friend, an African-American lady named Chico, and, in a scene that foreshadows what is to come, pays for their passage by having sex with a railroad worker who threatens to have them jailed.

Once in the Big Apple, Lily makes her way to the city's Gotham Trust Tower where she lures a man in the personnel department into an empty office. A quick romp with this fellow secures her a job in the firm's filing department, and from this point on, she quite literally sleeps her way to the top of the company. The viewer follows her progress through a very clever visual device in which the movie camera pans up the outside of the building, going floor by floor as she seduces her way up the corporate ladder.

Suffice it to say Lilly's rise to prominence is not without casualties. Office boys—including a youthful and quite handsome John Wayne—are seduced and quickly discarded once they have served their purpose. Young executives are lured into compromising positions that cost them their jobs. Marriages are ruined. One company CEO is murdered, and two others commit suicide. As for the femme fatale who is responsible for all this human misery, Lilly Powers ends up with an executive position in Paris, the hand in marriage of the wealthy grandson of the company's founder, and millions in stocks, bonds, and assorted gifts lavished on her by the assorted paramours she has ridden to the top of Gotham Trust.

Mention is made of *Baby Face* because it is a classic rendering in celluloid of the fatal woman as seductress and vampire. Its protagonist is aware of, and very comfortable with, her sexuality. She also understands the sexual needs and desires of the men around here, and she uses that knowledge to enslave and/or embarrass them so as to get what she wants in the way of pay and promotions. As with any cold-blooded predator—or Nietzschean *Übermensch* for that matter—she hunts efficiently and remorselessly, inured to the broken hearts, ruined relationships, destroyed careers, and lost lives that are attendant on her rise to power.

Increasingly in the modern period, when the expression femme fatale is used it is shorthand for seductresses in the mold of Lilly Powers, i.e., women who use their sexuality to ensnare and exploit the men around them. However, as noted above, from the latter half of the 19th century, it is also a rubric commonly associated with exotic female dancers, such as Salome, who used their "quivering bosoms, heaving belly and tossing thighs" to break the wills and master the minds of men. In what follows, we are going to examine the life and career of a historical figure who was the very embodiment of this dancing siren. Her name was Lola Montez, and as everyone who crossed her path would attest, she most definitely had *it* and knew how to make *it* pay.

Though she would pass herself off as a Spanish aristocrat for much of her life, Lola Montez was actually an Irish girl by the name of Marie Dolores Eliza Rosanna Gilbert, who was born into modest circumstances in County Sligo on February 17, 1821. Her mother was Elizabeth Oliver, the daughter of a sheriff and member of Parliament for County Limerick, and her father was Edward Gilbert, an ensign in the British Army. Neither side of the family was remotely royal.

At the age of two, Lola accompanied her parents to India where her father was billeted. Soon after their arrival, Edward Gilbert contracted cholera and died. His widow quickly remarried another officer by the name of Patrick Craigie, who appears to have been genuinely fond of his new stepdaughter. By all accounts, he spoiled her terribly, as did both the other members of her late father's regiment, and the Indian *ayahs* (governesses) hired to care for her. By the age of six, all of this pampering and indulgence is said to have transformed young Marie into something of a devil child, fond of roaming barefoot through jungles, swimming nude in nearby ponds, and chewing betel leaves.[36]

To ensure that she was raised in a manner more befitting a young lady, Lola was sent by her parents to live with Craigie's family in Scotland. Upon arriving in her new home, she proved herself to be just as intractable as she had been in India. To her Scottish relatives horror, she continued to delight in running about naked outdoors. Even worse, she enjoyed playing pranks on churchgoers during Sunday services.

Unable to control Lola at home, the Craigies sent her at the age of ten to a boarding school in England run by her stepfather's sister. Lola's aunt proved equally unsuccessful in her efforts to curb the young girl's fierce temper and "indomitable self-will." Indeed, a year later, the poor woman felt it necessary to transfer her niece to Aldridge Academy for Ladies, an institution in Bath noted for its success in taming troublesome girls.[37]

Lola's formal education ended in 1837 when her mother arrived in England, and informed her 16-year-old daughter that she had arranged for her to marry a 60-year-old judge in India. Horrified at the idea of being betrothed to a man so advanced in years, Lola seduced her mother's traveling companion, a Lieutenant Thomas James, and eloped with him to India. It was the first of a great many trysts that would take her around the world and up the social ladder.

This first marriage was not a happy one, and two years later Lola left her husband for England. On the voyage home, she took a wealthy cavalry officer as a lover, and with his help made her way to Cadiz, Spain to learn how to dance in the flamenco style. Blessed with "the eyes of a pre–Raphaelite sorceress—blue, black-lashed, and arched with flaring brows—and breasts 'that made madmen' everywhere,"[38] Maria James refashioned herself, Lola Montez, a noble Spanish widow and *danseuse*, who spoke English in a faltering manner with a heavy accent.

In 1843, she made her debut in London at Her Majesty's Theater. Though not an accomplished dancer, Lola's tight black bodice, short flounced pink silk skirt, shapely gams, and suggestive movements were an instant sensation. Typical of the reviews was the following:

> On Saturday last, between the acts of the opera, Donna Lola Montez was announced to appear on the programme at Her Majesty's. A thousand ardent spectators were in feverish anxiety to see her. Donna Lola enchanted everyone. There was throughout a graceful flowing of the arms—not an angle discernible—an indescribable softness in her attitude and suppleness in her limbs which, developed in a thousand positions (without infringing on the Opera laws), were the most intoxicating and womanly that can be imagined. We never remember seeing the habitués—both young and old—taken by more agreeable surprise than the bewitching lady excited. She was rapturously encored, and the stage strewn with bouquets.[39]

Unfortunately for Lola, there were also members of the audience who recognized her as "Betsy James, an Irish girl,"[40] who had abandoned her husband and committed adultery along the way, and these folks made their displeasure known by hissing her off the stage. As one of Montez's later biographers wittily noted, her "*première* had thus become her *dernière*."[41]

Though these revelations resulted in Lola's dismissal from Her Majesty's Theater, they also vaulted her to prominence. Abandoning London for the continent, she performed throughout Europe and attracted the attention of a great many notables, including Tsar Nicholas I of Russia and Frederick William IV of Prussia. The former found her charming, the latter declared her a veritable Lorelei.

5. *"Her arms are wicked and her legs are long"* 167

During this tour, Donna Montez also displayed a fiery temper, as well as a propensity for flamboyant behavior. In Berlin, she crashed a review held in honor of the Prussian King and his guest, the Russian Tsar. When a policeman attempted to stop her, she horsewhipped him. During the unveiling of a monument to Beethoven in Bonn, she forced her way into the event's official banquet, jumped on the table, while speeches were being delivered in honor of the composer, and danced for an audience that included Queen Victoria and Prince Albert (Vicky and Bertie were not amused). While visiting the German duchy of Reuss, she showed her displeasure with its ruler, Prince Heinrich LXXII, by riding across his flower beds and decapitating his prize roses. And when Warsaw's chief-of-police attempted to arrest her as an "undesirable," she pulled a pistol on him and instigated a riot that required an armed regiment to suppress. In short, wherever she went, trouble invariably followed.[42]

Lola also left in her wake "more lovers … than the legs of a centipede."[43] A wealthy "admirer" secured her comfortable lodgings in Brussels, her first port of call in Europe after her London fiasco. While touring Germany, she made the acquaintance of composer, Franz Liszt, who became so besotted with her that he dedicated a sonata to their love. During a trip to Russia, she was courted by a Prince Schulkoski, one of the great magnates of St. Petersburg. When this Russian dalliance failed to secure her a royal marriage, she made her way to Paris where she took up with Francis Leigh, a former English Hussar. After running him off with a pistol in a jealous rage, she became the mistress of a wealthy young journalist and newspaper owner named Charles Dujarier. His unfortunate death in a duel, led her back to central Europe where she finally hooked a king.[44]

Before turning to Montez's tumultuous affair with Ludwig I of Bavaria, we should take a moment to consider why men were so mesmerized by her. Though her dancing brought her to the attention of many of her paramours, she was not considered a very accomplished performer. As French writer and critic, Theophile Gautier, noted, "Mademoiselle Lola would do better on horseback than on a stage."[45] Be that as it may,

> Lola Montez was a charmer. There was something—I do not quite know what—about her appearance that was provocative and voluptuous, and which attracted one. She had a white skin, hair suggestive of the tendrils of honeysuckle, and a mouth that could be compared with a pomegranate. Added to this was a ravishing figure, charming feet, and perfect grace. Unfortunately, as a dancer, she had very little talent.[46]

Or, as Aldous Huxley would later note, "When you met Lola Montez, her reputation made you automatically think of bedrooms."

In addition to her obvious sex appeal, people were attracted to Lola Montez because she was a notorious *enfant terrible*. In the same review where he panned her ability as a dancer, Gautier also noted "that the public's curiosity aroused by her altercations with the police of the North and whip-cracking exploits among the Prussian gendarmes has not been satisfied."[47] Indeed, at a time when marriages were still arranged and women remained tethered to hearth and home, the former Marie Gilbert consciously chose to be a "bad girl," a "fallen woman" who reinvented herself as she saw fit, used her looks and sexual charms to advance her interests, and rejected any and all attempts to control her. More to the point, her open and unabashed concupiscence in an era characterized by crinolines and cant must have seemed a veritable tonic to the many men (and not a few women) who crossed her path.

This was certainly the case with King Ludwig I of Bavaria. Upon arriving in Munich in 1846, Montez went directly to the royal palace and demanded an audience with the 60-year-old ruler. A hopeless romantic, who was also no stranger to the ladies, Ludwig agreed to receive her in his private apartments. Accounts of their first meeting tell us that Lola not only danced for the aging monarch, but revealed her breasts to him when he asked her if they were real.[48]

From this moment on, Ludwig admitted to being utterly bewitched, and "in the grip of a passion like never before."[49] Five days after their initial meeting, and following her performance at the state theater, he introduced her to the officials of his court as "my best friend," and ordered them to "see to it that you accord her every possible respect."[50] Over the next 16 months, obeying that command entailed commissioning a portrait of her, which was hung in Ludwig's private "Gallery of Beauties"; making her a citizen of Bavaria; elevating her to the country's nobility as the Countess of Landsfeld; providing her with a generous yearly annuity; and building her a palace in Munich's fashionable Barerstrasse district. At 27, Marie Gilbert James had arrived.

In return for these many favors, Lola became Ludwig's devoted *Maîtresse du Roi* (Mistress of the King). Like a latter-day Pompadour, she coddled and flattered the aging king. She also indulged all of his sexual whims.

> At his request she gave him flannel swatches secreted in her vulva, let him suck her unwashed toes, and talked dirty. She wanted him to "besar [fuck] her with great gusto and pleasure"; she said her "cuno belonged to him."[51]

As Betsy Prioleau notes in her treatment of Lola, Montez was also fond of sharing her *cuno* with her many devotees in the Bavarian capital. When a group of university students founded a fraternity, the Alemmania, in her honor, she dubbed them her *Lolianer* (Lola's harem), and entertained them in her Barerstrasse palace. These entertainments included parties where the Alemmani would strip off their shirts and carry Lola up a crystal staircase to her private apartments, as well as one-on-one trysts with members of the group that she found particularly fetching.

Suffice it to say that in a deeply Catholic and traditional country such as Bavaria these shenanigans were not well received. Lola was shunned in public, "respectable women" were openly disdainful of her, both Bavarian aristocrats and their confreres in the other German states were scandalized by her elevation into their ranks, and Montez's loyal *Lolianer* were often set upon by the many students who regarded their mistress as little more than a whore. As for Ludwig,

> He was bombarded with anonymous letters and warnings, calling Lola by every evil name that occurred to the writers. She was La Pompadour and the Sempronia of Sallust in one, a "voluptuous woman," and a "flame of desire." There were also tearful protests from the higher clergy, who, headed by Archbishop Diepenbrock, were positive that the "dancing woman" was an emissary of Satan ... sent from England to destroy the Catholic religion in Bavaria.[52]

Even the highly respected German nationalist historian Heinrich von Treitschke felt compelled to raise his voice against the "shameless and impudent" Lola Montez. She was, he wrote,

> as insatiable in her voluptuous desires as Sempronia, she could converse with charm among friends; manage mettlesome horses; sing in thrilling fashion; and recite amorous poems in Spanish. The King, an admirer of feminine beauty, yielded to her magic. It was as if she had given him a love philter. For her he forgot himself; he forgot the world; and he even forgot his royal dignity.[53]

All of this ire came to a head when Ludwig insisted on naming Montez the Countess of Landsfeld. Pitched battles between her student supporters and opponents led to the closure of the national university. Three separate cabinets resigned, and a mob descended on Lola's Barerstrasse mansion demanding her blood. The situation was only made worse when Lola appeared on her balcony armed with a glass of champagne in one hand and a box of bon bons in the other. When she toasted her detractors and tossed chocolates at them, the crowd became even angrier and moved to storm the palace; an action that was only averted by the timely appearance of the king himself who escorted his mistress back to the royal palace. Disorder continued in the capital, however, and by March 1848, Lola felt compelled to flee Bavaria for Switzerland. Unable to envision life without her, Ludwig abdicated his throne soon thereafter.

Lola's stint as a royal mistress served to underscore Victorian era fears regarding the dangers attendant on uncontrolled female libidos. Over the course of a year-and-a-half, this Irish adventuress with her full figure and wanton ways was able to "bewitch" a king, and make herself the uncrowned queen of Bavaria. During her rather brief reign, conventional society was scandalized, church and state were at loggerheads, cabinets rose and fell, Munich was paralyzed by riots, and the country was plunged into a revolution that ultimately cost Ludwig I his throne. Indeed, Lola Montez proved herself a "fatal woman" in every sense of the word.

In the years following her affair with Bavaria's king, Lola made her way to the United States and Australia. She toured the outback of both countries, performing before appreciative audiences of prospectors, miners, ranchers, and cowboys. In addition to her usual flamenco numbers, she also introduced her new world patrons to something she called her "Spider Dance." This involved appearing on stage in a short ballet skirt on which hundreds of wire spiders were sewn. When any of these fell off, "she had to indulge in pronounced wriggles and contortions to put them back in position."[54] For the time, these movements were considered quite risqué.

Other than provocative dancing, Montez continued to horsewhip men who angered her, picked up two more husbands, spent some time in the Sierra foothills of California with a pet grizzly bear, wrote a book entitled *The Arts of Beauty or, Secrets of a Lady's Toilet, with Hints to Gentlemen on the Art of Fascinating*, and took to the American lecture circuit. In her capacity as a lecturer, she entertained audiences with presentations on her life, the secrets of seduction, the heroines of history (seductresses in the mold of Agnes Sorel and Catherine the Great), and the physical and intellectual qualities women needed to cultivate in order to play as well, if not better, than men. When she died in 1861 at the age of 39, her life was summed up as follows:

> This was one who, notwithstanding her evil ways, had a share in some public transactions too remarkable to allow her name to be omitted from the list of celebrated persons deceased in the year 1861.
> Born of an English or Irish family of respectable rank, at a very early age the unhappy girl was found to be possessed of the fatal gift of beauty. She appeared for a short time on the stage as a dancer (for which degradation her sorrowing relatives put on mourning, and issued undertakers' cards to signify that she was now dead to them) and blazed forth as the most notorious Paphian in Europe.
> Were this all, these columns would not have included her name. But she exhibited some very remarkable qualities. The natural powers of her mind were considerable. She had a strong will, and a certain grasp of circumstances. Her disposition was generous, and her sympathies very large. These qualities raised the courtesan to a singular position. She became a political influence; and exercised a fascination over sovereigns and ministers more widely extended than has perhaps been possessed by any other member of the demi-monde. She ruled a kingdom; and ruled it, moreover, with dignity and wisdom and ability. The political Hypatia, however, was sacrificed to the rabble. Her power was gone, and she could hope no more from the flattery of statesmen. She became an adventuress of an inferior class. Her intrigues, her duels, and her horse-whippings made her for a time a notoriety in London, Paris, and America.
> Like other celebrated favourites who, with all her personal charms, but without her glimpses of a better human nature, have sacrificed the dignity of

womanhood to a profligate ambition, this one upbraided herself in her last moments on her wasted life; and then, when all her ambition and vanity had turned to ashes, she understood what it was to have been the toy of men and the scorn of women.⁵⁵

Given the trajectory of Lola's life, it is difficult to believe that she would ever have believed it a waste. As even her mid–Victorian obituarist admits, this was no run-of-the-mill lady of the night. In her admittedly brief life, she circled the globe, danced for kings and cowboys, "went through men like cordwood," survived and thrived despite often-dramatic reversals of fortune, and ruled a kingdom. Far from being any man's toy, she made playthings of every male who fell into her orbit. As for remorse, one finds not a sign of it in either her actions, pronouncements, or writings. This was one proud courtesan.

What about the "scorn of women?" Undoubtedly, in the 19th century, Lola's more conventional and respectable sisters found her to be something monstrous. That said, by the latter half of the 20th century, a great many feminists regarded her as a liberated woman of the first rank. Indeed, one suspects lyricist Fred Ebb had the magnificent Montez in mind when he penned the lyrics to his famous song *Cabaret* in which he celebrates the life of a prostitute named Elsie. As the singer of the song makes clear, when this doyen of the demimonde dies she does so with a smile on her face, happy in the knowledge that she has lived her life according to her own rules. So inspired is the song's chanteuse by her friend's example, she decides that when it's her time to die, she too wants to go out like Elsie.

Doubtless Lola Montez would have concurred.

"I hate a woman who gads about and neglects her home": The Femme Fatale as Liberated Woman

The complaint about gadabout women that provides the title for this section was penned by Theognis of Megara, a sixth century BCE Greek poet and moralist. It captures in a very succinct way two deeply ingrained Western prejudices about the place and purpose of women in society. The first of these biases is that females should be confined to a male dominated household. The second is that their primary function is to care for that domicile and fill it with children.

Indeed, other than the fact that they were usurping traditional male roles, femme fatales in the mold of Cleopatra and Lola Montez were particularly worrisome because their lives were not limited to the care and maintenance of a household supervised by men. Instead, they were what Theognis derisively referred to as gadabouts, i.e., restless individuals flitting from one place and/or activity to another in search of power, pleasure, and entertainment. Should such behavior become commonplace among women, it was feared that the very foundations of human society would be undermined.

Given these prejudices and fears, it is not surprising that the suffragist and feminist movements of the modern period were greeted with considerable alarm by members of both sexes across all segments of society. Not only were the adherents of these causes calling for voting rights and equal pay for women, but they also wanted to eliminate the de jure and de facto social, political, economic, and cultural strictures that barred females from higher education, the professions, government, business, and the exercise of executive power. They were, in short, pressing for changes that would allow Western womenfolk to neglect their homes and become peripatetic gadabouts.

Even more worrisome for the opponents of these movements was their widespread appeal. Unlike the other ladies we have examined up to this point, the assorted suffragists and feminists of the late 19th and early 20th centuries were neither potentates nor prostitutes. Instead, they were mothers, wives, workers, intellectuals, artists, and reformers. Nor were these individuals interested in attaining the liberation of women via schemes aimed at dominating or seducing men. Rather, they envisioned a world where both sexes could achieve some measure of self-realization without recourse to either an aristocratic bloodline or the dispensing of sexual favors.

Perhaps no one better exemplified this ideal of liberated womanhood—as well as why it was so threatening to the West's social and sexual status quo—than Isadora Duncan. Dancer, teacher, inveterate bohemian, advocate of women's rights, and Communist sympathizer, Isadora was one of the most revered and reviled women of her time. She abhorred marriage, lived openly with three different men, sired two children out of wedlock, challenged Western dance conventions, and embraced the early Soviet state. For those of her compatriots with a more traditional view of a woman's place in society, she was the devil incarnate.

The youngest of four children, Isadora Duncan was born in San Francisco, California, in 1877. Following the divorce of her parents, Isadora's mother moved her children to Oakland where she tried to support them by teaching piano and knitting assorted caps and jackets for stores in the area. Looking back on this period, Duncan recalled:

> My mother was abandoned to fate with four small children on her hands. Although she was an educated woman, she was barely able to earn a bit of bread for herself and her children by giving music lessons. Her earnings were small and not enough to feed us. Whenever I remember my childhood, I see before me an empty house. With my mother at her lessons, we children sat by ourselves, generally hungry, and in winters generally cold.[56]

5. "Her arms are wicked and her legs are long"   173

Bereft of the toys and carefree fun normally associated with childhood, Isadora gravitated toward dance at a very early age. In her memoirs, she tells us that she was fond of going alone into the woods or down to the beach by the San Francisco Bay, stripping off her clothes, and moving in sync with the breaking waves and swaying trees. By age four, she was actually doing this kind of improvisational dancing for her neighbors. At six, she and her older sister Elizabeth, were supplementing the family income by giving dance lessons to local children.[57]

Growing up in an impoverished family supported by a single mother was also a radicalizing influence on Isadora. As she later noted:

> My mother was still young and beautiful but, cursed with the narrow bourgeois principles, she did not know how to use either her youth or beauty or indomitable intelligence or strength. She was in the prisonhouse of the days before the Emancipation of Women. Sentimental and virtuous, she could only suffer and weep.[58]

Weeping was not how Isadora chose to respond to the plight of her mother. Instead, she vowed at the tender age of 12 that she "would live to fight against marriage and for the emancipation of women and for the right for every woman to have a child or children as it pleased her, and to uphold her right and her virtue."[59]

In 1895, at the age of 18, with her mother in tow, Isadora set off for Chicago to make a name for herself in the world of dance. Though nothing materialized in the "Windy City," she did obtain an introduction to a New York theatrical producer by the name of Augustin Daly who was passing through town. He offered her a job, and over the next two years Duncan performed as a pantomime player in popularized renderings of Shakespeare plays, stories by Sir Walter Scott, and assorted productions with names like *Mme. Pygmalion* and *Geisha*. This experience left her with "a perfect nausea for the theatre: the continual repetition of the same words and the same gestures, night after night, and the caprices, the way of looking at life."[60]

Isadora's encounter with the American dance scene of the time was equally unsatisfying. Whereas Duncan viewed dancing as "the art that gives expression to the human soul through movement,"[61] her countrymen saw it as little more than a diversion or an entertainment. Indeed, insofar as dancers were featured on a stage at all, they were either ballet performers decked out in restricted garments executing a set of rigidly prescribed movements and pirouettes, or *danseuses* like Lola Montez, attired in scanty skirts putting on erotic or highly suggestive "spider dances." The kind of flowing, free improvisational movements that Isadora had perfected during her childhood in Oakland were nowhere to be found.

Unhappy with her lot in America, Isadora gathered up her family and booked passage for them on a cattle boat to England in 1899. Once settled in

London, she and her brother Raymond immersed themselves in the British Museum's vast collection of ancient Greek vases and bas-reliefs. They found these artifacts deeply inspirational, so much so that Duncan now opted to dress and dance only in a "Grecian mode," i.e., in loose fitting tunics, robes, silk veils, and, when not barefoot, sandals.

Other than examining ancient amphora with her brother, Isadora also spent considerable time in Kensington Gardens dancing amongst the flowers. It was during one of these impromptu performances that she made the acquaintance of Mrs. Patrick Campbell, the toast of the London stage. This actress was so impressed by Duncan's natural and unrehearsed movements that she took her under wing and introduced her to the city's cultural and social celebrities.

Success soon followed. Isadora's dance interpretations of various myths and musical compositions, usually barefoot and in loose fitting tunics that bared her arms and legs, were unlike anything that had ever graced the London stage. While some Londoners were positively scandalized by her free moving highly visible flesh, most were charmed. Indeed, by the end of 1900, her dance engagements were netting audiences that included no less a figure than the future Edward VII.[62]

This London success was soon followed up by a tour of Europe that included stops in Paris, Berlin, Budapest, Vienna, Munich, and Athens. Though critics in these cities were often less than laudatory about Isadora's performances, this did little to deter people from wanting to see her dance. Indeed, everywhere she went, enthusiastic fans greeted her. Students bedecked her carriages in flowers and escorted them through the streets. Artists, such as Auguste Rodin, Antoine Bourdelle, and Walter Schott, wanted to paint, draw, and sculpt her. The European intelligentsia vied for her attention.

Though her public performances were highly successful, Isadora viewed them as secondary to her real mission in life, which was "to restore the dance to its former high level of art."[63] Towards this end, she established in 1904 an Isadora Duncan School of Dance in a house she purchased in Berlin's Grunewald district. Though this institution would only last for three years and never counted more than 20 students in residence, it established the pattern for the three other schools that Duncan would found over the course of her career.

Isadora's pupils were young girls between the ages of four and eight from disadvantaged backgrounds where mothers were the primary breadwinners. They lived at the school, and their meals, housing, clothing, training, and education were free of charge. In return, they worked from 6:30 AM until the evening meal exercising on ballet barres, receiving instruction in gymnastics, learning the many different forms of the dance, and taking lessons

5. "Her arms are wicked and her legs are long" 175

in history, literature, mathematics, natural science, drawing, singing, languages, and music. They also spent a lot of time outdoors studying the surrounding environment.[64]

Duncan hoped that these lessons and exercises would create women that were self-sufficient, independent, and aware of the world around them. She also hoped that this regimen would help them "rediscover in its ideal form the beautiful rhythmic movements of the human body" and in so doing "resuscitate an art that has lain dormant for two thousand years."[65] In short, she was bent on creating a lot of gad about girls that were likely to neglect their homes.

While Isadora's dancing style and ideas regarding the education of women were unconventional and raised not a few eyebrows, her private life was nothing short of scandalous. From 1904 to 1908, she lived openly with the English stage designer Gordon Craig, who was the father of her first child Deirdre. When this relationship ended, she took up with Paris Singer, the American heir to a sewing machine fortune, with whom she had a second child, Patrick. Following the tragic death of her two children in a 1913 automobile accident, Duncan parted ways with Singer, and attempted to have a third child out of wedlock with a young Italian sculptor by the name of Romano Romanelli. Though she became pregnant, the baby died soon after birth.

Suffice it to say that all of these affairs and illegitimate children were grist for the penny press. As with present day celebrities, Isadora was dogged remorselessly by journalists seeking news about her love life. Though she deplored this invasion of her privacy, she would not back down in her defiance of what she regarded as oppressive social conventions. Indeed, many more lovers followed Romanelli, and the fourth estate gleefully expended ink on each one.

What ultimately turned the public against Isadora, however, was her embrace of Soviet Russia. In 1920, she was invited by the fledgling Bolshevik government to come to Moscow and open a school of her own. The Communist regime promised her a building, students, and resources sufficient to support her activities. It was an offer Duncan simply could not refuse.

Soon after her arrival in the Soviet capital, Duncan made the acquaintance of the Russian poet Sergei Aleksandrovich Esenin. Though he was 17 years her junior, the two became lovers. In 1922, they also became husband and wife so that he could join her in a tour of the United States that was intended to win public opinion over to the support of the new Soviet state.

Unfortunately, Isadora's American tour achieved the opposite effect. The U.S. was in the first of what would be many "red scares," and Duncan and her husband were regarded as little more than Communist agents. This suspicion was only strengthened when Esenin, a heavy drinker, would display red banners from the windows of the halls where Isadora was performing and drunkenly shout "Long live Bolshevism!" to people in the streets.

Matters only went from bad to worse on October 22nd when Isadora performed in Boston. While dancing to Tchaikovsky's Symphony No. 6 (the *Pathétique*), she raised a red Liberty scarf high over her head and shouted: "This is red! So am I! ... You were once wild here! Don't let them tame you!"[66] At the same moment, either by accident or design—accounts disagree—Duncan's breasts were exposed to the audience and she cried out: "You don't know what beauty is! This—this is beauty!"[67]

Both those attending her performance and the press begged to disagree. Most of her audience fled the theater, and newspapers across the nation greeted their readers with headlines such as "I'm Red! Cries Isadore Duncan. Stage Remarks Follow Repulsive Dance. Audience Is Disgusted!"

Another reporter noted, "She looked pink, talked red, and acted scarlet!"[68]

Though she managed to complete her tour, the damage was done. When she left the United States four months later, most of her countrymen regarded her as both a dangerous radical and a woman of loose morals. The U.S. government also concurred with this judgment and stripped her of her American citizenship on the grounds that she had forfeited it when she married Esenin. When her ship departed from New York, she waved a red scarf at the assembled press and pledged never to return. She never did.

The last few years of Duncan's life are rather sad. Her relationship with Esenin, stormy even in the best of times, deteriorated as he sank deeper into alcoholism and depression. Returning to Russia without her, he committed suicide in 1925.

As for Isadora, she retreated to the French Riviera where she lived a rather precarious existence. She drank heavily, relied on the kindness of friends who kept her housed and fed, gave the occasional interview, and worked on her memoir, *My Life*, which was never completed. On September 14, 1927, she met with a fatal accident when a scarf she was wearing became entangled in the rear wheel of a sports car in which she was riding. Just prior to her death, she cried out to her friends, "*Adieu, mes amis, je vais à la gloire!*" (Good-bye, my friends, I go to glory!) Actually, she was heading for what she hoped would be a romantic tryst with the car's driver, a garage owner named Bénoit Falchetto. All in all a dramatic and fitting end to a life always lived on its own terms.

Isadora Duncan was, without question, an acclaimed and significant artist. Her work and performances paved the way for the modern interpretive dance of Martha Graham, Mary Wigman, and a great many other directors and designers. At the time of her death, she was already a cult figure to Western intellectuals, writers, artists, and their bohemian imitators.

This said, she was also reviled by the public-at-large. For those who embraced a more traditional notion of a woman's place and role in society, she was little more than an advocate of free love, who lived and conducted herself like a whore. Her relationships and the children she bore out of wedlock were seen as a direct assault on the institution of marriage and motherhood, and Isadora would have agreed with her many critics on that score. Perhaps the following lines of André Maurois with regard to the French novelist, George Sand, are also applicable to Duncan, and explain to some degree why many regarded her as a very bad girl:

> Though not technically a chaste woman, she always looked upon an alliance as a marriage. She gave herself freely, entrusted herself wholly. She behaved like an honourable man.[69]

"Women are tired of being good all the time": The Problem of Female Bad Behavior

In a lecture she delivered on the problem of female bad behavior in literature, author Margaret Atwood noted that the advent of feminism raised the question of whether or not it was appropriate to continue to people the pages of novels and plays with "spotty handed villainesses" like Lady Macbeth. After all,

> is it not today—well, somehow unfeminist—to depict a woman behaving badly? Isn't bad behaviour supposed to be the monopoly of men? Isn't that what we are expected—in defiance of real life—to somehow believe, now? When bad women get into literature, what are they doing there, and are they permissible, and what, if anything, do we need them for?[70]

Her answer to these questions is that stories do indeed need bad girls who sleep their way to the top, seduce men for fun and profit, and flout social conventions without remorse. Not only are such characters necessary to the trajectory of a great many narratives, but they actually exist in life, and this being the case they should definitely show up in literature. Atwood also notes that there is more to women "than virtue. They are fully dimensional human beings; they too have subterranean depths; why shouldn't their many-dimensionality be given literary expression?"[71]

When we move from the world of fiction to that of fact, we are confronted with a very similar question, i.e., in the wake of the emancipation of women is it appropriate to regard the *Machtweibern*, seductresses, and liberated ladies of the past as villainous femme fatales? Especially in light of the fact that

> feminist analysis made some kinds of behaviour available to female characters, which, under the old dispensation—the pre-feminist one—would have been

considered bad, but under the new one were praiseworthy. A female character could rebel against social strictures without then having to throw herself in front of a train like Anna Karenina; she could think the unthinkable and say the unsayable; she could flout authority. She could do new bad-good things, such as leaving her husband and even deserting her children. Such activities and emotions, however, were—according to the new moral thermometer of the times—not really bad at all; they were good, and the women who did them were praiseworthy.[72]

While the three women addressed in the foregoing sections were not above bad behavior—Cleopatra was complicit in the murder of her siblings; Lola Montez was guilty of fraud and bigamy; Isadora left more than one bill unpaid—they also did much that was praiseworthy both in their own time and ours. When they were alive even their fiercest critics acknowledged their charm, charisma, and passion. Today a great many people, especially women, admire and even attempt to emulate them.

Whether one sees them as heroines or villainesses, however, during the times in which they lived, they were regarded, fairly or not, as agents of discord and disorder. In the wake of Cleopatra's successful courtship of Caesar and Antony followed civil war and the extinction of Egyptian independence. Lola's seduction of Ludwig plunged Bavaria into revolution and cost its king his throne. Duncan's dances and dalliances scandalized two continents and helped usher in an emancipation of women that continues to roil the West nearly a century after her death. In their time, they were what Huysmans says of Salome in the chapter's opening epigraph:

> The symbolic incarnation of world-old Vice, the goddess of immortal Hysteria, the Curse of Beauty supreme above all other beauties ... indifferent, irresponsible, insensible, poisoning.

They were, in short, women who were tired of being good all the time.

PART THREE

The Bad Seed
The Villain as Pathology

There are six things that the LORD strongly dislikes, seven that are an abomination to him: haughty eyes, a lying tongue, and hands that shed innocent blood, a heart that plots wicked schemes, feet that run swiftly to evil, the false witness who utters lies, and he who sows discord among brothers.
—Proverbs 6:16–19

Laudable as it may be to share your bread with beggars, you cannot trust everyone you meet along the road. Some strangers may turn into princes and good fairies; but others may be wolves and witches, and there is no sure way to tell them apart.
—Robert Darnton, *The Great Cat Massacre*

"These sociopaths," he said, "What do they feel like? Inside?" Isabel smiled. "Unmoved," she said. "They feel unmoved. Look at a cat when it does something wrong. It looks quite unmoved. Cats are sociopaths, you see. It's their natural state."
—Alexander McCall Smith, *The Sunday Philosophy Club*

Honestly, I don't understand why people get so worked up about a little murder!
—Patricia Highsmith, *Ripley Under Ground*

One of the great commercial successes of the 1950s was a psychological thriller by American writer William March entitled *The Bad Seed*. In March's novel, a mother named Christine Penmark discovers that her seemingly normal eight-year-old daughter, Rhoda, is a cold-blooded serial killer. The event that leads to Christine's discovery of her daughter's murderous nature is the drowning of Claude Daigle, one of Rhoda's classmates, at a school picnic. Christine later learns that this "accident" occurred after an argument between Claude and Rhoda over a penmanship medal he won, but which she regards as rightfully hers. Despite witnesses, Rhoda denies having been anywhere near Claude, and this lie triggers in Christine's mind memories of other troubling tragedies associated with her daughter.

Tellingly, these incidents also involved "accidents." One was the family dog falling to its death from an apartment window when Rhoda had grown tired of caring for the pet. Then there was an elderly babysitter who tripped down a flight of stairs and broke her neck after promising the girl a necklace in the event of her death.

Christine's suspicions are confirmed when she witnesses her daughter setting fire to the local caretaker, a less than savory fellow who sees through Rhoda's "innocent charm," and is convinced that she murdered the Daigle boy. When Christine finally confronts Rhoda about her crimes, the eight-year-old first denies her guilt, and then tries to manipulate her mother's affection for her. When she finally acknowledges that she did indeed kill the dog, the babysitter, and Claude, she insists that they were to blame for what befell them, i.e., her pet was annoying, the elderly lady did promise her a locket if she died, and everyone knew she deserved that best penmanship medal.

Suffice it to say that Christine is traumatized by the realization that her daughter is a remorseless cold-blooded murderer. Further, over the course of her investigation into Rhoda's crimes, Christine also learns that she herself was adopted, and that her real birth mother was a notorious serial killer by the name of Bessie Denker. Believing herself guilty for having passed on her "bad seed" to Rhoda, Christine feeds her daughter an overdose of sleeping pills and shoots herself. Unfortunately, while the mother dies, her murderous offspring survives to kill another day.

March's novel was both a critical and commercial success. His book was turned into a play that ran for 334 performances on Broadway, and was nominated for the Pulitzer Prize. Nancy Kelly, the actress who played Christine Penmark, went on to win the 1955 Tony Award for Best Actress in a Play, and Peggy McCormack, the child actress who played her daughter, Rhoda, was lauded for her performance.

Both women went on to star in the same roles in a 1956 black and white film version of the novel, which was produced by Warner Bothers and directed by Mervyn LeRoy. The movie was a box office hit. It grossed $4.1 million (a considerable sum in the 50s, especially for a black and white picture), and earned four Academy Award nominations, i.e., Best Actress, Best Actress in a Supporting Role (two nominees in this category), and Best Cinematography (Black and White). As with the Tonys, Nancy Kelly's portrayal of Christine Penmark won her the 1956 Academy Award for Best Actress.

 . Both the subject matter and the success of *The Bad Seed* speak very much to the subject of this section—the assorted villains responsible for so much of the chronic crime in our societies. Like Rhoda, these criminals commit their assorted misdeeds in a cold-blooded, premeditated manner without the slightest hint of remorse for the pain their actions inflict on others. Indeed, March's antagonist is a classic example of what the psychiatric profession first labeled a sociopath in the early half of the 20th century.

As with Rhoda, such a person appears to be both normal and free of any overt mental illness. He or she is also intelligent and capable of great charm. That said, as the second epigraph of this introduction reminds us, appearances can and often are deceiving. Like March's murderous antagonist, the sociopath also sees the rest of us as cats do birds and mice, as objects to be used, abused, and discarded as they see fit.

March's notion that there is some kind of genetic anomaly, or "bad seed," at work with these criminals is also a theory that has gained considerable credibility over the last half century. Though no one denies the importance of a person's social environment in determining how their genetic predisposition may be expressed, there is also agreement that many of these remorseless predators are, like Rhoda, from seemingly normal families and communities. In fact, as the following chapters attest, it is highly likely that a brain scan of *The Bad Seed*'s young villainess would reveal her to have low levels of serotonin, high levels of testosterone, and dysfunctional areas of the brain associated with empathy and feelings of remorse.

The phenomenal success of *The Bad Seed* speaks to another concern of this section, which is the ongoing fascination of the modern public-at-large with those who are regarded by all Western and non–Western cultures alike as the very embodiment of an abominable pathology. Since March's novel, and the various stage and screen adaptations of it, there have been almost 70 years of widespread morbid interest in assorted gangsters, grifters, rippers, and rapists whose crimes quite literally underscore what it means to be a lawful, decent, honest, empathic, and normal human being. Indeed, whether one is speaking of fiction, film, television drama, documentaries, or true crime stories, the villainy with which this section is concerned has become a multi-billion dollar growth industry. Why this is so and what it may portend for our societies are questions addressed in what follows.

March's novel and its successors to the side, it should be noted that while it has become fashionable in psychiatric circles to speak of all of the criminal types treated here as "antisocial personality types," this section distinguishes between sociopaths and what it labels psychopathic murderers. While both groups share many of the same behavioral and neurological characteristics, sociopaths are much like March's Rhoda. They are capable of murder, and are sometimes guilty of it, but killing is not a compulsion. Rather, it is what one might label an occupational hazard, i.e., something they feel compelled to do in order to acquire something they want, usually money. These are the so-called gangsters and grifters addressed in Chapter Six.

For the psychopathic murderer, however, killing is the be-all and end-all of their existence. For reasons that are still not completely understood, these individuals have a deep-seated, perhaps hard-wired, compulsion to seek out, stalk, capture, subdue, and murder strangers. They kill multiple times, in different places, usually with some cooling off period in between homicides. Unlike their sociopathic confreres, however, these serial killers do not commit their crimes for reasons of profit. Rather, they act as they do out of a desire to exercise domination and control over another human being. These are the rippers and rapists treated in Chapter Seven.

It should be noted here that whatever their label, the individuals addressed in the following pages are fully aware of the fact that their actions fly in the face of all moral and social strictures. A great many, in fact most sociopathic individuals, as well as a majority of those raised in the environmental conditions that often give rise to psychopathic serial killers, are not criminals. While they may not understand what they regard as "other people's confusing and emotion-driven social cues," they can distinguish between acceptable and unacceptable social behavior, and are capable, often with great difficulty, of living reasonably normal lives. This said, those among them who are incapable or unwilling to abide by those basic guidelines, perhaps best summarized in commandments six, eight, nine and ten of the Decalogue, are among the most frightening of the many villains addressed in this work.

6

Gangsters and Grifters
The Villain as Sociopath

> Sociopaths are "outstanding" members of society in two senses: politically, they draw our attention because of the inordinate amount of crime they commit, and psychologically they hold our fascination because most of us cannot fathom the cold, detached way they repeatedly harm and manipulate others.
>
> —Linda Mealey, *The Sociobiology of Sociopathy*

> I am a Sociopath. Remorse is alien to me. I have a penchant for deceit. I am generally free of entangling and irrational emotions. I am strategic and canny, intelligent and confident, but I also struggle to react appropriately to other people's confusing and emotion-driven social cues.
>
> —Diagnosed sociopath M. E. Thomas, author, law professor, and founder of Sociopathworld.com

> This biting of their toenails over what is the cause of badness is what turns me into a fine laughing malchik. They don't go into what is the cause of goodness, so why of the other shop. If lewdies are good that's because they like it, and I wouldn't interfere with their pleasures—and I was patronizing the other shop. Badness is of the self, the one, the you or me on our oddy knockies and that self is made by old Bog or God and is his great pride. But the not-self cannot have the bad, meaning they of the government and the judges and the schools cannot allow the bad because they cannot allow the self. And is not our modern history, my brothers, the story of brave malenky selves fighting these big machines? I am serious with you, brothers, over this. But what I do I do because I like to do.
>
> —Anthony Burgess, *A Clockwork Orange*

In Anthony Burgess' groundbreaking novel, *A Clockwork Orange*, readers are introduced to an urban society where gangs of stylishly dressed young men speak in a rhyming patois derived from Russian, congregate in so-called "milk bars," imbibe drug-laced dairy drinks, and roam the streets and surrounding suburbs in search of the old "in-out, in-out" and "ultra-violence." These latter activities involve brutal assaults on defenseless pedestrians and vagrants, savage street combat with other bands of likeminded thugs, and "surprise visits" that entail breaking into homes and then beating and raping the people living in them. All of this mayhem is lovingly described by the novel's narrator, a young man named Alex, who is the de facto leader of a particularly nasty group of "droogs" (mates) named Georgie, Pete, and Dim.

All of these individuals are fully aware of the fact that their actions are illegal and regarded as bad by society-at-large, and yet these strictures fail to deter them. Nor is their anti-social behavior driven by considerations of economic deprivation, political oppression, ideology, or social class. Alex hails from a comfortable home with two working parents who accede to his every wish. Though he has been something of a delinquent his whole life, he enjoys the services of a social worker intent on his rehabilitation. He has access to education and training, there are employment opportunities, and he is the citizen of a social welfare state governed by an elected government that accepts both freedom of speech and the press. He is by no means a victim of domestic abuse (though he visits it on his mother and father from time to time), a broken family, abject poverty, bigotry, or police brutality (at least not during the time in which he commits his crimes).

Why then do he and his droogs engage in these heinous actions? In part, they appear to be motivated by simple greed. Preying on helpless men and women affords them easy access to the money they need to pay for their wardrobes, designer drugs, and, in Alex's case, predilection for the high quality classical music of Ludwig van and company. Their ill-gotten gains also allow them to secure alibis from assorted barflies who frequent their favorite clubs, and are only too happy to trade false testimony to the police for free drinks and pub grub.

As this chapter's last epigraph makes clear, however, Alex does what he does because he believes *badness* to be his God-given nature, and, most importantly, he *enjoys* being bad. Whether it's *tolchocking* (hitting) one of his mates, stomping a vagrant, raping a *ptitsa* (woman), or slashing another gang member, violence excites him and affords him an electrifying *frisson*, or thrill. Even when listening to classical music and reading the Bible, his thoughts invariably turn to murder and mayhem. Indeed, Alex and his mates appear to be hardwired for deceitful, cruel, and predatory behavior.

The unsavory protagonist of *Clockwork Orange* is highlighted here because Alex is a perfect example of the sociopathic villains that are the subject of this chapter. Like him, these individuals are responsible for a considerable amount of the crime in their communities. They rob, steal, cheat, lie, beat, rape, and kill people, and they act in this manner fully aware of the fact that their conduct is regarded as morally and legally wrong by the societies in which they live and work. Also like Burgess' narrator, these sociopaths enjoy their criminal conduct, take pride in it, and, as with the above quoted sociopath, M. E. Thomas, are perplexed by other "people's confusing and emotion driven" aversion to their behavior.

As will be made clear in what follows, sociopaths also share a number of other behavioral attributes that make them fitting candidates for inclusion in any study of villainy.

They tend to be arrogant, callous, dominant, superficial, and manipulative. Their tempers are short and their capacity to form emotional bonds limited. They are completely lacking in empathy for others, and experience no guilt or remorse for the suffering they inflict on their victims. Like Alex and his droogs, they also behave in an irresponsible and impulsive manner that ignores and/or openly violates social conventions and mores.

It should be noted here that not all sociopaths are criminals, and most lawbreakers are not sociopathic. M. E. Thomas, the diagnosed sociopath quoted in the second epigraph, is a highly successful writer, professor, and lawyer with a webpage that celebrates his pathology. Frank W. Abagnale, one of the great con men of the late 20th century, is now a family man and the owner of a very successful secure documents corporation. While they may be deceitful and nonempathic, these folks can distinguish between acceptable and unacceptable social behavior and are capable of living reasonably normal lives.

That said, sociopaths perpetrate an inordinate amount of the crime committed in Western countries. In the United States, for example, where roughly four percent of the population is believed to be sociopathic (three perfect male, one perfect female), individuals who closely match the personality profile of the sociopath comprise 20 percent of the prison population and between 33 percent and 80 percent of chronic criminal offenders. Indeed, these individuals are believed to account for over 50 percent of all U.S. crimes.[1]

Despite this propensity for criminal behavior, or perhaps because of it, these individuals also enjoy a certain notoriety in Western culture. Picaresque literature—*Lazarillo de Tormes, Simplicius Simplicissimus, Moll Flanders, The History of Tom Jones, The Luck of Barry Lyndon, Vanity Fair, Flashman*— actually celebrates the misdeeds of assorted sociopathic servants, thieves, whores, gamblers, soldiers of fortune, and imposters. In these works, and others like them, authors use the decidedly dicey lives of knaves and scoundrels to highlight the moral hypocrisy of society's middle and upper classes, the sufferings of the poor, the horrors of slavery, and the monumental ineptitude and callous indifference to human life of so many of history's "great men."

In the 20th and 21st centuries, writers, television producers, and filmmakers have increasingly shown an inordinate fondness for actual outlaws whose sole motivation for wrongdoing was greed and whose only claim to fame was success in satisfying their avarice. Some of the notable criminals singled out for star treatment have been William Pierce, the mastermind of the great gold heist of 1855; Depression era bank robbers Bonny and Clyde; racketeers Al Capone, Legs Diamond, and Dutch Schultz; and the already mentioned forger, trickster, and imposter Frank Abagnale, Jr. Despite the fact that these individuals acted out of pure selfishness, and never shared their ill-gotten gains with anyone save themselves, they have all been celebrated as latter-day rebels and Robin Hoods. More to the point, the books, programs, and movies inspired by their careers have been well-received by the public-at-large. To paraphrase Mel Brooks, these days it's good to be a sociopath.

Why this is so is one of the issues to be addressed in what follows. Before turning to that query, however, we need to arrive at a clearer understanding of sociopathy itself. What do we mean when we speak of this condition, and how is it different (or not) from the psychopathy addressed in the next chapter? How are those diagnosed as sociopaths different from the population-at-large, and what is it about their personality traits and behavior patterns that mark them as "mad, bad, and dangerous to know?" Finally, what are the biological and environmental factors that play a role in making someone an "unprincipled scoundrel naturally disposed to base or criminal actions, or deeply involved in the commission of disgraceful crimes?"[2]

We will attempt to answer these questions in the following sections. The first of these will take a look at what psychologists, sociobiologists, and neuro scientists have uncovered in their researches into the traits, origins, and genetics of sociopathic behavior. This overview is then followed by case studies of two convicted felons and sociopaths: Mafia racketeer Joseph Valachi, and serial imposter Christian Karl Gerhartsreiter. Following this excursion into the world of gangsters and grifters, we will then return to the whole fraught question of why the villains addressed in this chapter are now celebrated by many as either heroic or anti-heroic figures.

"My name is legion, for we are many": Identifying and Explaining Sociopathy

Sociopathy is a term that appears to have been coined in 1909 by Karl Birnbaum, a German biological psychiatrist. It entered into widespread currency in 1930 when an American educational psychologist by the name of George E. Partridge recommended its use to describe socially maladjusted behavior characterized by actions that adversely affect others. In using this expression, both men were seeking an alternative to "psychopathy," a word derived from the Greek *psyche* (soul) and *pathos* (suffering), which was used to identify a wide range of mental disorders, including those involving the violation of social norms.[3]

For Birnbaum, Partridge, and others who followed their lead, sociopaths are individuals engaged in recurrent antisocial and criminal behavior. On an interpersonal level, these persons tend to be arrogant, superficially charming, extremely deceitful, irresponsible, lacking in guilt or remorse, and adept at conning others. Socially, they are prone to parasitic lifestyles, impulsivity, poor behavioral controls, juvenile delinquency, and habitual wrongdoing. Despite these traits, people with sociopathic personalities are capable of recognizing—if not understanding—the moral conventions of their respective societies. More to the point, depending on the social context within which they are born and raised, sociopaths are also able to behave in a non-psychopathological manner.[4]

Though many of these personality traits and antisocial behaviors can be, and are, applied to those labeled psychopaths, the term "sociopath" tends to be favored by psychologists and sociologists who believe that social conditions and early childhood environments are the agencies most responsible for people afflicted with this disorder. These professionals also prefer this term because of the popular association of psychopathy with "psychotics," i.e., individuals suffering from severe mental disturbances characterized by hallucinations, delusions, serial violence, and a complete lack of empathy or conventional morality. Further, as will become clear in the following chapter, those who study and treat chronically violent and/or murderous individuals tend to label them "psychopaths," and consider their behavior to be an innate characteristic that is the product of a complex set of biological, neurological, genetic, and environmental factors.

Despite these efforts to distinguish the two mental disorders from one another, both terms are often used interchangeably to describe the same complex of behaviors. In part, this has to do with the decision in the 1980s by both the American Psychiatric Association (APA) and the World Health Organization (WHO) to subsume both sociopathy and psychopathy under new more general categories. The former opted to dub these conditions "antisocial personality disorder" (ASPD) in its *Diagnostic and Statistical Manual of Mental Disorders* (DSMD), while the latter agency grouped them together as "dissocial personality disorder" (DPI) in the WHO's *International Classification of Diseases* (ICD).

It goes without saying that this disparate and often overlapping psychological nomenclature is confusing to the lay public. Nor are matters helped by the fact that the APA's ASPD and the WHO's DPI are also associated with paranoid, schizophrenic, narcissistic, histrionic, borderline, obsessive-compulsive, avoidant, and dependent personality disorders. Indeed, even professionals in the field of psychology often disagree on this matter, with some insisting that there are distinctive differences between sociopaths and psychopaths, and others arguing that they are merely two sides of the same coin. "We are legion," a demon tells Jesus when asked to identify himself, and much the same thing could be said about the difficulty of naming the individuals treated in this section.[5]

For the sake of simplicity and clarity, we will consider sociopaths and psychopaths to be two distinctive types. While acknowledging that these individuals do indeed share many of the same behavioral and neurological characteristics, this chapter treats sociopathy as a milder form of antisocial personality disorder characterized by a range of so-called "sinister" traits that are not necessarily criminal, nor beyond the capacity of the sociopath to control. Further, taking a leaf from psychologists Richard Christie, John W. McHoskey, and others, it also labels these sociopathic attributes Machiavellian, after the 16th century political theorist, Niccolo Machiavelli, who wrote extensively about the often unscrupulous and manipulative behavior of assorted Western statesmen.

According to Christie and company, Machiavellian personalities are individuals who

- consider their fellow human beings as objects to be manipulated, rather than as people with whom to empathize.
- are indifferent to conventional morality and consider deceit and other forms of miscreant behavior to be acceptable.
- do not manifest any obvious psychopathology, i.e., they are capable of behaving in a socially acceptable manner.
- eschew ideology, or any kind of idealism, in favor of purely self-interested actions.

While the majority of individuals who exhibit these "sinister" traits do not behave in a criminal manner, those that do are responsible for a considerable amount of the crime committed in the West, and they also tend to be chronic criminals. It is this subset of professional miscreants we are examining here.[6]

Who are these folks and why are they so prone to criminal antisocial behavior? During the ancient and medieval periods, the pat answer to this question would have been that these individuals were low born, ignoble persons unbounded by the accepted codes of aristocratic conduct and therefore "naturally disposed to base or criminal" activities. When Europe entered into Christian receivership after the collapse of the Roman Empire, both Catholic and Orthodox clergy acknowledged there were also scoundrels and unprincipled knaves to be counted among the nobility. However, being well born themselves, these clerics continued to subscribe to the notion that society's reprobates were found largely among the *vileins* of the world, who, in addition to being ignoble, were also simpleminded and easily tempted by Satan and his minions.

As the picaresque literature alluded to in the introduction attests, the modern period was more accepting of the idea that recurring antisocial and criminal behavior could be found among all classes of people. Further, the rise of Enlightenment era science and skepticism called into question the idea that individuals who behaved in this fashion were doing so because of some demonic influence. Nevertheless, despite these shifts in the West's intellectual landscape, the philosophes and scientists of the 18th and 19th centuries continued to see career criminals, cheats, and sharps as persons who largely hailed from the lower strata of Western society. Unlike their predecessors, however, these "enlightened" savants also attributed this misconduct to the less than savory environmental conditions in which peasants and urban laborers found themselves at this time. In their view, it was "social suffering" (sociopathy), rather than breeding and piety, which was responsible for criminal behavior. They also reasoned that if there were persons among the immiserated masses who were non-empathic, deceitful, manipulative, and prone to violence and chronic law breaking, it was because these traits allowed them to survive in impoverished, crime ridden, and violent communities where altruism, honesty, and the Golden Rule were in short supply.

This idea that society's miscreants were primarily people attempting to cope with highly stressful environments was widely embraced by 20th century social scientists. Not only did it appear to provide a clear answer as to who these newly minted "sociopaths" were, and where they came from, but it also proffered an explanation for their behavior that was not rooted in religious superstition or aristocratic prejudice. Further, if this mental disorder was essentially social in nature, then it was also possible to treat it by rectifying the poverty, domestic abuse, ignorance, and oppression responsible for it.

There were of course a number of problems with the notion that those guilty of recurrent criminal behavior were the products of lower class dysfunctional families and communities. Not the least of these was the simple fact that sociopaths are not concentrated in any one particular strata of society. While it is true that a great many criminals hail from the "wrong side of the tracks," and do indeed resort to crime as a means of addressing assorted social inequities and environmental pressures, the overwhelming majority of these individuals do not fit the sociopathic personality profile, i.e., they are capable of empathy, they do feel remorse or guilt for their actions, and, most importantly, they are neither inclined, nor likely to be, chronic criminals.[7]

Indeed, a great many of the sociopaths addressed here are from what can only be described as positive environments. Christian Carl Gerhartsreiter, the serial imposter and murderer addressed below, grew up in a prosperous, crime-free Bavarian village, in a stable home, with warm, loving parents. Many other predatory businessmen, corrupt politicians, or unethical and amoral professionals guilty of victimizing their clients, patients, and the general public also hail from similar backgrounds.[8]

Sociopaths are also still present in European social welfare states—Great Britain, France, Italy, the Benelux countries, Germany, Switzerland, Scandinavia—which have largely dispensed with the gross inequities and widespread human misery that were commonplace in Europe prior to the 20th century. Despite the fact that children in these countries are well-fed, housed, adequately clothed, educated, and have access to excellent health care services, gangs remain a fixture of urban life, and cons, carried out by clever grifters of one stripe or another, continue to be a staple of the popular press. As Anthony Burgess observed in *Clockwork Orange*, whatever the social environment, there appear to be people like Alex and his droogs who are just "bad to the bone."

Because of advances in genetics, neuroscience, and brain imaging, we now know that sociopaths are in fact hardwired to behave in socially inappropriate ways that have adverse effects on others. This has been demonstrated by magnetic resonance imaging (MRI) of the neural activity of career criminals and clinically diagnosed psychopaths, which has revealed that the brains of these individuals are markedly different from those of non-sociopaths. Specifically, these MRIs show deficiencies in such areas as the corpus collosum, a kind of nerve highway between the brain's left and right hemispheres; the amygdala and hippocampus, two of the brain's oldest organs responsible for anger, fear, and memory; and the prefrontal cortex, which enables us to exercise social control and appreciate the consequences of our actions. Damage or dysfunction to any one of these brain centers is known to cause antisocial behavior, problems with all of them are likely to produce personalities that are empathically impaired, lacking in fear or anxiety, incapable of learning from punishment, and bereft of conscience.[9]

Why the brains of socio and psychopaths are configured in this manner is a question for which there is, as yet, no definitive answer. In her study of *Evil Genes*, bioengineer Barbara Oakley argues that Machiavellian personalities are born with genotypes that fail to equip them with the full panoply of serotonin receptors, transmitters, and assorted enzymes that allow different areas of the brain to fully interact with one another and formulate socially appropriate responses to assorted stimuli from the surrounding environment.[10] These genetic deficiencies, in tandem with dysfunctional social circumstances—a childhood of parental abuse, coming of age and living in violent crime ridden communities—are believed to be the triggers that cause "some individuals to pursue a life strategy of manipulative and predatory social interactions."[11]

Perhaps the most disturbing aspect of this genetically based explanation for sociopathic behavior is the idea that these "evil genes" may actually confer certain evolutionary advantages on their recipients; advantages that have allowed these folks to pass on their genetic material over time. Indeed, in extreme environmental circumstances, such as wars, famines, or the ubiquitous "zombie apocalypses" routinely celebrated in franchises like *The Walking Dead*, it is easy to see how the non-empathic, amoral, "me first" behavior of a sociopath would help him or her survive, and, in some cases, even thrive. As Barbara Oakley notes:

> It might not be nice, for example, to steal food from your baby brother's mouth during a famine—but which of the two of you has a better chance of surviving?[12]

Add to this lack of affection for one's fellow human beings, a propensity for promiscuity, adultery, and coercive sexual behavior, and it is not hard to understand the reproductive success of sociopathic individuals.

There are also social environments that provide perfect evolutionary niches for those inclined to take advantage of the trusting natures and altruism of their neighbors. Populated urban areas with their large unrelated and anonymous crowds afford sociopaths with many opportunities to attack and steal from people who are unlikely to recognize or apprehend them. Tyrannies, such as those addressed in Chapter 3—or Wall Street on any given day of the week—actually encourage and reward amoral, selfish behavior that treats others as objects to be manipulated for one's own benefit. All of these places are for sociopaths "the equivalent of ponds and puddles for malarial mosquitoes."[13]

Whatever the environmental, genetic, and evolutionary reasons for sociopathic behavior and its persistence over time, individuals who fit this personality profile engender considerable unease and outright fear in human societies. Much of this anxiety stems from the sociopath's chameleon like nature. On the surface, such a person appears perfectly normal, and is in fact capable of great charm. He or she can also recognize moral and legal boundaries and behave accordingly. However, left to their own devices, a sociopath is also inclined toward predatory behavior that includes lying, cheating, theft, violence, and, in some cases, outright coldblooded murder.

Civilization has also made it more difficult to detect and apprehend these human chameleons. Unlike small hunting and gathering societies where it is relatively easy to recognize someone who "repeatedly lies and cheats and steals things and does not go hunting,"[14] large urban communities are places where most people are strangers to one another, social ties are looser, criminal activity is widespread and less difficult to conceal, and market economies accept and even reward some "sinister" behaviors. As already noted above, these places afford sociopaths ample opportunities to move around, blend in, and ingratiate themselves with individuals and groups that are unaware of their inclinations.

Historically, when sociopathic criminals are identified and apprehended, they can expect little in the way of mercy from the people they have wronged. In a traditional nomadic society, such as the Inuit, for example, the preferred way of dealing with someone labeled a *kunlageta*, i.e., one whose "mind knows what to do but he does not do it," was very straightforward. "Somebody would have pushed him off the ice when nobody else was looking."[15]

In more settled ancient and medieval societies ruled by law, what we label sociopaths would have been regarded quite literally as "villains," i.e., "unprincipled or depraved scoundrels naturally disposed to base or criminal actions, or deeply involved in the commission of disgraceful crimes." As such, when caught in acts deemed illegal, they were subjected to a wide range of often draconian punishments. These included crucifixion, hanging, mutilation, hard labor, and banishment for life.

Though certain of these penalties go out of style, throughout most of the modern period, criminal sociopaths continued to face retributive punishment for their acts. During the 20th century, however, the idea of rehabilitating criminals rather than just punishing them came into vogue. Unfortunately, as previously cited prison statistics demonstrate, sociopathic personalities that surrender to their inclination to violate legal and moral norms, continue to do so throughout their lives. Indeed, psychological studies have found that

> the violent recidivism rate of treated psychopaths was about 50% higher than that of untreated psychopaths. Therapy apparently made the psychopaths worse. But why? The simple answer is that group therapy and insight-oriented programs may help psychopaths to develop better ways of manipulating, deceiving, and using people, but do little to help them to understand themselves.[16]

Given the current findings of geneticists and neuroscientists, this outcome is not terribly surprising. For a sociopath to rehabilitate him- or herself, they quite literally have to go against their very nature. Many appear to be quite capable of doing this; others are just natural born villains.

How then does one deal with those that are quite simply bad to the bone? Barring currently unavailable genetic therapies, or drugs capable of altering their brain chemistry, incarceration continues to be the only method guaranteed to protect normal folks from sociopathic criminal predators. This said, an alternative to prison might be to place these individuals in supervised living and working arrangements that allow them to give expression to their natures.

Perhaps the best example of how this might work is the post-prison career of the previously mentioned master conman, Frank Abagnale. Upon release from federal custody in the 1970s, he was permitted by his parole officer to approach banks—many of which he had bilked—as a "white-collar crime specialist." In this capacity, he lectured to bank employees about how individuals like himself operate, as well as steps that they could take to protect their institutions from counterfeiting, fraud, and other cons. These lectures made him something of a star in the world of secure documents work, and he was soon in high demand by not only banks, but also hotels, airlines, and other businesses. Eventually, he ended up working with the FBI Financial Crimes Unit and teaching at the FBI Academy. He also married, sired three sons, and became the subject of a 2002 film by Steven Spielberg with himself played by Leonardo DiCaprio.[17]

Not bad for someone afflicted with evil genes.

Having addressed the psychological, neurological, and penal dimensions of sociopathy, it is now time to take a look at how one of these career criminals actually operates. To do that, we are going to spend some time in the New York underworld following the life trajectory of what can only be called a professional gangster. This person's name was Joe Valachi, and over the course of his lifetime he was a thief, getaway car driver, enforcer, soldier, racketeer, and family member of the dreaded *Cosa Nostra*. It is to his story that we now turn.

An Offer He Can't Refuse: The Sociopath as Gangster

When I was in high school, Mario Puzo's *The Godfather* was all the rage. My mother was one of the book's many fans, and it was on her recommendation that I read the paperback edition of the novel in 1970. Despite the fact that I have never been terribly fond of crime stories, I confess that I shared her liking for this particular yarn. It was well written, fast paced, suspenseful, had a satisfying, albeit disturbing ending, and, most importantly, revealed to me the shadowy realm of the Mafia, a world about which I knew nothing.

Looking back on this book nearly 50 years later, during a time when the Mafia is a ubiquitous presence in film, television, and literature, it is difficult to imagine that there was a time when I, or anyone else for that matter, could plead ignorance of this organization. Nevertheless, prior to the publication of Peter Maas' *The Valachi Papers* in 1968, and Puzo's novel in 1969, the public-at-large was largely ignorant about what Mafiosi called the *Cosa Nostra* ("our thing"). To be sure, U.S. Senate hearings in the 50s and 60s had conclusively established the existence of this crime syndicate, as well as its connection with Italian-Americans of Sicilian and Neapolitan descent. What was not so well known, however, was the inner workings of this criminal enterprise, i.e., how one entered into it, the codes of conduct that governed its membership, its social strata and relationships, and the culture within which so-called Mafiosi were inculcated, lived, worked, and died.

Puzo's novel addressed all of these questions by tracing the fortunes of a fictitious New York City mob family from the turn of the 19th century to 1955. Specifically, the book relates the life story of this family's founder, the orphaned son of a murdered Sicilian Mafiosi by the name of Vito Corleone, who is forced to immigrate to America in order to avoid the fate of his father. Upon arriving in his new home, Vito finds himself consigned to the crowded tenements of Hell's Kitchen where he and other Italian immigrants are denigrated, persecuted, and exploited by the city's established elites, businesses, police, and assorted gangs. Rather than submit to the authority of these self-styled *pezzonovantis* ("big shots"), our young migrant opts instead to build a criminal empire of his own encompassing protection rackets, bootlegging, gambling, and control of many of the city's unions. Vito's success in this enterprise makes him both a "man of respect" in New York's Italian-American community, and a formidable Don among the crime lords of the nation.

Don Corleone, however, is no mere thug, or flashy mobster along the lines of an Al Capone or a Legs Diamond. Rather, Puzo presents him as a kind of criminal prince and statesman who cares for his own and refuses to live by rules made by others, "rules which condemn him to a defeated life."[18] Nor does this recalcitrance, this "antisocial behavior," prevent him or those under his protection from prospering in their new home.

> The men of Don Corleone walked the streets with their heads held high, their pockets stuffed with silver and paper money. With no fear of losing their jobs. And even Don Corleone, that most modest of men, could not help feeling a sense of pride. He was taking care of his world, his people. He had not failed those who depended on him and gave him the sweat of their brows, risked their freedom and their lives in his service. And when an employee of his was arrested and sent to prison by some mischance, that unfortunate man's family received a living allowance; and not a miserly, beggarly, begrudging pittance but the same amount the man earned when free.[19]

Puzo's characterization of his fictitious Don as an underworld counterpart to Western society's "legitimate" presidents and prime ministers was further popularized by Francis Ford Coppola's 1972 film adaptation of *The Godfather* starring Marlon Brando in the title role. Not only did Brando look every inch the distinguished statesman in this movie, but his masterful interpretation of the character of Vito Corleone—an interpretation it should be noted that won him an Academy Award—conveyed to the film's audiences the idea that the Corleone family patriarch was really nothing more than a very gifted businessman who had earned his wealth by catering to the vices of the American people. Or as Puzo notes in his book's one epigraph taken from Balzac, "behind every great fortune there is a crime."

This portrayal of the gangster as a metaphor for corporate America was well received both in the United States and abroad. To date, Puzo's book has sold somewhere in the neighborhood of 20 to 30 million copies,[20] and Coppola's cinematic adaptation was one of the highest grossing movies of all time. *The Godfather* film also won three Oscars in 1973 for Best Picture, Best Actor (Brando), and Best Adapted Screenplay (Puzo and Coppola), was selected for preservation in the United States National Film Registry in 1990, and was ranked second only to *Citizen Kane* by the American Film Institute in 2007.[21]

I have gone on at such length about Puzo's novel and Coppola's film adaptation of it because these works not only popularized, but also rehabilitated what can only be described as criminal sociopaths. While it is true that gangsters like Al Capone enjoyed considerable notoriety, most of it infamous, during their lives, after *The Godfather*, these individuals became bonafied heroes with cult status. Indeed, as already mentioned, sympathetic portrayals of crime lords—*Godfather II* and *III*, *Goodfellas*, *Scarface*, *Bugsy*, *The Sopranos*—have become a mainstay of Western popular culture.

This said, is it appropriate to heroize or even sympathize with people who are, after all, unrepentant career criminals? Are these individuals simply "goodfellas" struggling to make a living by servicing the illicit desires of their countrymen, or are they instead "successfully sinister" sociopaths who should be regarded as villains? To answer these questions, it might be useful to turn our attention away from the glamorous gangsters of the silver screen, and examine instead the life of a real Mafiosi who was actually active in the underworld made famous by Puzo and Coppola's *Godfather*.

Joseph Michael "Joe Cargo" Valachi was born in 1903 in the Italian-American community of East Harlem. He was the second oldest of 17 children (of which only six survived) born to Dominick and Marie Valachi, two impoverished immigrants from Naples. Valachi's father was a vegetable pushcart peddler and then a laborer on a garbage scow. In the memoir he would later write with Peter Maas, Joseph reported that his family was terribly poor and constantly on the move from one unheated, bedbug infested, cold-water flat to another in the vicinity of East 108th Street. He also noted that the elder Valachi drank up most of his earnings, and regularly beat his wife and children.[22]

Up until the age of 11, Joe Valachi spent a considerable amount of time on the streets avoiding truancy officers. When he hit one of his teachers in the eye with a rock, he was sent to a Catholic reform school in the Bronx where the brothers who ran the place routinely beat him. After his release at 14, he returned home, dropped out of school at 15, and joined a burglary gang in East Harlem called the Minute Men (so-called because their assorted heists were usually completed in a minute's time or less). Valachi served as the "wheelman," or driver, of this group and participated in hundreds of robberies between 1919 and 1923, which largely involved tossing a garbage can through a store window and making off with the vandalized business's merchandise.

In 1923, a botched robbery led to Valachi's arrest, conviction on burglary charges, and a sentence of 18 months in Sing Sing. According to his memoir, he actually enjoyed his time in the penitentiary, and was out on parole after serving only nine months of his term. Returning to New York, he formed another gang of thieves, purchased a Packard, and began a whole new round of heists that involved breaking and entering into warehouses and lofts. One of these break-ins nearly cost him his life when a patrolman shot him in the head. Though he survived, he was arrested, tried once more for theft, and returned to Sing Sing, this time for four years.

Valachi later affirmed that this stint in prison was not only educational, but life changing. He completed the seventh grade in the prison school, learned how to read and write, survived a knife attack by another inmate, and, most importantly, made the acquaintance of one Alessandro Vollero, an Italian Mafiosi serving a life term for murder. It was Vollero who made him aware of the crime families of the Italian-American underworld, how they did business, and why it was good to be counted among their friends and allies.

When he was released from Sing Sing on June 15, 1928, Valachi had this to say about the experience:

> I came home with an education. I didn't learn much in that school, but at least I could read something and know what I was reading. Before I went back to Sing Sing, I could hardly make out street signs. But the real education I got was being worldly-wise. I could sit here all day and how am I going to explain what I mean? It's just all the things you lean about human nature in another world, and believe me, Sing Sing was another world.[23]

One of the things Valachi did not learn in Sing Sing about human nature was that for most folks, including a majority of those with whom he was incarcerated, it is normal to feel remorseful for criminal acts, and to empathize with those you have wronged.

What he did learn was the importance of being "mobbed up" if you were going to be a professional criminal. Consequently, upon his return to New York City, Valachi organized yet another burglary gang, but this time he tied its operations to a known Mafia crime figure named Dominick "The Gap" Petrilli, a member of the Lucchese Family, one of the principal Five Families of the New York underworld. This alliance landed him in the middle of the so-called Castellammarese War of 1930–31 between racketeers loyal to Joe "The Boss" Masseria and those aligned with the head of the Sicilian Castellammarese clan, Salvatore Maranzano. Because Petrilli was allied with Maranzano, Valachi found himself a "soldier" and enforcer in this crime lord's organization, and it was in this capacity that he was formally admitted into what Italian-American gangsters referred to as "this thing of ours," the *Cosa Nostra*.

Valachi's induction into this criminal society involved a Masonic like gathering complete with rituals that highlighted the violent and secret nature of the Mafia, the importance of its *Omertá*, or code of silence, and a pointed reminder that violating a member's wife meant death without trial. At this time, he was also introduced to other members of the Maranzano mob, and assigned a *gombah*, or godfather, by the name of Joe "Bananas" Bonanno, who would later head one of the five New York City crime families. Afterwards, everyone sat down to a formal Italian dinner with traditional pasta, chicken, and meat dishes, and a lot of Chianti and whiskey.[24]

During the Castellammarese War, Valachi distinguished himself as a reliable hit man who knew how to take orders and was cool under fire. Not only did he dutifully "hit the mattresses," an action which entailed literally taking a mattress with him as he moved from one apartment to another to keep an eye on Masseria's minions, but he was also responsible for directing the operations that took out a number of the opposition's top lieutenants in New York City. When this underworld conflict ended with Joe "The Boss's" murder in a Coney Island Italian restaurant, Joseph Valachi had been bloodied and was ready to take his place in the *Cosa Nostra* that Maranzano now set out to modernize.[25]

One suspects that Mario Puzo had Salvatore Maranzano in mind when he created his fictitious Don Corleone.[26] Like Puzo's protagonist, this crime lord was born into a Sicilian Mafia family and immigrated to the United States in the early part of the 20th century. He was also purported to be an elegant, educated, and modest man, who spoke seven languages and deeply admired Julius Caesar. Indeed, it was ostensibly from this Roman dictator that Maranzano got his idea to create a national syndicate of crime families with bosses, underbosses, *caporegimes* (lieutenants), and soldiers, all governed by a common code of conduct, and subject to his control as the *Capo di tutti Capi*, or "Boss of Bosses."[27]

Joseph Valachi was now a soldier of this modern Mafia, and in reward for his efforts during the war that had brought it into being, he was named a member of Maranzano's personal bodyguard. Unfortunately for Valachi, the "Boss of Bosses'" underlings were a young and restive lot who were not particularly enamored with the idea of owing fealty to a "Mustache Pete" from Sicily, who also fancied himself the Julius Caesar of organized crime. These men rallied around Charles "Lucky" Luciano, who, taking a leaf from Brutus and Cassius, assassinated Maranzano (with knives ironically enough) and some 40 *Cosa Nostra* leaders allied with him. It was a blood bath worthy of the last scenes in Puzo and Coppola's *Godfather*.

Luckily for Joe Valachi, Luciano was not averse to recruiting the soldiers of the old regime into what was now his syndicate. Consequently, Valachi became a soldier in the Genovese crime organization, married into a respected Sicilian Mafia family, and settled into a comfortable career carrying out contract killings on behalf of his employer. In return for his loyalty and proficiency as a mob enforcer, Valachi was rewarded with a share of such lucrative criminal sinecures as shylocking (loan sharking), numbers games, union racketeering, and black market operations during World War II. He was also able to become a shadow partner in a number of legitimate enterprises including restaurants, a dress factory, jukeboxes, and horse racing. By 1950, he was living in a suburban home in Yonkers, sending his only son to one of New York's best boarding schools, and keeping a mistress on the side. He was definitely what Barbara Oakley would call one of the "successfully sinister."[28]

These good times came to an end when Valachi got involved in the trafficking of heroin. Unlike the Mafia's other rackets—bootlegging, protection, prostitution, gambling, loan sharking—which were either tolerated or ignored by the public-at-large, the sale and use of addictive drugs was regarded by most Americans in the 1950s as a decidedly ignominious activity. More to the point, this sentiment was shared by the Federal Bureau of Narcotics, which was fully aware of the existence and operations of the *Cosa Nostra*, and also willing to take whatever steps it deemed necessary to put the kibosh on its illicit operations.

Unfortunately for Valachi, the Bureau was aware of his drug running activities, and decided to keep him and his associates under surveillance throughout the 50s. This watch paid off for them in 1959 when they were able to intercept one of his heroin shipments and arrest several of his colleagues. Though Joe went into hiding, he was eventually apprehended, charged with narcotics trafficking, and sentenced to 15 years in prison.

Valachi was incarcerated with his mob boss, Vito Genovese, who was also serving time for conspiring to import and sell narcotics. While in prison, Valachi was accused by a fellow Mafiosi of secretly working for the Bureau of Narcotics as an informer. Though there was no truth to this charge, Genovese decided that his longtime soldier had broken the Mafia's code of silence, and bestowed on him in public the dreaded "kiss of death."

Soon thereafter, Valachi bludgeoned to death an inmate that he mistook for someone in the mob commissioned by Genovese to kill him. Living on borrowed time and facing a death penalty for murder, Joseph Valachi cut a deal in 1962 with the U.S. Department of Justice to provide testimony regarding the existence, operations, and personnel of the *Cosa Nostra* in return for a life sentence in a secure federal facility. Attorney General Robert Kennedy agreed to this arrangement, and in October 1963, Valachi testified about the workings of the Mafia in a televised hearing before Arkansas Senator John L. McClellan's Permanent Subcommittee on Investigations. It was the first time, an actual member of this criminal organization had publicly acknowledged that it existed.[29]

Though the Mafia placed a $100,000 bounty on Valachi, it went uncollected because the Department of Justice insured his safety by locking him away in the maximum security cells of various federal prisons for the remainder of his life. Indeed, between the time he testified before Congress and his death from a heart attack on April 3, 1971, Joseph Valachi revealed to both American law enforcement and the public-at-large everything he knew about his former employers. He assisted police and the FBI in solving crimes that had remained open for years; exposed the inner workings of the *Cosa Nostra*; fingered those responsible for gangland murders, beatings, and extortion; and provided details about the mob's initiation rituals, including the ceremony where a burning paper is passed from hand to hand and the candidate swears: "This is the way I will burn if I betray the secret of the *Cosa Nostra*." To add insult to injury, he outlived his boss, Vito Genovese, by two years.

What are we to make of the life of Joseph "Joe Cargo" Valachi? That he was a criminal sociopath goes almost without saying. As was noted on the inside flap of the first edition of Peter Maas' *The Valachi Papers*:

> Joseph Valachi was the very epitome of the cold, seasoned criminal. His illustrious career encompassed burglary, slot machines, shylocking, numbers, narcotics, the protection racket, ration stamps (which in wartime netted him $150,000 in a good year), and, inevitably, murder. After completing the required gangland execution he was qualified for Cosa Nostra membership—and the Justice Department believes that in his lifetime he was involved in thirty-three murders.

One of Valachi's probation officers had this to say about him in 1960, while he was awaiting sentencing for his narcotics conviction:

> There is little to be said in his favor since he has failed to demonstrate any real semblance of moral conscience and social conformity. He has never been quite in tune with the society in which he lives, and at this late date there is little reason to indicate that he ever will.[30]

The federal agents who worked with Valachi while he was imprisoned came to similar conclusions. Indeed, it is striking how all of them concluded that he was not only rebellious against all constituted authority, but was also a devious, unrepentant killer capable of extreme violence.

Though we are unable to scan Valachi's brain, one suspects that MRIs would have demonstrated that it was deficient in those neuro transmitters and enzymes that insure a certain level of altruistic and trusting behavior in most of us. Add to this defective neurological makeup what can only be described as an abusive, fearful, and violent childhood environment, and it is not terribly surprising that Joseph Valachi turned out the way he did. That said, did his life really rate an action movie with no less a star than Charles Bronson in the title role? We will return to that question after examining "the astonishing rise and spectacular fall of a serial imposter."

"The man in the Rockefeller suit": The Sociopath as Grifter

One of the great classics of the science fiction genre is the novella *Who Goes There?* by John W. Campbell, Jr. Later adapted three times as a motion picture entitled *The Thing*, this story recounts the misfortunes that befall a group of Antarctic scientists when they uncover an alien spaceship that crashed into the South Pole some 20 million years ago. Though their efforts to secure the craft result in its destruction, they do discover and retrieve the body of its pilot frozen in a block of ice not far from the crash site.

Unbeknownst to these scientists, this extraterrestrial is not dead. Instead it has been hibernating in its icy prison for millennia awaiting an opportunity to thaw out; something that it does upon arriving in the much warmer confines of the researchers Antarctic base. After freeing itself, this "Thing" proves to be a remarkable creature that is capable of assuming the form, memories, and personality of any living being that it consumes. And because it is able to retain its original body mass for further reproduction, it is also able to assume multiple identities.

Suffice it to say, the chameleon-like nature of this alien Thing makes it a veritable wolf among the sheep. In short order, it begins to kill and imitate not only members of the research team, but their sled animals as well. When the beleaguered scientists realize what they are up against, they find themselves in a state of near paralysis as no one can be sure who is truly human and who is not. Some individuals even go insane because they find themselves wondering if they are the last human being in the station, and, if so, how they would even know.

Campbell's creature is not altogether different from the sociopaths that are the subject of this section. Like the Thing that preys on the Antarctic research team, grifters are amoral predators who survive by assuming multiple false identities and taking advantage of those who are unaware of their true nature. They single out individuals they regard as vulnerable, study them assiduously, gain their confidence, and then exploit them for their personal benefit. Unfortunately for the victims of these sociopaths, this exploitation usually involves theft of one form or another, and sometimes murder.

No less than with the traitors examined earlier, the deceit practiced by grifters undermines the bonds of trust and loyalty that are central to any social order. The lies and machinations of these individuals sow discord among families and friends, deprive people of their livelihoods, add to the security burdens of businesses and governments, and often lead to sexual aggression, physical violence, and death. Indeed, those victimized by these so-called con artists often find themselves reduced to a state of social paralysis, in which it becomes difficult, if not impossible, to enter into any relationship predicated on accepting the full faith and credit of another human being.

Perhaps the most pernicious aspect of this particular group of sociopaths is their apparent normalcy and great charm. A cursory examination of the lives of some famous con artists—Jeanne de la Motte, perpetrator of the affair of the diamond necklace in late 18th century France; Victor Lustig, the man who auctioned off the Eiffel Tower twice; George C. Parker, an American confidence man who sold such New York City landmarks as Madison Square Garden, the Metropolitan Museum of Art, Grant's Tomb, the Statue of Liberty, and the Brooklyn Bridge; Fernand Waldo Demara, a fellow who passed himself off as everything from a monk to a prison warden; and Sante Kimes, a notorious American female grifter convicted of murder, robbery, violation of anti-slavery laws, forgery, and a veritable slew of other crime—reveals that these individuals tend to hail from relatively normal middle class families. Most of them also have some formal education, are quite intelligent, tend to be good listeners, appear to be quite empathic, and are excellent raconteurs. Finally, though capable of remorseless violence, these folks prefer more subtle ways of fleecing their victims. Unlike their gangster counterparts, murder is seldom their occupation of choice.[31]

Perhaps one of the best examples of how grifters operate, and the havoc they leave in their wake, is the 30 year career of serial imposter, Christian Karl Gerhartsreiter. Born in 1961 to Simon and Irmgard Gerhartsreiter, Christian was raised in the village of Bergen in the German state of Bavaria. His father was a well-respected carpenter and house painter with a steady income, and his mother was a traditional housewife who took in tailoring jobs for extra money. As his only other sibling was 12 years younger, he was essentially an only child who was adored and doted upon by his parents. By all accounts, his childhood was comfortable, trouble free, and very happy.[32]

At an early age, Gerhartsreiter developed a fondness for reading and watching old American movies, particularly those directed by Alfred Hitchcock.

He could recall everything that he read or watched with little difficulty, and enjoyed quoting extensively from classical works of literature. Former German friends also report that he was an excellent speaker, a very good story teller, and something of an actor.

> "Christian liked to play games in which he adopted another identity," said Thomas Schweiger, a onetime close friend.
> At thirteen, Mr. Schweiger said, Christian telephoned a government office that registered cars, "and he changed his voice and said that he was a millionaire from Holland and that he wanted to register his two Rolls-Royces." Although the clerk was skeptical, Christian persuaded him, his friend said. "He really played the role perfect."[33]

On a less sanguine note, the young Gerhartsreiter was also spoiled, lazy, temperamental, and openly contemptuous of his neighbors and teachers. He showed little regard for the feelings of others, ignored any rules or strictures that restricted his freedom, and failed to apply himself in school. Indeed, he was such a hellion, that his own father was heard to remark *"Er ist ein verrückter Hund"* (He is a crazy dog).[34]

Soon after completing high school, Christian focused all of his attention and energy on getting out of Bergen and making his way to America. Towards this end, in 1978, he befriended an American couple, Elmer and Jean Kelln, who were traveling in Germany. Following their departure from Bavaria, and without their knowledge, he entered their names as his sponsors on a tourist visa application to the United States. He also told his parents at this time that he had a job lined up in New York City as a DJ, and got them to agree to give him $250 a month until he could get settled in his new home. An elderly aunt, who lived with the family, also agreed to send money.

With a six-month tourist visa in hand, and a modicum of family financial support, Gerhartsreiter packed up his belongings, and, at the age of 17, flew from Munich to Boston in the fall of 1978. From this point until his arrest in 2008 at age 47, he would assume up to seven false identities while crisscrossing the United States. From 1979 to 1981, he was Christopher Kenneth Gerhart, the scion of old German money. Under this name, he passed himself off as a foreign exchange student at a high school in New Berlin, Connecticut, and later the University of Wisconsin in both Stevens Point and Milwaukee. As Chris Gerhart he also entered into a green card marriage with a 22 year old woman in Madison, Wisconsin, whom he promptly abandoned after the wedding. In the mid–1980s, while living in the wealthy community of San Marino, California, he assumed the name Christopher Mountbatten Chichester, a relative of the British royal family. After murdering a young couple sometime in 1985—more on this below—he absconded to New York and became Christopher Chichester Crowe, computer programmer and financial securities expert. By 1992, he was Clark Rockefeller of the Percy Rockefeller branch of the Rockefeller clan. In this persona, he married well, sired a child, and became the toast of Manhattan society. Following his divorce in 2007, he morphed into Charles "Chip" Smith, a wealthy ship's captain and resident of Baltimore, Maryland. It was in this last alias that he was arrested for assault and battery and parental kidnapping in 2008.[35]

Though Gerhartsreiter's aliases changed during this 30 year period, his modus operandi remained remarkably consistent. Wherever he set down roots, he would affect the airs of an eccentric man of wealth with a preppy manner of dressing and speaking, which put many in mind of Thurston Howell III, the millionaire castaway in the television comedy *Gilligan's Island*.[36] As such, his grooming was always perfect, his clothes expensive, and his manners impeccable. He also sought out those churches that catered to the upper crust of the communities within which he was living, and then ingratiated himself with the older women among their clientele. Once ensconced within the social circles of these society dames, he would regale their members with stories about his family's wealth and connections with the rich and powerful of Europe and America. He would also tell them about his stint as a TV producer of *The Prisoner* and *Hitchcock Presents* series; the work that he did as a high level computer programmer; his management of the debt of various third world nations; the many securities deals he had executed; his membership in the Trilateral Commission; and the jet propulsion system he had invented.

Though these personas were completely false, and even a cursory background check would have revealed that Gerhartsreiter was not who he claimed to be, no one seems to have noticed that the "emperor had no clothes." This appears to have been due to a number of distinct, albeit related, factors. First among these was the simple fact that the people who came within Gerhartsreiter's orbit were largely trusting folk who had grown up in communities where predators such as himself were in short supply. Secondly, he was an accomplished actor and storyteller, who was very intelligent and highly knowledgeable about a wide range of topics. Finally, with one notable exception, Christian Gerhartsreiter largely contented himself with scams that involved getting others to voluntarily take care of his needs.

Perhaps the best example of Gerhartsreiter's ability to con people into supporting him was his marriage to Sandra Boss. The daughter of a Boeing engineer, Boss was raised in a devoutly Christian (Episcopalian) upper-middle-class family in Seattle, Washington. She was by all accounts a highly accomplished young woman. Indeed, when she met Christian Gerhartsreiter, or, as he was styling himself at the time, Clark Rockefeller, in New York City in 1993, she was a Stanford graduate finishing up an MBA at Harvard's School of Business.

Actually, it would be more correct to say that she met the man who was to become her husband through her sister, Julia, who had gotten to know him as a regular parishioner at St. Thomas Episcopal, a venerable New York church with a well-heeled congregation. For a good Episcopalian girl like Sandra Boss, Gerhartsreiter's regular attendance at her sister's parish spoke very highly of him. It also did not hurt that he was ostensibly the scion of George Percy Rockefeller (of the William line of the Rockefellers), was reputed to be terribly wealthy, and had entered Yale at 14.

Indeed, for a shy, private young woman like Sandra, whose intelligence and business acumen intimidated most of the men she met, Clark Rockefeller was a dream come true. At Gerhartsreiter's trial in 2009, she testified:

> He was well read. He had read a lot of classic literature, which I liked. He was quite interested and dedicated to the church. We had a lot of similar philanthropic values and aspirations. He was very attentive, very polite, very kind—very complimentary to me.[37]

Boss was also impressed by the fact that her new boyfriend was not concerned about material wealth—hardly surprising given the fact that he did not have any—and that he claimed to be helping developing nations reduce and renegotiate their debts to banks.

Whatever her reasons for being attracted to Clark Rockefeller, Sandra fell in love with him and married him in a Quaker ceremony that had no legal status in 1995 (Gerhartsreiter never filed the forms necessary to obtain a license so as to keep his name and personal information out of the public record). Shortly thereafter, she was hired by the prestigious multinational management consulting firm, McKinsey & Company, as an associate starting at approximately $80,000 a year. At the same time, her new husband decided to quit his fictitious debt renegotiation work so that he could do more independent consultancy work for Third World countries experiencing economic problems. It would be the last job, imaginary or otherwise, that he would hold for the duration of their marriage.

In the years following their wedding, Sandra Boss carved out a highly lucrative career in the municipal derivatives market. By 1999, she was made a partner of McKinsey & Company—one of the youngest in the firm's history—holding down a six-figure salary. While she was working long hours and rising in the business world, her husband was busy walking his dog in Central Park and collecting an eclectic mix of friends who he entertained in private New York clubs on Sandra's dime. Indeed, in so far as Clark Rockefeller had a job, it was controlling his wife's money, which he spent freely on expensive food and wine, antique cars, club memberships, apartments in New England resort towns, and a ramshackle house in Cornish, New Hampshire, where he played at being a country squire.

In addition to her earnings, Gerhartsreiter controlled all the particulars of his wife's life. As Boss later testified:

He cut off my contact with my friends. He cut off my contact with my family. He wouldn't let me make long-distance calls. He would scream at my friends.... He's, as I learned, capable of being an extremely scary and intimidating guy. He would scream at me and scream at me and scream at me until I couldn't resist.[38]

When asked why she stayed with him, Boss' response was very revealing about how con men like Gerhartsreiter maintain control over their victims:

One, I was terrified. I could tell that he wasn't going to let me go. I didn't know why I had been picked for this situation, but I could tell that he was really strong, and I couldn't figure out how to get out. The other thing was that, you know, I had this upbringing, which is very much about duty and honor, and you're supposed to work on your marriage. My parents had a horrible marriage and stayed together thirty-five years. I was taught life is hard—suck it up.[39]

Further complicating matters for Sandra Boss was the unexpected birth of a child in 2001. Though she and her husband used condoms for birth control, Boss was convinced that he tampered with them in 2000 in order to get her pregnant and thwart any plans she might have had about divorcing him. Whether or not this was actually the case, the couple had a girl, Reigh Storrow Rockefeller, whose care was left largely in the hands of Boss's stay-at-home partner. Surprisingly, Gerhartsreiter proved to be a doting, if highly possessive father, and he developed a strong rapport with "Snooks," the nickname he bestowed on his daughter. For Sandra, this bond was yet another reason why she felt trapped in her marriage.

In 2007, Boss finally filed a petition for divorce. She also hired a private detective to look into her husband's financial dealings and transactions in order to ascertain how much of her money he might have squirreled away over the years of their marriage. Though her PI did not find any evidence that Rockefeller had hidden away any of her assets, he did uncover the fact that he

had no employment history, no relatives, no addresses, no passport, and no credit cards that weren't paid by Sandra Boss. There was not even a marriage license issued to Clark Rockefeller and Sandra Boss. He had, in short, absolutely no trace of a pre–Sandra life.[40]

In the face of these revelations, Gerhartsreiter quickly decided to settle the divorce out of court. In return for $800,000, two cars, a dress, and her engagement ring, he surrendered custody of Reigh to Sandra and also left her with the various properties he had purchased in her name over the years. Boss was also granted the right to take their child with her to London, where she had arranged to take a position in her company's British office, and Rockefeller was limited to three court-supervised visits with "Snooks" a year.

It was during one of these supervised get-togethers in 2008 that Gerhartsreiter assaulted a court appointed social worker and kidnapped his daughter. He fled with her to Baltimore where he had purchased a house and a catamaran under yet another alias, Charles "Chip" Smith. In the course of the ensuing manhunt, Gerhartsreiter's true identity and two of his past personas—Christopher Chichester and Christopher Crowe—were revealed. Within a week he was tracked down to Maryland, apprehended, and charged with custodial kidnapping, assault and battery, and assault with a deadly weapon. In the trial that followed, his many aliases and machinations were finally revealed and a jury found him guilty as charged. The judge presiding over the case sentenced him four to five years for kidnapping and two to three years for assault, to be served concurrently.

Four years later, Gerhartsreiter was back in court, this time for the murder of Jonathan Sohus, the adopted son of his former landlady in San Marino, California, Didi Sohus. In the ensuing trial, it was revealed that during Gerhartsreiter's stint as Christopher Mountbatten Chichester in the early 1980s, he had ingratiated himself with Jonathan's mother, who was a reclusive alcoholic suffering from dementia, and gotten her to agree to let him live rent-free in her home's guesthouse. While living there, he also befriended Jonathan and his wife, Linda, who were also residing with Didi at this time.

What followed is like something out of a Hitchcock movie. It appears that at some point Gerhartsreiter decided that he needed to get Jonathan and his wife out of the way so that he could better manipulate and control Didi Sohus. Towards that end, he convinced what appears to have been a highly gullible young couple that he was actually a secret agent involved in sensitive undercover work in Europe. He also "recruited" them for a mission that required them to relocate to France. After the couple had informed Didi and their friends in the area that they were moving overseas, Gerhartsreiter bludgeoned John Sohus to death in the guesthouse, and quite likely killed his wife Linda at the same time. He then dismembered Jonathan's body, wrapped the pieces in two book bags he had brought with him from his "student days" at the University of Wisconsin–Milwaukee and the film school at the University of Southern California, and buried them in the back yard. Though Linda vanished without a trace, police associated with the case conjecture that she is dead and probably interred somewhere in the mountains or desert surrounding the LA basin.

Afterwards Gerhartsreiter apparently took control of Didi Sohus's affairs and introduced her to Don and Linda Wetherbee a couple involved in the business of selling trailers in the city of La Puente. These individuals befriended Didi and convinced her to sell her home and buy a trailer in the park where they lived. They also borrowed $40,000 from her, which they gave to Gerhartsreiter as his fee for introducing them to the elder Sohus. With this money and the murdered couple's pickup truck, Christopher Chichester was able to make his way to Connecticut where he now became Christopher

Crowe. The Wetherbees, on the other hand, became Didi's caregivers in her final years, and were rewarded for their efforts by being named the administrators and beneficiaries of her will.[41]

Though most of the evidence presented at Gerhartsreiter's trial for murder was largely circumstantial—the body buried in the backyard could not be definitively identified as that of John Sohus—the jury found him guilty of first-degree murder. Two pieces of evidence appear to have been critical in the jury's deliberations. First "Christopher Crowe" was in possession of the Sohus's pickup truck following their disappearance; secondly, the dismembered corpse was found buried in Christopher Chichester, aka Chris Gerhart's university book bags. On August 15, 2013, Christian Gerhartsreiter was given a maximum sentence of 27 years to life. He will be eligible for parole in 2035.

What to make of this "man in the Rockefeller suit"? That he was a sociopath is obvious. During his 30 year stint as a serial imposter, Christian Karl Gerhartsreiter behaved in a manner that was completely contrary to accepted social and moral norms. He repeatedly lied, engaged in deceitful subterfuges, bilked people that trusted him, and cold bloodedly murdered an innocent young couple for $40,000 and a pickup truck. Nor does he appear to have suffered any guilt or remorse for his actions. Instead, he regarded his victims as little more than prey to be used and dispensed with as he saw fit.

What makes Gerhartsreiter's case particularly disturbing is how easy it was for him to get away with his serial impostures and crimes. On the surface, he appeared to be a perfectly normal, though somewhat eccentric, individual. The older women he preyed on found him charming, courteous, a good listener, and an entertaining storyteller. Others accepted at face value his claims of great wealth and worldly experience. His partner and wife of 15 years, Sandra Boss, was a graduate of Stanford and Harvard, an economist, and a major consultant for a high end financial consultancy business, and yet she had no idea if Gerhartsreiter even had a bank account. When confronted with this glaring ignorance at her husband's trial, all she could say was:

> I think consistently you're making a connection between business intelligence and personal intelligence. I mean, I came from a place where people don't jaywalk—it's a very honest place. It never in my entire life occurred to me that I could be living with someone who was lying about such basic stuff.[42]

Indeed, the fact that Gerhartsreiter was able to pull the wool over so many people's eyes for such a long period of time has worked to make him something of a celebrity. Besides journalist Mark Seal's *The Man in the Rockefeller Suit*, novelist Walter Kirn has written an account of his friendship with Gerhartsreiter from 1998 until his arrest in 2008 entitled *Blood Will Out: The True Story of a Murder, a Mystery, and a Masquerade*. In this "intimate portrait of a professional confidence man,"[43] Kirn goes so far as to label the German imposter a "literary psychopath who had killed for literature."[44] This despite the fact that

> many of his lies were lifted wholesale from episodes of *Knight Rider*, *Frasier*, and *Star Trek*. The main inspiration for his Rockefeller persona, it was revealed at his trial, was Thurston Howell III, "the Millionaire" of *Gilligan's Island*.[45]

Other accounts of Gerhartsreiter's scams include a 2010 *Lifetime* movie, *Who is Clark Rockefeller?* with Eric McCormack in the title role, and a 2013 novelized version of his life entitled *Schroder: A Novel* by American author Amity Gage. This latter work was lauded by the *Los Angeles Times* as "absorbing, with a propulsive plot and a narrator who is charming, ambivalent, and searching—a man driven by love who understands that love cannot save him."[46]

Perhaps the most disturbing aspect of this sordid grifter's life is how much sympathetic attention he has received since his apprehension and imprisonment. Nowhere is this more evident than in the following remarks by one of Gerhartsreiter's friends, the architect Patrick Hickox:

> Hickox compared his friend's American odyssey to something out of the novel *Tom Jones*, or a book by Joseph Conrad. "There is a phrase of Truman Capote's: 'a genuine fraud.'" He continued. "Not that the person is a complete fraud. Quite the reverse. It's a person who actually may be genuine, but built upon a fictional armature. I think all Americans are our own inventions. That's part of the allure of this country. And in some ways one has to see Clark as an archetypal immigrant who constructs a new life and a new persona, free of the constraints of the country he left behind."[47]

To go from murderous con man to "archetypal immigrant" is quite an apotheosis. Figuring out how such a transformation is possible is the question to which we will now turn.

Howling with the Wolves: The Sociopath as Anti-Hero

As mentioned in the introduction to this section, the individuals treated in this chapter and the next are very much the embodiment of what Westerners believe to be villains. Attitudes may change with regard to the natural world and those that hail from different cultures, tyrants can and are sometimes considered "great," some traitors may pass for patriots or even heroes, and femme fatales are now regarded as "career girls," but people who purposely and chronically break the law, and violate the moral underpinnings of society, are typically adjudged to be villainous folk. Certainly, a gangster like Joe Valachi, who was guilty of theft, loan-sharking, heroin smuggling, and 33 mob hits, and a grifter in the mold of Christian Karl Gerhartsreiter with seven false identities and a heinous murder to his credit should not be regarded as anything other than base, despicable criminals.

And yet, as we have seen, both these men and other sociopaths like them enjoy a certain celebrity status in Western culture. Joe Valachi's life story was turned into a bestselling movie with action-adventure star, Charles Bronson, in the title role. Christian Karl Gerhartsreiter, on the other hand, has intellectuals likening him to an "archetypal immigrant," or a latter day Raskolnikov. Indeed, many seem to regard these sociopaths as something akin to heroes, or at the very least anti-heroes.

Why this is so may have something to do with the fact that these individuals are free of the constraints that inhibit most of us from engaging in criminal acts. Just as tyrants excite us because they "seem unconstrained and unconcerned about our persistent questions of morality," sociopaths fascinate us for much the same reason. They act on their impulses, do as they please, and are often quite successful in their endeavors. This was definitely the case with the men treated here prior to their apprehension and conviction.

These criminals are also the beneficiaries of a Western anti-heroic tradition that comes to the fore in the modern period. Confronted with a reality in which heroes were either the stuff of fantasies or a bunch of murderous megalomaniacs eager for gold and glory, a great many Westerners from the 16th century to the present have embraced figures of folklore—Tom Thumb, Puss 'n Boots, Petit Jean—fiction—Becky Sharp, Tom Sawyer, Huck Finn, Jack Crabb (*Little Big Man*), Harry Flashman—and film—Keyser Söse, Bonny and Clyde, Butch Cassidy and the Sundance Kid, Don Corleone—who appear to be everymen like themselves. These characters are fixated on survival rather than fame. They lack all resources save their wits. And they are not above committing immoral acts and capital crimes to fill their bellies and defend themselves against the depredations of their social superiors. They are, in short, heroic types perfectly suited to a time where a great many people see themselves as underdogs in a game of life where hypocrisy is rampant and virtuous behavior is no guarantee of success. Indeed, in a cruel world ruled by vicious predators, these anti-heroes know how to "howl with the wolves," and, in the process of doing so, secure a "piece of the action" for themselves.

Perhaps nothing illustrates this kind of bandit worship better than the affection many residents of rural Washington State continue to feel towards air highwayman D. B. Cooper. In November 1971, Cooper successfully hijacked a Boeing 727 jet, ransomed it for $200,000, and parachuted over Clark County, Washington, never to be seen again. As a journalist reporting on this story noted:

The guy pulled a daring stunt, hurt no one and took the government for a couple of hundred thousand dollars. [Quipped a local resident of the area into which Cooper parachuted:] "Around here, we got a name for someone like that. Hero. And you're invited to the next party."[48]

In the end, it is this sense of familiarity, this idea that one could socialize, or "party" with these reprobates—real or fictitious—that makes them such attractive figures. Their efforts to survive and get ahead in a world dominated by wealthy and powerful elites is an experience with which most can identify. Similarly, their roguery rings true to any person who has ever felt it necessary to feign ignorance, pretend competence, be less than forthcoming about taxes, or refrain from telling the whole truth. Most importantly, their success in using their native intelligence to best their betters and secure a room of their own affirms the idea that there is indeed something remarkable, something heroic about the ongoing efforts of ordinary folk to just stay alive.[49]

Be this as it may, the sociopaths treated here are really anything but ordinary people. Because of "evil genes" or abusive environments, or a combination of the two, they have opted not to hold legitimate jobs, or play by the rules. They are also selfish, amoral, and devoid of conscience. Altruism is alien to their natures, and deceit is the very air they breathe. Consequently, to heroize or in some way rehabilitate the reputations of such individuals does a grave disservice to both society at large and their hapless victims. Whatever the glamor surrounding their fictional counterparts, the rogues examined in these pages are very real and extremely dangerous. And for that reason, they very much deserve to be labeled villains.

7

Rippers and Rapists
The Villain as Psychopathic Murderer

Serial killers would seem to be born without the capacity to develop a normal range of emotion. They seem unable to recognize that other people have feelings as important as their own. They are impervious to remorse or guilt. They neither give love nor receive it. Often the adults they become have an intense need for excitement. They may also feel "society" has let them down or failed to give them the acclaim they merit. These are the budding serial killers, psychopaths and sociopaths.

—Dr. Paul Britton, forensic psychologist

Murder is not about lust and it's not about violence. It's about possession.

—Theodore Robert Bundy, serial murderer

A census taker once tried to test me. I ate his liver with some fava beans and a nice Chianti.

—Hannibal Lecter, *Silence of the Lambs*

If it bleeds, it leads.

—News media saying

On December 10, 1999, at roughly 4:00 in the morning, an 18-year-old UCLA freshman music major named Michael William Negrete finished playing a computer game with a friend and fellow resident of Dykstra Hall, a dormitory on campus. Sometime between 4 a.m., when Michael logged off his computer, and 9 a.m., when his roommate discovered him missing, Negrete left his dorm room and disappeared, never to be heard from again. He did not leave behind any notes as to his whereabouts, and his personal belongings, including his clothing, shoes, wallet, and musical instruments, were still where he had left them the day before.

In the ensuing investigation, the police brought in search dogs that tracked Negrete's scent to Sunset Boulevard and Bellagio Street on the northern border of the UCLA campus, but they did not turn up any additional evidence regarding the young man's disappearance. Authorities also released a sketch of an unidentified Caucasian male in a grey jacket seen inside Dykstra Hall at 4:35 a.m. on December 10. He was described as being around 35 years old, of medium height (5'7" to 5'8" tall), with a heavy build. To date, this person has yet to be found.

Following his disappearance, there was speculation that Michael Negrete may have been depressed and/or troubled by some secret that caused him to run away and assume a different identity elsewhere. Both Negrete's family and police investigators dismissed this conjecture on the grounds that Michael had no history of depression, was quite close to his family, and did not appear to have any "secrets" that were troubling him. Michael's teachers and friends at UCLA also affirmed that he was a good student (he was awarded a music scholarship), and a sociable fellow who made friends easily. In fact, he appears to have been a fairly normal well-adjusted young man who sang jazz songs to himself, enjoyed the *Simpsons* television series, played trumpet and steel drum, and was an avid gamer. Police also note that if he did run away with the aim of starting a new life, it was odd that he did not take anything with him—no money, clothes, shoes, or any other personal possessions—that might have helped him make such a transition. Indeed, since Negrete vanished in 1999, there has been no activity on his bank account, credit cards, or Ralph's club card.[1]

The other explanation for Michael Negrete's disappearance was that he was the victim of a serial killer, that is "someone who has murdered three or more victims, with a cooling off period in between each of the homicides."[2] This frightening supposition was based on a number of considerations. The first of these was that as a college student, Michael was a member of one of the so-called "vulnerable communities" often targeted by these murderers, i.e., vagrants, the homeless, prostitutes, migrant workers, homosexuals, missing children, single women (out by themselves), elderly women, and hospital patients. Secondly, as is often the case with the victims of these killers, Negrete also appears to have been lured from his room by someone he either knew and trusted, or believed to be unthreatening (perhaps the unidentified white man seen inside Dykstra Hall at 4:35 a.m. on December 10). Finally, the complete absence of evidence in Michael's dorm, or anywhere else in the surrounding area, pointed to the methodical handiwork of an experienced predator who knew how to clean up after himself.

If this was indeed Michael's fate, he joins a long list of unfortunate souls who have run afoul of men, and some women, who hunt, snare, torment, and kill individuals with whom they have no relationship. Like their sociopathic brethren, these murderous individuals are non-empathic and remorseless. They view their fellow human beings as little more than objects to be used and discarded as they see fit. And any pain and suffering they inflict on their victims arouses in them neither sympathy nor any sense of guilt.

Unlike the sociopaths treated in the last chapter, these psychopathic killers do not violate and murder people for occupational reasons, or as a necessary step in an elaborate con game. In fact, with the notable exception of so-called "black widows," most serial murderers do not kill in order to enrich themselves. Rather, their murder sprees are motivated by a compulsive desire to seek out vulnerable strangers over whom they can exercise power or dominance.

Though these serial rippers and rapists behave in a profoundly inhumane, and by normal standards irrational manner, they look and act like everyone else around them. As with Joe Valachi and Christian Karl Gerhartsreiter, the murderers treated in this chapter appear to be perfectly normal, even harmless, individuals. They do not manifest any serious mental problems, and many of them are model citizens. Serial killer John Wayne Gacy, for example, owned a construction business, lived in the suburbs of Chicago, and dedicated his free time to humanitarian activities raising money for homeless children. Though he appeared to be a genuinely good man, he was also busy filling a crawlspace under his house with the bodies of 33 young men he brutally murdered.

In addition to their ability to pass themselves off as just plain folks, serial killers are also an elusive target for the authorities seeking to identify and apprehend them. Aside from having no overt mental illnesses, or distinguishing physical characteristics, these murderers usually do not have a prior relationship with the people they kill. They are also very meticulous about not leaving anything at crime sites that might incriminate them. Consequently, law enforcement agencies are bereft of the "usual suspects" or pieces of evidence they would normally rely on to locate a guilty culprit.

Matters are further complicated by the tendency of these killers to dispatch their victims at different times and in different geographical locations. This penchant for mobile murder brings into play multiple police departments that do not normally share or coordinate their criminal investigations. What then ensues is something Professor Steven A. Egger refers to as "linkage blindness," or an inability on the part of the authorities to detect "linkages between similar crime patterns or modi operandi" across different areas of a given state or country.[3]

The victims in these killings also tend to live alone and/or hail from marginalized communities such as college students, vagrants, prostitutes, single women, homosexuals and the elderly. Unfortunately, the disappearance of individuals from these groups often goes unnoticed, or worse, is regarded as a low priority by law enforcement. If indeed Michael Negrete was the victim of a serial killer, he would be one of a long line of trusting young people lured to their death by someone they did not really know, who then moved on to kill others like him somewhere else.

Though few would disagree with the characterization of these psychopathic murderers as villains, if not out-and-out monsters, it is also important to note here that contemporary Western society appears to be in love with them.

> In the eighties 23 movies on serial killers were produced. In the nineties, there were 54 movies.... There is not one serial killer in recent North American history whose story has not been turned into a film.[4]

In addition to these movies and television shows, whole sections of bookstores are dedicated to so-called "true crime" literature, which is largely concerned with the grisly deeds of assorted serial rippers and rapists. And when authorities are lucky enough to apprehend one of these killers, their trials often become media circuses that attract large audiences of what can only be described as avid fans. Indeed, serial murderers have not only become celebrities, but in the case of the fictitious Hannibal Lecter of *Silence of the Lambs* fame, actual heroes.

Why these individuals receive such star treatment, and what this may portend for our society, are concerns we will attempt to address in what follows. Prior to that, however, we need to consider a number of distinct, albeit related questions regarding the villainous type we label the psychopathic serial killer. Among these queries are the following: What are the distinguishing characteristics of these murderers, and how are they alike and different from the other chronic criminals addressed in the last chapter? Who do they victimize and why? How do these latter-day rippers get away with their crimes? And finally, are there ways to identify and apprehend them?

After addressing these questions, we will examine in some detail the life and crimes of serial murderer Theodore "Ted" Bundy. Attractive, intelligent, charming, and seemingly harmless, Bundy raped and murdered 30 women in seven states between 1974 and 1978. When he was finally apprehended, 250 reporters from five continents covered his trial. The proceedings were also nationally televised and watched by millions. Indeed, Bundy's celebrity was such that, prior to his execution in 1989, heart throb, Mark Harmon, played him in a television miniseries, *Deliberate Stranger*, which highlighted his crimes and sensational trial. Given his career as both a savage serial killer and a mass media star, Ted Bundy provides us with a perfect case study of this chapter's villainous type, as well as those among the public-at-large who find these killers fascinating and even glamorous.

Predators and Prey: Making Sense of the Serial Killer

Though the historical record is replete with men and women who have killed acquaintances and strangers multiple times—Gilles de Rais (15th century French nobleman who raped and murdered over 140 children); Elizabeth Bathory (16th century Hungarian countess who bathed in the blood of servant girls she tortured and killed); Sarah Jane Robinson (19th century black widow and "Massachusetts Borgia" who administered arsenic to friends and family in order to cash in on their life insurance policies); Jack the Ripper (infamous and unapprehended turn-of-the-century murderer and mutilator of five prostitutes in London's Whitechapel district)—the term "serial killer" was not coined until the latter half of the 20th century. As is often the case with words of this nature, its authorship is a contested matter. Some attribute this expression to FBI special agent, Robert Ressler, because he used the term "serial homicide" in the 1970s. Others argue that criminal investigative pioneer Pierce Brooks, the founder of the Violent Criminal Apprehension Program (VICAP), first used the word in his efforts to define the phenomenon of individuals who kill strangers for pleasure. Whoever came up with "serial killer," it is now the label of choice for the criminals addressed in this chapter.[5]

The FBI defines a serial killer as "someone who has murdered three or more victims, with a cooling off period in between each of the homicides." In the manual for multi-agency investigative teams, which he prepared for the U.S. Department of Justice in 1988, criminal investigator Pierce Brooks added the following details to the FBI's brief definition:

> Serial murder is a series of two or more murders, committed as separate events, usually, but not always, by one offender acting alone. The crimes may occur over a time ranging from hours to years. Quite often the motive is psychological, and the offender's behavior and the physical evidence observed at the scene will reflect sadistic, sexual overtones.[6]

The most detailed definition of the phenomenon labeled serial murder is the one developed by professor of Criminal Justice, Steven A. Egger. He argues that investigators are likely dealing with a serial killer in their jurisdiction if the following seven conditions are present:

- One or more persons (usually male) commit a second and/or subsequent murder.
- There is usually no prior relationship between the victim and the killer.
- Murders occur at different times without any apparent connection to the initial killing.
- Killings usually occur in different geographical locations.

- The motive for the murder is not material gain. Rather, it is committed out of a desire by the murderer to exercise power and domination over a victim.
- Killers select their victims because they have symbolic value for them, or they are perceived to be lacking in worth. Individuals who are unable to defend themselves or alert others are also prime targets.
- Those who fall prey to a serial killer usually come from the following vulnerable communities: vagrants, the homeless, prostitutes, migrant workers, homosexuals, missing children, single women (out by themselves), elderly women, college students, and hospital patients.[7]

What kind of person engages in serial murder and what is their modus operandi? To date there is no empirical data base on serial killers. That said, a number of researchers in psychology and criminal justice have compiled case studies of apprehended individuals guilty of murdering multiple strangers, and compared and contrasted their social environments, family backgrounds, interpersonal relationships, criminal records, and operational methods. This process has revealed a number of commonalities among these murderers, as well as differences in how and why they kill people.[8]

While there are female serial killers, the overwhelming majority of these murderers are heterosexual men. They also tend to be males from working class or lower socioeconomic status families where one or both parents are alcoholic, fathers are usually abusive, and mothers often form unusually close and dominant relationships with their sons. At some point in their childhood, all of these individuals appear to suffer from some kind of health trauma, often brought on by being severely beaten by a parent.

The teenage years of serial killers usually involve some kind of juvenile delinquency and run-ins with the law. In high school, these individuals are either "loners" or find it difficult to establish lasting and meaningful relationships with their peers. They experience sex for the first time as teens, and it is often associated with some form of violence. A disproportionally high number of these murderers develop a keen interest in law enforcement at this time in their lives.

As adults, serial killers often marry and then divorce their wives. Like their sociopathic cousins, they are regarded by their peers as manipulative and dishonest. This said, they pass as perfectly normal, even harmless, individuals who hold jobs, work hard, and own homes. They also have reputations for being extremely neat and orderly in their lifestyles. Going back to the example of John Wayne Gacy, though there were bodies decomposing under his house, above floors everything was spic and span. This was also the case with Jeffrey Dahmer, a cannibal who kept body parts in his refrigerator, while maintaining a very clean and tidy apartment.

When these individuals begin killing people they usually use some kind of lure to attract their victims. Ted Bundy, for example, would wear a fake leg or arm cast and ask women to assist him with putting packages in his car. Others pose as police officers and use their ostensible legal authority to coerce people into accompanying them. Those who primarily kill within a certain geographic area lure young men and women to their deaths with offers of money or a job. All of these killers prey on people that are vulnerable and easily abducted, e.g., single women who are by themselves, young gay men cruising for sex, elderly shut-ins, hitchhikers, homeless vagrants.

These murderers are also quite mobile, and as already noted tend to kill in different geographical locations. As such they all use cars—windowless vans being a favored mode of transportation—to abduct victims and dispose of their corpses. They use a variety of deadly weapons—pipes, clubs, knives, and guns—on those they kidnap, but their preferred method of killing is strangulation.

When apprehended serial killers display no self-remorse and actually blame others for their crimes. They often taunt their captors and the various psychologists that are called in to examine them. When interrogated they reveal themselves to be compulsive and obsessed with controlling others. And it goes without saying that they love the "celebrity" their crimes and high profile trials bring them.

Psychologists who study the phenomenon of serial murder have identified different types of serial killers. For example, there appear to be sedentary and migratory murderers. The former kill within a specific area—home, hospital, city, or region—while the latter roam from place to place seeking out victims.[9]

Researchers Ronald M. Holmes and James De Burger further subdivide these killers according to their motive for murder. To date, they have identified four distinct kinds of serial murderers, which they label visionary, mission-oriented, power/control, and hedonistic. Those they designate as visionary murderers are ostensibly following orders, or obeying the dictates of some vision or voice. This kind of killer sees himself as an agent of either good or evil. The mission-oriented killer is akin to the Travis Bickle character in Martin Scorsese's *Taxi Driver*, who kills as a way of ridding the world of individuals he perceives to be human trash. Power/control serial killers are individuals who derive pleasure from dominating a helpless person. Hedonists, who were once labeled "lust murderers," are sensationalists who receive a sexual *frisson* from the suffering of their victims.[10]

José Sanmartín, an international authority on serial murder and its perpetrators, also distinguishes between the psychotic and psychopathic serial murderer. The former is someone who suffers from a severe mental illness, usually some form of schizophrenia, which is accompanied by visions or hallucinations. These individuals kill ostensibly on orders from God or Satan, and are notable for the disorganized nature of their crimes. The psychopath on the other hand is the embodiment of the cold-blooded, organized, and methodical killer. He

> plans his crimes with clearness of mind and attention to the smallest detail. He knows what he will do and does not want to fail. His longstanding deviant fantasies guide him in the selection of a victim.... The organized serial killer not only chooses victims for a common physical feature, but he also chooses easily controllable victims. Absolute control over the victim is, moreover, one of the main objectives of the organized serial killer.[11]

Sanmartín also notes differences in how psychotic and psychopathic serial killers commit murder and clean up afterwards. Psychotics do not plan their crimes beforehand. They select whoever has the misfortune of crossing their path, use whatever means are available to murder them, are not particularly meticulous about disposing of the body, and often have sex with the corpse. As already noted above, the organized psychopathic killer follows a well-thought out scheme aimed at capturing and controlling his victims. He tends to favor "tool kits" containing such materials as rope, handcuffs, blindfolds, scalpels, and the like. Once he has subdued and abducted his prey, he usually rapes them, and then keeps them alive long enough to carry out whatever aberrant fantasies are causing him to kill in the first place. These psychopathic killers are also fond of collecting souvenirs from those they murder, such as underwear, necklaces, shoes, body parts.[12]

Suffice it to say that psychopathic rippers and rapists terrify us. Whereas psychotics are obviously in the grip of a mental illness over which they exercise little if any control, psychopaths do not suffer from such a disorder. Indeed, with the exception of their murderous proclivities, they behave in a perfectly normal fashion. As with the sociopaths treated in the last chapter, these killers are fully aware that their deeds are regarded as immoral, reprehensible crimes, but because they lack an ability to empathize with their victims, this makes no difference to them. Instead

> they treat them as predators would their prey. It is as if their victims do not belong to the same species. They play with them like a cat plays with a mouse. They want to keep them alive as long as possible in order to prolong the pleasure of total control and domination. They kill when they want to kill, when they believe they have reached the summit of pleasure, which almost always coincides with the union of sex and death.[13]

Why do these people kill and then kill again? The consensus among the researchers who study serial killers is that these individuals are dealt a kind of "poker hand of criminality" that includes all the requisite cards necessary to produce a psychopathic multiple murderer. Among these is a genetic predisposition inclining such a person to antisocial behavior and violence. Brain imaging scans and other tests on convicted murderers indicate that they have low levels of serotonin, a neurotransmitter necessary for the control of impulsivity, as well as abnormally high levels of testosterone, a steroid hormone which fuels aggression. There is also evidence of dysfunction in those areas of the brain associated with empathy and feelings of remorse.

The brains of serial murderers, however, are markedly different from those of so-called "impulse killers who kill only once and for reasons of passion or anger. Whereas brain scans of the latter show depressed levels of activity in the prefrontal cortex, which is responsible for planning and behavior regulation, those who murder multiple times have considerable activity in this part of their brains. All of which explains how and why these predators are able to meticulously plan and execute their crimes."[14]

Another card these individuals are dealt is a formative social environment that appears to activate their biological proclivities for violence and murder. For example, case studies of apprehended serial killers show that the majority of them are raised in what can only be described as dysfunctional families. During childhood and adolescence, it is not unusual for these nascent murderers to be verbally and physically abused by parents or others designated to care for them. What this entails is best captured in the following remarks by Dr. Park Elliot Dietz regarding what it takes to create a Ted Bundy, John Wayne Gacy, or Edmund Kemper (serial murderer of six female hitchhikers as well as his own mother):

> Start with an abusive, criminal father and a hysterical, alcoholic mother; torture the boy as erotically as possible; have the naked mother spank him and sleep with him until age 12; bind and whip him regularly; have the mother sexually arouse him and punish him for his erections; let the mother appear promiscuous while condemning prostitutes; leave detective magazines around the house for him to find; and encourage him to watch R-rated slasher films and violence against glamorous women.[15]

It is important to keep this level of abuse in mind because serial killers by and large do not kill for reasons of material gain, or sexual pleasure. As previously mentioned, these individuals murder because they relish exercising control and domination over others. And this enjoyment appears to be fueled by formative experiences — such as those addressed by Dr. Dietz — that leave these murderers feeling as if they are powerless nobodies.

Indeed, in her interviews with convicted psychopathic multiple murderers, criminologist Candice Skrapec has been struck by how all of these individuals tend to see themselves as victims who feel a need to kill in order to defend themselves from a threatening world that makes them feel inconsequential. She notes, for example, that though these killers are fully aware of the moral, social, and legal strictures that condemn and proscribe what they do, they nonetheless feel that they are entitled to mete out punishment to those they feel have wronged them in some way, or who are representative of others who have humiliated or harmed them at some point in their lives. By killing people they believe are deserving of what they get, serial murderers feel empowered and in control of their immediate environment. They also feel more consequential because they are doing something that others will or cannot do; a feeling, it should be noted, that is only increased when they are apprehended and turned into celebrities by the media. In addition to this sense of potency, these individuals experience a feeling of euphoria at being able to vent their violent anger on a stand-in for all of those things that make them feel like "nothing" in their lives.[16]

Before continuing, it should be noted here that whatever their brain chemistry or formative influences, the decision to become a serial killer is very much a matter of choice. As noted in the previous chapter, though sociopaths may not be hardwired like the rest of us, most of them manage to avoid becoming gangsters or grifters. It also goes without saying that literally millions of people grow up in abusive, dysfunctional environments and still manage to build for themselves, often with great difficulty, normal, fulfilling, and successful lives.

Concurrently, most of us believe ourselves entitled to certain things— equal rights, education, health care, opportunities for advancement—for which we are willing to fight if we feel they have been denied to us. Similarly, it is quintessentially human to seek some measure of control over the world around us and to experience pleasure when we feel our lives empowered in some manner. While serial killers may be motivated by these same feelings and desires, we should underscore that they experience and address them in markedly exaggerated and distorted ways.

Whatever the reasons for a serial killer's decision to abduct, torture, and kill another human being, who is likely to fall victim to his violent rage and aberrant fantasies? Criminologist Steven Egger argues:

> In most cases, victims are selected solely on the fact that they crossed the path of the serial murderer and became a vehicle by which hypo-arousal occurred for his pleasure. Victims are self-selecting only due to their existence at a place and point in time.[17]

This said, as we have noted repeatedly, these predators prefer certain kinds of prey, who are members of communities that Steven Eggers also identifies as the "less-dead":

> Marginalized groups of society who comprise the majority of the serial killer's victims. They are called the "less-dead" because before their death, they "never were" according to society. In other words, this group is basically ignored and devalued by their own communities or members of their neighborhoods. The "less-dead" victims are not missed and basically ignored by

society. Examples of the "less-dead" are prostitutes, the homeless, vagrants, migrant farm workers, homosexuals, the poor, elderly women, and runaways.[18]

Analysis of data collected by psychologist Kim A. Egger on 1,246 serial killers from 1900 to 1999, bears out Steven Egger's findings with regard to those who most commonly fall victim to the predations of these murderers. Without question, the largest number of these victims are women (65 percent), most of whom are prostitutes. In addition to these sex workers, elderly females and women who live alone are also commonly targeted.[19]

Male homosexuals are also at special risk, especially when the serial killer preys exclusively on males. In such a situation, 48 percent of those killed will be gay prostitutes, or young gay men cruising for sex in local clubs. It should also be noted here that though the majority of the murderers treated in this chapter are heterosexual, the roughly five percent that are homosexual include in their ranks some of the most prolific killers of men—Donald Harvey (50),[20] John Wayne Gacy (33), Dean Corll (27), Juan Corona (25), Patrick Kearney (28), Jeffrey Dahmer (17), William Bonin (10), and Randy Kraft (suspected of 51 murders).[21]

Age also plays a role in determining who a serial killer will victimize. Six percent of those murdered are either elderly or children. Of these victims, children are most at risk because they are often unaware of the peril posed by strangers, are easily lured away from their parents, friends, and caregivers, and can be subdued with little effort.

Seven percent of serial murder victims are selected on the basis of their race. Not surprisingly, serial killers count among their ranks white racists, e.g., Joseph Paul Franklin, who target black men, especially those seen with white women. Concurrently, there have been African-American murderers, such as Hubert Gerald, who specifically go after black females.

Hospital patients sometimes find themselves victimized by so-called "angels of mercy," or medical personnel who use their access to patients' rooms and medications to select and murder those people they deem no longer worthy of life. This category of victims make up about 3% of those killed by so-called "sedentary" serial killers, both male and female. Exemplary of this kind of multiple medical murder are the careers of Jane Toppan and Harold Frederick Shipman. The former was a late 19th century American nurse who administered a fatal drug mixture to 31 patients, with whom she got into bed and held close to her as they died. Toppan revealed during her trial that this kind of fatal intimacy gave her a sexual thrill. Shipman, on the other hand, was a British doctor who murdered over 200 patients (80 percent of them women) by injecting them with lethal injections of diamorphine, and then falsifying their medical records to make it look as if they died of natural causes.

Lest those readers who do not belong to any of the abovementioned communities think themselves immune to the predations of serial killers, it should also be noted that at least two percent of victims appear to be chosen solely because of their location. These people are

> in the right house, or working in the right shop, or living in the right alley, or shopping the right mall, or working the right street corner. They are chosen simply because they happen to be in or live in the place where the serial killer is hunting—where he feels most comfortable and safe in killing.[22]

As Kim Eggers reminds us, in the end, we are all at risk from these monsters, especially if we happen to have the misfortune of crossing their path at an opportune moment for them to act.

Why is serial murder so difficult to detect and stop? To a large degree, we have already answered this question in our consideration of serial killer profiles, motivations, methods, and victims. As with sociopaths, there is nothing that really distinguishes these individuals from anyone else around them. Nor do they behave like their messy psychotic confreres who feel that they are compelled by voices and visions to murder multiple times. Rather, the psychopathic serial killers treated here do not exhibit any noticeable mental illnesses, and are also quite meticulous about not leaving anything at a murder site that might link them to their crimes.

While most female serial killers usually murder strangers, acquaintances, and family members for material gain (and normally employ some kind of poison to do so), their far more numerous male counterparts kill for reasons other than greed. As anyone familiar with the detective story genre is aware, most criminal investigations are guided by the question "Who benefits from the crime?" While the answer to that query is more forthcoming in cases involving a mobster like Joe Valachi, or a con man such as Christian Karl Gerhartsreiter, it is less apparent in a case with a victim that shares no relationship with their killer save being in the wrong place at the wrong time.

Serial murderers can also hunt in areas where they will not be noticed, or appear different from others around them. These include red light districts, businesses operating along major interstate highways—convenient food marts, service stations, rest areas—shopping malls, parks, public pools, fairs, and parking lots. In all of these places, it is the norm for strangers to interact with one another, and for people to remember little of what is going on around them.

Serial killers also operate much like the vampires of fiction. They kill varied strangers at different times and in disparate locations. These victims also tend to hail from fringe communities that are shunned and/or ignored by society at large. Indeed, the general attitude with regard to these "less-dead" that end up very dead is either "they brought this on themselves," or "they had it coming to them." In the face of such bigotry, it is hardly surprising that serial murders often go unnoticed and unsolved.

Finally, there is the whole phenomenon of "linkage blindness." Law enforcement agencies throughout the West are assigned specific jurisdictions—local, state, regional, national—with varying responsibilities. Collaboration between these groups is limited, and often discouraged for reasons of "boundary maintenance, jurisdictional integrity, or turf protection."[23] In the absence of such cooperation, it is often impossible for criminal investigators to discern connections between murders occurring at different times and locations. As we have noted, serial killers tend to take a keen interest in police procedurals, and are fully aware that those charged with tracking and apprehending them do not share or exchange information pertaining to unsolved murders with their fellow officers in different jurisdictions.

What if anything is to be done with regard to psychopathic murderers who kill strangers for pleasure? Barring some kind of *Brave New World* scenario wherein neurological anomalies are eliminated at conception, and every child is guaranteed a secure and loving formative experience, we are likely to have these "killers among us" well into the foreseeable future. This said, there are steps we can take to better protect ourselves from these predators. Among them:

- Members of vulnerable communities need to be made aware of the fact that they are often targets for serial killers, and law enforcement agencies should afford more effective protection to these groups.
- Everyone should be conscious of the possibility that they could be at risk of running afoul of one of these murderers. As such, we should all be aware of our surroundings, and exercise due caution when interacting with strangers (particularly men asking for assistance in or near a windowless van).
- More research needs to be done with regard to the background, motivations, and modus operandi of these killers.
- Regional, national, and international data bases with extensive and detailed information on serial killers should be created to facilitate correlations aimed at tracking and identifying these criminals.
- Law enforcement officers at all levels and in every jurisdiction should be familiarized with what has been learned from serial murder investigations, and encouraged to work closely with one another when there is a possibility that such a case is afoot in their area.
- Respecting the value of any person, regardless of their community, who falls victim to these killers.

- Holding news outlets and the entertainment industry accountable for the myths they propagate with regard to serial killers and their victims (more on this in the concluding remarks of this chapter).

Having examined what we know in general about this chapter's villainous type, let us now examine in some depth the life and career of Theodore "Ted" Bundy, one of the most prolific serial killers of the 20th century.

"We all go a little mad sometimes": The Case of Ted Bundy

Perhaps the most fascinating thing about Ted Bundy is how little we actually know about the man, despite three trials, 12 books, and a plethora of newspaper and magazine articles about him and his crimes.[24] Much of this mystery stems from the fact that he often gave his many interrogators conflicting accounts of everything from the particulars of his childhood to the details of his many homicides. For example, while he confessed to 30 murders committed in seven states between 1974 and 1978, he hinted at having slain many more young women earlier in his life, and the investigators who worked on his case did not think this was idle boasting.

This said, Bundy's life does fit the general profile of the serial killer. Like his fellow murderers, his early family life was far from idyllic. He was born in 1946, the illegitimate child of Elizabeth Louise Cowell and a man whose identity has never been confirmed. Some members of Elizabeth's family suspect that the father was none other than Bundy's grandfather, Samuel Cowell, a violent and abusive parent who was fond of beating his wife and daughters.[25]

Whatever Bundy's paternity, he and his mother lived in her parents' home in a working class neighborhood of Philadelphia during the first three years of his life. In order to avoid the stigma associated with being born out of wedlock, the boy was passed off as the son of his grandparents, and his mother pretended to be his older sister. It is not clear when or how Bundy discovered that he was a bastard, and that his sibling was actually his mom, but he later acknowledged a lifelong resentment of Elizabeth Cowell for lying to him about his parentage.

Though Bundy told one biographer he was quite fond of his father/grandfather, he also later acknowledged to other chroniclers of his life that Samuel Cowell was not a pleasant fellow.[26] In addition to regularly beating his wife, daughters, and the family dog, Cowell was a nasty bigot with a pronounced dislike for most of his fellow Philadelphians. While we do not know if he visited violence on his grandson, it seems likely given his behavior with everyone else under his roof.

7. Rippers and Rapists 225

By the time Bundy was four, his mother had had enough of family life with her father and moved with her now acknowledged son to Tacoma, Washington. Here she married a hospital cook named Johnny Culpepper Bundy, who adopted Ted as his son. Bundy's stepfather appears to have been a decent fellow who made every effort to treat his stepson in the same manner as the four children he had with his mother Elizabeth. That said, Bundy never warmed to his new father and remained distant from his siblings.

Despite conflicting accounts that he gave to various biographers and interviewers about his adolescence and teen years in Tacoma, Bundy was not a "good boy." He was arrested at least twice on suspicion of burglary and car theft, was fond of roaming the streets at night looking into undraped windows at women undressing, and he drank heavily. He also appears to have developed a liking for true crime literature and films at this time, particularly those stories which dealt with sexual violence and featured photos of mutilated corpses.

In high school, Bundy was found to have a high IQ (he tested at 122), but he performed at a B- level. He played Little League baseball, was part of his school's football team, ran cross-country, and was a Boy Scout. He was also an avid skier. Though he later claimed to be a loner who didn't fit in with his peer group, he was recalled as someone who was by and large well-liked by his peers. Bundy's neighbors remembered him as "serious, nice and polite, not a troublemaker, and rather quiet."[27]

Bundy attended a number of universities and studied a wide array of subjects. He spent a year at the University of Puget Sound in Tacoma and then transferred in 1966 to the University of Washington (UW) in Seattle to major in Asian studies. During the summer of 1967 he attended the Stanford Chinese Institute in Palo Alto, California. He returned to UW in the fall and changed his major to urban planning and sociology. Between 1968 and 1970, Bundy dropped out of school and traveled across country to Philadelphia where he visited his grandparents and attended Temple University for a semester. Upon his return to Washington, he re-enrolled at UW, this time majoring in psychology, and graduated in 1972. Two years later, he was studying law, first at the University of Puget Sound and then at the University of Utah. Throughout these college years, he was also quite active in Washington State GOP politics, working actively in the campaigns of Governor Dan Evans and presidential candidate Nelson Rockefeller.[28]

No one knows what triggered Bundy's murderous propensities, or even when he actually started acting on them. He may have started killing while he was a teenager and there is some circumstantial evidence linking him to the abduction and murder of an eight-year-old girl in Tacoma in 1961. It should be noted here, however, that Bundy denied having anything to do with this killing.[29] The critical moment may have been in the summer of 1967 when his first girlfriend, an older coed from a wealthy San Francisco family, broke up with him. Family members recall that he was extremely upset and moody, and Bundy himself confessed that this period was "absolutely the pits for me—the lowest time ever."[30] Soon thereafter, he dropped out of school and headed across the country where it is likely he began to develop the skills that he would later use to such deadly effect during his killing spree in the mid to late 70s. This supposition is based on Bundy's admission, following his apprehension, that he had killed two women and unsuccessfully tried to abduct another one in 1969 while he was visiting his grandparents in Philadelphia.[31]

Bundy's documented murders began in 1974 and only ended with his apprehension in Florida in 1978. During this time period, he abducted, beat, raped, and strangled at least 17 young women. Law enforcement officers believe that he likely committed many more murders, and Bundy himself hinted that there were indeed other victims than the ones formally credited to him.

Rather than go into the gruesome details of each killing—something that has been done exhaustively in all of the accounts on Bundy cited in this chapter—or rehash the particulars of his arrests (he was incarcerated in eight different jails and prisons between his first arrest in 1975 and conviction in 1979), escapes (two in Colorado), and trials (one in Utah for attempted kidnapping, one in Colorado for murder, and two in Florida also for homicide), we will focus instead on Bundy's modus operandi, the type of person he hunted, why he killed, and how he was able to get away with these murders for years.

Like other psychopathic serial killers, Bundy was a well-organized and methodical predator (he was also extremely neat, orderly and impeccably groomed). His last attorney, Polly Nelson, noted that he meticulously researched the areas in which he was hunting so as to enhance his chances of abducting his victims, making a clean getaway, and having safe sites in which to kill them and dispose of their corpses.[32] Because he was also versed in police investigative procedurals, Bundy was quite good about not leaving any fingerprints or incriminating evidence at his crime scenes. Indeed, he was so fastidious on this score that he would remove and burn the clothes (or in one case donate them to Good Will) of his victims, so as to avoid any fibers that might link him to their murder.

Ted Bundy was also a mobile, migratory serial killer. He favored a nondescript tan colored Volkswagen Beetle because it got good gas mileage and the seats could be removed when loading and unloading what he euphemistically referred to as his "cargo." In this car, he kept a "tool kit" that included such items as a ski mask, pantyhose, a crowbar, handcuffs, trash bags, rope, and an ice pick. Thus equipped, he drove across country in the late 1960s, and later roamed over wide stretches of Washington, Oregon, Utah, Colorado, and Florida from 1974 to 1978 looking for victims. As we will see below, much of his luck in evading capture for as long as he did stemmed from the fact that his crimes encompassed very large geographical distances that crossed multiple police jurisdictions.

As with other serial killers, Bundy's methods of killing evolved over time. Initially, he favored locating women who lived alone in out-of-the-way basement apartments that were easy to break into at night. Once inside, he would bludgeon, rape (usually with some kind of instrument that would cause internal damage), strangle his victims, and then dispose of their corpses in surrounding wilderness areas. Soon thereafter he graduated to choosing a young female who was alone, approach her while wearing a false cast on his arm or leg that concealed a small crowbar, ask her to help him open the door to his car, and, when she bent over to do so, knock her senseless, push her into the auto, secure her with handcuffs, and then take her to a pre-arranged site some distance away. Once there, he would usually sodomize and strangle the unfortunate woman, mutilate her sexual organs, and bite off pieces of flesh from her belly and thighs. Bundy was also fond of revisiting these secondary crime sites and engaging in necrophilia with the corpses, an act which often entailed redressing and grooming the bodies. On a couple of occasions that we know of, he would also dress up as a police officer and persuade victims to accompany him to his vehicle. Later, when he was on the run from authorities in Florida, he reverted to his earlier modus operandi of breaking into Florida State University's Chi Omega sorority house at night, and then savagely beat five girls in their beds, two of which he strangled with panty hose. Typical of psychopathic multiple murderers, he also kept souvenirs of these killings, which included photos and even heads.[33]

To the best of our knowledge, all of Ted Bundy's victims were young white females between the ages of 15 and 25. The vast majority were college students who were usually out alone at night. In addition to their similarity in age, race, and occupation, these women had long straight hair, which they parted in the middle. Much has been made of the fact that Bundy's first girlfriend, the one who broke up with him in 1968, also wore her hair in the same fashion.

No one really knows why Bundy hunted and killed these women in such a horrendous fashion. While he was obviously a violent and vicious misogynist, he had several long term relationships with women, and dated a great many others without incident all the way up until his first arrest in 1975. True crime writer Ann Rule, who actually worked alongside Bundy as a volunteer at the Seattle Crisis Center in the early 70s, conjectures that his misogyny stemmed from the lifelong resentment he felt towards his mother for both his illegitimacy and the fact that she kept this knowledge from him until his adolescence. Rule also believes this deep seated anger was stoked into a murderous rage against females in general when Bundy's first girlfriend—a white college age girl with long hair parted in the middle—rejected him.[34]

It may also be that Bundy was yet another example of a serial killer who believed himself threatened by a world that made him feel of little consequence. We know that his illegitimacy troubled him, doubtless because of the stigma associated with children born out of wedlock. While his bastardy does not appear to have been held against him by family, peers, or partners, he may still have felt that his lack of paternity made him an outcast, and this sense of alienation was probably heightened when he was rejected by a woman who was well-born and loved by her legitimate parents. As is often the case with psychopathic murderers, once apprehended, Bundy expressed no remorse for the women he killed and tried to lay blame for what he did to them on everything from his lack of a father figure to the pornography he was fond of watching as a youth.

Whatever triggered Bundy's murderous rage, we know from his death row confessions that he was driven to kill for much the same reason as others of his ilk, that is he got a thrill from exercising complete control over another human life. Indeed, in discussions with two of his biographers, Stephen Michaud and Hugh Aynesworth, he acknowledged that whether he was stealing something or abducting someone, "the big payoff for me, was actually possessing whatever it was I had stolen. I really enjoyed having something that I had wanted and gone out and taken."[35] And what greater thrill for such a man than to take complete possession of a young woman by assaulting and killing her and then defiling her remains.

Looking over Bundy's modus operandi and victims, it is not difficult to understand how he was able to get away with murder for almost a decade. By killing unrelated strangers at different times and in disparate places, which also crossed multiple police jurisdictions, he essentially insured the kind of "linkage blindness" that prevents law enforcement agencies from discerning connections between seemingly unrelated capital crimes. His choice of a tan VW Beetle, while often commented upon by witnesses and the occasional survivor, was not an unusual sight on the road in the 60s and 70s, and eyewitnesses could never agree on its color. By relying on surprise, blunt force trauma, and strangulation, Bundy guaranteed that his crimes were neither noisy nor likely to leave any incriminating evidence at abduction sites. He also made it harder to pin anything on him by murdering the women he kidnapped in out-of-the-way places, such as wilderness parks, and then disposing of their clothing and personal possessions.

Ted Bundy was also able to pass himself off as a perfectly normal, even upstanding member of society. He was handsome, educated, well-groomed, sociable, polite, and at least in Washington state, connected to high ranking members of the Republican party. All of this worked to deflect attention from him during his murder spree in Washington and Oregon during 1974. When police released a sketch of the primary suspect in the various abductions that summer, as well as a description of the tan VW he was driving, Bundy's girlfriend, Elizabeth Kloepfer, his workmate Ann Rule, and one of his former UW psychology professors contacted authorities and reported that Bundy fit the profile. Local law enforcement ignored their tip believing it unlikely that a young, clean-cut, politically active law student without a prior record (Bundy's juvenile arrests had been expunged when he turned 18), was likely to be such a cold calculating murderer.[36]

Finally, it was also difficult for witnesses to identify Ted Bundy because he had what can only be described as a chameleon-like ability to make himself look different with minor changes to his appearance. Looking at the many photographs taken of him during his arrests, incarcerations, and trials, it is striking how a change in hairstyle, the growth of a mustache, or losing weight could make him look like a completely different person.[37] More to the point, Bundy was aware of the fact that he had easily altered, anonymous features, and he used this trait to his advantage throughout his criminal career.

In the end, Bundy's ability to seemingly kill at will and evade detection and capture for years helped make him a media sensation. As already noted, when he was finally apprehended, Bundy's life, crimes, modus operandi, escapes, and trials were front page news. Journalists, true crime writers, psychologists, and criminal justice experts flocked to the various cells in which he was held during his hearings and pending his execution, for interviews, biographical tidbits, and insights into how other serial killers "tick." Hollywood even made a mini-series about him.

Surprisingly absent in all of this coverage was much, if anything, about the different women he had brutally abducted, beaten, raped, sodomized, strangled, partially devoured, and defiled in death. Why this monster became a celebrity and his victims ciphers is the question to which we will now turn.

"If not 'evil,' what?": Demystifying the Serial Killer

One suspects that author Thomas Harris had Ted Bundy in mind when he created the two serial killers featured in his bestselling book, *The Silence of the Lambs*. Like Bundy, Harris' "Buffalo Bill" lures unsuspecting young women to his vehicle by pretending to be injured and in need of assistance. When a female opts to assist him, he savagely beats her into unconsciousness, secures her in his van, and drives her to his house, where she is held captive pending death by strangulation. Afterwards, Bill appropriates parts of his victim's skin for a "woman suit" he is manufacturing in the hopes of changing his gender identity.

While Buffalo Bill's modus operandi is very much akin to that used by Ted Bundy, the other serial killer in Harris' story, Hannibal Lecter, captures much of what made Bundy such a compelling figure to the public. Like his real life counterpart, Lecter is handsome, intelligent, courteous, well-groomed, socially connected, and a student of psychology. In all respects, he appears to be a seemingly normal, upwardly mobile young professional. Unfortunately, Hannibal also has Ted's down side, i.e., he is a cold-blooded, remorseless psychopathic murderer who hunts, kills, and devours his victims.

One other similarity shared by Bundy and Harris' characters is their celebrity. *Silence of the Lambs* was a hit in print and on the big screen. The book sold at least 1.3 million copies worldwide and won the 1988 Bram Stoker Award and the 1989 Anthony Award for best novel of the year. The film version, which was released in 1991, grossed $227.7 million worldwide and won five Oscars (Best Picture, Best Actor, Best Actress, Best Director, Best Adapted Screenplay).

Suffice it to say that this success invited imitation. Indeed, since Buffalo Bill and Hannibal Lecter were introduced to the public, there have been a veritable slew of films, television series, and documentaries about serial killers. Studios have produced and released such box office hits as *Basic Instinct* ($352 million),[38] *Seven* ($327 million), *Hannibal* ($351 million), *Red Dragon* ($209 million), and *Scream* ($173 million). Broadcast and cable networks have followed suit, commissioning and airing prime time dramas—*Hannibal, Dexter, Bates Motel, The Following*—in which the central characters are psychopathic murderers. Even independent filmmakers and documentarians have gotten in on the act by producing "in-depth" treatments of real life serial murderers such as *The Search for the Yorkshire Ripper* (1999), *Son of Sam Speaks: The Untold Story* (1997), *The Killer Clown* (2002), and *Confessions of the Boston Strangler* (2014).

When it comes to serial killers the purveyors of printed material have not been far behind their visual media colleagues. Whether one is talking about a chain like Barnes & Noble, or a neighborhood store selling second hand novels, all book sellers now feature special sections that provide prospective readers with true crime stories highlighting the careers of assorted gangsters, grifters, rippers, and rapists. In short, the villains treated in this section have become a multi-billion dollar industry.

Why is the public so enamored with these murderous predators? To some degree, this fascination is akin to the phenomenon of "rubber necking," or slowing down to take in the particulars of a bad traffic accident. People are curious about the carnage that has occurred and the deaths and injuries that accompany it. They also derive some satisfaction in knowing that on this occasion at least, they avoided a similar fate.

People also share with serial killers a sense of entitlement to certain things, as well as a desire to be in control of their lives. Further, when folks actually realize these desires, they too experience the same intense sense of well-being and accomplishment that these murderers feel when they hunt and kill their victims. Unlike the sociopaths and psychopaths addressed in this section, however, normal human beings recognize restraints on their behavior, which often make it more difficult for them to accomplish their aims and achieve the *frisson* that accompanies such an achievement. Given these difficulties, it is not terribly surprising that the law abiding, morally bound general public is not only horrified, but also fascinated, perhaps even a little envious, of individuals who blithely dismiss any strictures on their behavior, and experience no remorse in doing so.

Whatever the psychological reasons that attract us to these killers, there is also the simple fact that it is almost impossible to avoid hearing or reading about them in today's 24-hour news cycle. "If it bleeds, it leads," is a common refrain in the media, and so the press—print and otherwise—affords considerable coverage to violent crime and its practitioners. Indeed, in a comparative analysis of newspaper crime coverage in the U.S. and other countries from 1960–1989, criminal justice researcher, Harry L. Marsh, found that

> there is an overrepresentation of violent crimes and an underrepresentation of property crimes; the percentages of violent crimes reported in newspapers do not match official crime statistics; crime coverage presents a false image of the effectiveness of police and courts in controlling crime and punishing criminals; and newspaper coverage fails to educate readers as to the causes of crime or how to avoid personal victimization.[39]

One consequence of all of this misinformation is that a great many people believe that they are quite literally surrounded by super savvy serial killers scheming to off them and their loved ones at an opportune moment. In the face of this conviction, it is difficult for authorities to reassure the general public that (1) there are not that many of these killers afoot; (2) their ability to evade notice and capture has little to do with any intellectual superiority on their part; (3) the probability of crossing paths with one of these individuals is low; and (4) only a small percentage of homicides are the handiwork of serial murderers. Given this level of ignorance about the facts of serial murder, it is hardly surprising that these criminals loom large in the popular imagination.

In addition to all the attention these killers receive in the press and on TV news, the film industry routinely presents serial murderers in a manner that cannot help but arouse feelings of admiration for them. The psychopaths in many of the abovementioned blockbuster movies, for example, are played by handsome leading men who are remarkable actors. This is best exemplified by Sir Anthony Hopkins' dramatization of Hannibal Lecter in *Silence of the Lambs*. From the moment Hopkins' Lecter appears on the big screen, he is a larger-than-life figure—handsome, suave, intelligent, charming, witty, and, despite the fact he is behind bars, definitely in control of the situation. Small wonder that a great many viewers of this movie regard Lecter, rather than the protagonist of the story, Clarice Starling (played by Jodie Foster), to be the hero of the movie.[40]

Hollywood also ramps up, one could even say glorifies, the violence we see these virile, smart, and sexy serial killers commit on screen. Films by directors like Quentin Terantino, Zack Snyder, Wes Craven, and John Carpenter are literally awash in blood, brain matter, and viscera. Indeed, these folks and their imitators have created an entire cottage industry of so-called "slasher films"—*Halloween, Friday the 13th, Nightmare on Elm Street, The Texas Chain Saw Massacre, Hostel, Saw*—that are essentially snuff movies in which hapless teenagers and undergraduate college students fall into the clutches of terribly nasty psychos, who then proceed to visit great violence on their bodies with an assortment of knives, razors, machetes, buzz saws, nail guns, meat hooks, and other blunt instruments and edged weapons.

Perhaps the most disturbing aspect of all these sensational crime stories, best-selling novels, Oscar nominated films, B grade slasher movies, TV series, and documentaries is their lack of concern for the hapless victims of these murderers. With the exception of detailed descriptions and/or close up shots of their mangled and mutilated corpses, or mention of where they number in the murderer's list of kills, the men, women, and children that fall prey to these criminals are largely ignored. In part, this omission is because many of these unfortunates are counted among what Egger calls "the less dead," or members of marginalized communities considered expendable and not worthy of coverage. More often than not, however, those murdered fall victim yet a second time to the gross indifference of journalists, authors, producers, and filmmakers who opt to sell papers, tickets, and advertising with serial killer centered stories that downplay the fact that their prey are actually someone's mother, father, husband, wife, daughter, or son.

In the end, all of this "coverage" works to desensitize the public to violence and devalue the serial killers' victims. It also contributes to the heroization of what is without question a truly villainous type. While it could be argued (and I have done so in an earlier work) that Achilles and his ilk were often savage killers responsible for a great many deaths and much suffering, these "heroes" did not lurk in the shadows awaiting a helpless stranger that they could bludgeon, rape, cannibalize, and defile in death (Hector's corpse being the notable exception to the rule). Rather, they were public figures who sought out willing foes worthy of combat and an honorable demise. Even referring to these figures as "anti-heroes" is problematic given the fact that the picaroons, survivors, and assorted oddballs that have been the historic recipients of this rubric never engaged in gratuitous violence, killed only in self-defense, and were completely uninterested in "celebrity" of any kind.[41]

Instead of heroizing or sensationalizing these killers, it might be better to acknowledge, as psychopathic murderers often do, that for reasons genetic, social, or otherwise, they are the unapologetic representatives of a deep seated pathological viciousness that resides in every human being. These individuals give expression to a truly bestial nature that some 50,000 years of evolution, and over five millennia of civilization, religion, philosophy, and science, has been unable to eradicate. As Philip Jenkins, the Distinguished Professor of History at Baylor University, notes:

> When the 20th century began, it was obvious to all educated people that this would be a great age of science and enlightenment. As this black age slouches towards its conclusions, it is clear that science has failed either to understand or to subdue the beast within humanity and the highest form of enlightenment might be to admit this fact. At the very least, let us agree on the failure of language to offer an acceptable terminology for the beast, the darkness, for whatever metaphor we choose to employ for that intuitively obvious reality. If not "evil," what?[42]

Or, to put this question another way, if psychopathic murderers are not villains, who is?

Epilogue

Marplots and Madmen
The Villain as Metaphor

> *From ghoulies and ghosties*
> *And long-leggedy beasties*
> *And things that go bump in the night,*
> *Good Lord, deliver us!*
>
> —Scottish Prayer

> *Monsters are metaphors, and we are crawling with them because obviously we are very afraid of many things.*
>
> —Mary McNamara, LA Times TV critic

> *Life is, in fact, a battle. Evil is insolvent and strong; beauty enchanting but rare; goodness very apt to be weak; folly very apt to be defiant; wickedness to carry the day; imbeciles to be in great places, people of sense in small, and mankind generally unhappy. But the world as it stands is no illusion, no phantasm, no evil dream of a night; we wake up to it again for ever and ever; we can neither forget it nor deny it nor dispense with it.*
>
> —Henry James

This book grew out of a freshman seminar that focused on how villainy is defined and represented over the course of Western history. Over the years I have offered this seminar, I always kick off the first class meeting by asking my students to share with me what comes to mind when they think about villains and villainous behavior. With the notable exception of Adolf Hitler, they invariably reference fictional characters associated with assorted movies, TV series, comic books, and video games. These include the likes of Darth Vader, Magneto (and the evil mutants allied with him), Lex Luthor, Aladdin's nemesis Jafar, *Game of Thrones*' Cersei Lannister and her loathsome son Joffrey, *Nightmare on Elm Street*'s Freddy Krueger, and anyone who messes with Spider Man. When I press them as to why they select these figures, they usually note their amazing powers, cool clothes, and over-the-top, unabashedly evil behavior.

This association of villains with fictitious felons who dress and behave in a manner that clearly identifies them as the "bad guys," is an interesting historical development because in the past villainy was very much associated with individuals, groups, and natural forces that were in and of the real world. Persons and objects identified as villainous were not imaginary constructs but actual people, places, and phenomena that were regarded as threats to the physical survival, sense of identity, internal harmony, moral order, and social relations of human society. While the fables and fictional accounts of Western culture have always abounded in malicious characters, these imaginary antagonists were also largely derived from the types addressed in the preceding pages—animate and inanimate nature, sybaritic "Oriental" peoples, nomadic tribes, illiterate and ill-washed peasants, abusive tyrants, intrusive bureaucrats, those who betray kith and kin, "uppity" women, and chronic criminals.

Why villainy is now largely associated with metaphorical monsters, marplots, and madmen appears to have something to do with the inverse relationship that now exists between modern notions of who is worthy of being regarded as either a hero or a villain. Whereas the heroic pantheon has expanded in a rather dramatic fashion to accommodate men *and* women who are commoners, martyrs, athletes, artists, researchers, explorers, rebels with or without a cause, entrepreneurs, survivors, and even successful dieters, what is regarded as villainous has narrowed considerably. As we have seen above, the natural world is now regarded in a positive light, Orient and Occident are increasingly intertwined, most Western families hail from nomadic and peasant stock, some tyrants are still considered "great," bureaucratic domination is a fact of life in modern urbanized society, traitors come in different flavors, so-called power women are now career girls, and serial offenders cannot seem to help themselves.

Perhaps the best way to understand how these shifts in thinking about heroes and villains came about is to consider what these words first signified, and then consider how their meaning changed in response to such developments as Christianity, the scientific and political revolutions of the modern period, and the various "isms" of the 19th and 20th centuries. As noted in the introduction, "villain" is derived from the Latin *villanus*, which was used to describe someone who labored on one of the large country farms known as *villas* in ancient Italy. Even during the medieval period, when *vilein* or *villain* became the established rubric for any unprincipled or depraved scoundrel, the word continued to be a term for people who were "low-born," menial in their habits, and "ignoble" in their actions. In fact, up until the 20th century, it was commonplace to assume that someone guilty of base and criminal actions was also likely to hail from the wrong side of the tracks.

Much the same thing can be said about the rubric "hero," which was originally an honorific for aristocratic warriors and a subset of the gods. Though this term gradually becomes associated with mere mortals and the non-martially inclined, there remains an expectation throughout most of Western history that anyone dubbed heroic will also boast an impeccable pedigree. Even in cases where the hero is a commoner, he or she is still expected to comport themselves in the manner of someone with blue blood on at least one side of the sheets.

Christianity, however, with its messiah born in a stable and its promise of a heaven open to all, ushers in a certain measure of egalitarian thinking among Westerners. This egalitarianism is further strengthened by the successful scientific, industrial, and political revolutions of the modern period that usher in our present day mass society. Not only do these developments work to democratize the heroic pantheon by making it possible for those other than the well-born to be heroized, but they also rescue from ignominy a great many people who were once villainized simply because of their ethnicity, class, and gender.

This social leveling was further assisted by assorted "isms"—liberalism, socialism, communism—that were committed, in theory at least, to the proposition that every life is worthy of respect and should be accorded the opportunity to realize itself. Two of these isms—romanticism and environmentalism—went a step further and extended this idea to the non-human world as well. Indeed, after two centuries of romantic poetry and environmental activism, mountains, forests, rivers, oceans, and wild life once regarded as red in tooth and claw, and in need of taming and ruthless exploitation, are now viewed as the epic and sublime elements of a mother nature besieged by a rapacious and villainous humanity.

Even our thinking with regard to chronic criminals who were once regarded as the very embodiment of villainy has changed markedly with advances in medicine, genetics, and neuroscience. Whereas in the past, such repeat violators of the law were regarded as either ignoble commoners naturally inclined towards crime, or as the possessed minions of some fell spirit, we now know these miscreants are actually hardwired to behave in socially inappropriate ways. While this certainly does not justify or excuse their crimes, it does make us aware of the fact that these individuals really do not understand the moral and legal boundaries that constrain their more altruistic neighbors from visiting harm on one another. Rather, they appear to be afflicted with an anti-social personality disorder that makes them naturally inclined toward such predatory behavior as lying, cheating, theft, violence, and, in some cases, outright coldblooded murder.

Further complicating this whole business with criminals is the West's ongoing love affair with anti-heroes. Though this category encompasses everyone from concentration camp survivors to unhappy, depressed, and confused slackers, it also counts in its ranks quite a few rogues and reprobates. These include the low born tricksters of peasant folk stories, the picaroons of picaresque literature, and the real life highwaymen, bank robbers, gangsters, and forgers celebrated in a great many films and television programs. While most of these figures are little more than selfish sociopaths, their struggles to survive and get ahead, by whatever means necessary, in a world dominated by wealthy self-centered elites appears to have struck a sympathetic chord among a great many Westerners who see themselves as underdogs in a game of life that is rigged against them.

Added to these class resentments is also the fact that conventional heroes are not only terribly difficult to emulate, but are often guilty of unethical and even criminal behavior. Homer's Odysseus lies, steals, rapes, and murders his way across the Mediterranean during his two decades away from Ithaca. Yahweh's beloved David, king and champion of Israel, does a stint as a bandit, works as a hired hand for the Philistines, and has no qualms about arranging the death of a man whose wife he covets. Knightly crusaders pledge themselves to defend the church, widows, orphans, and the weak, and then pillage, sexually abuse, and slaughter defenseless Christian and non-Christian men, women and children alike. Explorers such as Columbus and Cortes sail off into the horizon, discover unknown peoples, and enslave them. Brilliant scientists—Fritz Haber, Edward Teller, Andrei Sakharov—break new ground in the sciences while also helping the military establishments of their countries turn their discoveries into weapons of mass destruction. Given the suffering and death these "great men" have visited on others, it is hardly surprising that many people now prefer to heroize rather than villainize people who concentrate on getting a "piece of the action" for themselves while tweaking the noses of their betters.

Though all of these historical developments have made it increasingly difficult to clearly delineate who and what is villainous, as Mary McNamara reminds us in the second epigraph of this chapter, we still remain afraid of a great many things. For example, everyone may now be a tree hugger, but we are also terrified of pandemics, climate change, and super storms. Barbarians may now be nothing more than the hirsute Vikings of Capital One commercials, but Islam and immigrants still arouse ominous talk about the "clash of civilizations." We may concede that intrusive bureaucracies, the worldwide web, and secret surveillance programs make modern civilization possible and safe, but they also put many in mind of Orwell's Big Brother. Law enforcement authorities tell us that there are fewer crimes being committed, and they also assure us that serial killers are not very numerous or bright, but our news and entertainment media feature stories that imply murder and mayhem are all around us. And so on, ad infinitum.

Whereas in the past we could associate these very real fears with villains of flesh and blood (or soil and sinew), and actually do battle with them, we are now living in a world where the "lines in the sand" delineating insiders and outsiders, order and disorder, lawful and criminal, normal and abnormal are blurred and frequently overlap with one another. For a species that tends to view the world in what social anthropologist Claude Lévi-Strauss termed "binary oppositions," this is an unsatisfactory, even maddening reality. Or to put this another way, just as we continue to yearn for heroic champions who help us define the meaning of excellence and virtue, so do we also need villainous types to highlight the dangers of unlawful conduct, absolute power, mendacity, betrayal, and amoral behavior.

So where does one find villains in a time where certainty is in short supply and ambiguity is the rule? If the students in my seminars are any indication, we appear to be finding them in worlds other than the one in which we live. As for why this is happening, perhaps the best explanation is the one TV critic Mary McNamara makes when attempting to explain the literal explosion of monsters in the popular media:

> So how much easier for everyone if those figures we considered Satan became literally Satan? Or one of his minions? How much clearer the roles if the "us" were simply humans, the "them" a bunch of decaying corpses/bloodsucking vampires/uncool werewolves?
> These are battles we can all get behind. Families are strengthened, unlikely alliances are formed to fight real evil, even when that "evil" is the stereotyping of all vampires as predators or all witches as cruel.
> In the world of horror, even the notion of social tolerance is simpler, represented by the recognition of "good" monsters (those still in touch with their humanity), and "bad" humans (those who behave more like monsters).[1]

Or to put this another way, if you fear nature, strangers, tyrants, traitors, women, and chronic criminals, but recognize these categories have become far too complicated to simply villainize, the easiest way to address your unease is to translate these types into something metaphorical. Thus *Sharknado* becomes a stand-in for the natural environment. The zombies of *Walking Dead* are the new barbarians. Darth Vader and his Sith emperor represent everything we dread about big government, and Anakin Skywalker is *the* traitor most foul. *The Devil Wears Prada*'s Miranda Priestly is the epitome of the emasculating bitch. And Hannibal Lecture is the very definition of the psychopath, albeit one with panache and excellent table manners. Because these characters are not real, we can also fear and loathe them without guilt.

As Henry James reminds us, however, life is a battle, "evil is insolvent and strong," and wickedness often carries the day. While it is certainly laudable that our civilization has progressed to a point where nature, people that are different from us, and women are no longer assumed to be likely villains, there are real monsters around us and they are not evil mutants. Perhaps no one captures this reality better than that master of modern horror Stephen King. In novellas like *Rita Hayworth and Shawshank Redemption*, *Apt Pupil*, and *The Body*, King reminds us that there are actual Nazis, racists, psychopaths, corrupt officials, sadistic guards, and schoolyard bullies who seek power and relish the suffering of others. These are not phantasms or "evil dreams of a night." These are actual inhabitants of the world we "wake up to … for ever and ever; we can neither forget" this fact "nor deny it nor dispense with it." To do so is to open the door to terrors that are far worse than anything we see on a TV screen or read in a comic book.

This said, it might also be time for us to acknowledge the simple fact that if all of us are now deemed capable of heroism, we are all certainly capable of villainy. As Mary McNamara notes at the end of her article on the proliferation of "ghoulies and ghosties and long-leggedy beasties":

> Most modern horror series acknowledge the fragility of the line between monster and human, but none more than the "The Walking Dead." As deadly as the zombies remain, they have never been the true monsters of the piece, as each season makes clear. The real monsters are the living who succumb to rage or despair or their own dark natures. The real battle, for survival, for resources, for a stable, thriving society, is not "us" versus "them"—but "us" versus "us."
>
> We just need to figure out how to talk about it all without the vampire fangs, the hexenbiests and the crazy cannibals.[2]

Hopefully this book will help its readers take part in that conversation.

Chapter Notes

Chapter 1

1. An excellent summary of Ice Age climatology can be found in Brian Fagan, ed., *The Complete Ice Age* (London: Thames and Hudson, 2009).
2. On the Mount Toba eruption, see Brian Fagan, *Cro-Magnon: How the Ice Age Gave Birth to the First Modern Humans* (New York: Bloomsbury Press, 2010), 93–97; Michael Rampino and Stanley Ambrose, "Volcanic Winter in the Garden of Eden: The Toba Supereruption and the Late Pleistocene Human Population Crash," *Geological Society of America Special Paper 345* (2000); and Henry and Elizabeth Stommel, *Volcano Weather: The Story of 1816, the Year Without a Summer* (Newport, RI: Seven Seas Press, 1983).
3. See R. Dale Guthrie, *The Nature of Paleolithic Art* (Chicago: University of Chicago Press, 2005) for a professional paleontologist's description of Ice Age fauna.
4. Richard G. Klein and Blake Edgar describe language as a "knowledge sense" in their *The Dawn of Human Culture* (New York: John Wiley & Sons, 2002), 146.
5. Fagan, *Cro-Magnon*, 14.
6. In their *The Dawn of Human Culture*, Klein and Edgar do a particularly good job of underscoring the significant role culture plays in both insuring human survival and inculcating a sense of otherness between early humanity and the non-human environment. The last chapter in this book, "Nature or Nurture: Before the Dawn," is also an excellent introduction for non-specialists to the continuing debate surrounding what sparked early modern human cultural development, i.e., shifts in technology and organization in the aftermath of the Mount Toba catastrophe or some kind of fortuitous neural mutation in the human brain. Another excellent treatment on this subject from a historical point of view can be found in J.R. McNeill and William H. McNeill *The Human Web: A Bird's-Eye View of World History* (New York: W.W. Norton, 2003), 9–24.
7. McNeill and McNeill, in *The Human Web*, do an admirable job of summarizing what was entailed with the shift to an agricultural way of life in the second chapter of their book "Shifting to Food Production, 11,000–3,000 Years Ago," 25–40. More exhaustive accounts include Bruce D. Smith, *The Emergence of Agriculture* (New York: Scientific American Library, 1995); Jack R. Harlan, *Crops and Man* (Madison, WI: American Society of Agronomy: Crop Science Society of America, 1992); and Juliet Clutton-Brock, *A Natural History of Domesticated Mammals* (Cambridge: Cambridge University Press, 1999).
8. *Myths from Mesopotamia: Creation, the Flood, Gilgamesh, and Others*, ed. and trans. Stephanie Dalley (Oxford: Oxford University Press, 1989. Reissued 2008), 53.
9. Ibid., 63.
10. God of war, hunting, and the plague.
11. Ibid., 115.
12. Genesis 3:17–19. These and subsequent quotations are from *The New American Bible* (Washington, D.C.: Catholic Publishers, 1971).
13. Deuteronomy 8:15.
14. Isaiah 42:15, 5:6.
15. Roderick Frazier Nash, *Wilderness and the American Mind* (New Haven: Yale University Press, 2001), 14–15.
16. As punishment for conspiring to overthrow him, Zeus compelled his brother Poseidon and another high-ranking co-conspirator, his son Apollo, to work for King Laomedon of Troy. Laomedon ordered them to build a fortified wall around his city, after which he refused to pay for their services. Thus the longstanding hatred by the Greek god of the sea for all things Trojan. Homer, *The Iliad*, Book VII,

451–453. These and subsequent quotations are from *The Iliad of Homer*, trans. Richard Lattimore (Chicago: University of Chicago Press, 1951).

17. Homer, *The Iliad*, Book XII, 15–30.

18. Homer, *The Odyssey*, Book XVIII, 130–31. These and subsequent quotations are from *The Odyssey of Homer*, trans. Richard Lattimore (Chicago: University of Chicago Press, 1951).

19. For an erudite and exhaustive treatment of the place of nature in classical Greek literature (as well as in the Archaic and later Hellenistic periods) see Charles Paul Segal's "Nature and the World of Man in Greek Literature," *Arion*, Vol. 2 No. 1 (Spring 1963), 19–53.

20. *Beowulf: A Prose Translation*, trans. E. Talbot Donaldson (New York: W.W. Norton, 2002), 24.

21. *Ibid.*, 25.

22. Edward Cuthbert Butler, "St. Anthony," *The Catholic Encyclopedia*, Vol. 1 (New York: Robert Appleton Company, 1907). See also St. Athanasius' "The Life of Saint Antony" in Phillip Schaff and Henry Wace, eds., *Athanasius: Select Works and Letters* (New York: C. Scribner's Sons, 1897) http://www.fordham.edu/halsall/basis/vita-antony.html.

23. Augustine's "zoophobia" is apparent throughout his *Confessions*, particularly in Book X of that work.

24. "Be fertile and multiply; fill the earth and subdue it. Have dominion over the fish of the sea, the birds of the air, and all the living things that move on the earth."

25. Nash, *Wilderness*, 19.

26. Eugen Weber, "Fairies and Hard Facts: The Reality of Folktales," *Journal of the History of Ideas*, XLII (1981), 97. See also Robert Darnton's essay "Peasants Tell Tales" in his *The Great Cat Massacre: And Other Episodes in French Cultural History* (New York: Random House, 1985) for an equally enlightening and entertaining exposition on how peasants used folktales during the early modern period and what these stories also tell us about conditions during that time.

27. For an account of how the natural philosophers of the Enlightenment and their counterparts in the 19th century fashioned themselves into heroic figures doing battle with the natural world see M. Gregory Kendrick, "'To boldly go where no one has gone before': The Hero as Explorer," in *The Heroic Ideal: Western Archetypes from the Greeks to the Present* (Jefferson, NC: McFarland, 2010).

28. Daniel Worster, *Nature's Economy: A History of Ecological Ideas* (Cambridge: Cambridge University Press, 1994), 173. The quoted material in this selection is taken from George Perkins Marsh, "The Study of Nature," *Christian Examiner* (January 1860), 35.

29. Quoted in Worster, *Nature's Economy*, 176–77.

30. The idea that romanticism is characterized by a love of the "unclassifiable" was put forward by R. R. Palmer and Joel Colton in their *A History of the Modern World* (New York: Alfred A. Knopf, 1978), 428.

31. The reader interested in the history of romanticism and its premier artists is directed to the following works: M. Cranston, *The Romantic Movement* (Oxford: Oxford University Press, 1994); Roy Porter and Mikul Teich, eds., *Romanticism in National Context* (New York: Cambridge University Press, 1988); Nicholas V. Riasanovsky, *The Emergence of Romanticism* (New York: Oxford University Press, 1992); and H. G. Schenk, *The Mind of the European Romantics* (Garden City, N.Y.: Doubleday, 1969).

32. Nash, *Wilderness*, 44–47.

33. *Ibid.*, 47–49. The quote is from John Muir's essay on national parks found in *John Muir: The Eight Wilderness-Discovery Books* (London: Diadem Books, 1992), 480.

34. *Los Angeles Times*, 1934. Quoted on the cover page of Mike Davis' *Ecology of Fear: Los Angeles and the Imagination of Disaster* (New York: Vintage, 1999).

35. *Ibid.*, 9.

Chapter 2

1. Bruce J. Malina, *The New Testament World: Insights from Cultural Anthropology* (Louisville, KY: Westminster/John Knox Press, 1993), 29.

2. I am using the translation of *barbaros* found in Richmond Lattimore's *The Iliad of Homer* (Chicago: University of Chicago Press, 1961), 99.

3. This section's discussion of the lexicology of the term "barbarian" owes much to Arno Borst's "Barbarians: The History of a European Catchword" in his *Medieval Worlds: Barbarians, Heretics and Artists in the Middle Ages* (Cambridge: Polity Press, 1991), 3–13. The tendency of Herodotus to distinguish between "hard" and "soft" peoples is noted in an article by James Redfield "Herodotus the Tourist" in *Greeks and Barbarians*, ed. Thomas Harrison (Edinburgh: Edinburgh University Press, 2002).

4. Herodotus, *The Persian Wars*, trans. George Rawlinson (New York: The Modern Library, 1942), 535.

5. *Ibid.*, 536.

6. Redfield, "Herodotus the Tourist," 41–42.

7. Herodotus, op. cit., 497–8.
8. Redfield, op. cit., 39–43. See also in the same collection of essays Pierre Briant's "History and Ideology: The Greeks and 'Persian Decadence'" and Wilfried Nippel's "The Construction of the 'Other.'" Though an older work, Helen H. Bacon's *Barbarians in Greek Tragedy* (New Haven: Yale University Press, 1961) also offers insightful observations regarding how the soft barbarians of Asia are portrayed in classical age Greek drama.
9. Edward Said, *Orientalism* (New York: Vantage, 1979), 55–60.
10. Virgil, *The Aeneid*, trans. Robert Fitzgerald (New York: Vintage, 1990), 254 (Book VIII, 931–2).
11. Cassius Dio, *Roman History*, trans. E. Cary (Cambridge: Harvard University Press, 1960–1969) 50.5, 24–25.
12. *Ibid.*, 50.5.
13. *Ibid.*, 50.27, quoted in Prudence Jones, *Cleopatra: The Last Pharaoh* (London: Haus, 2006). It should be noted that Jones' biography of Cleopatra, though brief, is an excellent summation of what both ancient and modern sources tell us about Egypt's queen and her efforts to maintain Egyptian independence. It is also beautifully illustrated.
14. Michael Grant, *Cleopatra* (New York: Barnes & Noble, 1995), 235. While Grant's biography is relatively old, I find his appraisal of Cleopatra and Antony's actions prior to the final break with Octavian both sensible and compelling.
15. Said, *Orientalism*, 287.
16. See Redfield's "Herodotus the Tourist," for an excellent discussion on the differences Herodotus draws between the Egyptians and the Scythians, pages 36–39.
17. For the reader interested in examining Roman accounts of these different barbarian tribes, the following primary sources are recommended: Julius Caesar, *The Gallic War*, trans. H. Edwards (Cambridge: Harvard University Press, 1917); Cassius Dio, *Roman History*, trans. E. Cary (Cambridge: Harvard University Press, 1960–1969); Diodorus Siculus, *Library*, Volumes III and VI, trans. F. Watson (Cambridge: Harvard University Press, 1933); Livy, *History of Rome*, Vol. III, trans. B. O. Foster (Cambridge: Harvard University Press, 1982–98); Pliny, *Natural History*, trans. H. Rackham and W. Jones (Cambridge: Harvard University Press, 1938–63); Sallust, *The Histories*, trans. J. Rolfe (Cambridge: Harvard University Press, 1965); Tacitus, *Agricola and Germania*, trans. M. Hutton (Cambridge: Harvard University Press, 1970). A really excellent secondary source on this subject is Thomas S. Burns, *Rome and the Barbarians 100 B.C.–A.D. 400* (Baltimore: John Hopkins University Press, 2003).
18. Tacitus, *Agricola and Germania*, revised translation with an Introduction and Notes by J. B. Rives (London: Penguin, 2009), xlii.
19. *Ibid.*, 41–42.
20. *Ibid.*, 52.
21. Bitter friends is the expression historian Thomas S. Burns uses in his *Rome and the Barbarians*, cited above, to describe the often complicated relationship between the Romans and their Celtic, German, and Gothic neighbors.
22. Ammianus Marcellinus, *History*, trans. John C. Rolfe (Cambridge: Harvard University Press, 1982–1986).
23. Ibn Fadlan, "A Viking Funeral," in *Chronicles of the Barbarians: Firsthand Accounts of Pillage and Conquest, From the Ancient World to the Fall of Constantinople*, ed. David Willis McCullough (New York: History Book Club, 1998), 223.
24. *Ibid.*, 224.
25. From the "Annals of St. Bertin: The Northmen in Frankland 843–859" and "The Anglo-Saxon Chronicle 994–1016" in *Chronicles of the Barbarians*, 215–217, 219.
26. John P. McKay, Bennett D. Hill, John Buckler, *A History of Western Society* (Boston: Houghton Mifflin, 1987), 741.
27. The bracketed remarks are from Leon Trotsky's *Literature and Revolution*, quoted in my *The Heroic Ideal: Western Archetypes from the Greeks to the Present*, 147. For an exhaustive discussion of heroic vitalism and its progeny, see "Black Angels and New Men: Heroism in a Totalitarian Context," in the same work, 146–183.
28. Nietzsche coined the expression "beast of prey" to describe the kind of *Übermensch*, or "Over man" that he had in mind for the future. The quoted phrase "violent, domineering, undismayed, cruel" is from Hitler's *Mein Kampf*.
29. Internet Movie Database, "Memorable quotes for Serenity," http://www.imdb.com/title/tt0379786/quotes.

Chapter 3

1. Roger Boesche, *Theories of Tyranny From Plato to Arendt* (University Park: Pennsylvania State University Park, 1996) 456.
2. One finds this quote cited in every major account of the Greek tyrants. This particular iteration comes from A. Andrewes, *The Greek Tyrants* (London: Hutchinson & Co., 1956) 21.
3. *Ibid.*, 137.
4. This is certainly the judgment of M. I.

Finley in his *The Ancient Greeks* (New York: Penguin, 1985), 40. Andrewes also considers that *tyrannos* might have initially been used to designate a usurper, though she finds it equally likely it is another neutral expression for king. See also John V. A. Fine, *The Ancient Greeks: A Critical History* (Cambridge: Harvard University Press, 1983), 685–687.

5. Perhaps the best modern account of Gyges' coup and subsequent rule is found in Robert Drewes' article "The First Tyrants in Greece," *Historia* 21, no. 2 (1972): 129–44. Ancient authors, such as Nicolaus of Damascus, Herodotus, Plato, and Plutarch, also write about him but their accounts largely focus on his alleged passion for Candaules beautiful queen, a passion that leads him to first betray and then murder his king.

6. A. Andrewes is particularly good on the social and political significance of these hoplite armies. See pages 31–38 in her *The Greek Tyrants*.

7. Fine, 131–134.

8. *Ibid.*

9. *Ibid.* See also A. Andrews treatment of the foreign and domestic policies of the many tyrants addressed in her work, as well as Chapter 2 "Tyranny in the Early Peloponnese" and Chapter 6 "The Peisistratidae and the Reforms of Cleisthenes" in Raphael Sealey's *A History of the Greek City States ca. 700–338 B.C.* (Berkeley: University of California Press, 1976) for additional information on the colonizing and public works efforts of these men.

10. Fine, 132.

11. Andrewes and Fine both examine the nature of these party divisions in considerable detail in their sections dealing with the Pisistratid tyranny. See also Book I of Herodotus' *Histories* 59–64 (Loeb edition) and Aristotle's *Athenian Constitution* 13 (Loeb).

12. Andrewes, 100–107; Fine, 212–214; Also see Herodotus (I.59–64) and Aristotle, *Athenian Constitution*, 14–16 for a detailed description of Pisistratus being escorted to Athens by Athena.

13. Fine, 214.

14. *Ibid.*, 214–215.

15. Fine, 215. See also A. Andrewes, 111.

16. Fine, 218–219. A. Andrewes, 111, 113–114.

17. Fine, 216–218, A. Andrewes, 112.

18. See Fine, 222–224, for an exhaustive account of the events leading up to the deposition of Hippias.

19. *Ibid.*, 222–225.

20. *Ibid.*, 226.

21. Herodotus, *The Persian Wars*, trans. George Rawlinson (New York: The Modern Library, 1942), see in particular the conversations and events highlighted in Book Seven found on the following pages, 496–502; 511–514; 534–535. Creon's quote regarding his ownership of Thebes is part of an exchange with his son Haemon that underscores the tyrant's conviction that the *polis* is his to rule as he sees fit. It can be found on page 97 of the following edition of the play: Sophocles, *The Three Theban Plays*, trans. Robert Fagles (New York: Penguin, 1984).

22. For the general reader interested in Plato's pronouncements on tyrants and tyranny, see the following excellent translations: Plato, *Republic*, trans. Allan Bloom (New York: Basic Books, 1968); *Laws*, trans. Thomas Pangle (New York: Basic Books, 1980); and *Gorgias* in *The Collected Dialogues of Plato*, ed. Edith Hamilton and Huntington Cairns (Princeton: Princeton University Press, 1961). Roger Boesche's chapter "Plato: The Political Psychology of Tyranny" in his *Theories of Tyranny* also provides an excellent summation and critical analysis of Plato's thinking on this subject.

23. Quoted in Boesche's chapter "Aristotle: Tyranny as Unnatural," 50. All of Aristotle's pronouncements on tyrants and tyranny are found in either his *Politics* or *The Athenian Constitution*. Readers interested in these documents can find translations of them in *The Complete Works of Aristotle*, ed. Jonathan Barnes, the revised Oxford translation, 2 vols. (Princeton: Princeton University Press, 1984).

24. Fine does a good job of summarizing the different historical explanations for the rise of Archaic Greek tyranny, as well as the paucity of primary sources on the subject. See in particular 106–108 in his *The Ancient Greeks*. For a very detailed discussion of the racial factors that may have played a role in the rise of these men, see Andrewes, 54–65.

25. Drews, 131.

26. The subtle distinctions Aristotle and other political thinkers have made between tyrants and despots is addressed in-depth in Melvin Richter's treatment of "Despotism" in the *Dictionary of the History of Ideas: Studies of Selected Pivotal Ideas*, 5 vols. (New York: Charles Scribner's Sons, 1973), 2: 1–18.

27. To get some idea of just how durable autocratic rule in the West has been, see Arno J. Mayer, *The Persistence of the Old Regime: Europe to the Great War* (New York: Pantheon Books, 1981).

28. There is a sizable literature on Peter the Great, and it continues to grow. For the reader interested in a more substantial treatment of this figure than that found here, the following works are recommended: Nicholas V. Riasanovsky's *A History of Russia* (Oxford: Oxford University Press, 2010) contains the best concise treatment of Peter and his place

in the larger context of Russian history. For an exhaustive treatment of Peter's reforms and their overall effect on Russian life and culture, see the following works by James Cracraft, *The Church Reform of Peter the Great* (Stanford: Stanford University Press, 1971); *The Petrine Revolution in Russian Architecture* (Chicago: University of Chicago Press, 1988); *The Petrine Revolution in Russian Imagery* (Chicago: University of Chicago Press, 1997); *The Petrine Revolution in Russian Culture* (Cambridge: Belknap Press of Harvard University Press, 2004); and *The Revolution of Peter the Great* (Cambridge: Belknap Press of Harvard University Press, 2003). Among biographies, Vasili Klyuchevsky's *Peter the Great* (Boston: Beacon Press, 1984), though old, is still well regarded by historians and is an excellent Russian treatment of this remarkable Tsar, and Robert K. Massie's *Peter the Great: His Life and Work* (New York: Modern Library, 2012, c1980) is also very well written and quite thorough as well.

29. R.R. Palmer and Joel Colton, *A History of the Modern World* (New York: Alfred A. Knopf, 1978), 234.

30. These numbers are cited by Nicholas V. Riasanovsky in his *A History of Russia* (Oxford: Oxford University Press, 1969), 253–54.

31. Palmer and Colton, *Modern World*, 232–233.

32. Quoted in Riasanovsky, *A History of Russia*, 266–267.

33. For those interested in Hitler's life and career, the most current and best biography of the German Führer is Ian Kershaw's two volume *Hitler: 1889–1936 Hubris* and *Hitler: 1936–1945 Nemesis*. Kershaw's work is exhaustive, addresses past and contemporary interpretations of the Nazi dictatorship and its leader, and focuses considerable attention on forces external to Hitler's personality that shaped his policies and those of his regime. Older biographies that still merit attention are Alan Bullock, *Hitler: A Study in Tyranny* (New York: Harper and Row, 1964); Joachim Fest, *Hitler* (New York: Harcourt Brace Jovanovich, 1974); and William Carr, *Hitler: A Study in Personality and Politics* (New York: Harper and Row, 1964).

34. The idea of "working towards the Führer" is the motif and organizing principle of Ian Kershaw's aforementioned two-volume biography of Hitler. He used this expression, articulated by a minor Nazi functionary in 1934, as a way to explain both the nature of Hitler's extraordinary power and the ensuing radicalization of his regime.

35. A recent work that focuses on the many commonalities of these totalitarian movements and regimes is Vladimir Tismaneanu, *The Devil in History: Communism, Fascism, and Some Lessons of the Twentieth Century* (Berkeley: University of California Press, 2012). For an excellent review of this work, see William Pfaff's "Pure, Purifying, and Evil," *The New York Review of Books*, 20 June 2013, 58–59.

36. George Orwell, *1984* (New York: The New American Library of World Literature, 1961), 220.

37. Boesche, *Theories of Tyranny*, 236. For a much more in-depth look at this idea of a tyranny without a tyrant, also see the following chapters in Boesche's book: "Tocqueville: The Pleasures of Servitude; " "Marx: Despotism of Class and Workplace"; "Freud: The Reproduction of Tyranny"; and "Weber: The Inevitability of Bureaucratic Domination."

38. Boesche, *Theories of Tyranny*, 472.

Chapter 4

1. *The Divine Comedy*, Dante Alighieri, trans. John Ciardi (New York: W.W. Norton, 1970), 179.

2. Chapman Pincher, *Traitors* (London: Sidgwick and Jackson, 1987).

3. Floyd Seyward Lear, *Treason in Roman and Germanic Law* (Austin: University of Texas Press, 1965), xvi, 13.

4. *Ibid.*, 3–48.

5. *Ibid.*, 73–107.

6. On the traits of "anti-social" personalities, see Barclay Martin, *Abnormal Psychology* (New York: Holt, Reinhart and Winston, 1981), 431–432.

7. For a much more in-depth account on the collaboration of the Mafia and the U.S. military during World War II, see British military historian Tim Newark's *Mafia Allies: The True Story of America's Secret Alliance with the Mob in World War II* (Saint Paul: Zenith Press, 2007).

8. See Eric Carlton, *Treason: Meanings and Motives* (Aldershot: Ashgate, 1998), 1–16; and Nachman Ben-Yehuda, *Betrayal and Treason: Violations of Trust and Loyalty* (Boulder: Westview Press, 2001), 105–127.

9. Nachman Ben-Yehuda, *Betrayal and Treason*, 309.

10. Herodotus, *The Persian Wars*, trans. George Rawlinson (New York: The Modern Library, 1942), 583.

11. *Ibid.*

12. The Wikipedia entry on Judas is actually quite thorough, and does an admirable job of addressing the etymological debate surrounding Judas' surname on page one of http://en.wikipedia.org/wiki/Judas_Iscariot.

13. John 12:5.
14. John 12:7–8.
15. Edward D. Freed's entry "Judas Iscariot" in *The Oxford Guide to People and Places of the Bible*, Bruce M. Metzger and Michael D. Coogan, eds. (Oxford: Oxford University Press, Current Online Version, 2012) gives a very succinct and cogent overview of the conflicting biblical accounts of Judas and his actions.
16. Pages 5 and 6 of the abovementioned Wiki entry (http://en.wikipedia.org/wiki/Judas_Iscariot) provide a fairly exhaustive list of how Judas has been represented in western art and literature from the medieval period through the present.
17. Philip Shenon, "In Short: Non Fiction," *New York Times*, 4 January 1987.
18. There are a number of accounts of Walker's life, the three most prominent being Howard Blum, *I Pledge Allegiance: The True Story of the Walkers, an American Spy Family* (New York: Simon & Schuster, 1987); Jack Kneece, *Family Treason: The Walker Spy Case* (New York: Stein and Day, 1986); and Pete Early, *Family of Spies: Inside the John Walker Spy Ring* (New York: Bantam, 1999). The account given here is largely drawn from Richard Sale's highly readable distillation of these sources, i.e., "The Traitor as Petty Thief and National Catastrophe: John Walker, Jr.," in his *Traitors: The Worst Acts of Treason in American History from Benedict Arnold to Robert Hanssen* (New York: Berkeley Books, 2003), 184–186.
19. Sale, *Traitors*, 190–191.
20. On the importance of these keylists, see Sale, *Traitors*, 191–195.
21. *Ibid.*, 202.
22. *Ibid.*, 208.
23. *Ibid.*, 180.
24. *Ibid.*, 248.
25. *Ibid.*, 249.
26. Plutarch, *Makers of Rome: Nine Lives of Plutarch*, trans. Ian Scott-Kilvert (New York: Penguin, 1983), 16.
27. *Ibid.* Most of the information that we have on Coriolanus, whom some believe to be little more than a legend, come from his biography in Plutarch's *Lives of Noble Romans and Greeks*, as well as the account of his life that is given in Livy's history of Rome, *Ab Urbe Condite*.
28. *Ibid.*, 25–32.
29. *Ibid.*, 25.
30. *Ibid.*, 31.
31. *Ibid.*, 34.
32. *Ibid.*, 35.
33. *Ibid.*, 35–37, 39–47.
34. *Ibid.*, 48.
35. *Ibid.*
36. *Ibid.*, 51–52.

37. Sale, *Traitors*, "The Traitor as Hero: Benedict Arnold," 18–19. For more in-depth accounts of Arnold, see the following: James Thomas Flexner, *The Traitor and the Spy* (New York: Syracuse University Press, 1991); James Kirby Martin, *Benedict Arnold: Revolutionary Hero* (New York: New York University Press, 1997); Willard Sterne Randall's *Patriot and Traitor* (New York: Quill, 1999); Barry K. Wilson, *Benedict Arnold: A Traitor in Our Midst* (Quebec City: McGill-Queens University Press, 2001).
38. *Ibid.*, 20.
39. Quoted in "Lost to All Sense of Honour: Benedict Arnold America's hero-turned-villain," in Ian Crofton, *Traitors & Turncoats: Twenty Tales of Treason, from Benedict Arnold to Ezra Pound* (London: Quercus, 2009), 76.
40. *Ibid.*
41. *Ibid.*, 75.
42. *Ibid.*, 77.
43. Perhaps the best account of the conspiracy against Caesar is to be found in Christian Meier's superb biography *Caesar*, trans. David McLintock (New York: Basic Books, 1982), 479–486.
44. *Ibid.*, 479.
45. Sale, *Traitors*, "Rebel Rose: Rose O'Neal Greenhow," 90.
46. *Ibid.*, 91.
47. *Ibid.*, 93.
48. *Ibid.*, 95.
49. Readers interested in a more in-depth account of Rose O'Neal Greenhow's life as a Washington hostess and spy for the Confederacy are directed to the following: Rose O'Neal Greenhow, *My Imprisonment and the First Year of Abolition Rule at Washington* (London: Richard Bentley, 1863); Ann Blackman, *Wild Rose: The True Story of a Civil War Spy* (New York: Random House, 2006); Ishbel Ross, *Rebel Rose: Life of Rose O'Neal Greenhow, Confederate Spy* (New York: Harper, 1954); Michael Farquhar, "Rebel Rose, A Spy of Grande Dame Proportions," *Washington Post*, 18 September 2000. There is also an Official "Rebel Rose" O'Neal Website with links to a wide array of material on this spy for the Confederacy.
50. Sale, *Traitors*, "The Third Man: Kim Philby Double agent par excellence," 171.
51. *Ibid.*, 173.
52. *Ibid.*
53. Quoted in Sale, *Traitors*, 169.
54. The reader interested in a more in-depth account of Kim Philby's life is directed to the following: Kim Philby, *My Silent War* (London: MacGibbon & Kee, 1968); Genrikh Borovik, *The Philby Files* (New York: Little, Brown, 1994); Philip Knightley, *Philby: KGB Masterspy* (London: Andre Deutsch, 2003);

Richard C.S. Trahair and Robert Miller, *Encyclopedia of Cold War Espionage, Spies, and Secret Operations* (New York: Enigma Books, 2009).

55. Frank Herbert, *Dune* (Philadelphia: Chilton Books, 1965), 19.

56. Readers interested in a more in-depth account of John Vassal's life are encouraged to take a look at the entry on him in the abovementioned (note 54) *Encyclopedia of Cold War Espionage, Spies, Secret Operations*. Chapman Pincher also addresses him in his *Too Secret Too Long: The Great Betrayal of Britain's Crucial Secrets and the Cover-Up* (London: Sidgwick & Jackson, 1984). And then there is Vassall's take on his treason in his autobiography *Vassall: the autobiography of a spy* (London: Sidgwick & Jackson, 1975).

Chapter 5

1. Hesiod, *Theogony and Works and Days*, trans. M. L. West (Oxford: Oxford University Press, 2008), 39.

2. Ibid.

3. This scene can be found in *Myths from Mesopotamia: Creation, The Flood, Gilgamesh, and Others*, trans. Stephanie Dalley (Oxford: Oxford University Press, 2008), 77–79. The quoted passage is on pages 78–79.

4. Nancy Hathaway, *The Friendly Guide to Mythology: A Mortal's Companion to the Fantastical Realm of Gods, Goddesses, Monsters, and Heroes* (New York: Penguin, 2001), 186.

5. All of these examples are addressed in more detail in Hathaway's *Friendly Guide to Mythology*, 185–186.

6. Aeschylus, *The Oresteia*, trans. Robert Fagles (New York: Penguin Books, 1979), 264.

7. Hathaway addresses the problem of the Athena woman in her *Friendly Guide*, 219–220. See also Sarah Pomeroy, *Goddesses, Whores, Wives, and Slaves: Women in Classical Antiquity* (New York: Schocken Books, 1995), 4–5.

8. Phyllis Bird, "Images of Women in the Old Testament," in *Religion and Sexism: Images of Woman in the Jewish and Christian Traditions*, ed. Rosemary Radford Ruether (New York: Simon & Schuster, 1974), 56–57.

9. The particulars of Jezebel's story are scattered across several different chapters in the First and Second Book of Kings. In the first book, they are 16:29–32; 18:1–40; 19:1–2; 21:1–29. 2 Kings 9:30–37.

10. Kings 16:33.

11. Kings 21:22.

12. Kings 11:20. Everything we know about Athaliah is found in 2 Kings 8:25–27 and 11:1–20.

13. Pandraic Colum, *The Children of Odin* (New York: Macmillan, 1964), 241.

14. This admittedly brief and truncated version of the events that occur in the *Völsunga* and *Nibelungenlied* are based on the older Norse and German variants of these stories. The two translations used in this work are *The Saga of the Volsungs: The Norse Epic of Sigurd the Dragon Slayer*, trans. Jesse L. Byock (Berkeley: University of California Press, 1990) and *The Nibelungenlied: The Lay of the Nibelungs*, trans. Cyril Edwards (Oxford: Oxford University Press, 2010).

15. Mark 6:23.

16. Mark 6:24.

17. Mark 6:25–29.

18. The text of Wilde's play consulted for this section is *Salome* (London: Faber and Faber, 1989).

19. Toni Bentley, *Sisters of Salome* (Lincoln: University of Nebraska Press, 2005), 46. This work does an admirable job of addressing the role Wilde's *Salome* plays in the development of modern exotic dancing and its attraction not just for men, but for some of its most prominent performers as well.

20. There is a considerable literature on femme fatales in the movies, particularly those classified as film noir. Recommended for the general reader are the following: *The Femme Fatale: Images, Histories, Contexts*, eds. Helen Hanson and Catherine O'Rawe (New York: Palgrave Macmillan, 2010); M. Bould, *Film Noir: From Berlin to Sin City* (London: Wallflower, 2005); E. Cowie, "*Film Noir* and Women," in J. Copjec, ed., *Shades of Noir* (London: Verso, 1993); H. Hanson, *Hollywood Heroines: Women in Film Noir and the Female Gothic Film* (London: I.B. Tauris, 2007); E. A. Kaplan, ed., *Women in Film Noir* (London: BFI, 1978).

21. F. E. Adcock, *Greek and Macedonian Kingship* (London, 1953), 171.

22. Prudence Jones, *Cleopatra: The Last Pharaoh* (London: Haus, 2006), 16–19.

23. Plutarch, *Mark Antony* in *Makers of Rome*, trans. Ian Scott-Kilvert (New York: Penguin, 1983), 294.

24. Jones, *Cleopatra*, 19–20.

25. For a very detailed discussion of Cleopatra's use of traditional Egyptian religion to advance her various agendas, see Michael Grant, *Cleopatra* (New York: Barnes & Noble, 1972). On the significance of Memphis and the installation of the Buchis bull, see pages 42–48.

26. Plutarch, *Antony*, 302.

27. This is the argument that Stacy Schiff makes in her wonderful biography *Cleopatra: A Life* (New York; Little, Brown, 2010), 36–40.

28. Suetonius, *Julius Caesar*, 52.

29. Schiff, *Cleopatra*, 74.
30. *Ibid.*
31. Quoted in Jones, *Cleopatra*, 40.
32. For a more detailed rendering of Cleopatra's actions at this time, see Schiff, *Cleopatra*, 133–139.
33. Plutarch, *Mark Antony*, 332 (passage 66).
34. Schiff, *Cleopatra*, 5.
35. *Ibid.*, 301–2.
36. Betsy Prioleau, *Seductress: Women Who Ravished the World and Their Lost Art of Love* (New York: Viking, 2003), 245. Prioleau's very brief, albeit highly entertaining, treatment of Lola Montez is largely taken from Bruce Seymour's exhaustive biography *Lola Montez: A Life* (New Haven: Yale University Press, 1996). An older bio of Montez that is an enjoyable read is Horace Wyndham, *The Magnificent Montez: From Courtesan to Convert* (New York: Benjamin Blom, 1935).
37. *Ibid.*, 245–246.
38. *Ibid.*, 246.
39. Wyndham, *Montez*, 55.
40. *Ibid.*, 54.
41. *Ibid.*, 56.
42. Regarding Lola Montez's "passionate pilgrimage" through Europe after being hooted off the stage in London, see Wyndham, *Montez*, 61–74, 91–94.
43. Prioleau, *Seductress*, 247.
44. Wyndham, *Montez*, 61–74.
45. *Ibid.*, 66.
46. From the *Souvenirs* of Gustave Claudin quoted in Wyndham, *Montez*, 72.
47. *Ibid.*, 66.
48. Seymour, *Lola Montez*, 103.
49. *Ibid.*, 108.
50. Wyndham, *Montez*, 102.
51. Prioleau, *Seductress*, 247–248.
52. Wyndham, *Montez*, 111.
53. *Ibid.*, 103.
54. *Ibid.*, 218.
55. *Ibid.*, 13–14.
56. *Isadora Speaks: Writings and Speeches of Isadora Duncan*, ed. Franklin Rosemont (Chicago: Charles H. Kerr, 1994), 23.
57. *Ibid.*, 24.
58. *Ibid.*, 28.
59. Isadora Duncan, *My Life* (New York: Boni and Liveright, 1927), 17.
60. *Ibid.*, 41.
61. Rosemont, *Isadora Speaks*, 31.
62. For a more thorough treatment of Isadora's stay in London, as well as the state of dance in that city prior to her arrival, see Peter Kurth, *Isadora: A Sensational Life* (Boston: Little, Brown, 2001), 55–67.
63. Rosemont, *Isadora Speaks*, 37.
64. Kurth, *Isadora*, 165–169.
65. Rosemont, *Isadora Speaks*, 37.
66. Kurth, *Isadora*, 461.
67. *Ibid.*
68. *Ibid.*, 461–462.
69. *Encyclopaedia Britannica*, 15th ed., s.v. "Duncan, Isadora," 272.
70. Margaret Atwood, "Spotty-Handed Villainesses: Problems of Female Bad Behaviour in the Creation of Literature." http://gos.sbc.edu/a/atwood.html.
71. *Ibid.*
72. *Ibid.*

Chapter 6

1. Linda Mealey, "The Sociobiology of Sociopathy: An Integrated Evolutionary Model," *Behavioral and Brain Sciences* 18 (1995): 523.
2. The definition of villain found in the *Oxford English Dictionary*, Oxford University Press, 2010.
3. Steve Rutter, *The Psychopath: Theory, Research, and Practice* (Mahwah, NJ: Lawrence Erlbaum Associates, 2007), 37.
4. These traits are taken from Robert D. Hare's Psychopathy Checklist-Revised (PCL-R) in "Psychopaths and Their Nature: Some Implications for Understanding Human Predatory Violence," in *Violence and Psychopathy*, ed. Adrian Raine and José Sanmartín (New York: Kluwer Academic/Plenum Publishers, 2001), 9. It should be noted here that while Hare believes that socio- and psychopaths share many of these traits, they are also distinct disorders. See especially his *Snakes in Suits: When Psychopaths Go To Work* (New York: HarperCollins, 2006).
5. To get some sense of the various personality disorders associated with psycho- and sociopathy (or antisocial personality disorder) see Barbara Oakley's summary of the Axis I and Axis II mental health conditions found in the DSM-IV in her *Evil Genes: Why Rome Fell, Hitler Rose, Enron Failed, and My Sister Stole My Mother's Boyfriend* (Amherst, NY: Prometheus Books, 2008), 133–136.
6. The Machiavellian personality traits listed here are taken from Oakley, *Evil Genes*, 42. For more information on this subject, see Richard Christie, "Why Machiavelli?" in *Studies in Machiavellianism*, ed. Richard Christie and Florence Geis (New York: Academic Press, 1970); and John W. McHoskey, William Worzel, and Christopher Szyarto "Machiavellianism and Psychopathy," *Journal of Personality and Social Psychology*, Vol. 74. No. 1, 192–210.
7. Mealey, "Sociobiology," 523; Hare, "Psychopathy," 7–8.
8. Hare, "Psychopathy," 7.
9. Oakley, *Evil Genes*, 89–108. Adrian

Raine, "Psychopathy, Violence, and Brain Imaging," in *Violence and Psychopathy*, 35–55.
10. Oakley, *Evil Genes*, 59–88.
11. Mealey, "Sociobiology," 524.
12. Oakley, *Evil Genes*, 255. Also see her entire chapter on "Evolution and Machiavellianism," 253–283.
13. *Ibid.*, 266.
14. *Ibid.*, 265.
15. *Ibid.*
16. Hare, "Psychopaths," 19.
17. Frank W. Abagnale with Stan Redding, *Catch Me If You Can: The True Story of a Real Fake* (New York: Broadway Books, 1980), 279–285.
18. Mario Puzo, *The Godfather* (Greenwich, CT: Fawcett, 1969), 365.
19. *Ibid.*, 215.
20. Wikipedia, List of Best-Selling Books, http://en.wikipedia.org/wiki/List_of_best-selling_books.
21. *Ibid.*, The Godfather, http://en.wikipedia.org/wiki/The_Godfather.
22. On the particulars of Joe Valachi's childhood see Peter Maas, *The Valachi Papers* (New York: G. B. Putnam's Sons, 1968), 61–64.
23. *Ibid.*, 77–78.
24. *Ibid.*, 95–99.
25. *Ibid.*, 99–105.
26. Actually, Maranzano is featured in *The Godfather* as Vito Corleone's principal rival for power. Like Joe Masseria, he is rubbed out after a gang war.
27. *Ibid.*, 106–107.
28. Valachi's various contracts, business interests, and move to the suburbs is chronicled in some detail in chapters 7–9 of *The Valachi Papers*.
29. The particulars of Valachi's arrest, imprisonment, and cooperation with federal authorities can be found in Chapters 1, 2, and 12 of *The Valachi Papers*.
30. *Ibid.*, 37.
31. Those interested in the nefarious career of Jeanne de la Motte and the famous Diamond Necklace Affair of 1785 should take a look at Jonathan Beckman's book *How to Ruin a Queen: Marie Antoinette, the Stolen Diamonds and the Scandal that Shook the French Throne* (London: John Murray, 2014), and Motte's own account of the affair *Authentic Adventures of the Celebrated Countess De Le Motte (1787)* (London: Kessinger, 2010). For detailed information on the remarkable career of Victor Lustig see James F. Johnson, *The Man Who Sold the Eifel Tower* (Garden City, N.Y.: Doubleday, 1961). The career of George C. Parker is treated in Carl Sifakis' *Hoaxes and Scams: A Compendium of Deceptions, Ruses and Swindles* (New York: Facts on File, 1994). Fernand Waldo Demara's exploits are exhaustively examined in Robert Crichton's *The Great Imposter* (New York: Avon Books, 1968). And the truly monstrous life of Sante Kimes is addressed in her oldest son, Kent Walker's *Son of a Grifter* (New York: HarperCollins, 2009).

32. Almost all of the biographical details of Gerhartsreiter's life are taken from journalist Mark Seal's *The Man in the Rockefeller Suit: The Astonishing Rise and Spectacular Fall of a Serial Imposter* (London: Penguin Group, 2012).
33. *Ibid.*, 25.
34. *Ibid.*, 24.
35. Again, the most detailed account of Gerhartsreiter's peregrinations across the U.S. and the different identities he assumed during these journeys is Seal's *The Man in the Rockefeller Suit*.
36. This is not surprising in light of the fact that he spent a considerable amount of time after his arrival in the U.S. watching this show and imitating its millionaire for the American family that put him up in New Berlin, Connecticut.
37. *Ibid.*, 158.
38. *Ibid.*, 196.
39. *Ibid.*
40. *Ibid.*, 272.
41. The particulars of this murderous confidence game can be found in *The Man in the Rockefeller Suit*, 178–183.
42. *Ibid.*, 200.
43. Nathaniel Rich, "A Killer Con Man on the Loose," review of *Blood Will Out: The True Story of a Murder, a Mystery, and a Masquerade*, by Walter Kirn, *New York Review of Books*, Volume LXI, Number 8 (May 8, 2014): 24.
44. *Ibid.*, 25.
45. *Ibid.*
46. Wikipedia, Christian Gerhartsreiter, http://en.wikipedia.org/wiki/Christian_Gerhartsreiter.
47. Seal, *The Man in the Rockefeller Suit*, 259.
48. Tomas Alex Tizon, "Hijacker's trail may be warming," *Los Angeles Times*, 30 March 2008, sec. A15.
49. I have written extensively about this anti-heroic tendency in modern western history in my *The Heroic Ideal: Western Archetypes from the Greeks to the Present* (Jefferson, NC: McFarland, 2010), 184–200. Much of what is written above is taken from this book.

Chapter 7

1. Information on Michael William Negrete and his case can be found at the following websites: The Charley Project http://www.charley

project.org/cases/n/negrete_michael.html; The North America Missing Persons Network http://www.nampn.org/cases/negrete_michael.html; California Attorney General's Office/California Missing Persons http://oag.ca.gov/missing; University of California at Los Angeles *Daily Bruin* http://dailybruin.com/search/Michael+Negrete.

2. This is the FBI definition of a serial killer. Quoted in Steven A. Egger, *The Killers Among Us: An Examination of Serial Murder and its Investigation* (Englewood Cliffs, NJ: Prentice Hall, 2002), 6.

3. *Ibid.*, 242.

4. José Sanmartín, "Concept and History of the Serial Killer," in *Violence and Psychopathy*, ed. Adrian Raine and José Sanmartín (New York: Kluwer Academic/Plenum, 2001), 95.

5. Egger, *Killers*, addresses the problem of attribution in his section on "Defining Serial Murder" on page 4 of his book. Criminal Justice historian, Peter Vronsky, argues that the term was actually coined in 1966 in John Brophy's book *The Meaning of Murder*, and was later brought into wider usage by the *New York Times* in the 80s. Vronsky's arguments on this matter can be found in his "Serial Killer Zombie Apocalypse and the Dawn of the Less Dead: An Introduction to Sexual Serial Murder Today," in *Serial Killers: True Crime Anthology* (Toronto: RJ Parker, 2014).

6. P. R. Brooks, M. J. Devine, T. J. Green, B. J. Hart, and M. D. Moore, *Multi-Agency Investigation Team Manual* (Washington, D. C.: U.S. Department of Justice, 1988), vii.

7. Egger, *Killers*, 5.

8. Most of what follows is taken from Steven Egger's excellent cross-case analysis of seven serial killers in his book *The Killers Among Us*, 230–236.

9. Sanmartín, "Concept and History of the Serial Killer," 96–97.

10. R. M. Holmes and J. De Burger, *Serial Murder* (Newberry Park, CA: Sage, 1988), 46–60.

11. Sanmartín, "Concept and History of the Serial Killer," 97.

12. *Ibid.*, 97–98.

13. *Ibid.*, 99.

14. Candice A. Skrapec, "Motives of the Serial Killer," in *Violence and Psychopathy*, ed. Adrian Raine and José Sanmartín (New York: Kluwer Academic/Plenum, 2001), 107–110.

15. Quoted in R. I. Simon, *Bad Men Do What Good Men Dream* (Washington, D.C.: American Psychiatric Press, 1996), 311.

16. Skrapec, "Motives of the Serial Killer," 112–121.

17. Steven Egger, *Research in Progress: Preliminary analysis of the victims of serial murderer Henry Lee Lucas*. Paper presented at the annual meeting of the American Society of Criminology, Cincinnati, Ohio, October, 1984.

18. Quoted in Eggers, *Killers*, 88.

19. These numbers and the ones that follow are found in Kim A. Egger's chapter "Victims: The 'Less-Dead,'" in Eggers, *Killers*, 91–93.

20. The number in each parenthesis corresponds to the number of male victims attributed to these serial killers.

21. *Ibid.*, 84.

22. *Ibid.*, 92.

23. Eggers, *Killers*, 242.

24. Bios and true crime books include the following: George R. Dekle, Sr., *The Last Murder: The Investigation, Prosecution, and Execution of Ted Bundy* (Santa Barbara: Praeger, 2011); Laura Foreman, *Serial Killers—True Crime* (Alexandria, VA: Time-Life Books, 1992); Elizabeth Kendall, *The Phantom Prince: My Life with Ted Bundy* (Seattle: Madrona, 1981); Robert Keppel, *The Riverman: Ted Bundy and I Hunt for the Green River Killer* (New York: Simon & Schuster, 2005) and *Terrible Secrets: Ted Bundy on Serial Murder* (Irving, TX: Authorlink Press, 2011); Richard W. Larsen, *Bundy: The Deliberate Stranger* (Englewood Cliffs, New Jersey: Prentice Hall, 1980); Stephen Michaud and Hugh Aynesworth, *The Only Living Witness: The True Story of Serial Sex Killer Ted Bundy* (Irving, TX: Authorlink Press, 1999) and *Ted Bundy: Conversations with a Killer* (New York: Signet, 1989); Polly Nelson, *Defending the Devil: My Story as Ted Bundy's Last Lawyer* (New York: William Morrow, 1994); Ann Rule, *The Stranger Beside Me* (New York: Pocket Books, 2009); Kevin M. Sullivan, *The Bundy Murders: A Comprehensive History* (Jefferson, NC: McFarland, 2009); Steven Winn and David Merrill, *Ted Bundy: The Killer Next Door* (New York: Bantam, 1980). Bundy's Wikipedia entry runs 26 pages.

25. Michaud and Aynesworth, *The Only Living Witness*, 56.

26. Rule, *The Stranger Beside Me*, 9; Michaud and Aynesworth, *The Only Living Witness*, 330.

27. Egger, *Killers*, 162.

28. *Ibid.*, 162–163.

29. Keppel, *The Riverman*, 387.

30. Eggers, *Killers*, 166.

31. Sullivan, *The Bundy Murders*, 57.

32. Nelson, *Defending the Devil*, 257.

33. For the particulars of Bundy's modus operandi, see Michaud and Aynesworth, *The Only Living Witness*; Rule, *The Stranger Beside Me*; and Nelson, *Defending the Devil*. All are quite thorough in detailing the ways in which he preyed on, murdered, and defiled the bodies of his many victims. Actually, all of the above mentioned treatments of Ted Bundy in note

23, spend considerable time on Bundy's many crimes and how he committed them.

34. Rule, *The Stranger Beside Me*, 51–52, 431–432.

35. Michaud and Aynesworth, *The Only Living Witness*, 41.

36. Rule, *The Stranger Beside Me*, 103–105.

37. To get some sense of his chameleon-like features, see the photos of Bundy in Holmes and De Burger, *Serial Murder*, 124–125.

38. Worldwide box office gross.

39. Harry L. Marsh, "A Comparative Analysis of Crime Coverage in Newspapers in the United States and Other Countries from 1960–1989: A Review of the Literature," *Journal of Criminal Justice* 19, no. 1 (1991): 67.

40. This is certainly the case in classes where I have shown this movie.

41. For a more in-depth treatment of the heroic types addressed here, see my *The Heroic Ideal: Western Archetypes from the Greeks to the Present* (Jefferson, NC: McFarland, 2010).

42. Philip Jenkins, "The Inner Darkness: Serial Murder and the Nature of Evil," *Chronicles: A Magazine of American Culture*, 19 (1995): 19.

Epilogue

1. Mary McNamara, "TV Conjures Halloween Year-Round: Witches, Zombies, Vampires and Other Frights Crowd the Nightly Lineup," *Los Angeles Times*, October 21, 2014, sec. D.

2. *Ibid.*

Bibliography

Abagnale, Frank W. *Catch Me If You Can: The True Story of a Real Fake.* New York: Broadway Books, 1980.
Adcock, F. E. *Greek and Macedonian Kingship.* London: Reprinted from Proceedings of the British Academy, London, v. 39, 1954.
Aeschylus. *The Oresteia.* Translated by Robert Fagles. New York: Penguin, 1979.
Alighieri, Dante. *The Divine Comedy.* Translated by John Ciardi. New York: W. W. Norton, 1970.
Andrewes, A. *The Greek Tyrants.* London: Hutchinson & Co., 1956.
Bacon, Helen H. *Barbarians in Greek Tragedy.* New Haven: Yale University Press, 1961.
Barclay, Martin. *Abnormal Psychology.* New York: Holt, Reinhart and Winston, 1981.
Barnes, Jonathan, ed. *The Complete Works of Aristotle.* Princeton, NJ: Princeton University Press, 1984.
Beckman, Jonathan. *How to Ruin a Queen: Marie Antoinette, the Stolen Diamonds and the Scandal That Shook the French Throne.* London: John Murray, 2014.
Ben-Yehuda, Nachman. *Betrayal and Treason: Violations of Trust and Loyalty.* Boulder: Westview Press, 2001.
Bentley, Toni. *Sister of Salome.* Lincoln: University of Nebraska Press, 2005.
Bird, Phyllis. "Images of Women in the Old Testament." *Religion and Sexism: Images of Woman in the Jewish and Christian Traditions*, edited by Rosemary Radford Ruether. New York: Simon & Schuster, 1974.
Blackman, Ann. *Wild Rose: The True Story of a Civil War Spy.* New York: Random House, 2006.
Blum, Howard. *I Pledge Allegiance: The True Story of the Walkers, an American Spy Family.* New York: Simon & Schuster, 1987.
Boesche, Roger. *Theories of Tyranny From Plato to Arendt.* University Park: Pennsylvania State University Park, 1996.
Borovik, Genrikh. *The Philby Files.* New York: Little, Brown, 1994.
Borst, Arno. *Medieval Worlds: Barbarians, Heretics and Artists in the Middle Ages.* Cambridge: Polity Press, 1991.
Briant, Pierre. "History and Ideology: The Greeks and 'Persian Decadence.'" In *Greeks and Barbarians*, edited by Thomas Harrison. Edinburgh: Edinburgh University Press, 2002.
Brooks, P. R., M. J. Devine, T. J. Green, B. J. Hart, and M. D. Moore. *Multi-Agency Investigation Team Manual.* Washington, D. C.: U. S. Department of Justice, 1988.
Bullock, Alan. *Hitler: A Study in Tyranny.* New York: Harper and Row, 1964.
Burns, Thomas S. *Rome and the Barbarians 100 B.C.–A.D. 400.* Baltimore: John Hopkins University Press, 2003.
Byock, Jesse L., trans. *The Saga of the Volsungs: The Norse Epic of Sigurd the Dragon Slayer.* Berkeley: University of California, 1990.

Caesar, Julius. *The Gallic War*. Translated by H. Edwards. Cambridge: Harvard University Press, 1917.
Carlton, Eric. *Treason: Meanings and Motives*. Aldershot: Ashgate, 1998.
Carr, William. *Hitler: A Study in Personality and Politics*. New York: Harper and Row, 1964.
The Catholic Encyclopedia, s.v. "St. Anthony." New York: Robert Appleton, 1907.
Clutton-Brock. *A Natural History of Domesticated Mammals*. Cambridge: Cambridge University Press, 1999.
Colum, Pandraic. *The Children of Odin*. New York: Macmillan, 1964.
Cowie, E. "*Film Noir* and Women." *Shades of Noir*. Edited by J. Copjec. London: Verso, 1993.
Cracraft, James. *The Church Reform of Peter the Great*. Stanford: Stanford University Press, 1971.
_____. *The Petrine Revolution in Russian Architecture*. Chicago: University of Chicago Press, 1997.
_____. *The Petrine Revolution in Russian Culture*. Cambridge: Belknap Press of Harvard University Press, 2004.
_____. *The Petrine Revolution in Russian Imagery*. Chicago: University of Chicago Press, 1997.
_____. *The Revolution of Peter the Great*. Belknap Press of Harvard University Press, 2003.
Cranston, M. *The Romantic Movement*. Oxford: Oxford University Press, 1994.
Crichton, Robert. *The Great Imposter*. New York: Avon Books, 1968.
Crofton, Ian. *Traitors & Turncoats: Twenty Tales of Treason, from Benedict Arnold to Ezra Pound*. London: Quercus, 2009.
Dalley, Stephanie, ed. *Myths from Mesopotamia: Creation, the Flood, Gilgamesh, and Others*. Translated by Stephanie Dalley. Oxford: Oxford University Press, 1989.
Darnton, Robert. *The Great Cat Massacre: And Other Episodes in French Cultural History*. New York: Random House, 1985.
Davis, Mike. *Ecology of Fear: Los Angeles and the Imagination of Disaster*. New York: Vintage, 1999.
De la Motte, Countess. *Authentic Adventures of the Celebrated Countess De La Motte (1787)*. London: Kessinger, 2010.
Dekle Sr., George, R. *The Last Murder: The Investigation, Prosecution and Execution of Ted Bundy*. Santa Barbara: Praeger, 2011.
Dio, Cassius. *Roman History*. Translated by E. Cary. Cambridge: Harvard University Press, 1960–1969.
Drewes, Robert. "The First Tyrants in Greece." *Historia* 21, no. 2 (1972): 129–44.
Early, Pete. *Family of Spies: Inside the John Walker Spy Ring*. New York: Bantam, 1999.
Edwards, Cyril, trans. *The Nibelungenlied: The Lay of the Nibelungs*. Oxford: Oxford University Press, 2010.
Egger, Steven A. *The Killers Among Us: An Examination of Serial Murder and Its Investigation*. Englewood Cliffs, NJ: Prentice Hall, 2002.
_____. *Research in Progress: Preliminary Analysis of the Victims of Serial Murderer Henry Lee Lucas*. Paper presented at the annual meeting of the American Society of Criminology, Cincinnati, Ohio, October 1984.
Farquhar, Michael. "Rebel Rose, A Spy of Grande Dame Proportions." *Washington Post*, 18 September 2000.
Fest, Joachim. *Hitler*. New York: Harcourt Brace Jovanovich, 1974.
Fine, John V. A. *The Ancient Greeks: A Critical History*. Cambridge: Harvard University Press, 1983.
Finley, M. I. *The Ancient Greeks*. New York: Penguin, 1985.
Flexner, James Thomas. *The Traitor and the Spy*. New York: Syracuse University Press, 1991.
Foreman, Laura. *Serial Killers—True Crime*. Alexandria, VA: Time-Life Books, 1992.
Fragan, Brian. *Cro-Magnon: How the Ice Age Gave Birth to the First Modern Humans*. New York: Bloomsbury Press, 2010.
_____, ed. *The Complete Ice Age*. London: Thames and Hudson, 2009.

Freed, Edward D. "Judas Iscariot." In *The Oxford Guide to People and Places of the Bible*, edited by Bruce M. Metzger and Michael D. Coogan. Oxford: Oxford University Press, Current Online Version, 2012.
Grant, Michael. *Cleopatra*. New York: Barnes & Noble, 1995.
Greenhow, Rose O'Neal. *My Imprisonment and the First Year of Abolition Rule at Washington*. London: Richard Bentley, 1863.
Guthrie, R. Dale. *The Nature of Paleolithic Art*. Chicago: University of Chicago Press, 2005.
Hanson, Helen. *Hollywood Heroines: Women in Film Noir and the Female Gothic Film*. London: I. B. Tauris, 2007.
Hanson, Helen, and Catherine O'Rawe, eds. *The Femme Fatale: Images, Histories, Contexts*. New York: Palgrave Macmillan, 2010.
Hare, Richard D. "Psychopaths and Their Nature: Some Implications for Understanding Human Predatory Violence." In *Violence and Psychopathy*, edited by Adrian Raine and José Sanmartin. New York: Kluwer Academic/Plenum, 2001.
_____. *Snakes in Suits: When Psychopaths Go To Work*. New York: HarperCollins, 2006.
Harlan, Jack R. *Crops and Man*. Madison, WI: American Society of Agronomy: Crop Science Society of America, 1992.
Harrison, Thomas, ed. *Greeks and Barbarians*. Edinburgh: Edinburgh University Press, 2002.
Hathaway, Nancy. *The Friendly Guide to Mythology: A Mortal's Companion to the Fantastical Realm of Gods, Goddesses, Monsters, and Heroes*. New York: Penguin, 2001.
Herbert, Frank. *Dune*. Philadelphia: Chilton Books, 1965.
Herodotus. *The Persian Wars*. Translated by George Rawlinson. New York: The Modern Library, 1942.
Hesiod. *Theogony and Works and Days*. Translated by M. L. West. Oxford: Oxford University Press, 2008.
Holmes, R. M., and J. De Burger. *Serial Murder*. Newberry Park, CA: Sage, 1988.
Homer. *The Iliad*. Translated by Richard Lattimore. Chicago: University of Chicago Press, 1951.
_____. *The Odyssey*. Translated by Richard Lattimore. Chicago: University of Chicago Press, 1951.
Internet Movie Database. "Memorable quotes for Serenity." http://www.imdb.com/title/tt0379786/quotes.
Jenkins, Philip. "The Inner Darkness: Serial Murder and the Nature of Evil." *Chronicles: A Magazine of American Culture* 19 (1995): 16–19.
Johnson, James F. *The Man Who Sold the Eifel Tower*. Garden City, NY: Doubleday, 1961.
Jones, Prudence. *Cleopatra: The Last Pharaoh*. London: Haus, 2006.
Kaplan, E. A., ed. *Women in Film Noir*. London: BFI, 1978.
Kendall, Elizabeth. *The Phantom Prince: My Life with Ted Bundy*. Seattle: Madrona, 1981.
Kendrick, M. Gregory. *The Heroic Ideal: Western Archetypes from the Greeks to the Present*. Jefferson, NC: McFarland, 2010.
Keppel, Robert. *The Riverman: Ted Bundy and I Hunt for the Green River Killer*. New York: Simon & Schuster, 2005.
_____. *Terrible Secrets: Ted Bundy on Serial Murder*. Irving, TX: Authorlink Press, 2011.
Kershaw, Ian. *Hitler: 1889–1936 Hubris*. New York: W. W. Norton, 2000.
_____. *Hitler: 1936–1945 Nemesis*. New York: W. W. Norton, 2000.
Klein, Richard G., and Blake Edgar. *The Dawn of Human Culture*. Chicago: University of Chicago Press, 2005.
Klyuchevsky, Vasili. *Peter the Great*. Boston: Beacon Press, 1984.
Kneece, Jack. *Family Treason: The Walker Spy Case*. New York: Stein and Day, 1986.
Knightley, Philip. *Philby: KGB Masterspy*. London: Andre Deutsch, 2003.
Kurth, Peter. *Isadora: A Sensational Life*. Boston: Little, Brown, 2001.
Larson, Richard W. *Bundy: The Deliberate Stranger*. Englewood Cliffs, NJ: Prentice Hall, 1980.
Lear, Floyd Seyward. *Treason in Roman and Germanic Law*. Austin: University of Texas Press, 1965.

Livy. *History of Rome*. Translated by B. O. Foster. Cambridge: Harvard University Press, 1982–98.
Maas, Peter. *The Valachi Papers*. New York: G. B. Putnam's Sons, 1968.
Malina, Bruce J. *The New Testament World: Insights from Cultural Anthropology*. Louisville, KY: Westminster/John Knox Press, 1993.
Marcellinus, Ammianus. *History*. Translated by John C. Rolfe. Cambridge: Harvard University Press, 1982–1986.
Marsh, Harry L. "A Comparative Analysis of Crime Coverage in Newspapers in the United States and Other Countries from 1960–1989: A Review of the Literature." *Journal of Criminal Justice* 19, no. 1 (1991): 67–79.
Martin, James Kirby. *Benedict Arnold: Revolutionary Hero*. New York: New York University Press, 1997.
Massie, Robert K. *Peter the Great: His Life and Work*. New York: Modern Library, 2012.
Mayer, Arno J. *The Persistence of the Old Regime: Europe to the Great War*. New York: Pantheon Books, 1981.
McCullough, David Willis, ed. *Chronicles of the Barbarians: Firsthand Accounts of Pillage and Conquest, From the Ancient World to the Fall of Constantinople*. New York: History Book Club, 1998.
McKay, John P., Bennett D. Hill, and John Buckler. *A History of Western Society*. Boston: Houghton Mifflin, 1987.
McNamara, Mary. "TV Conjures Halloween Year-Round: Witches, Zombies, Vampires and Other Frights Crowd the Nightly Lineup." *Los Angeles Times*, October 21, 2014, sec. D.
McNeill, J.R., and William H. McNeill. *The Human Web: A Bird's-Eye View of World History*. New York: W.W. Norton, 2003.
Mealey, Linda. "The Sociobiology of Sociopathy: An Integrated Evolutionary Model." *Behavioral and Brain Sciences* 18 (2006): 523–599.
Meier, Christian. *Caesar*. Translated by David McLintock. New York: Basic Books, 1982.
Michaud, Stephen, and Hugh Aynesworth. *The Only Living Witness: The True Story of Serial Sex Killer Ted Bundy*. Irving, TX: Authorlink Press, 1999.
_____. *Ted Bundy: Conversations with a Killer*. New York: Signet, 1989.
Muir, John. *The Eight Wilderness-Discovery Books*. London: Diadem Books, 1992.
Nash, Roderick Frazier. *Wilderness and the American Mind*. New Haven: Yale University Press, 2001.
Nelson, Polly. *Defending the Devil: My Story as Ted Bundy's Last Lawyer*. New York: William Morrow, 1994.
The New American Bible. Washington, D. C.: Catholic Publishers, 1971.
Newark, Tim. *Mafia Allies: The True Story of America's Secret Alliance with the Mob in World War II*. Saint Paul: Zenith Press, 2007.
Nippel, Wilfried. "The Construction of the 'Other.'" In *Greeks and Barbarians*, edited by Thomas Harrison. Edinburgh: Edinburgh University Press, 2002.
Oakley, Barbara. *Evil Genes: Why Rome Fell, Hitler Rose, Enron Failed, and My Sister Stole My Mother's Boyfriend*. Amherst, NY: Prometheus Books, 2008.
Orwell, George. *1984*. New York: The New American Library of World Literature, 1961.
Palmer, R. R. and Joel Colton. *A History of the Modern World*. New York: Alfred A. Knopf, 1978.
Pfaff, William. "Pure, Purifying, and Evil." *The New York Review of Books*, 20 June 2013: 58–59.
Philby, Kim. *My Silent War*. London: MacGibbon & Kee, 1968.
Pincher, Chapman. *Traitors*. London: Sidgwick and Jackson, 1987.
_____. *Too Secret Too Long: The Great Betrayal of Britain's Crucial Secrets and the Cover-Up*. London: Sidgwick & Jackson, 1984.
Plato. *Laws*. Translated by Thomas Pangle. New York: Basic Books, 1980.
_____. *Republic*. Translated by Allan Bloom. New York: Basic Books, 1968.
_____. *The Collected Dialogues of Plato*. Edited by Edith Hamilton and Huntington Cairns. Princeton: Princeton University Press, 1961.

Pliny. *Natural History.* Translated by H. Rackham and W. Jones. Cambridge: Harvard University Press, 1965.
Plutarch. *Makers of Rome: Nine Lives of Plutarch.* Translated by Ian Scott-Kilvert. New York: Penguin, 1983.
Pomeroy, Sarah. *Goddesses, Whores, Wives, and Slaves: Women in Classical Antiquity.* New York: Schocken Books, 1995.
Porter, Roy, and Mikul Teich, eds. *Romanticism in National Context.* New York: Cambridge University Press, 1988.
Prioleau, Betsy. *Seductress: Women Who Ravished the World and Their Lost Art of Love.* New York: Viking, 2003.
Puzo, Mario. *The Godfather.* Greenwich, CT: Fawcett, 1969.
Rampino, Michael, and Stanley Ambrose. "Volcanic Winter in the Garden of Eden: The Toba Supereruption and the Late Pleistocene Human Population Crash." *Geological Society of America Special Paper* 345 (2000).
Randall, Willard Sterne. *Patriot and Traitor.* New York: Quill, 1999.
Redfield, James. "Herodotus the Tourist." In *Greeks and Barbarians*, edited by Thomas Harrison. Edinburgh: Edinburgh University Press, 2002.
Riasanovsky, Nicholas V. *The Emergence of Romanticism.* New York: Oxford University Press, 1992.
———. *A History of Russia.* London: Oxford University Press, 2010.
Rich, Nathaniel. "A Killer Con Man on the Loose." Review of *Blood Will Out: The True Story of a Murder, a Mystery, and a Masquerade*, by Walter Kirn. *New York Review of Books* LXI, no. 8 (May 8, 2014): 24–26.
Richter, Melvin. "Despotism." *Dictionary of the History of Ideas: Studies of Selected Pivotal Ideas.* New York: Charles Scribner's Sons, 1973.
Rosemont, Franklin, ed. *Isadora Speaks: Writings and Speeches of Isadora Duncan.* Chicago: Charles H. Kerr, 1994.
Ross, Isabel. *Rebel Rose: Life of Rose O'Neal Greenhow, Confederate Spy.* New York: Harper, 1954.
Rule, Ann. *The Stranger Beside Me.* New York: Pocket Books, 2009.
Rutter, Steve. *The Psychopath: Theory, Research, and Practice.* Mahwah, NJ: Lawrence Erlbaum Associates, 2007.
Said, Edward. *Orientalism.* New York: Vantage, 1979.
Sale, Richard. *Traitors: The Worst Acts of Treason in American History from Benedict Arnold to Robert Hanssen.* New York: Berkeley Books, 2003.
Sallust. *The Histories.* Translated by J. Rolfe. Cambridge: Harvard University Press, 1965.
Sanmartin, José. "Concept and History of the Serial Killer." In *Violence and Psychopathy*, edited by Adrian Raine and José Sanmartin. New York: Kluwer Academic/Plenum, 2001.
Schaff, Phillip and Henry Wace. *Athanasius: Select Works and Letters.* New York: C. Scribner's Sons, 1890–1900.
Schenk, H. G. *The Mind of European Romantics.* Garden City, N.Y.: Doubleday, 1969.
Schiff, Stacy. *Cleopatra: A Life.* New York: Little, Brown, 2010.
Sealey, Raphael. *A History of the Greek City States ca. 700–338 B.C.* Berkeley: University of California Press, 1976.
Seal, Mark. *The Man in the Rockefeller Suit: The Astonishing Rise and Spectacular Fall of a Serial Imposter.* London: Penguin Group, 2012.
Segal, Charles Paul. "Nature and the World of Man in Greek Literature." *Arion* 2, no. 1 (1963): 19–53.
Seymour, Bruce. *Lola Montez: A Life.* New Haven: Yale University Press, 1996.
Shenon, Philip. "In Short: Non Fiction." *New York Times*, 4 January 1987.
Siculus, Diodorus. *Library.* Translated by F. Watson. Cambridge: Harvard University, 1933.
Sifakis, Carl. *Hoaxes and Scams: A Compendium of Deceptions, Ruses and Swindles.* New York: Facts on File, 1994.
Simon, R. I. *Bad Men Do What Good Men Dream.* Washington, D. C.: American Psychiatric Press, 1996.

Skrapec, Candice A. "Motives of the Serial Killer." In *Violence and Psychopathy*, edited by Adrian Raine and José Sanmartin. New York: Kluwer Academic/Plenum, 2001.
Smith, Bruce D. *The Emergence of Agriculture*. New York: Scientific American Library, 1995.
Sophocles. *The Three Theban Plays*. Translated by Robert Fagles. New York: Penguin, 1984.
Stommel, Henry and Elizabeth. *Volcano Weather: The Story of 1816, the Year Without a Summer*. Newport, RI: Seven Seas Press, 1983.
Suetonious. *Lives of the Caesars*. Translated by J. C. Rolfe. Cambridge: Harvard University Press, 1959.
Sullivan, Kevin M. *The Bundy Murders: A Comprehensive History*. Jefferson, NC: McFarland, 2009.
Tacitus. *Agricola and Germania*. Translated by M. Hutton. Cambridge: Harvard University Press, 1970.
———. *Agricola and Germania*. Revised translation with an Introduction and Notes by J. B. Rivers. London: Penguin, 2009.
Tismaneanu, Vladimir. *The Devil in History: Communism, Fascism, and Some Lessons of the Twentieth Century*. Berkeley: University of California Press, 2012.
Tizon, Alex Tomas. "Hijacker's trail may be warming." *Los Angeles Times*, March 30, 2008, sec. A15.
Trahair, Richard C. S. and Robert Miller. *Encyclopedia of Cold War Espionage, Spies, and Secret Operations*. New York: Enigma Books, 2009.
Vassall, John. *Vassall: The Autobiography of a Spy*. London: Sidgwick & Jackson, 1975.
Virgil. *The Aeneid*. Translated by Robert Fitzgerald. New York: Vintage, 1990.
Vronsky, Peter. "Serial Killer Zombie Apocalypse and the Dawn of the Less Dead: An Introduction to Sexual Serial Murder Today." *Serial Killers: True Crime Anthology*. Toronto: RJ Parker, 2014.
Walker, Kent. *Son of a Grifter*. New York: HarperCollins, 2009.
Weber, Eugen. "Fairies and Hard Facts: The Reality of Folktales." *Journal of the History of Ideas* XLII (1981): 93–113.
Wikipedia. "Judas Iscariot." Last modified August 7, 2015. http://en.wikipedia.org/wiki/Judas_Iscariot.
———. "Christian Gerhartsreiter." Last modified August 15, 2015. http://en.wikipedia.org/wiki/Christian_Gerhartsreiter.
Wilde, Oscar. *Salome*. London: Faber and Faber, 1989.
Wilson, Barry K. *Benedict Arnold: A Traitor in Our Midst*. Quebec City: McGill-Queens University Press, 2001.
Winn, Steven and David Merrill. *Ted Bundy: The Killer Next Door*. New York: Bantam, 1980.
Worster, Daniel. *Nature's Economy: A History of Ecological Ideas*. Cambridge: Cambridge University Press, 1994.
Wyndham, Horace. *The Magnificent Montez: From Courtesan to Convert*. New York: Benjamin Blom, 1935.

Index

Abagnale, Frank 186,193
Age of Enlightenment 24–25, 51
Annals of Imperial Rome 79
Anthony the Great, Saint 22
Anti-social personalities 108–109
Antony, Mark 44–45, 154; *see also* Cleopatra VII; Octavian; Ptolemaic Egypt
Aphrodite 142, 144–146
Aristotle 75–76, 78–79
Arnold, Benedict 104, 110, 118–119, 123–126, 138
Athaliah 142, 148–149
Athena 142, 144–147
Atwood, Margaret 177

Baby Face 164
The Bad Seed 179–180
Barbarous 38
La Belle Dame sans Merci 142, 151
Beowulf 22
Blair Witch Project 11–12
Brave New World 4, 98, 209
Brutus and Cassius 102–103, 110, 126–128, 160
Brynhild 150–151
Bundy, Theodore 214, 217, 219, 224–229
Bureaucratic domination 98

Campbell, John W.: *Who Goes There* 200
Capital One barbarians 46–47
Castellammarese War 197
Celts 38, 47–49
Cleopatra VII 44–45, 141–142, 171, 178; alliance with and marriage to Mark Antony 160–163; childhood and youth 154–155; civil war and relationship with Julius Caesar 156–159; physical appearance and character traits 154–155; *see also* Antony, Mark; Octavian; Ptolemaic Egypt
A Clockwork Orange 183–184, 190
Collins, Suzanne: *The Hunger Games* 97, 105
Coriolanus 104, 110, 118–123
Cosa Nostra ("our thing") 193–194, 197–198
Cro-Magnon 8–9

Dante: *Inferno* 101–103
Darwin, Charles 26
Davis, Mike: *Ecology of Fear* 30–31
Delilah 135, 142, 147
Despot 78–80, 86, 88
The Devil Wears Prada 139
Dictatorships 90, 93, 95
Dominii 79
Duncan, Isadora 141–142, 178; childhood and youth 172–173; lovers 175; relocation to England and tour of Europe 173–174; scandalous dance in Boston 176; schools of dance 174–175; support of the Soviet Union 175–176
Dune 133–134

"Eastern" barbarism 43–45
Ecology of Fear 30–31
Ephialtes 110, 112–114, 138
Epic of Gilgamesh 18–19, 143, 152
Eve 142–143, 147

Feminism 62, 172
Femme fatale 60, 62
Film noir 142, 153
Firefly 56–57
Francis of Assisi, Saint 13, 23–24

Gacy, John Wayne 213, 216, 219, 221
Genovese, Vito 198–199
Gerhartsreiter, Christian Karl 201–209, 222
German barbarians 35, 38, 47–49
Germania 39, 40, 49, 55
The Godfather 193–195, 198
Greco-Persian Wars 38, 74–75, 110
Greenhow, Rose O'Neal 104, 128–130
Grifters 200–201
Grimmhild 150
Gudrun 150–151
Gyges 68–69

Herbert, Frank: *Dune* 133–134
Hesiod: *Works and Days* 142–143

259

260 Index

Hitler, Adolf 4, 65–66, 68; childhood, youth, wartime experience 91; personality traits 91; rise and consolidation of power 91–92; similarities and differences with despots of past 93–95; successes and downfall 92–93
Hebrew books of the Bible 19, 20
Hera 142, 144–145
Herodotus 38, 41–43, 47, 49, 55, 75, 78, 112–113
Heroic vitalism 53, 89
Hippias 73–75
The Hunger Games 97, 105
Huns 33, 35, 49,
Huxley, Thomas 26–27

Iliad 20–21, 38
Inferno 101–103
Ishtar 142, 144, 152
Islam 35–36, 45, 46

Jezebel 142, 148–149
Judas Iscariot 101–103, 110, 114–115, 138

Keats, John: *La Belle Dame sans Merci* 142, 151
Koros, atē, and *hubris* 42–43, 57

Lecter, Hannibal 214, 230, 232
Lilith 147
Lord of the Flies 55
Louis XIV 67, 85–88

Maas, Peter: *The Valachi Papers* 193
Machtweiber 62
Mafia 193, 196–199
Maiestas 107
Maranzano, Salvatore 197
MICE (money, ideology, compromise, ego) 104, 110
Montez, Lola 141–142, 171, 178; career as dancer 166–168; childhood and youth 165–166; flamboyant behavior 167; life in the United States and Australia 170; lovers 167; obituary 170–171; relationship with Ludwig I of Bavaria 168–169
Mount Toba eruption 15

Napoleon I 85–87, 89
Nationalism 52–53
Neanderthal 7–9
Negrete, Michael 211–
1984 4, 97
"noble savage" 40

Octavian 44–45; 160–163; *see also* Antony, Mark; Cleopatra VII; Ptolemaic Egypt
Odyssey 21

Paleolithic 9, 13–14
Pandora 142–143
Perduellio 107

Peter I (the Great) 4, 60, 68, 88; family intrigues and early education 81; military measures and foreign policy 83; Petrine reforms 82–83; seizure of power and the "Grand Embassy" 82; titles and legacy 84–87
Petty and high treason 108
Philby, Kim 104, 130–133
Philotimia 77, 100
Pisistratus 4, 67, 69; foreign policy 73; reforms and public works 71–72; rise to, and consolidation of, power in Athens 71–72
Plato 75
Priestly, Miranda 139–141
Principate 79
Ptolemaic Egypt 43–44; *see also* Antony, Mark; Cleopatra VII; Octavian

Romanticism 27–28, 52, 89

Said, Edward 43, 46
Salome 142, 151–152
Samson 104,134–135, 137, 147
Scythians 47
Seductress 62
Serial killers: brain chemistry 218–219; definition 212, 215–216; detection and apprehension 222–223; distinguishing characteristics 216, 218; family and social environments 219; modus operandi 213, 217–218; motivations 213, 217, 219–220; popular culture 214, 230–233; types 217–218; victims 213–214, 217, 220–222
Signy 150–151
Silence of the Lambs 214, 229–230, 232
Sociopathy: environmental niches for sociopaths; genetic factors 190; evolutionary advantages of sociopathy 191; Machiavellian behavior 188, 190; origin of term 186–187; relation to psychopathy and anti-social personality disorder 187–188; religious and social explanations for sociopathy 188–190; treatment 192–193
Sophocles 75
Stalin, Joseph 66–67, 95–96
Star Wars 1–2

Tacitus: *Annals of Imperial Rome* 79; *Germania* 39, 40, 49, 55
Thermopylae, Battle of 41, 112; *see also* Aeschylus; Herodotus; Xerxes
300 41, 113
The 300 Spartans 113
Treubruch 107
Tyrannos 67–68, 75
Tyrannoi 71, 75–76, 94, 100

Vader, Darth 1–3
Valachi, Joseph Michael 195–200, 209, 222
The Valachi Papers 193
Vassall, John 104, 135–137

Vikings 35, 49–50
Villanus 2, 235
Volsung Saga 142, 150

Walker, John Anthony 104, 110, 116–118
Walking Dead 191, 238–239
Weber, Max 4, 68, 98, 109

Who Goes There 200
Wilde, Oscar: *Salome* 142, 151–152
Wilderness 21–22, 24
Works and Days 142–143

Xerxes 41–42, 46, 74–75, 112; *see also* Aeschylus; Herodotus; Thermopylae, Battle of